Made from scratch:
Daily Bread Bakery & Cafe

3rd Edition - 2010

Skidmore
WOOFers
Betsy Bott

Betsy Bott

Get a Way Press
PO Box 1258
Blue Hill, Maine

Get A Way Press
P O Box 1258
Blue Hill, ME 04614

Printed in Lewiston, Maine, USA
by Penmor Lithographers
Third Printing, November 2010

Library of Congress Cataloging-in-Publication Data
Bott, Betsy, 1948-
Made from scratch: daily bread bakery & cafe/ Betsy Bott
p. cm.
Includes bibliography, appendices and index.
ISBN: 978 0-9764381-4-4

Contents

Cafe Recipes

Dedication

To my grand-
parents who
shared whatever
they had with
neighbors,
who cheerfully
set another
place at the
table, who sang
while they
worked and
took time to set
and listen.

Acknowledgements

This project began twenty years ago, in 1985, before Daily Bread Bakery had a cafe. Judy Bush provided much enthusiasm and did most of the original breakdown of recipes and tested them out on her family. Thank you Judy.

Daily Bread's food, politics, philosophy, finances and atmosphere were shaped by the over 160 bakers, cooks and counter people who worked there from 1979 to 2000. They generously shared their recipes, time and skills to make the Bread the legendary eatery it was. I have given credit throughout the text to the best of my memory. Any mistakes or oversights were unintentional. Thanks to all of you.

By 2000, printing was a digital business. My immediate and extended family showed me the rudiments and offered technical and moral support along the way. Thank you Patti Bott, Robert Bott, Tobe Bott-Lyons, Dave Stafford, Henry, Ben and Chelsie Bush.

The Blue Hill Public Library let me use their public computer before I had my own. Nancy Guy, Gayle Durnbaugh, Heather Rowe and Sheri Sweet-Holcomb taught me word processing and held my hand through lost files and other minor setbacks. Sheri was indispensable in getting my files to the printer. Thank you for your support.

Jeb Bush gave me the time and space to bring this project to fruition. He gave every word a critical read and kept me focused. He suffered through my frustrations with computers, printers and software. He started the generator when the batteries wore down, and reminded me that this was worth the effort. Thank you Jeb.

Trisha Terwilliger, a chance laundromat acquaintance and professional copy editor, proofread the manuscript for errors and style. Thank you Trisha.

Thank you to all the known and anonymous photographers, whose work is scattered throughout the book.

Ed Miller and the folks at abco Printing were extremely patient in turning my files into a real book. Thank you Gladys, Carmen and everyone else at abco.

Over 200 old customers, family and friends showed their faith in the project by investing in the original printing. Thanks to each and every one of you.

2nd edition help

For Betsy Orvis, my Vermont representative and salesperson. Her cheerful efforts connected most Vermont books with their outlets, making posssible this second printing.

The folks at abco encouraged me to go through the effort to make the book more user friendly.

Autograff's Richard Merrill set up the new templates for the friendlier format.

Jane Crosen applied her cracker-jack editing skills to assemble full indexes: a general people, place, thing; a second spefically recipe-related. Things will be easier to find.

Close to 1,000 copies of the first edition are in the hands of happy readers, eaters and cooks. Your interest, support and feedback have been invaluable.

Daily Bread Bakery & Café was a popular eatery in a small northern Vermont town at the turn of the 21st century. It began as a part time wholesale bread bakery and evolved into a legendary bakery café with a small breakfast and lunch dining room open seven days a week, plus Thursday evening for acoustic music. It baked itself into the hearts and stomachs of neighbors and people from all over the world from 1979 to 2000 because its food was both everyday and not just something to eat. It served up comfort food with a twist. It was about local food and alternative food options, hearty food in generous portions. We baked with maple syrup, honey and molasses, and we weren't afraid of sugar. Our café menu was mostly vegetarian, with a few chicken and fish soup and salad options. The environment was nurturing for workers, customers and neighbors, and inspired others to create the same. After years of promises, here are the recipes and reminiscences.

The Bread, seasoned liberally with eclectic personalities and alternative political perspectives, grew from seeds planted in childhood, which is where I'll begin.

Oyster Bay

Newlyweds Mary and Johnnie Bott pose in Washington Square Park, 1944.

I was born Betsy Jean Bott in 1948, in New York City to Mary Dow McLeroy Bott, the eighth of nine living children of Tobe and Mattie McLeroy, Texas dirt farmers and Eugene V. Debs socialists, and John R. Bott, a newspaperman and only child of Katherine and Alfred Bott, a partner in Grand View Bottling Co. near Nyack, New York. I spent my childhood in Oyster Bay, on the north shore of Long Island, thirty-five miles from "the" city, middle child with an older brother Robert, and a younger sister Patti. We spent a lot of time in the kitchen. We read lots of newspapers, magazines and books. And we enjoyed all kinds of music. Debs was quoted as saying: "Years ago I recognized my kinship with all living beings, and I made up my mind that I was not one bit better than the meanest on earth." **(1)** I never heard it said so clearly, but that belief seemed to inform the way my folks lived their lives.

The post-war era brought great changes in the way food was grown and delivered. DDT promised to spare grain crops from destructive pests, while it deprived the landscape of indigenous species. "New" fertilizers grew bigger corn crops, encouraged larger dairy operations and drove many small farmers off their land. Trains and trucks from California, Texas and Florida filled midwestern and eastern market shelves with fresh produce year round. Government subsidized irrigation and migrant labor kept the trucks full and the prices low. Bulk holding tanks for milk were required to replace cans. Local market growers and small dairy farmers could not compete.

Families traded their home gardens for lawns; mom and dad gave up their big garden when dad went from night city editor to days in 1953. Suburban tract housing with government guaranteed loans made home ownership available to the masses. A chicken in every pot made way for a car in every garage.

Local butchers, green grocers and general merchants lost out to "super" markets, where in exchange for the "low, low prices," as humorist Lord Richard Buckley used to say, "Now you are pushing the mother cart."**(2)** Frozen food was available, increasing winter vegetable and meat options without time-consuming home-canning. Factories cranked out "wonder" bread, from which all nutrition was removed and then "fortified" with vitamins and minerals. Cake mixes simplified baking. No more anxiety over whether or not the pudding would set; use the "instant."

Proximity to the ethnic neighborhoods of "the" city and to family friends Bea Markowitz and Sally Fox, who baked their own, exposed me to a variety of breads at an early age. Our neighbor Mr. Mac grew sweet corn and tomatoes long after my folks had given up their vegetable garden. The diversity of cuisines which showed up on our dinner table matched that of the guests who ate there--a newspaperman meets and works with a wide cross section of the community.

Food and friendship

Getting together for shared meals was a frequent family event. Mom's brother Stanley brought a carload of food with him for holiday meals while he and his family still lived in New Jersey. He and his brother Uncle Jim spent most of their working lives in the restaurant trade. Neighborhood clambakes on the nearby shore were an annual event. Our friends Eleanor and "Stape" Stapleford had a great yard for summer picnics; I have never come close to how delicious Eleanor's macaroni and cheese and scalloped potatoes tasted.

Mom met Howard Mitcham, chef and woodcut artist, doing defense work during World War II. He made beautiful woodcuts and ran at least two restaurants, one in Provincetown and one in New Orleans. His book, *Creole Gumbo and All That Jazz,* inspired me with its mouth watering recipes, original artwork and personal homage to our American jazz heritage.

Dad's friend Eng Boy Hong invited us to elaborate family events and to special dinners at his Chinatown restaurant. Arthur and Sil Massolo worked at *The New York Post* with Dad and phoned when "Mama" made one her special dinners, completely from scratch. My childhood ballet teacher, Frances deLagrange, boarded with our family on Friday nights for years. She and her husband Jean grew up in France and introduced us to authentic provincial French food.

Old Texas friends of mom's moved to neighboring Huntington. Desi and mom cooked up pots of beans, vats of potato salad, cold fried chicken, and hot barbecue. Family friend Bea Markowitz met some Japanese exchange students who sharpened all of mom's knives, fired up the Hibachi and served us Sukiyaki, complete with raw egg added at the last minute to make rich gravy.

My friend Kathy Higgins and I baked brownies and birthday cakes, from mixes to start with. We branched out to frosting and eventually to breads and fruitcake from scratch. My brother Robert went to work at the local IGA market. He brought home various items and set about ways to cook them up.

We went to public school. Jean Williams' chef's course for boys gave my brother Robert a firm culinary back-

Gretchen Myers, Mom, Ann Moran & Bebe Freilinghaus check the clambake.

ground. It served him well in collective houses, as "Cooky" for the horse-drawn traveling Caravan Stage Company two summers in Western Canada and with enough recipes to write a weekly "Bachelor Bob" column in the *Calgary Herald*.

Mom and Dad enjoyed entertaining. Our house was an old carriage house with the living quarters upstairs. They renovated the carriage rooms downstairs into a large living room, perfect for big crowds. That room hosted many parties and receptions for visiting performers, including Teddy Wilson, Josh White and Jean Leon Destine. Robert and I spied on the adults from upstairs when we were supposed to be asleep, and passed trays of treats once we were older.

Rising Consciousness

About 1960, I turned in my band instrument, the flute, for a guitar. We played folk songs and copied blues licks from Dave van Ronk and Mississippi John Hurt and thought we were pretty cool by 1962. Claudia Jacobs, Sally Baron and I formed a group "The Bacchantes." We heard many of our musical heroes in person as they played the round of fundraisers for the Student Peace Union, the Congress of Racial Equality and the Student Non-Violent Coordinating Committee.

Voter registration drives were going on down south to open the voting booth to everyone, regardless of race. School segregation had been outlawed and public institutions were finally accessible to all, but not without a fight. Many lives were lost in the crossfire.

Martin Luther King Jr. had worked tirelessly to bring voting rights and equal access. He called people to march on Washington, D.C. in 1963, and inspired the world and the country with hope, giving voice to the dream we all prayed would unfold.

President Kennedy was shot in November, 1963. The shock of the assassination was magnified with the on-air gunning down of the only suspect in the shooting, Lee Harvey Oswald. My dad the newspaper editor was either on the phone, eye to the television or ear to the radio during the entire week following the assassination.

The American dream and its rewards were still out of reach to many. Ghettoes erupted in riots and fires from Newark to Los Angeles.

The Wechsler's cousin, John Wiesenthal, showed up from California to spend the next summer. I already had gained a reputation as a baker. He gave me Henry Miller's essay "The Staff of Life" to read. Already a doubting teenager, my mind was opened by Miller's premise that the bread a people eats tells much about the people. See what you think:

> Bread: prime symbol. Try and find a good loaf. You can travel fifty thousand miles in America without once tasting a piece of good bread. Americans don't care about good bread. They are dying of inanition but they go on eating bread without substance, bread without flavor, bread without vitamins, bread without life. Why? Because the very core of life is contaminated. If they knew what good bread was they would not have such wonderful machines on which to lavish all their time, energy and affection. A plate of false teeth means much more to an American than a loaf of good bread…Start with the American loaf of bread so beautifully wrapped in cellophane and you end on the scrap heap at forty-five. The only place to find a good loaf of bread is in the ghettos….
>
> "The Staff of Life"
> Henry Miller (3)

Our American bread was quite horrible. It gave me a new perspective, a new lense with which to view the world. I started thinking differently about bread and food.

The words of dissident Soviet poet Yevgeny Yevtuschenko reaffirmed that perspective in his poem, "Zima Junction":

> There's truth enough where there's enough bread,
> See to the bread and truth sees to itself.
>   Yevgeny Yevtuschenko (4)

My German family: Ingala, Mutti, Vati and Gretel Eisenkramer outside their Bensberg-Refrath home

For a lark and because I was pretty bored with school, I applied and was accepted to the American Field Service foreign exchange program. I spent my senior year of high school, 1965-'66, living with the Eisenkramer family and attending an all girls' high school, called a Gymnasium, outside Cologne, Germany. The bread there was the real thing, a meal in itself. And the weekly outdoor village market with fresh produce, meats and baked goods, provided fresh, tasty, local food. There were supermarkets, but my German "mother" Mutti used them primarily for stocking up on dry and canned goods.

Culture shock

Back in the states, I was in culture shock. Our cars seemed gargantuan. The food was tasteless and stale. Cities continued to burn. I went off to Harpur College, which was already expanding to become the State University of New York at Binghamton. Students and professors expected and delivered rigorous debate and study. The theater and dance programs, heady with new studios and theaters, pushed the limits to provide professional performances. Visiting artists provided inspiration and honed our skills. Radicals sabotaged the defense-related computer experiment at the college. Philosophy professors discussed altered states of consciousness, and marijuana smoke became a familiar aroma.

Lyndon Johnson's Great Society programs provided food stamps, Medicaid and Aid to Needy Families with Children to the poor and began Medicare health benefits to seniors and those unable to work. Funds went to poor schools and to low-income housing. The Voting Rights Bill outlawed poll taxes and other indirect barriers to voting. These measures helped reduce some of the volatility of the time.

I married Dan Mayer, brother of a college friend, and moved to New York City in 1968. His Orthodox Jewish family exposed me to their ceremonial cycle, very much based around the seasons and, of course, food. Celebrating at home with your immediate family was a wonderful way of honoring the passage of time and our human connection to the sacred.

Dan was at Columbia University during the 1968 student takeover. At Hunter College, where

Dan and unidentified *Post* reporter on the
Columbia campus, 1968

I finished my degree, a B.S. in German with an elementary education minor, lesson plans were tossed aside for open-ended discussion circles. I taught at P.S. 168 on E. 105th St. between First and Second Avenues in east Harlem. I went to Hunter at night to get my Masters in early childhood education. We played music all the time.

Dan moved on to Albert Einstein Medical School. We lived in the Bronx. We became involved with the Medical Committee for Human Rights and started working as a medical presence first aid team for street demonstrations; we met some of the Vermont health teams, who had been training themselves. We shared what we knew. We supported hospital workers organizing a union at Lincoln Hospital in the South Bronx. We helped to gather equipment and train Black Panther Party members who were setting up a neighborhood free clinic.

Dan's brother Jack did rotations at Mary Fletcher Hospital in Burlington, Vermont and then Goddard College student health service in Plainfield as part of his medical training. We met many Vermont radicals as they traveled between the Green Mountains and the nation's capitol. During these tumultuous years we used a large street presence to make our voices against war, racism, oppression and sexism heard by those in power.

We formed a tight cadre of friends through a "con-sciousness-raising" group and lived collectively for one year. Housemates Sally and Steve Jaspan started baking our bread-- we even prepared and canned a batch of ketchup from Connecticut tomatoes.

Our medical presence group huddles before a march on Camp Dix, a New Jersey Army base.

Free Vermont, State of Mind

By 1971, budget cutbacks began to gut some of the social programs which had eased hunger and poverty. Class sizes increased; staff were cut. There was a shoot-out in the courtyard of my school. Neighbor kids carried .357 magnum pistols to protect themselves in the growing cocaine trade. An overnight guest in our apartment turned out to be a police informant. The rural vision of growing your own food and building communities sounded like a more promising option. We began looking for a new home.

Burlington had much of what we needed to make a move: Dan needed to finish his medical training and there was a "street" clinic in town; and I wanted to find an alternative school setting, of which there were many.

We visited the Burlington suburb Richmond on a scouting expedition and met a few of the residents of Green Mountain Red, the commune on Browns Trace, where original communard Roz Payne still lives. In June 1972, we picked up stakes and moved to Burlington.

In a letter to Burlington newspaper *Seven Days* twenty-five years later, I described that first summer:

> Burlington in 1972 was an exciting place to be. From the burned out shells of Strong Hardware, St. Paul's and other arsons' victims of Urban Removal, many Burlington institutions took root: Community Health Center, Burlington College, Onion River Coop and Vermont Women's Health Center. …The raw "can do" power of that experience inspired and influenced many and spawned numerous careers and businesses, including my own, Daily Bread. (5)

Barbara Nolfi, who was part of Free Vermont, a loose association of Vermont communes, and instrumental in the formation of the People's Free Clinic, stated in a 1984 interview, "We wanted to make a better life for everyone, make things accessible to people without bureaucracy, profit-making and distortion. We were anti-capitalists. We intended to change the world." **(6)**

Women took chances to return birth to the home because doctors and hospitals refused to take away the straps and sedatives. Lay midwives trained and studied with whoever would share information. A British nurse-midwife who practiced at the Burlington hospital in the 1960s and 1970s was very generous. While many families continue to choose to give birth at home, the medical profession has made progress since then to make more humane options available in the hospital.

We rented an apartment in Burlington that first summer. In between meetings, looking for work and exploring the new neighborhood, I joined the group who baked desserts for the Fresh Ground Coffee House, a quasi-collective cafe and hangout. After a few months, Dan and I put a down payment on a house in Richmond, which we shared with Berta, Henry and their 18-month-old son Jeremy Geller. I worked at The Children's School, a Montessori-based private preschool. Dan worked at the People's Free Clinic as an alternative military service. We were pregnant, and chose a home birth. Our daughter Half Moon was born there in Richmond. She died quite suddenly of crib death at 3 1/2 months. Dan finished his internship in Boston. I stayed in Vermont, and began to work at the Womens Health Center.

The Free Clinic and the Health Center ran by consensus. There was a dedication and effort to hear every voice. A great deal of time and energy were devoted to process.

Dan and I divorced in 1975. Dan left Vermont with his new wife Julia. He has continued to teach and doctor and currently lives and works in Albany, New York.

Richmond, Vermont

Richmond is located about 16 miles east southeast of Burlington, Vermont, on the banks of the Winooski River. The Abenaki, Vermont's first people, camped on the river's banks and islands for millennia before Europeans settled there in the late 18th century. Settlers cleared land for farms and many small mills sprang up along Richmond's streams and rivers. The old turnpike, later U. S. Route 2, runs through the village, as do the railroad tracks. Travelers stopped at its hotels and taverns for more than a century. According to local historian Harriet Riggs, "in 1904 it had three hotels, a high school, district schools, industries employing over 200, a sawmill and box factory, a jeweler, liveryman, stationer, clothier, grocery store and hardware store. Population was about one thousand." **(7)** A 1908 fire destroyed much of the downtown, and the historic flood of 1927 took out old mills and bridges for the last time.

The Huntington River, which meets the Winooski a few miles up-river, had power enough to spawn early electric generating plants. John Baker brought power to the village from Ransom Robinson's Huntington River dam for his underwear factory. Many local women earned money in Baker's and other factories.

Seventy percent of Vermont's landscape was clear at the end of the 19th century, and small dairy farms dotted the surrounding hills. River bottom soil nourished corn and hay crops. The vagaries of the grain, wool and livestock markets and cheap land to the west drew many Vermonters off the land. Hill farms were marginal to begin with. The Depression, tractors and then bulk tanks forced even more small farmers to give up.

IBM built a chip manufacturing plant ten miles away in the early 1960s. General Electric's large Burlington plant provided many jobs and continues as a major local corporate player under yet another new name. While many businesses disappeared from the Richmond landscape, many new residents moved in, dotting pasture land with raised ranch homes. Twenty farms remained. There were also back-to-the-land-ers and at least one commune attracted to Richmond's rural landscape and village center. FBI agents roamed the streets of Richmond throughout the 1970s in search of subversives. Hippies and locals alike stonewalled them, recognizing the outsiders by the shine on their shoes.

Friends celebrate one of the marriages performed by the Reverend Tom Nagle in the courtyard of the Shady Deal Welding Parlor in Richmond.

Burlington and Montpelier were close enough to Richmond for culture. Five colleges in Burlington, including the University of Vermont, and two in the Montpelier area made northern Vermont a lucrative enough stop for performers of everything from chamber music to rock. Clubs were small where you could see legendary blues artists and locals up close and personal. The local bands were high calibre too, playing every weekend: Road Apple, John Cassel, the Enzones, Sass, Zzebra and Pure Pressure were just a few.

Artists and Woodburners

Artists of all sorts set up shop in the out-lying communities surrounding Burlington. There were fine woodworkers, post and beam builders, blacksmiths and welders. Through the 1970s and early 1980s, Tom Nagle's Richmond welding shop, the Shady Deal Welding Parlour served as a local community center.

There were potters and batik artists, wood cut printers and soft sculpture seamstresses. Three or four of them revived an Old Shirt Factory in the center of Richmond village into a thriving bee hive of activity and creativity. The Bead Parlour and Sewing Saloon occupied the back of the ground floor, future home of Daily Bread.

Ironically, many passers-by entered the bead shop disappointed that there were no fresh loaves of bread!

Local artists displayed their work for a holiday sale at the Old Shirt Factory in December of 1976. I met Judy Bush there through her pottery and woodcuts.

She and husband Jeb bought their land in 1971. They designed and built their own house:

Jeb and Judy Bush

"We have no one to blame, but we can also take all the credit." They also built shops: pottery for Judy, wood and metal for Jeb.

They were ridiculed at first as the "wood-burners." By 1976, their son Ben was four and Jeb was building wood burning stoves for many for whom oil heat had become too expensive. Jeb and Judy believed that anything was possible, that small was good, and recycling was where it was at.

Jeb acquired local

Jeb tests out a new jack jumper with both feet off the ground!

fame building jack jumpers, a seat on a single ski used to ride down snowy hillsides. It is said they were invented by loggers for riding down out of the woods at the end of a winter day. They were lots of fun and brought old and young together on the neighborhood slopes, from backyards to ski areas. He also repaired and fabricated farm machinery.

Judy knew (as a second or third grader in Minnesota) that she wanted to be an artist. Despite her parents' and teachers' advice to the contrary, she became an accomplished print-maker, potter, batik and graphic artist.

Judy's art classes have sparked many young people to pursue careers as artists and inspired many adults to find hidden creative talents. Judy continues to teach young and old and create original ceramic works at her Richmond home.

The twins Henry and Chelsie were born in 1977. Besides raising three boys and abundant gardens, Judy and Jeb found time to support Daily Bread from its inception to its sale.

Jeb constructed most of the first and last renovations. The name Daily Bread was his suggestion. Many of the functional and beautiful fixtures were his work: pot racks, cooling racks, shelf brackets, fan brackets, exhaust hoods, table bases, roll divider bases and granola funnel.

Judy worked at the bakery off and on through the late 1990s. The bread label and the original T-shirt art are her designs. She did much of the recipe breakdowns for the cookbook. Ben, Henry and Chelsie all worked at the Bread. Ben's wife Raechel even worked a few college summers.

Time for a Change

Working at the Health Center had been extremely educational and satisfying work for me, though I realized I was not cut out to be a primary care giver such as a physician's assistant. And it was a forty-minute commute. A catastrophic 1977 fire destroyed the Health Center building in downtown Burlington. To rebuild, we purchased and renovated a brick house on North Avenue in Burlington. The staff had to become general contractors and property owners. It was a challenging transition. I was ready to trade in my commute to Burlington's North End for something closer to home.

What to do? The 1974 oil crisis and growing families found many women turning to the workplace seeking job security and higher wages to support rising costs. I enjoyed baking, and thought perhaps all the people returning to the workplace would still enjoy home-baked bread. Judy had often dreamed of a bakery, and we began fantasizing. Richmond boasted a population of only 3,000, but people from Huntington, Hanksville, Jonesville, Bolton and parts of Jericho funneled through Richmond to get to their new jobs in Essex Junction, Burlington, Colchester and Winooski.

A Bakery Takes Shape

I began experimenting with recipes, trying them out on my housemates and friends to see which would sell. I had a route of customers and sometimes hitch-hiked to deliver my bread and buy more ingredients.

I looked at buildings in Richmond, Jonesville and Huntington. I approached Charles Ross about the Old Shirt Factory in Richmond. He had rented to seamstresses, the bead shop, a leather shop, a secondhand clothing shop, a mime artist-- why not a bakery? He was not receptive, adamantly opposed in fact.

I continued to work out of Wendy Weldon and Terry Bachman's house on the Dugway Road, where I was the woman who came to house sit and stayed two years. Their house was off the power grid, and I baked up to ninety-six loaves by hand per day, three days a week from there. I needed to liberate Wendy's kitchen and find larger quarters.

Just when I had given up hope and taken a medical secretary job, Mr. Ross contacted me to see if I was still interested in renting space in his Richmond building. After doing research on what might be necessary for improvements, we struck a deal. I started paying rent in January of 1979.

I had collected an ancient 20-quart Hobart mixer, two Blodgett deck ovens, some mixing bowls and bread pans, a small stainless table and a few galvanized trash cans for flour storage.

I scrambled to borrow enough money to get started, what amounted to $5,000. My investors were family and friends, no one putting in more than a few hundred. Jeb and Judy helped me to

Don Robbins visits with Onnie, Tony and Andy Palmer at the opening April Fools party.

design the initial kitchen space. We divided off a hall to access Lael Livack's Sewing Saloon and to create a retail display which served us well for the first nineteen years. Terry, Jeb and Andy Palmer donated their skill, tools and labor to do the basic carpentry. I had my first and last experience mudding sheetrock. We used what we had, old four-light storm windows to divide hall from kitchen. It gave cooks and bakers a connection to the outside, and offered the public a glimpse of the inner sanctum of the kitchen while satisfying health regulations.

There were time-consuming and expensive skirmishes with various state agencies involved with sanctioning and regulating food service establishments. The health people stipulate "smooth, cleanable surfaces." The fire code specifies 5/8 thick fire code Sheetrock. We had to remove the old pressed tin ceilings and fill in all the cracks in the old wooden floor. I found local contractors to do the work: Cottie Bressor did the wiring, Ted Sargent the plumbing.

Jeb fashioned an oven hood from 16-gauge steel. Wendy and Terry donated maple boards for the work table. Jeb put together the top and made the base. I found an old home-size refrigerator, bought galvanized trash cans, a two-bay utility sink, an old enamel hand sink, a few more stainless bowls and assorted baking pans.

We had a kick off party April Fool's Day 1979, and officially opened for business April 2.

Jeff Nagle and Ben Bush admire the baked goods

Randall Gillett reviewed the early Daily Bread in a June l979 *County Weekly* newspaper article:

> The most recent addition to Richmond's retail trade began in April with the opening of the town's first bakery….Daily Bread is the result of customer demand, requiring an expansion of her previous wholesale trade into a retail store. …
>
> "I originally planned this as a part-time occupation," admitted Betsy, "I thought it would involve only three working days plus maybe a couple of hours one other day."
>
> Her Daily Bread products are so popular; however, she finds it rare to have two days off. Another surprise is that while she uses only natural and wholesome ingredients in her whole grain products, she has found that there is no way to ignore people's sweet tooth. (8)

In October, 1979, I moved to my own place, a little hunting camp on Texas Hill Road in nearby Hinesburg--wood heat, outhouse, carry-in water. I moved up the road a year later to an old tenant house, reportedly built in 1820, on thirty acres, mostly perpendicular--wood heat, outhouse and intermittent water.

The old tenant house on Texas Hill Road, with garden and array of 1960s heavy Chevy's.

A Few Main Characters

Judy Bush provided inspiration, perspiration and a common sense approach to business, making a living, not a killing. She offered many recipes which were bakery favorites, such as the Orange Tea Cake and Poppy Seed Pound cake. She tested many recipes on her family. She did the bookkeeping for the first few years and taught me record keeping. Judy's artwork graced Daily Bread signs, labels, T-shirts and walls. Many of Judy's after-school-art-kids became high school employees at the Bread.

Alison Forrest is a legendary Vermont cook. She began her career making ice cream for Ben and Jerry when they opened their first scoop shop on Burlington's St. Paul Street in an old gas station.

She baked for Daily Bread in the early 1980's and was a prime mover in the 1986 cafe addition. Alison gave generously of her favorite recipes, most prominent in the muffin chapter. Alison, partner Bart Howe and son Sam live in a little house in the woods. Alison became the school cook at nearby Brewster Pierce Elementary School. She took her love and appreciation for fresh, wholesome food to school, winning over even the staunchest meat and potatoes eaters. She has worked with the Northeast Organic Farmer's Association to help school lunch programs purchase from local farmers and to extend food education into the classroom.

Lynn E Alden & Mare Kuhlman

Mare Kuhlman came to Vermont to study with the Sunray Meditation Society just before the cafe took shape, and was instrumental in setting up the kitchen. Mare cooked professionally, from "gonzo" vegetarian cuisine in Oregon to chicken fried steak at an Arizona cowboy cafe, and shared many of her favorites. She created the basic Daily Bread breakfast and brunch menus, and taught many of us the fine art of short order cooking.

Heidi Champney made a brief appearance in the early cafe days. She brought many recipes from her experience cooking in a coop dining hall at Oberlin College. Many favorites are from her collection: the TLT, Creamy Onion Soup and a number of casseroles. Heidi is an accomplished musician, violin and voice her primary instruments. She is a healer and helper, providing kind and considerate care for many differently abled adults in Addison County.

Heidi accompanies Dan Cox, JB Bryan and Betsy at Richmond's band shell

Krista Willett is a woman of many talents. She taught skiing to the blind, elementary school in Marshfield, promoted cheese and milk for the dairy council, baked at Bolton Valley Resort, waitressed at Howard Johnson's and sold Carvel ice cream. Krista brought many recipes and techniques to Daily Bread, sharing her expertise and doing research when we ran into trouble. Many recipes came from her collection. She joined the staff as a breakfast cook, a spot she filled

off and on for years. She held down regular early morning or afternoon baking shifts and taught many new and old bakers the fine points. She is also an avid origami artist; she folded individual ornaments for every staff member for years.

Rose Lovett quietly joined our staff a few years into the cafe. Rose grew up in Richmond, and cooked around the corner at the pizza shop Papa Louis' for years. Rose held down the lunch shift, took care of many ordering details and kept track of the Meals on Wheels senior lunches. She was a steadying influence for us all, and taught many young people how to work.

Krista, Rose, Dylan, Betsy and Malcolm pose with Senator James Jeffords for a campaign publicity shot.

Rose "Rosa" Warnock worked nine years as breakfast cook at the Bread. It was the breakfast cook's job to make the soup, and Rosa was expert at fine-tuning recipes to our ingredients and our setting. Rosa was always on the lookout for new recipes, and helped adapt others for less fat and dairy. Rosa challenged many a customer to just *try* a TLT (the Tofu, Lettuce & Tomato sandwich) once! Just about everyone agreed they never realized tofu could taste so good.

Andrew Paschetto cooked and baked professionally in a number of venues before arriving at Daily Bread in the 1990s. He studied with Anne Marie Colbin at her New York City cooking school. I met Andrew the first summer he cooked at the Sunray Meditation Society Peace Village in Lincoln. The kitchen there was an outdoor, temporary affair, with all water carried in and out. Andrew concocted beautiful and delicious food on a shoestring budget, using garden produce as much as possible. His love

of food and joyful cooking were infectious. Andrew contributed many breads, cakes, soups and main dishes. He was a gentle mentor to many high school students during his afternoon bake shifts. His kind and devoted caretaking of our friend Marcia Rhodes was inspirational to all of us.

Dwayne Doner did not arrive at the Bread until the late 1990s, just in time to add many vegan (no eggs, no dairy) dishes to the menu. Dwayne is a master of vegetarian comfort food. His stews and chilis are memorable, and his marinated tempeh and seitan sandwiches will become legend with your friends and family.

These are just a few of the many--about 180 over twenty-one years--individuals who made invaluable contributions of their time and talents to Daily Bread. You will meet many of them as you meet their recipes.

Kitchen Basics
Tools

Before you get started, there are many movers and shakers which will greatly ease production and cleanup of baking and other kitchen projects. Here are a few.

Work surface/s of the proper height will add enjoyment and physical well-being to cooking and baking. Your kneading surface should be ideally the same height as your belly button. For chopping vegetables, you want it a little higher, a little above your waist. Experiment with what you have available. Your back, wrists, elbows and neck will thank you.

A big enough bowl to work in is essential. Like the old James Brown tune says, "I can't do my best unless I got room to move." You need space to develop the gluten for a well-risen loaf of bread; space to beat air into cake batters for a light, fluffy product; space to toss to just combine scone or pastry dough. A properly sized bowl allows you to involve your larger muscle groups, cutting down on tendonitis and carpal tunnel syndrome. A 12-13 quart bowl is really nice for 3 or more loaves of bread, about 14 inches across, 6 inches deep. A 4-6 quart bowl, 12 inches across, 3-4 inches deep is useful for smaller batches. At home, I knead my bread right in the bowl, saving one round of counter clean up.

Two large measuring cups (with at least a 4-cup capacity) help so you have one for wet ingredients and one for dry.

A bench scraper or bench knife, a 4-inch by 6-inch stiff rectangular metal blade with wooden or plastic handle, works well for dividing bread dough, pie dough or scones. Or lift pastry from your counter with it to transfer pieces to waiting pie tin or baking sheet. It also works for peeling up recalcitrant traces of dough from your counter for clean up.

A pastry blender helps to cut shortening into flour. You may also use two table knives, held together in one hand. Or just use your fingers for this if you work quickly.

A heavy wire whisk is my tool of choice for beating air into cakes, batters and eggs. Some bakers preferred a heavy wooden or metal spoon for this. Electric mixers and food processors work for many recipes, but take care not to over work. Whichever tool you choose, just beat it!

Rubber spatulas are very handy for cleaning out bowls and cups and are essential for folding beaten egg whites into batter, gently moving good-sized volumes of whites without breaking apart their structure.

A small aluminum shaker with a screw top saves a lot of mess when kneading, dusting pans, rolling out dough or dusting hands before beginning to knead sticky dough.

Glass canning jars with screw rings work quite well topped with a piece of window screen for sprinkling cinnamon sugar on sweet rolls.

Large and small loaf pans: 9 5/8"x5 1/2"x2 3/4" and 7 3/8"x3 5/8"x2 1/4", or that range.

Assorted pans and sheets: 8"x8" or 9"x9"; an 8", 9" or 10" pie tin; a 10"x14" sheet pan and cookie sheet; and 9" layer pans. A 9" spring form pan for large cheesecakes is also good to have.

A rolling pin. Bakers have their favorites. I prefer the "french" style, one piece roller. Other bakers preferred the ball-bearing model, where the roll turns while your hands stay stationary on the handles.

A pastry bag, a coated fabric or plastic funnel with interchangeable tips for fancy decorating, is nice to have. You can also create your own out of waxed or parchment paper.

Muffin tins. Ours were large, at least 1 1/2" across the bottom. Our 12 muffin recipe will fill 18 regular home-sized tins. Grease and flour muffin tins for easier removal. A fork or table knife will help the stubborn ones out.

An assortment of covered sauce pans and stock pots: a 1 1/2 quart, 4, 6, and 8 quart. You need these to cook glazes, prepare fruit, for soups, stocks and stews, for cooking potatoes and pasta.

An assortment of light 8-inch saute pans to 12- or 14-inch cast iron skillets. These are essential for omelets, for crisping or caramelizing vegetables, for pan-toasting spices or nuts. They also work for grilling potatoes or sandwiches.

A steamer insert or basket which will fit your pans. These help vegetables to cook without becoming mushy. It helps retain more of the fresh nature of the vegetable.

A double boiler or some combination of metal bowl and saucepan allows cooking over not in boiling water. Custards and some fillings need this treatment to avoid curdling or separating.

A 4-6 quart colander, 8- to 12-inches accross, for draining pasta or vegetables.

A flame diffuser or "tamer" to keep those thick sauces, rouxs or beans from scorching, which could ruin hours of preparation. Reduce heat to low, put diffuser on the burner under your pot or skillet.

An assortment of knives, from 3-inch paring to 12-inch chef's. I find good, affordable knives harder and harder to find. Our old favorite Russel 2332, affectionately known as "Stubby," was truly irreplacable. The model disappeared from the market. There are excellent knives available. They are worth the investment, especially for the home kitchen. Find out how to sharpen a carbon steel knife, and have, to my mind, the best cutting edge for kitchen work.

Garlic press, the vegetable peeler, the graters, the small strainers. These are not essential but make cooking faster and more enjoyable. From grating cheese to grating ginger, or for getting every seed out of the lemon juice, it's great to have these around.

Blender or food processor. These are not inter-changeable. We worked without a food processor for years. We used it all the time once we had one. Blending or processing tofu with some accompanying liquid gives the end product a smoother texture. The food processor also makes stocking chopped nuts much quicker, saving the baker's time for more goodies.

Leftover containers with lids of a variety of sizes. They are handy for storing prepared batters or ingredients planned for later. Reuse yogurt and cheese containers. We bought only a few very large containers at the Bread. We used enough dairy, nut butters, oils and sweeteners that we always had extra buckets around.

Baking Ingredients

Flour usually refers to wheat flour. Hard, spring wheat yields the best bread flours, both whole and unbleached. These are high in protein to develop the gluten structure which holds up the dough. Loaves will be crunchy on the outside, light on the inside.

Whole wheat bread flour is best used freshly ground. It has many oils which oxidize over time, giving the flour a rancid off taste. 100 per cent whole wheat doughs will feel sticky even when they have enough flour. A little handful added to basic white French doughs gives the gluten a little more to hang onto. Check with your local health food store or bakery for local sources.

Unbleached flour refers to a "bread type" unbleached flour. There are many choices on supermarket shelves, at health food stores and from specialty catalogues. We baked everything except a few specialty breads with King Arthur special unbleached: cakes, pies, breads, muffins, everything.

Whole wheat pastry and all purpose flour are lower in protein, milled from soft spring wheat and good for tender cakes, pastry and cookies.

Cereal Grains
Wheat flakes, rye flakes, rolled oats, wheat bran, cornmeal, brown rice and millet as well as many seeds such as sesame, sunflower, poppy and caraway may be added to bread for additional texture and nutritional value. Many are on supermarket shelves, though some are only available at specialty shops.

Liquids
Most tap water, for baking, will suffice. The key, one of the most important, is starting with perfectly warm water. Water too hot will kill off yeast, a very common mistake. Err on the side of slightly cool. It will take a little longer, but it will work. You can test it like a baby's bottle, on the inside of your wrist; it should feel neither hot nor cold.

Hard water may need a little acid, vinegar or juice, to please the yeast. Soft water may be offset by a little extra salt to strengthen the gluten. Heavily chlorinated water may inhibit the activity of the yeast, too; use filtered water if this seems to be an issue.

Potato water drained off boiled potatoes is excellent for yeast and sourdough breads. Yeast loves potato starch. It is very simple and readily available to the yeast. It will start the yeast working before the wheat starches have even shown up at the dance.

Milk, sour cream or powdered milk will give a fine texture to your finished loaf. Milk also adds nutritional value: protein, calcium, iron, B-vitamins. Powdered milk is easy to have on hand. It may be added with other dry ingredients, and it saves the time of heating and cooling required of liquid milk (there is some debate whether this step is necessary as almost all milk is now pasteurized).

Eggs add color, texture, nutritional value and loft. Egg breads such as Herb and Challah or Brioche will surprise you with their oven spring! These are high risers! Egg wash or glaze, made by beating a few drops of water with an egg, gives baked products a beautiful shiny finish; use it on breads, pies, turnovers and rolls.

When using whole eggs, the fresher the better. If you can find eggs from chickens fed on greens and more than just grain, you will notice how orange the yolks are; this shows that they are higher in vitamins A and B. If beating egg whites for maximum rise, older are better. Take refrigerated eggs out long enough to come to room temperature to give beaten eggwhites plenty of loft.

Soy milk is useful for non-dairy cooking. It needs the addition of acid like vinegar or lemon juice to truly replace milk. We found that using toasted soy flour and water the same way you would use dried milk and water, was less expensive than liquid soy milk: 1/3 cup flour plus 3/4 cup water to equal 1 cup liquid. Add 1/2 teaspoon vinegar per cup.

Leavening: we make it rise!

Yeast is a simple organism, a fungus actually, which feeds on sugars and starch to produce carbon dioxide gas. That gas gets trapped in bubbles of gluten to rise your loaf of bread. Yeast will find enough sugar for this reaction from flour alone, but will be quicker to act with the assistance of sweeteners such as honey, maple syrup, molasses or barley malt. Yeast prefers a warm moist atmosphere and welcomes the Dog Days of August. Commercial baker's yeast has been dehydrated, waiting for you to add food and water.

The most common killer of yeast is excessive heat. This can happen from the liquid being too hot to start with or can come from over working with an electric mixer.

At least some of my fascination with yeast and fermentation is genetic. The following reference to my great grandfather appeared in a Walkerville, Ontario brochure published by the Windsor Architectural Conservation Advisory Board,

> John Bott…achieved a measure of fame for his prize-winning malt at the Chicago World's Fair in 1893, (and) was manager of the Walkerville Brewing Company. He was a member of the first town council with his friend, Thomas Reid, and was elected mayor in 1896. (9)

Yeast does not give up easily, and will rise again and again after being punched down or worked on the table. Oven heat eventually kills the yeast, leaving the pockets behind which it generously formed for us. These are the little pockets which trap melted butter, honey or jam!

Sourdough is a moist colony of your own wild yeasts with enough flour and water to keep them alive until you are ready to use it again. (see page 36)

Baking Powder and Soda are both used as leavening, or risers, for quick breads such as muffins, cakes, tortillas and scones. Baking powder needs heat and moisture to activate it. Soda needs moisture and some acid, often provided by buttermilk, yogurt or sour cream. A soda-risen product must be baked right away once the liquid has been added. Powder-risen items can sit a while without diminishing the end result.

Salt is a simple mineral basic to our existence. It contributes flavor and helps to rein-in the wild yeast, exuberant with sugars. As salt toughens meats and beans, it also toughens yeast dough, giving the gluten bubbles a little extra support. Breads without salt may fall more easily. Salt also helps keep mold from growing on your finished loaves. Add a little extra in the warmer months.

David Young, Franklin Heyburn and Tim Jennings play a set.

Sweeteners. Daily Bread chose to use natural sweeteners for its breads early on for nutritional and political reasons. Complex sugars generally take longer to break down, cause less of a sugar rush and provide many other trace elements. Natural sweeteners help breads stay fresher longer. Honey and maple syrup were available from local producers. We supported our local farmers and tried to keep some of our dollars in our local community. The sugar trade was built upon slavery.

Daily Bread used about 30 gallons of maple syrup and 20 gallons of honey every month once the bakery and café were in full swing.

We purchased our honey from Franklin Heyburn, the "honey man," who is also a fine fiddler. Almost all of our maple syrup came from the Taft farm of Huntington. We also used small quantities of barley malt in our brownies and granola.

We certainly used plenty of refined white and brown sugar in our cakes and brownies, though most of our muffins and scones were naturally sweetened.

The Tafts

The Taft farm sits on a scenic hillside rising up towards the local landmark Camels Hump in Huntington Center. Gentle Jersey cows dot the steep pastures. Bruce and Mary, and now their son Tim, milk 365 days a year, with very occasional help from neighbors or hired hands. Maple syrup provides a cash infusion which helps purchase seed and fertilizer going into the more productive summer season.

Their maple syrup is legendary, winning prizes year after year. They used to barrel up their B-grade (now called Dark Amber) with Daily Bread in mind, and keep it in their cool cellar until we were ready for it. Bruce and Tim always helped muscle the heavy barrels down into our cellar, the only place cool enough to keep it from spoiling.

Steam rising up from the sugar house on cold spring evenings, backlit by flames shooting up the stack, creates eerie clouds visible from miles around. The boiling is fired by dead wood cut during January's slack time. Bruce designed a special splitter to handle the long pieces. It is all part of the natural cycle of farming.

Most of their taps are set up on tubing, though they still collect from a few hundred buckets. Tractors make the rounds now. Bruce has fond memories of working with the horses his father used.

One year I stopped out to the sugar house to taste that year's crop. Bruce offered me samples from a number of barrels, more than a cup of pure syrup by the time I left. By the time I got home, I was woozy. I had to lie down with one foot on the ground to keep the room from spinning around.

Global warming has taken its toll. A dependable sugaring season is no longer a sure thing.

Warm days and cold nights are needed to produce good sap. Sudden warm ups cause trees to bud out, resulting in low volume and an off taste.

Shortening increases a bread's tenderness and keep-ability. It also adds flavor and slows down yeast's exuberant activities. In your home kitchen, wait until after you have worked your dough in the bowl to add the oil or butter. This will yield a flakier result, since you have already created a network of gluten strands.

We used mostly butter in the early days. A combination of customer requests for lower fat and no dairy caused us to change from butter to oil in our standard loaves. Butter still gives holiday Stollen its characteristic flavor.

Light oils will add tenderness without flavor; we used primarily sunflower and canola. A full bodied fruity olive oil will make your Rosemary Olive or Pesto loaves more memorable.

Chocolate and Cocoa come in many forms: sweetened, unsweetened, solid, powder. We used Baker's unsweetened baking chocolate and "ruddy red" Dutch process cocoa. Experiment with what is available and you'll find your favorites.

Zest is called for in a number of recipes, lemon or orange. This refers to the outermost layer of citrus skin without the bitter under layer.

Other staples

It is always helpful to have a wide assortment of basic grains, beans, and pasta plus fresh and canned or frozen vegetalbes. Your particular cupboards and coolers will reflect your household preferences.

Grains:
basmati rice
brown rice, short and long
wild rice
pearled barley
bulgur

Seeds:
sesame
sunflower
poppy

Pasta:
spirals/rotini
linguini
lasagna
soba

Beans:

pinto
kidney
black turtle
Great Northern
garbanzo/ chick peas
green split peas
yellow split peas
green lentils

Canned or frozen:

whole tomatoes in juice
black olives
tomato sauce
green olives
artichoke hearts
green peas
kernel corn
spinach

Sea vegetables:

dulse
kombu/ kelp

Fresh vegetables:

potatoes
celery
garlic
tomatoes
red peppers
kale
lettuce

carrots
onions
parsley
green peppers
cabbage
spinach

Bread

Why did I begin with bread? Bread, the Staff of Life! "Man can not live by bread alone…," but can do pretty well with a little something to go on it. The daily sustenance provided by bread inspired Jeb Bush to come up with the name Daily Bread. Bread is the "everyday" of food.

Bread, beer and agriculture appeared about the same time in human history, about 4,000 BC. The mystery of fermentation, of risen bread and bubbly beer, has inspired bakers and brewers ever since. Working with living dough, nurturing all the ingredients into tasty, satisfying food, inspired me to consider life as a baker, as it still does.

Daily Bread came to be known locally as the Bread, and rightly so. Bread formed the centerpiece. It was the only product to begin with, and we continued to bake bread every day. The café menu was built around it: toast, French toast, sandwiches, soup, croutons, pizza, and calzones.

Ethnic urban neighborhood bakeries introduced me to flavorful dark loaves which earned the name "staff of life." I literally grew fat on all the hearty bread and cakes I encountered during my senior year of high school in Germany as a foreign exchange student. Our 1960's counter culture experimented with and embraced whole foods whole-heartedly, and that sparked a widespread resurgence of home baking. Many of us persevered to turn out tasty loaves that even the kids would eat.

Yeast breads do require time and elbow grease. But once you have the basics down and get to know when "enough" is enough, yeast baking is not difficult and can be worked around any schedule. Many types of dough can be refrigerated overnight or all day, and then raised and baked at the next block of time available. Filling your home with the aroma of fresh-baked bread is worth the effort. Witness the popularity of bread machines! Why not take advantage of an opportunity to zone in to the dough and zone out for a while? You and your family and friends will be happier for it.

Which Bread? •

The giant puppets which are now prominent at all political demonstrations and deemed effective enough to be seized by the police, VT were inspired by Peter Schumann and the many other puppeteers of the Bread and Puppet Theater of Glover. Since the late 1960's the company has created its larger than life puppets for parades, demonstrations, street theater, school programs, international theater festivals and their once annual Domestic Resurrection Circus, a two day outdoor extravaganza of puppets, poetry, music and community.

Many families set the time aside each year and camped out for the weekend to renew old friendships and to be rejuvenated. Others came for the day to feast on the bread smothered in garlic butter and the camaraderie of fellow travelers. We tried to remember the punch-lines from the afternoon circus and mulled over the "meaning" of the evening pageant for weeks. While Glover was two hours away from Richmond by car, Bread and Puppet's influence was felt far and wide. At least once a year, people ate the old bread. Larger and larger crowds gathered in the late '90's; the annual event ended after a visitor was killed on a nearby campground. All the puppets of all those years are displayed in tableaus in the museum barn at the home place in Glover.

In the 1984 Bread and Puppet Press pamphlet Bread. Schumann writes of his own bread history:

A late 1990's circus act at Bread and Puppet's Glover arena.

I come from a stretch of land where bread meant bread, not the pretext for a hot-dog nor a sponge to clean up sauces with, but an honest hunk of grainy, nutty food which had its own strong taste and required a healthy amount of chewing. Until the end of the 18th century most bread eaters ate such

The big bread oven used to bake bread for the annual gathering.

bread, bread on which you could live. With the French Revolution people got what they needed, and more than they needed: the bread of the kings, or the delicate pastry which the kings called bread. And that is mostly what they eat ever since….In 1963 in a loft on Delancey Street in New York, as a normal frustrated city-artist and esoteric puppet show-maker, I decided to connect the bread with the puppets… The bread has its own contradictions: it's the old bread, the staff of life, designed to keep body and soul together, meant to feed the hungry. But it's baked in the country of a million gimmicks and distributed to overeaters.

Peter Schumann (10)

At Daily Bread, we chose the middle path. We based many of our standard loaves on cereal grains: wheat flakes, rolled oats, corn meal and bran. We used some whole wheat bread flour, grown and ground by Ben Gleason in Bridport, located in the fertile Champlain Valley. And we finished off with about 2/3 King Arthur unbleached bread flour, a good high protein flour commercially available. The result is a freckled, light bread which hangs together for a sandwich or French toast, and not so heavy that two slices are too much. These loaves appealed to a wide variety of customers and to many tastes within one household.

General bread instructions

Flour, yeast--cultivated or wild--salt and water are enough to produce the most basic French-style loaf. It is fabulous right out of the oven, but does not keep. It will dry out in one day, and will only be good for French toast, croutons, bread pudding or crumbs.

Cracked cereal grains, coarse meal, sweeteners and shortening all add to the moisture and longevity of your finished loaves. Some bread will keep a week or more.

1. Soak grain, if using a cereal-based recipe. Pour boiling water or very hot tap water over grain in your bread mixing bowl and allow the mixture to cool to room temperature. This step softens the grain and releases some of the starches, getting them ready for the yeast.

2. Activate yeast. This step is called "proofing." Measure out a portion of the liquid with a little sweetener, making sure the temperature is just lukewarm, neither hot nor cold. Add yeast and wait for it to foam up. This assures you that the yeast is active. Some yeast sits on shelves for a long time and will act sluggish. Use a little extra if this seems to be the case. Health food stores and food co-ops generally have fresh stocks since they sell proportionately more.

Add the proofed yeast to the other liquid and/or soaked grain.

3. Stir in whole wheat or the first 1/3 of your flour; this is also called a "sponge." A sturdy wooden or metal spoon works well. Give this a vigorous workout, 50-100 strokes to get the yeast going and to start the gluten structure forming. Gluten is very elastic. As you work the dough, you stretch and stretch the gluten strands. When you slice a loaf of bread, you can see them. You can give your bread a boost if you allow this sponge to rise once before proceeding.

4. Mix. Add the rest of the flour, salt and shortening. Add the flour a few cups at a time, working the dough into a ball, stirring up from the bottom and folding it over. Add the salt and shortening and more flour. Continue with the spoon until dough becomes too stiff to work.

5. Knead. You can do this in your bowl if it is big enough, or turn it out onto your counter. Dust your hands with flour and begin to knead the dough. Lift up, fold towards you, and push on it. Turn it a quarter of a turn. Fold, push, turn. Think round. Get your whole body into it. Stand firmly on both feet. Use both hands. Lean into it. Put some muscle into it and enjoy this break.

It usually takes about ten minutes to knead dough to its final stage. You want a smooth, springy ball that just barely sticks to your hands. This is where you can really feel gluten's elastic nature; if you push on it, it pushes back!

6. Set to rise. Scrape your mixing bowl with a rubber scraper or spoon. Grease or oil it and place your kneaded dough into it. Turn the ball over so it is greased top and bottom. Cover with a damp cloth and place in a draft-free warm place to rise until doubled in size. This usually takes

an hour, but depends on the dough and environmental factors. Old-style pilot lights provided the perfect warmth to raise a small batch of bread. A corner near the wood stove works well. The Dog Days of summer do it with no extra assistance.

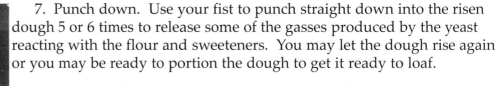

7. Punch down. Use your fist to punch straight down into the risen dough 5 or 6 times to release some of the gasses produced by the yeast reacting with the flour and sweeteners. You may let the dough rise again or you may be ready to portion the dough to get it ready to loaf.

8. Divide and "boule" or round. Turn the risen dough out onto your floured counter. Use a sharp knife or bench scraper to cut the dough into the number of loaves you plan to make. Form each piece into a smooth ball by kneading it lightly into a cohesive piece. Allow to rise till doubled, about 35 to 40 minutes.

9. Rest and rise. Cover the rounds with a warm damp towel. Let rise till doubled in size. Poke a finger into the ball up to your first knuckle. If the hole fills up right away it is still rising. If it fills slowly, it is ready to loaf.

10. Loafing. Grease bread pans.

For pan or box loaves, flatten each ball out into a rectangle with the short side facing you. It should be about as wide as your pan is long. If bubbles squeak and pop as you press this out, you have hit the jack pot; you and the yeast have done your jobs. Grab the end closest to you and roll it tightly into a cylinder. Tuck the ends in and pinch the seam along the bottom. Roll the loaf a few times under your hands to even it out. Place it seam down in the prepared pan. Put in a warm place to rise. Preheat oven to 350 degrees or desired temperature.

For hearth style French loaves or "batards," press your ball out into a flat oval with the long side towards you. Grab the edge closest to you and roll up, stretching as you go, without tearing the dough. Tuck in the ends and pinch the seam. Give it a roll to even out any lumps. Place seam side down on a flat baking sheet. A tight roll here will stand up in the oven. A loose roll will spread out in a pancake.

11. Final rise. Cover with a damp towel and let loaves rise till doubled or peeking above the tops of your pans. Do not let them rise too much or they may cave in when they hit the heat, stretched literally to the breaking point. Preheat oven fifteen minutes before baking.

12. Bake. Place in the middle of preheated oven and bake forty-five minutes to an hour. Let loaves bake thirty minutes undisturbed before rotating loaves from one side to the other or from one shelf to the other, depending on whether or not your oven has hot spots. Loaves should be aromatic, lightly browned and sound hollow when tapped.

13. Cool and eat! Remove from baking pans and cool on a wire wrack. Enjoy the results of your handiwork.

These are basic instructions. Humidity and temperature will make a difference. Amounts will vary. Yeast doughs are forgiving and can withstand a little tampering.   Experiment with your own variations.

They thought I was crazy

Fifth grade historians Sarah Curtis and Tucker Andrews wrote a piece for their class book called *Richmond, a Community with Pride:*

When Betsy Bott started the Daily Bread fifteen years ago, people thought she was crazy. When you look at the Daily Bread now, it's very popular. As you probably know, Betsy feels her customers that come in and out are one of the things she likes most at the Daily Bread....
There are several job shifts at the Daily Bread. The morning bakers get there at 4 a.m. They have to take care of opening procedures and bake rolls, muffins and bread. The afternoon baker has to bake and bag granola....

Sarah Curtis and Tucker Andrews (11)

Daily Loaves

True to our name, we baked bread every day. We developed a schedule of regulars, and worked in specials according to holidays or availability of seasonal ingredients. We'll go through the regular daily offerings first.

Monday

Maple Wheat (3 loaves or 2 loaves plus 8 rolls or English muffins)

This was by far our most popular loaf, and one which I can call an original. From the beginning, Daily Bread was committed to buying local and supporting local agriculture. Besides dairy and eggs, maple syrup was an important part of our local farm economy. We developed a large repertoire of maple-sweetened items from bread to cakes to granola. Maple wheat makes excellent English muffins and rolls. It is also a great candidate for French toast, and we offered it for toast, English muffins or French toast every Saturday brunch.

4 cups hot water
2 1/2 cups wheat flakes
2 tablespoons butter or 2 tablespoons oil
1/2 cup maple syrup

1 cup warm water
1 1/3 tablespoon yeast
2 cups whole wheat bread flour
1 tablespoon salt
6 1/2 to 7 cups unbleached flour

If you are new to yeast baking, read the general instructions on page 30 before you begin. Pour hot water over wheat flakes, butter or oil and maple syrup. Allow to stand until room temperature. Dissolve yeast in warm water till it begins to foam, or proof. Add the proofed yeast to water and flakes. Stir in whole wheat flour. Beat 50 to 100 strokes. Stir in unbleached flour, a little at a time to a kneadable consistency. Turn out onto a floured surface or work it in your bowl if it is big enough. Knead in salt and enough flour to form elastic, springy dough. Lightly oil both top and bottom of dough. Set to rise, covered with a damp cloth. Let rise until doubled in size.

Turn out onto floured surface. Divide into three equal pieces. Knead each piece until it becomes a smooth round ball. Let rise until doubled. Preheat oven to 350 degrees. Grease pans. Form loaves. Place in greased pans. Let rise until doubled. Bake 45 minutes to one hour until golden brown and hollow-sounding when tapped. Turn out onto wire racks. Cool and eat!

English muffins:

Divide one third of the risen dough into six pieces. Knead each of these into a smooth ball. Let them rest at least 15 minutes. Pour a handful of cornmeal onto your counter or into a small bowl. Flatten each round and press into the cornmeal, so both sides are dusted. Place on a plate or pan to rise. On top of the stove, preheat a fry pan or griddle to medium heat. Place the risen rounds on the pre-heated pan or griddle and grill till browned on one side, 5 to 10 minutes. Turn over to brown on the other. They should feel firm, not soft when gently pressed. Allow to cool before splitting to toast.

Jim Painter •

Jim worked for a year as a breakfast cook while recovering from one skirmish with the cancer which took his life in 1997. Grilling all 36 English without burning any was a challenge. Jim sent us this solstice poem:

In Celebration of the Life of

Jim Painter

Hi Daily Bread! Fellow transmitters of light & love!
Season Greetings
Life Greetings Death Greetings
Dark Greetings Light Greetings
Maine Greetings!
Blessings on your work and burn an E-muff for me once in a while.
Jim (12)

1961 - 1997

French Baguette (2 loaves)

1990's baker David Lanxner wanted to make a "real" French bread. He worked from the basic method given in John McLure's *Baba a Louis Bakery Bread Book,* recipes from another Vermont landmark. This loaf needs all day or overnight to rise. It has a thick, brittle crust that can about cut your mouth. Because it has no oil or sweetener, it will not keep long. It is perfect with any number of cheeses, an oily antipasto, soup, salad or casserole.

1 2/3 cups warm potato water
1 1/2 teaspoon yeast
4 teaspoons salt (yes, this is the correct amount)
4 3/4 to 6 cups unbleached flour

Night before:

Dissolve yeast in water till it foams. After the yeast has bubbled, add the salt and flour and work with spoon or hands into a stiff dough. Turn out onto a floured surface or use your bowl, and knead till it is smooth. It doesn't seem possible that this will turn into anything edible, but have faith. Place in a lightly greased bowl, cover lightly and let rise in a cool place or the refrigerator overnight or all day.

Next morning or later that day:

Voila! Turn out onto floured surface. Divide into two and knead each into a smooth ball. Let rise till doubled. This may take a while depending on the temperature. The warmer the room is, the quicker the rise will be. Stretch each piece into a long, almost rectangle, using your hands or a rolling pin. With the long side toward you, roll up very tightly, working back and forth across each piece, pinching as you go to form a long, skinny roll about 18 inches long. Place seam side down on a lightly cornmealed baking sheet.

Preheat oven to 425 degrees. Let rise. Brush or spray heavily with water. Slice deep diagonals into the tops with a sharp knife. Spray oven with water or throw a few ice cubes into the bottom just before you start bread baking. This is the secret to a chewy, authentic Baguette crust. Bake 35-45 minutes until tops are golden brown and crackly.

Whole Grain Whole Wheat (2 loaves)

This recipe closely resembles the classic Tassajara wheat bread. Tassajara is a Buddhist retreat center in California. Edward Espe Brown's original *Tassajara Bread Book,* of bread and goody recipes served at the center, was published in 1969. It was required reading for hippies and health food eaters who wanted to bake breads, muffins and sweets which appealed to the general palate, things their kids would eat without protest. This is about as basic as a whole wheat bread can be. The additional rise of the sponge helps make this light enough for sandwiches. Spelt flour works well with this recipe for those who are wheat sensitive.

4 cups warm water
1 1/2 tablespoon yeast
1/4 cup honey
8 cups whole wheat bread flour
3 tablespoons oil
1 tablespoon salt

Mix water, yeast, honey and 4 cups of the flour together. Beat 50 to 100 strokes with a spoon. Let sit about one hour until lots of bubbles are in evidence and it has risen up the sides of the bowl. This is the sponge. Add oil and salt, and stir into the sponge. Add the remaining flour a little at a time till it is a knead-able consistency. Turn out onto a floured surface and knead well until dough is elastic and springy. This dough will continue to feel stickier than most. Place in a lightly greased bowl and let rise till doubled, about one hour.

Punch down using fists to collapse dough in on itself. Let rise again till doubled. This will not take as long--20 to 30 minutes.

Turn out onto floured surface and divide into two equal parts. Knead each piece into a smooth round ball. Let rise again till doubled. Preheat oven to 350 degrees. Form into loaves. Let rise. Bake 45 minutes to 1 hour until light brown and hollow when tapped.

Tuesday
Oatmeal (2 loaves)
Richmond resident Louise Freer gave me this recipe when I first started. It became a bakery regular with many fans of it plain or as Oatmeal Raisin (see below). Moist and chewy, the molasses gives it an old-fashioned flavor.

   3 cups hot water
   2 tablespoons butter or oil
   1/2 cup molasses
   2 1/4 cups regular rolled oats, not instant
   3/4 cups warm water
   1 tablespoon yeast
   2 teaspoons salt
   6 to 7 cups unbleached flour

Use basic method for cereal grain dough, such as Maple Wheat.

Oatmeal Raisin (2 loaves)
How did oatmeal and raisins become such a popular couple? I don't know, but the addition of a little cinnamon and raisins to Oatmeal made excellent toast or a base for sweet sandwiches. For a special breakfast, try it as French toast.

   1 recipe oatmeal dough, uncooked
   1 to 1 1/2 cups raisins (depending on how fond you are of raisins)
   3/4 teaspoon cinnamon

When dough is pressed out into a rectangle and ready to loaf, sprinkle 1/4 teaspoon cinnamon and 1/3 to 1/2 cup raisins on top. Leave a border at the top edge so dough will still stick to itself. Roll up as usual. Let rise. Slice diagonally into tops with a sharp knife. Bake.

Sourdough

Before baker's yeast was grown commercially, cooks used a little dough saved from the previous batch called "starter." Some starters have provenance back centuries. If you are located near an artisan bakery, you might coax the baker to give you a little piece to start your own. Otherwise, you will have to collect your own wild yeast. These will vary from place to place. There is plenty in the air of any commercial bakery or home kitchen where regular yeast baking takes place. Outdoor types of yeast are good to attract to your trap. Make sure you cover the container with cheesecloth or other slightly porous cloth when you leave it outside, or you may have uninvited guests.

Simple Starter: stalking the wild yeast
1 cup potato water or milk
1 cup whole wheat bread flour

Stir liquid and flour together in a small bowl or wide-mouthed jar. Cover loosely and allow the mixture to stand out overnight or as many as three days. Put your container outside for one day if the temperature is above 65 degrees. Bubbles should appear on the surface. It may collapse. That is OK. It should sheet off your spoon like jam or jelly. If a little mold appears on the surface, scrape it carefully off and discard. Always save a few tablespoons of starter before adding sweetener, oil or seeds. Keep in a loosely covered jar in the refrigerator for your next sourdough adventure.

Sourdough French (2 loaves)
I concocted this one. It is not a true sourdough like the Artisan breads which gained popularity in the 1990's, since it relies on baker's yeast for some of its rise. It is soft with a mild tang. It makes nice dinner rolls, burger rolls or even pita bread.

Note: You need sourdough starter for this. Use some held back from your last episode or you will need a few days to season a new starter. See above.
Day One:
2 tablespoons sourdough starter
1 cup warm potato water
1 cup whole wheat bread flour

Stir together starter, water and flour to make a thick batter. Follow general sourdough directions. Remember to take out some starter!
Day Two:
1 cup warm water
1 tablespoon yeast
3 tablespoons honey
1 1/2 tablespoons oil
3/4 teaspoon salt
2 1/2 to 3 1/2 cups unbleached flour
Additional 1 egg and water for glaze

Dissolve yeast in warm water. Let proof. Add yeast mixture to sour mix and stir well. Stir in honey, oil, salt and half the unbleached flour. Beat well. Add the rest of the flour, a little at a time, to a kneadable consistency. Turn out onto a floured surface or use your bowl. Knead in enough flour to form elastic, springy dough. Let rise until doubled. Turn out onto floured surface. Divide into two equal pieces and knead into rounds. Cover and let rise until doubled. Preheat oven to 350 degrees. Form each ball into a box, round or oval loaf. Place on greased baking sheet, lightly dusted with cornmeal. Let rise until doubled. Beat egg with a little water. Brush with egg glaze. Make three diagonal slices with a sharp knife into the top of each loaf. Bake 45 minutes to 1 hour.

Employees ·

Even though I enjoy my work as a massage therapist very much, I'm so used to describing my time at the Daily Bread as "the best job I ever had" that it's easy to think of it that way. It is, indeed, a cherished memory.

    Rosie McLaughlin, Therapeutic Massage
    practitioner in Portland, Oregon (13)

While my original plan was for a sole proprietorship with myself as the one and only worker, it quickly became apparent that I required assistance if I wanted to survive the first year. My parents visited the first summer, and they helped at the shop with labels and bagging. Judy took over the accounts. Heidi Racht and Alan Campbell started delivering bread. Seamstress neighbor Lael Livack and Tanya Clark closed once a week and did the big clean-up. Soon Pat Bates started the long line of Granola queens and kings. And so it began.

Then it became obvious that traditionally bakers worked at night to have product for morning customers. I hired Jeffrey Nagle as the first dough boy to get things going so there would be sweet rolls for the early customers at 6 and fresh bread for lunch. Judy baked off and on for the next 18 years. The next morning bakers were Sandra Heath and her husband Bill Owens, who lived right across the street and were just starting their jewelry business, Silverwear, still thriving in Benson, VT.

Jeff Nagle was the first dough person to hold down the early morning baker position.

Kids and other work drew these early people away, and the business grew enough to need a half-time person. I advertised formally only once in 21 years. I asked people to write a brief note about themselves, their skills and their reasons for wanting to work there. I usually went on personal vibe and enthusiasm for food.

By the end of the first seven years, with just the bakery, the Bread was open six days, with two people on shift each day, over-lapping an hour or so through the noon hour. Each was his or her own boss.

For many years we had this quote on the wall:
(14)

Lael Livack had her sewing shop next door during the early years and often helped out.

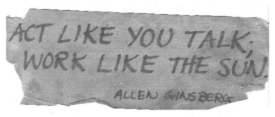

Wednesday

Maple Bran (3 loaves or 2 loaves plus 8 English muffins or rolls)

This is a variation on the Maple Wheat, substituting bran for wheat flakes. We baked Maple Wheat on Mondays and Fridays, Maple Bran on Wednesdays. Some customers will remember coming in for one and finding the other. Four in the morning found many of us not as awake as we thought.

5 cups warm water
2 cups wheat bran
1/3 cup maple syrup
1 1/3 tablespoon yeast
1 1/2 cups whole wheat bread flour
2 tablespoons butter or 2 tablespoons oil
1 tablespoon salt
6 1/2 to 7 cups unbleached flour

Combine water, bran, syrup and yeast. Allow yeast to proof. Add whole wheat flour. Beat vigorously 50-100 strokes. Stir in unbleached flour a little at a time till dough is knead-able. Turn onto floured surface or use your mixing bowl. Knead in salt and enough flour to form springy dough. Follow general bread instructions (page 29) for rising, forming and baking.

New York Rye (2 loaves)

Yes, I did grow up on Long Island, and a favorite, light weekend meal was from the Jewish deli in the next town. Seeded light rye was a major part of the experience. I searched a long time before discovering the basic inspiration and method in James Beard's *Beard on Bread*. I will include our original version and 1990's baker Andrew Paschetto's changes.

Note: These are sourdough breads which require starter, prepared the first time a few days ahead.

Method One:
Day One:
1 cup sourdough starter
2 cups warm water
2 cups rye flour, coarse if you can find it

Stir together starter, water and flour in a medium bowl to make thick slurry. Cover loosely and allow the bowl to sit out overnight.

Day Two:
1/2 cup warm water
1 tablespoon yeast
2 tablespoons honey
1 1/2 tablespoons caraway seed
2 tablespoons oil
2 teaspoons salt
4 to 5 cups unbleached flour
Additional 1 egg and water for glaze

Dissolve yeast in warm water. Let proof. Add to overnight mix after taking out starter for the next time. Add honey, caraway, oil, salt and half the unbleached flour. Beat well with a spoon, 50-100 strokes. Add the rest of the flour a little at a time until dough is kneadable. Turn out onto a floured surface. Knead till dough is smooth and elastic. Place in oiled bowl, lightly covered with a damp towel. Let rise till doubled in size. Divide into two parts. Knead into rounds. Let rise till doubled. Preheat oven to 350 degrees. Form loaves, whatever your choice: box, round or oval (*batard*). Let rise till doubled. Brush with egg glaze and slash with a sharp knife just before baking. Bake 45-50 minutes.

Method 2:
Andrew's changes. This yields a chewier loaf

Day One:
1 cup sourdough starter
2 cups warm potato water
1 cup rye flakes
1 cup rye flour

Stir together starter, water, flakes and flour to a thick slurry. Cover lightly and allow to stand overnight. Three hours will do, but will not give as much flavor.

Day Two:
1/2 cup warm water
1 tablespoon yeast
2 tablespoons honey
1 1/2 tablespoons caraway seed
2 tablespoons oil
4 1/2 cups unbleached flour
1 egg and a little water for glaze

Follow method on page 39. Remember to take out starter to save for your next batch! For a more flavorful loaf, add other seeds such as flax, dill, poppy or cumin.

Pumpernickel (2 loaves)

I loved the dark, moist, grainy Pumpernickel loaves which also came from the deli when I was a kid. This is the closest we ever came at the Bread. Andrew Paschetto is responsible for this version. Hammelman's Bakery, which operated during the same time period as Daily Bread but in Brattleboro, made the real thing. They used a recipe passed along to them by a German minister. It baked over night in a very slow oven and was dense, dark and chewy with cracked grains.

Note: This requires prior planning to have sourdough starter already prepared.

Day One:
2 1/4 cups rye flakes
3/4 cup rye flour
1 tablespoon caraway seed
1 tablespoon unsweetened cocoa
2 1/4 teaspoons salt
2 tablespoons sourdough starter
3/4 cup water
1 1/2 tablespoons oil
1/2 cup warm water
1 tablespoon molasses
3 tablespoons barley malt
1 tablespoon yeast

Combine flakes, flour, caraway, cocoa, salt, starter, 3/4 cup water and oil in your regular bread-mixing bowl. Stir water, molasses, barley malt and yeast together in a large cup. Let yeast bubble up. Combine this mixture with the flakes and flour mix. Work this into a thick gooey glop with a heavy spoon, heavy whisk or your hands. It doesn't seem that it will turn into bread, but have faith. It is the mingling of all these flavors into the rising batter that gives this its authentic taste.

Day Two:
3/4 cup warm water
3 3/4 cups +/- unbleached flour
1 egg and a little water for glaze

Save a few tablespoons of your overnight mix for starter. Add water and half the flour to the overnight mix. This is stiff dough. Add rest of flour, a little at a time, until dough is kneadable dough. Turn out onto floured surface. Knead in more flour until dough is springy and beginning to feel elastic. Let rise until doubled. Turn out onto a floured surface. Divide into two equal pieces. Knead into rounds. Let rise till doubled. Form loaves into rounds or ovals and place on a baking sheet, lightly sprinkled with cornmeal. Preheat oven to 350 degrees. Let loaves rise till doubled. Brush with an egg wash or spray with water. Slice a crisscross or a few diagonals into tops with a sharp knife. Bake 45-50 minutes.

Onion Rye (2 loaves)

Krista Willett contributed this recipe, which she received from a co-worker of her mother's at a small college in mid-state Pennsylvania. Andrew Paschetto changed it a little, with the addition of sourdough starter. The sweetness of the onions and the honey give this rye variation a rich taste. It makes an excellent Reuben sandwich base, with either the traditional corned beef or the tempeh variety we served (see page 269).

Day One:
1 1/3 cups potato water
1/3 cup sourdough starter
3/4 cups rye flour
3/4 cups rye flakes

Stir together water, starter, flour and flakes to a thick slurry. Cover and let stand out overnight.

Day Two:
1/3 cup warm water
1 tablespoon yeast
3 tablespoons honey
3 tablespoons oil
2 teaspoons salt

2 tablespoons caraway seed
2/3 cup chopped raw onions
4 to cups unbleached flour

Use sourdough method as for New York Rye.

Fellow Travelers. ·

Upland Bakery's Jules and Helen Rabin baked legendary bread from their Plainfield home. The crunchy crust surrounded chewy bread with lots of holes to hold butter or whatever-- artisan loaves before their time. Shoppers planned their coop trips to coincide with Rabin's deliveries. When I made the ocaasional granola delivery to Buffalo Mountain Coop, I always looked for their loaves.

Jules was a Goddard College faculty member until the college fell on tough financial times in the late 1970's. Rabins had built a fieldstone oven at their Plainfield home after visiting a Ghandian community in France where members all brought their bread to a central oven for baking. The concept didn't catch on in Plainfield, but the Rabins put the oven to use when they needed an alternative to Jules' salary.

Upland bread is only baked three days a week. Both Helen and Jules share in the work. They have their specialties. They found working at home gave them time with their children when they were young, now for their other interests and pursuits. And life centered around their homestead fit with their basic beliefs.

If you are lucky, you may still find their bread in Central Vermont food coops and stores.

Jules called me occasionally to ask for donations for striking union workers or flood victims. Knowing they were there gave me strength to follow my own beliefs.

Thursday
Molasses Bran (2 loaves)

This recipe came to us through Onnie Palmer. She found the original, which at the time (1978) was her family's favorite, in Delores Casella's *A World of Breads* and called Butter Bran. Following customer demand, we substituted oil for butter and changed its name.

3 1/2 cups warm water
1/3 cup molasses
1 1/2 tablespoons yeast
3 cups wheat bran
1 1/2 teaspoons salt
4 tablespoons oil or butter
6 to 8 cups unbleached flour

Follow straight dough method, such as Maple Bran on page 38, for mixing, forming and baking.

Plain French (2 loaves or 1 loaf plus 6 calzone wrappers)

This is your classic French loaf: water, yeast, a little sweetener, salt and flour. It is great for a day, maybe two. It is not a keeper. We replaced our original calzone dough with this after staff and customers requested a breadier wrapper. This is the basis for the famed Garlic French, below.

2 1/2 cups warm potato water, plain tap water will do in a pinch
1 tablespoon yeast
1 1/2 tablespoons honey
1 1/2 teaspoons salt
5 1/2 to 7 cups unbleached flour
1 egg and water for glaze

Follow straight dough method. To form loaves, press your rounds into ovals, long side towards you. Roll up, pulling fairly tightly. This will keep loaves from spreading out in the oven. Pinch the seam; give a roll to even out the loaf. Grease a flat baking sheet. Sprinkle it with cornmeal. Place loaves seam side down on the sheet to rise. Preheat oven to 350 degrees. Let loaves rise, 30-40 minutes. Brush with egg glaze before putting in the oven to bake. Bake 40-50 minutes.

Garlic French (2 loaves)

Fresh chopped or "slushed" garlic (garlic pureed with a touch of olive oil) and lots of it, baked right into each loaf, made this a garlic-lover's delight. Thick slices of garden ripe tomatoes on a slice are to live for. Hundreds of loaves over the years accompanied the spaghetti at fourth grade fund-raisers.

One recipe unbaked Plain French dough
6 cloves garlic, chopped fine or pureed into slush
1 egg and water for glaze

When you are ready to loaf, press each piece out into an oval, long side toward you. Spread half the prepared garlic on each piece, leaving room at the top empty so the dough will stick to itself and hold together in the oven. Roll up as tightly as is possible, beginning with the edge towards you. Pinch the seam. Place seam down on a lightly cornmealed baking sheet. Preheat oven to 350 degrees. Let rise. Brush with egg glaze, water, or nothing. Slice diagonally across the top of each loaf two or three times with a sharp knife. Bake 45-50 minutes.

Jonesville friends the Minards, Grants and Lowes took bread to new heights: the top of Mount Mansfield!

Equipment

The old 20-quart Hobart mixer I had purchased from Ruth Cobb's Lincoln, Vermont home bakery, was working way too hard to keep up with orders. Someone sent me to retired baker Ray LeBlanc. He had a garage full of equipment and a cautionary tale to tell. He was disabled by trying to catch a 20-quart mixer which was walking itself across the counter. I purchased his old 80-quart Hobart mixer, many pans and small items. That mixer, vintage 1930s, served us well. It let us down only once when an old break let go. Jeb took the old shaft part to Tom Drake in Burlington who machined us a replacement.

The Blodgett ovens were also old, having served the Ecole Champlain school, now Kingsland Bay State Park. They required occasional replacement of the thermo-couple.

I replaced a long line of ancient Sunbeams with a Kitchenaid mixer for small batters. Jeb fabricated cooling racks. He found and restored a roll divider in the scrap pile at the steel yard, which divides a lump of dough into 36 equal pieces. Other than shelving and storage containers, we did not add to the bake shop equipment until the 1999 expansion. Employees and customers enjoyed the beauty and utility of our handmade fixtures.

Baker LeBlanc's tale led me to lecture every new hire: do not risk harm to yourself or anyone else to save a utensil or piece of equipment. Most equipment can be repaired. It's not so easy with human beings.

Friday
Maple Wheat (see page 32)
Baker's Choice (see next section for Specials)

Saturday
Portuguese White (3 loaves)

The original recipe called for boiling the water, butter and salt and allowing them to cool before adding the remaining ingredients. This is what made it authentically "Portuguese." Terry Bachman's family came from Portugal, and they were fond of this type of bread. So were customers. This was our Saturday bread, which many customers drove long distances to purchase. It is what you always wanted white bread to be.

    4 cups warm water
    2 tablespoons honey
    2 tablespoons yeast
    2 teaspoons salt
    4 tablespoons butter
    9 to 11 cups unbleached flour

Combine warm water, honey and yeast in a medium to large mixing bowl. Let stand until the yeast has foamed, or proofed. Add 5 cups flour and beat vigorously with a wooden spoon 50-100 strokes. Add salt and butter and the rest of the flour, two cups at a time until the dough is beginning to come away from the bowl. Use your hands to finish mixing and to knead. Oil the kneaded dough and set to rise. Allow to double in size. Punch down and turn out onto your counter. Cut into three pieces. Knead each piece into a ball. Let rise till doubled. Preheat oven to 350 degrees. Grease three bread pans. Form each round into a loaf. Let rise. Bake 40-50 minutes till it's golden brown and it sounds hollow when thumped.

Marie Whiteford's 1999 Job Application . . . .

Dear Betsy,

I can remember getting up on Saturday morning when I was six or seven and realizing, "It's Saturday-- Corn Molasses day." I used to love walking to the bakery in the morning (we used to live in that big yellow house on the corner of Main and Baker Street) and waiting in line admiring the cakes and pastries, trying desperately to make a decision as to what to get. It was always, "Cakes or rolls? With raisins or without? What kind of bread?" Of course Saturdays were a no-brainer in that aspect as Corn Molasses was our absolute favorite. (15)

Corn Molasses (3 loaves)

My mom was very fond of cornbread. This yeasted variety, similar to what is often called Anadama, was one of the first successful yeast loaves I baked as a teenager. The original inspiration came from a recipe in *Uncle John's Bread Book*. It is sweet, moist and a good keeper.

2 2/3 cups hot water
1 1/2 cups cornmeal
1/3 cup molasses
2/3 cup warm water
1 tablespoon yeast
1 cup whole wheat bread flour
3 tablespoons oil
2 teaspoons salt
5 to 7 cups unbleached flour

Use standard cereal-based method as for Maple Wheat (page 32).

Sunday
Honey Oatmeal (3 loaves)

Judy Bush created this version of oatmeal bread. It became her house standard, and she served it to her hungry art students before their after school art classes. Judy's son Chelsie and I agree that no one can make this bread the same as Judy's. Some of Judy's art kids requested her bread at the bakery. It soon joined the ranks of regulars, becoming Sunday's offering and Monday's toast.

3 cups hot water
2 1/4 cups regular rolled oats
3 tablespoons honey
1 1/2 tablespoons oil
3/4 cup warm water
1 tablespoon yeast
1 tablespoon salt
3/4 cup whole wheat bread flour
6 to 7 cups unbleached flour

Use cereal grain based dough method such as Maple Wheat.

Der Beck	The Baker
Zu mir rein/ wer hat Hungers not	You who are hungry/ through my door tread
Ich hab gut Weiss und Ruecken Brot	I have good white and whole grain bread
Aus Korn/ Weitzen und Kern backen	Baked from rye, whole wheat and bran
Gefaltzen recht/ mit allen sachen	All ingredients kneaded right in
Ein recht Gewicht/ das recht wol schmeckt	A proper weight that tastes just so
Semel/ Bretzen/ Laub/ Spuln un' Weck	Crumb buns, pretzels, loaves, twists and rolls
Dergleich Fladen und Enerkuchn	At Easter time they come to buy
Thut man zu Ostern ben mir suchn	Things like layer cakes and pies (16)

Traditional German rhyme given to me by a customer, translated by myself.

Special Breads

Ｗe baked specials at least once a week, usually on Friday for a weekend treat. We also baked seasonal recipes such as Crown Challah, Pan de Dio de los Muertos, Stollen and Russian Easter Bread for holidays. First the baker's choices, followed by the holiday specials.

Herb (2 small loaves or 1 dozen sandwich rolls)

Huntington naturalist and writer Gale Lawrence passed this recipe on to me in the very early days of the bakery. The unusual combo of nutmeg and basil make an excellent accompaniment to anything savory. The egg makes it light in texture. This also makes excellent sandwich rolls.

2 1/2 cups warm water
1 tablespoon yeast
1/4 cup honey
3/4 teaspoon nutmeg
1 1/2 teaspoons basil
1 egg
2 teaspoons salt
2 teaspoons oil
1 cup whole wheat bread flour
4 to 6 cups unbleached flour
1 egg and water for glaze

Use straight dough method as for Portuguese White.

Sour Cream Sage (2 small loaves or 1 dozen dinner rolls)

This recipe was adapted from the original in Delores Casella's *A World of Breads*. It became a standard for holiday dinner rolls, and had many fans. It makes a yummy base for leftover Thanksgiving turkey or Easter ham. The sage flavor comes through, but is not overpowering. Make sure to give a full last rise before baking for a light end result.

1 2/3 cup warm water
1 tablespoon yeast
2 1/2 tablespoons honey
2/3 cup sour cream
1/3 cup powdered milk
1 tablespoon sage
1 tablespoon salt
1/4 cup oil
1 1/2 cups whole wheat bread flour
5 to 7 cups unbleached flour
1 egg plus water for glaze

Use straight dough method.

To make rolls, divide dough into twelve pieces after dough has risen once, as equal as you can make them. Knead each of these into a small ball. Place onto greased baking sheet. Preheat oven to 350 degrees. Let rise till doubled. Brush with egg glaze and bake 25-30 minutes. Bake bread 45-50 minutes.

Pesto (2 small loaves)

Andrew Paschetto contributed this recipe. It calls for dry basil and garlic powder, so can be prepared in any season. It smells divine while baking. A good quality olive oil rounds out the pesto flavors.

1 1/2 cups warm water
1 tablespoon yeast
1 tablespoon honey
3 tablespoons olive oil
1/3 cup dried basil
2 teaspoons garlic powder
1/3 cup walnut pieces
2 teaspoons salt
2/3 cup whole wheat bread flour
3 1/2 to 4 cups unbleached flour

Use straight dough method.
Form into round or box loaves.
Preheat oven to 350 degrees. Let
rise. Brush with olive oil before
baking. Bake 350 degrees for 45-50 minutes.

Scallion Dill (2 small loaves)

Baker Cindy Bramon brought us this recipe for a special. It is a light loaf with a surprisingly sweet flavor. We had many requests for this, especially in the summer, always a popular potluck offering. The flavors blend nicely with fresh garden vegetables, many cheeses and a variety of savory dishes.

1 2/3 cup warm water
1 1/3 tablespoon yeast
1/3 cup powdered milk
3 tablespoons honey
1 tablespoon salt
10 scallions, finely chopped
1 1/3 tablespoon dried dill weed/ 3 tablespoons fresh
1 tablespoon dill seed
1 egg
4 cups unbleached flour
1 egg and water for glaze

Use standard bread method such as Portuguese White (page 44). Form into small box loaves or rounds. Brush with egg glaze just before baking. Bake 40 minutes at 350 degrees.

Rosemary Black Olive (2 loaves)

Baker Jean Kelly, who later gained local culinary fame as "Pizza Genie," suggested this recipe to try as her baker's choice. It is as flavorful as your ingredients. Briny Kalamata olives and a full-bodied olive oil are the best. Experiment with your own choice of herbs, or add chopped fresh garlic! Also check the strength of your fresh rosemary, and adjust accordingly.

Day One: (or at least three hours before you plan to mix your dough)
2 tablespoons sourdough starter
1 cup potato water
1 cup whole wheat bread flour

Mix starter, water and flour to a loose slurry. Cover loosely and let stand overnight or a few hours.

Day Two: (or later that same day)
1 cup warm water
1 tablespoon yeast
3 tablespoons honey
1 cup coarsely chopped black
    olives
1 tablespoon dried rosemary/
    2 tablespoons fresh
1/2 teaspoon dried oregano/
    1 teaspoon fresh
1/8 teaspoon black pepper
2 teaspoons salt
1 tablespoon olive oil plus extra
    for brushing loaves
5 to 6 cups unbleached flour

Follow general method for yeasted sourdough, such as New York Rye.

Charthouse Rye (2 loaves)

Krista Willett brought in this recipe, which she received from a Bolton Valley Resort co-worker. It is a chewy, sweet, dark rye bread. Knead it long and hard, and give it lots of time to rise. Some people like to add raisins. Butter a slice to eat with a bowl of soup or stew, and you have a satisfying meal.

2 cups warm water or potato water
1 tablespoon yeast
1/3 cup molasses
1/2 cup brown sugar
1 tablespoon barley malt (not essential)
1 1/2 cups rye flour
3 cups whole wheat bread flour
Unbleached flour for kneading

Use straight dough method. The dough will be stiffer than most. Give it lots of time to rise. Form loaves into rounds or ovals. Preheat oven to 350 degrees. Bake 50-60 minutes.

Golden Corn (2 loaves)

Richmond farmer George Safford was well known for his bountiful crops of winter squash and his boundless generosity. Daily Bread was a frequent recipient of both. While searching for ways to use our supply, I discovered the original for this "Yeasted Cornbread" in Delores Casella's *A World of Breads.* The squash serves as the only sweetener, and I added the soy flour for additional protein. Baker Lynn E. Alden noticed that the loaf contained the Native American food staples of corn, beans (soy), and squash, known as the Three Sisters since their combination of sweet, vitamins and protein are life-sustaining. So we began calling this Three Sister's Bread. Unlike powder- or soda-risen cornbreads, this slices well and holds together for sandwiches or toast. The dough can be a little finicky, so don't give up on your first try.

1 1/2 cups hot water
1 1/2 cups cornmeal
1/2 cup cooked and mashed winter squash or pumpkin
1/2 cup warm water
2 1/2 teaspoons yeast
1 teaspoon salt
1 1/2 tablespoons oil or 3 tablespoons butter, soft
1/2 cup whole wheat bread flour
1/4 cup soy flour
4 to 5 cups unbleached flour

Use the soaked grain method as for Maple Wheat (page 32). This dough is stickier than many. It wants to have spring, despite its moisture. Knead well and let rise fully before baking. Bake 45-55 minutes at 350 degrees

8-Grain (2 loaves)

Cheesetraders, a wine and foods store in South Burlington, Vt. approached us to produce some of their breads in the late 1990s. Owner Steve Leidell gave us this recipe to try. Customers (and staff) looking for a hearty, full-grain bread were delighted with this one. The seeds and grains must be soaked overnight or all day before they are soft enough to add to the dough. This is not for the soft of tooth! Even after soaking, the barley can be very crunchy.

Day One:
1/3 cup rolled oats
1/3 cup millet
1/3 cup bulgur
1/3 cup pearled barley
1/3 cup hulled sesame seeds
1/3 cup poppy seeds
1/3 cup sunflower seeds
1 2/3 cups cold water

Soak grains overnight or all day in cold water. Hot water will keep grains from softening, especially the barley.

Day 2:
1/2 cup warm water
2 teaspoons yeast
1/3 cup honey
1 1/4 cups whole wheat bread flour
2 1/2 cups unbleached flour
1 teaspoon each of poppy seeds, sesame seeds and sunflower seeds for the rolling

Let yeast proof in water and honey till foamy. Add to soaked grains. Add whole wheat and unbleached flours, can be all at one time. Stir or use hands to work into sticky dough. Turn out onto floured surface. Knead till dough feels springy. Note that it may continue to be a little sticky. Let rise. Divide into two pieces. Knead each into a round. Let rise. Grease one or two baking sheets. Preheat oven to 350 degrees. Flatten each risen piece into an oval. Roll up tightly into an 8-inch long loaf. Pinch seam on bottom. Mix the seeds on a plate or baking sheet. Roll each loaf in the seeds to cover all around. Place, seam side down, on a greased baking sheet. Let rise. Bake for 50-60 minutes.

Peanut Butter (2 loaves)

This follows closely a recipe from Frances Moore Lappe's *Diet for a Small Planet*, whose basic premise is that we can feed ourselves very well with less degradation to the planet by combining "complementary" plant proteins rather than relying so heavily on animal proteins for nutrition. Plants are efficient producers, using less energy to grow and less energy to store. This recipe combines milk, peanut, soy and wheat proteins.

While the concept seems weird, the nutty sweetness is quite nice with cheese, ham, bacon, tempeh, tofu or just plain peanut butter and jelly.

2 cups warm water
1/4 cup powdered milk
3 tablespoons molasses
1 1/2 tablespoons yeast
1/3 cup peanut butter
1/4 cup soy flour
3/4 teaspoon salt
4 1/2 cups unbleached flour

Follow instructions for a straight dough such as Portuguese White.

Lemon Almond Braid (2 small loaves)

This was inspired by a recipe in the original *Tassajara Bread Book*. We altered it some. It is a sweet, rich loaf especially nice for holidays or weekend brunch. The braids, brushed with egg wash before baking, are shiny and aromatic. If there's any left over, it makes extravagant French toast.

1 1/4 cup warm water
3 tablespoons powdered milk
1/4 cup honey
1 tablespoon yeast
2 eggs
1 cup whole wheat bread flour
3/4 teaspoon nutmeg
1/4 cup chopped almonds
1 teaspoon grated lemon zest
1 teaspoon lemon juice
4 tablespoons melted butter
1 teaspoon salt
3 to 4 cups unbleached flour
Additional water and egg for glaze

Use straight dough method. This dough becomes smooth as a baby's bottom. Divide risen dough into 2 equal pieces and knead each into a ball. Let rest at least 15 minutes. To form braids, roll each ball into a long snake. Cut each into three pieces and braid, beginning at the middle, so the middle will be thick and the ends tapered (see illustration on page 54).

Preheat oven to 350 degrees. Let rise. Bake 40-50 minutes till golden brown and it sounds hollow when thumped.

Baking, an Act of Love..

Yeast is a gift, It is a gift of life.
Yeast lives, it moves and has its being.
God gave us yeast, so we could feel how to work with a living thing.
Give us this day,
Our daily bread.
And accept our thanks for the life that is in it.

We put ourselves into it.
We arise early, out of warm beds
To come and bring life into our bread.
And our bread makes our rising worth the while.

Leave me alone, in front of a board,
With a mound of living dough.
Let it feel my touch,
And spring back to me with its ready love.

"Loave" must be some
Forgotten participle of "love."
For that is what my bread insists that I feel.
We are in love, there at my board.
    Paul Benzaquin (17)

Excerpted from a longer poem Paul wrote after spending a morning bake shift with me. Used with his permission.

Holidays

Challah (2 loaves)

This light braided bread, usually topped with a sprinkling of poppy seeds, is the traditional Friday evening Sabbath loaf served at Jewish tables around the world. I was told that true Challah was a braid of seven strands, one for each day of the week. It represents the fruits of the earth for which thanks is given. Everyone at the table gets a piece. The mother of the house is always given the first piece, and then according to age, eldest first.

1 1/2 cups warm water
1 tablespoon yeast
2 eggs
1/4 cup honey
1/4 cup oil
2 teaspoons salt
1 cup whole wheat bread flour
3 to 4 cups unbleached flour
1 egg and water for glaze
1 teaspoon poppy seeds for tops

Mix according to a straight dough method, noting that it will be softer than most when it reaches its smooth stage. Let rise. Divide risen dough into two equal pieces and knead each into a ball. Let rest at least 15 minutes. To form braids, roll each ball into a long snake. Cut each into three pieces and braid, beginning at the middle, so the middle will be thick and the ends tapered. Preheat oven to 350 degrees. Let rise. Bake 40-50 minutes till golden brown and it sounds hollow when thumped.

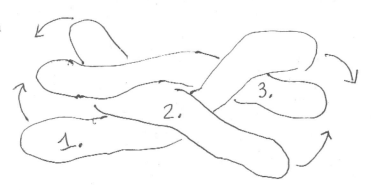

Round Crown Challah (2 large loaves)

Rosh Hashanah, the Jewish New Year, which falls around the time of the autumnal equinox, celebrates the fullness and sweetness of the year. For this holiday only, the Challah is extra sweet, with raisins and sometimes nuts, and round to signify the full circle of the seasons. Andrew Paschetto brought in this version. He cautions against adding too much flour to this or other sweet doughs. They want to feel soft and almost greasy.

    1 2/3 cups warm water
    1 1/3 tablespoons yeast
    2 eggs
    2/3 cup honey
    1 teaspoon nutmeg
    Grated zest of 1 lemon
    1/2 cup raisins
    1/2 cup coarsely chopped almonds
    1 1/2 teaspoons salt
    1/3 cup oil
    1 1/3 cups whole wheat bread flour
    4 3/4 to 5 1/4 cups unbleached flour
    1 egg and water for glaze

Use straight dough method, adding only enough flour to make smooth, soft dough which will not quite stick to your hands. Let rise till doubled; give it time. Form loaves into rounds or save about one quarter of the dough to braid. Form the larger pieces into rounds. Grease one or two baking sheets. Place rounds on sheet/s. Divide the smaller pieces, each into three. Roll out each piece into a long snake. Form two braids. Wrap each braid into a circle, pinching the ends together. Place one circle on each round. Preheat oven to 350 degrees. Let rise till doubled. Brush with egg glaze. Bake 40-50 minutes.

Pan de Dio de los Muertos/ Mexican Day of the Dead Bread (2 large loaves)

November 1 is the day after Halloween and is celebrated in many cultures. Some know it as All Souls' or All Saints' Day. In Mexico, and some other South and Central American countries, it is called the Day of the Dead. Elaborate shrines appear at grave sites, covered with all variety of sweets and flowers. Home altars are decorated in a similar fashion. Sugar skulls are sold in every market and shop. All these goodies are to feed the spirits of those who have come before, and to laugh at death. This subtly flavored loaf is baked for the holiday, and is often formed into the shapes of skulls and bones. I have also seen it baked in clay bowls. Cook and Spanish instructor Sherry Pachman brought us this recipe.

1 1/2 cups warm water
1 tablespoon yeast
3 tablespoons honey
2 eggs
6 tablespoons soft butter
1/4 cup powdered milk
1 1/2 teaspoons anise seed
1 pinch nutmeg
1 teaspoon grated orange zest
5 to 6 cups unbleached flour
1 egg and water for glaze
1 tablespoon confectioner's sugar for dusting finished loaves

Mix to a soft dough using straight dough method as for Portuguese White. Divide dough into two or three pieces after its first rise. Knead each piece into a smooth round and allow to rest 15 minutes. To form skulls, knead a small round. Pinch across the lower portion to create the jaw. Use your finger to poke eye holes and nostrils. You get the picture. Use a sharp knife for more detail. For bones, press out into a long oval. Roll very tightly into a long French-style loaf. Bulge out both ends. Slice each end through with a knife. Grease one or more baking sheets. Place loaves on the prepared sheets. Preheat oven to 350 degrees. Let rise till doubled. Brush with egg glaze. Bake 40-50 minutes until golden brown and aromatic. Dust with confectioner's sugar while loaves are still hot.

Holiday Stollen (2 large or 3 medium loaves)

Stollen was an essential part of my childhood Christmas experience ever since I can remember. I think it staved off hunger while we went through opening presents Christmas morning before the family had a real breakfast. My year abroad in Germany as a senior in high school gave this traditional German holiday bread even more meaning. When I returned from Germany, I started baking it myself for family and neighbors. When I began baking professionally, it remained a traditional holiday offering. It is rich and fruity and smells wonderful while baking or toasting later on.

1 cup water
1 tablespoon yeast
1/3 cup honey
1/4 cup powdered milk
2 eggs
12 tablespoons soft butter/ 1 1/2 sticks
Grated zest of 1/2 lemon
Grated zest of 1/2 orange
1/2 cup raisins
· 3/4 cup chopped almonds
3 to 4 cups unbleached flour
2 tablespoons melted butter for brush-
      ing tops
2 tablespoons confectioners sugar for
      tops

Original artwork by Lynn E Alden.

Follow straight dough method to form soft greasy dough. To
form loaves, flatten each round into an oval. Fold almost in half, the long way. Preheat oven to
425 degrees. Let loaves rise. Bake 10 minutes at 425 degrees. Reduce heat to 350 and bake another 35-45 minutes until well browned and sounds hollow when tapped.

Russian Easter Bread (2 loaves)

Judy Bush got this recipe from a family in Franconia, New Hampshire, when she and Jeb
lived there in the late 1960's. She baked it as gifts for Easter and other holidays. It is similar to
Stollen, but sweeter and lighter. At the bakery, we formed the loaves into egg shapes and cut decorative designs in the tops before baking.

3/4 cup warm water
1 tablespoon yeast
4 eggs, separated
3 1/2 tablespoons honey
1/3 cup powdered milk
8 tablespoons soft butter/ 1 stick
Grated zest of 1 lemon
1 pinch salt
1/2 cup raisins
1/2 cup chopped almonds
5 to 7 cups unbleached flour
3 1/2 tablespoons sugar, to beat with the egg whites
1 egg and water to make glaze

Proof yeast in warm water. Add egg yolks, powdered milk, butter, lemon zest, salt, raisins, almonds and half the flour to make a soft batter. Beat sugar and egg whites with an electric mixer or wire whip, to form stiff peaks. Fold the beaten whites and enough flour to make soft but kneadable dough. Turn out onto floured surface and knead. Place in greased bowl to rise. Turn out onto floured surface. Divide into two pieces and shape into ovals, egg-like in appearance. Preheat oven to 475 degrees. Let rise. Brush with egg glaze and cut designs into the top with a small sharp knife or single edged razor blade. Bake 5 minutes at 475 degrees. Reduce oven to 350 degrees and bake an additional 35-45 minutes until the bread sounds hollow when tapped on the bottom.

No Donuts

How can an establishment calling itself a bakery exist without frying doughnuts? Somehow, Daily Bread managed to stay in business twenty-one years without ever frying one.

Housemate Wendy Weldon's father Jack ran a bakery supply company in Indiana, America's heartland, which wholesaled King Arthur flour, among other products. Jack was an astute economist and business-man, and no stranger to the financials of commercial baking. He could not believe that I was not going to make doughnuts! He told me that 80% of bakery business (in 1979) was doughnuts!

Deep fat frying is dangerous business, creating potentially flammable greasy vapors and a nasty mess. State regulations require that one have automatic fire extinguishing and an exhaust hood of very particular specifications. It would have cost me $5,000 (in 1979) to set up for frying. It cost me $5,000 for everything else!

Heart healthy is not what comes to mind when you think "doughnut." They are high in carbohydrates, sugars and fats--all the things our doctors warn us against. They also have a very short shelf life. There is nothing worse than a sinker of a doughnut past its prime.

No doughnuts--and they said it couldn't be done.

Rolls, sweet rolls, soda bread and pretzel

Irish Soda Bread (2 loaves)

This recipe is a tip o' the hat to my Irish ancestors. I don't know where I first got this recipe. We baked it every Saint Patrick's Day. It is a quick bread with baking soda and cream of tartar for leavening, so there is no rising time. The raisins and caraway give it its tell-tale flavors. It is best straight out of the oven with butter. And of course, it is the perfect accompaniment to corned beef and cabbage or a nice hearty cabbage or kale soup. There's no reason other than tradition to only bake it once a year.

    2 cups buttermilk
    1 cup raisins
    1/2 tablespoon caraway seeds
    4 cups unbleached flour
    1 tablespoon sugar
    1 tablespoon baking soda
    3/4 teaspoon cream of tartar
    1 teaspoon salt
    1 tablespoon melted butter for tops

Preheat oven to 350 degrees. Grease a baking sheet. Mix raisins and seeds with buttermilk. Combine all dry ingredients and stir to combine well. Add to the wet and mix only until all ingredients are thoroughly moistened. Turn out onto a well-floured surface. The dough will be sticky. Dust hands with flour to knead lightly into two rounds. Place on greased baking sheet. Cut a cross into the top of each loaf with a sharp knife. Bake 45 minutes. Brush tops with melted butter while hot out of the oven.

Hot Cross Buns (12, one dozen)

These were one of my dad's favorites. When Lent came around each year, he would bring them home for a treat. I altered a version given in Delores Casella's *A World of Breads*. These are buttery and light, with touches of lemon, cinnamon and, of course, raisins. For the perfect result, let these rise especially well the final time before baking. The dough can be refrigerated if you wish to bake only half, or if you want to do the hard part the night before. Remember to give the chilled dough time to return to room temperature and rise before baking.

    2/3 cup warm water
    1 tablespoon yeast
    1/4 cup honey
    3 tablespoons powdered milk
    2 eggs
    5 tablespoons butter, melted
    1/3 cup raisins

Grated zest of 1/4 lemon
1 pinch cinnamon
2 2/3 cups unbleached flour
1 egg and water for glaze
1 cup confectioner's sugar and water for "crosses"

Use straight dough method, being careful not to add too much flour. This dough wants to feel a little greasy and be soft, but kneadable. Turn out onto floured surface and knead till smooth and springy. If you are refrigerating the dough, do it now. If continuing, place in an oiled bowl to rise till doubled. Turn out onto floured surface and roll out into a long snake about 2 inches in diameter. Cut into twelve equal pieces. Round each piece into a smooth ball and place one inch apart on a greased baking sheet. Preheat oven to 375 degrees. Let rise well; be patient! Brush with egg glaze. Bake 10 minutes. Reduce oven to 350 degrees and continue baking another 10-15 minutes. While buns are in the oven, make a thick but spreadable paste of confectioner's sugar with a little water. Fill pastry bag (see Tool section), using a simple round tip. After buns have cooled slightly, use bag to make a frosting cross on each one.

We often used a fork to drizzle the frosting; it's not as neat, but works and tastes just fine.

Parker House Rolls (36, three dozen)

This is your classic dinner roll. Light and buttery, they are the perfect vehicle for gravy of any kind. In a pinch, you can make little sandwiches out of them. We offered these for special order every holiday of feasting, and they were by far the customer favorite. This recipe is a slight reworking of the one from the original big blue *New York Times Cookbook.*

2 1/2 cups warm water
2 tablespoons yeast
1/2 cup powdered milk
1 tablespoon honey
8 tablespoons butter, melted/ 4 for dough, 4 for tops/1 stick
1 1/2 teaspoons salt
6 to 6 1/2 cups unbleached flour

Use straight dough method, keeping dough on the soft side. Turn out onto floured surface and knead to a smooth ball. Let rise till doubled. Turn out onto floured surface. Use rolling pin to roll out to slightly more than 1/2 inch thick. Cut out circles about 2 1/2 inches in diameter using a biscuit cutter or floured water glass. Fold each circle in half, crease down the middle, and place on greased baking sheet. Preheat oven to 350 degrees. Let rolls rise till doubled. Melt second 4 tablespoons butter and brush tops before baking. Bake 20-30 minutes.

Brioche (6 rolls or crust for 10x14 Garlic Gateau)

This is a short method version of the classic French roll with a top-knot, which grew out of the *New York Times Cookbook*'s American Brioche recipe. The extra egg yolk and the butter make these a decadently rich choice for brunch or tea. They go equally well with sweet or savory accompaniments. With a chunk of good chocolate baked inside, this becomes the infamous Pain au Chocolate. The high fat content in these turns unbelievably large amounts of garlic sweet in Garlic Gateau (see page 123-24). The dough refrigerates well, but remember to give it time to return to room temperature before rising and baking.

    1/2 cup warm water
    2 teaspoons yeast
    3 tablespoons honey
    1 egg yolk plus 2 whole eggs
    6 tablespoons butter, melted
    1 teaspoon salt
    2 2/3 to 3 cups unbleached flour
    1 egg and water for glaze

Proof yeast in warm water till foamy. Add yolk and whole eggs, salt and butter. Add flour a little at a time till you have a soft dough. Turn out onto a floured surface and knead in just enough flour to keep it from sticking to your hands. It should feel springy but greasy to the touch. Too much flour will keep these from rising to their highest level! Place in greased bowl and let rise till doubled; this can happen overnight in the refrigerator.

Turn dough onto a floured surface. Divide into 6 equal pieces and knead each piece into a round. Cover and let rise till doubled. Grease and flour muffin tin. To form, divide off about 1/8 of the piece and ball it separately (see above). Place large piece in muffin tin, and make a deep dent in the center. Place small piece in the resulting indentation and press down in. Repeat with other five rounds. Preheat oven to 350 degrees. Let rise till doubled. Brush tops with egg glaze. Bake 25 minutes.

Pain au Chocolate (6)

    1 recipe Brioche, above
    1 good 8 oz. chocolate bar

Follow recipe and method for brioche through second rising. Grease and flour muffin tin. Press each round out into a 3-4 inch circle. Place 1/6 chocolate bar in the middle of each circle. Bring outside of round around chocolate and pinch together to completely surround chocolate. Place pinched side down into greased muffin tin. Continue as above.

Golden Harvest (12, one dozen)

Baker Heidi Racht brought in this recipe for a vegan (no dairy, no eggs) dinner rolls option. The cooked winter squash (or pumpkin) gives these a beautiful golden color.

1 cup warm water
1 tablespoon yeast
1 cup cooked and mashed winter squash or pumpkin, room temperature
1/4 cup honey
1/4 teaspoon salt
4 tablespoons soy margarine, melted
2/3 cup whole wheat bread flour
3 1/3 cups unbleached flour

Follow straight bread method to make soft dough. Let rise till doubled. Turn out onto floured surface. Roll out into a long snake 2 inches in diameter. Cut into twelve equal pieces. Knead each piece into a smooth round and place on greased baking sheet about 1 inch apart. Preheat oven to 350 degrees. Let rise till doubled. Bake 25 minutes.

Sesame Soft Pretzels (9 large)

These are another Krista Willett contribution. Krista attempted to recreate day-old soft pretzels sold during school recess in Lancaster, Pennsylvania, where she grew up. She says, "These are not it, but they are good." They are low in fat, high in flavor. They received high marks from customers, and became a regular Tuesday offering.

1 cup hot water
1/4 cup bulgur or cracked wheat
1 1/2 cups warm water
1 tablespoon yeast
1 tablespoon salt
1/2 cup whole wheat bread flour
3 cups unbleached flour
1/4 cup sesame seeds
1 tablespoon kosher or other coarse salt
1 egg white and water for glaze
1/8 teaspoon pickling lime and water (gives authentic pretzel flavor, but not essential)

Pour hot water over bulgur and let cool to room temperature. Proof yeast in warm water till foamy. Add to soaked bulgur. Add salt and whole wheat flour. Stir 25-50 strokes. Add unbleached flour a little at a time to form a soft dough. Turn out onto floured surface and knead well into a smooth round. Place in greased bowl and let rise till doubled. Turn dough onto floured surface. Roll out into a snake about 2 inches in diameter. Divide into nine equal pieces. Knead each piece into a smooth round. Preheat oven to 400 degrees. Let rounds rise till doubled.

To form, roll each piece out into a snake about 12 inches long. Tie into a pretzel knot (see illustration). Press into a plate of sesame seeds and place on a lightly greased baking sheet to rise. Let rise. Brush with egg white and pickling lime, and then sprinkle with salt and additional sesame

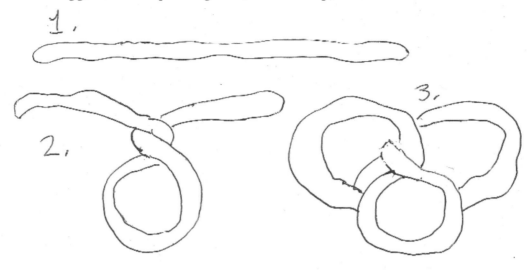

seeds. Bake 15 minutes.

Roving Review I. . . . .

You can't sit down to eat at the Daily Bread Bakery, but don't pass it up if you don't mind munching in the car, on the bakery steps, or along the banks of the Winooski River.

...It's the brightest spot in this well-weathered town, and it's got the people of Richmond hooked on breads, cakes, pies, cookies and croissants. We sampled some almond sweet rolls that were as good as any we've had anywhere. Betsy also sells coffee, milk, and mint tea (brewed right in your cup in a bamboo strainer).

Interstate Gourmet-New Haven to Burlington   1981(18)

Sweet Rolls (12 and 24, 1 dozen or 2)

These were the Daily Bread hallmark, the standard morning offering, baked every day. The recipe began with one from Delores Casella's *A World of Breads*. I altered it some, and a succession of other Bread bakers gave it their own touches. The mashed potato in the recipe is the secret ingredient. This dough rises in the refrigerator, so plan ahead. The result is well worth it. The dough may be filled with your choice, from the basic cinnamon and sugar, to decadent cream cheese concoctions, to

apples and cheddar cheese. Experiment! Delight family and friends with fresh sweet rolls some weekend or holiday morning. The dough holds well in the refrigerator for 2 to 3 days.

12	**24**
Dough:	
1 1/4 cup warm potato water	3 cups
1 1/2 teaspoons yeast	1 tablespoon
1/4 cup honey	1/2 cup
1 egg	2 eggs
1/2 cup mashed potatoes, room temp.	1 cup
4 tablespoons melted butter/ 1/2 stick	8 tablespoons/ one stick
1/3 cup wheat bran	2/3 cup
4 cups unbleached flour	8 cups
For rolls:	
4 tablespoons melted butter	8 tablespoons
1/4 cup cinnamon sugar	1/2 cup (1 tablespoon cinnamon/ 1 cup sugar)
and/or	
2 cups raisins	4 cups
or	
4 tablespoons melted butter	8 tablespoons
2 cups chopped nuts	4 cups
or	
2 cups apples, peeled, cored & diced	4 cups
1 cup cheddar grated cheese/ 4 ounces	2 cups/ 8 ounces
Glaze:	
1 cup powdered sugar	2 cups
1 1/2 tablespoons + /- water	3 tablespoons +/-
Vanilla extract, if desired	

Day One:

Proof yeast in potato water till foamy. Add honey, egg/s, potato, butter, bran and half the unbleached flour. Beat 50-100 strokes. Add remaining flour to make soft dough. Work the dough with spoon or hands till it feels "velvety." Grease another bowl and turn dough into it. Turn piece over once so top is oiled too. Cover with waxed paper and refrigerate overnight.

Day Two:

Take dough out of refrigerator and allow it to warm 30 minutes to one hour if you are in a hurry, or to room temperature if you have the time. Turn out onto a lightly floured surface. Pat out into an approximate rectangle, long side toward you. Use a rolling pin to square up your rectangle, 12 inches long for 12, 24 inches long for 24. Melt butter and brush onto surface of the rectangle. Make sure you leave an inch accross the top butter-free so you can seal the edge.

Sprinkle desired filling over the butter. Roll up, jelly-roll style, beginning with edge nearest you. Pinch the seam to seal. Slice into 12 or 24 pieces with a sharp knife. Place, cut side down on a greased baking sheet. Preheat oven to 350 degrees. Let rise till doubled.   Bake 20 minutes. Glaze with powdered sugar and water mix or brush with maple syrup.

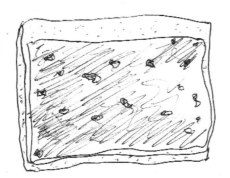 

CINNAMON RAISIN ROLL

Empty Bread Baskets. . . . .

On bakery shelves
behind thick glass,
willow bread baskets

yawn, empty of grain
loaf or crumb.

The baker's pleasure
the baker's pain,
the eternal mound of dough
to knead and name.

One father
alone at the east wall
of the shop
hears hunger's hollering call.
In answer, from his
hands fall round bagels,
mint cookie discs, plump whole wheat
loaves from old groaning stoves.

A parade of wandering children
run sticky fingers
across steaming glass,
wondering how long
a sticky bun will last.

One goddess, resurrected
falls into the morning coffee line,
singing softly, she receives
a poppy seed bun.

Under the warming Sun
she returns to the wandering,
bathed in cool spring rains.

Sherry Pachman peeks through a window FULL of scones, sweet rolls and Brioche.

Breath of new green, sprouting, shouting
searching for work, she wanders
among old clapboard houses

and the stony hay fields
of this Green Mountain town.

    diane nazarowitz mortier, April 1997, used with the author's permission **(19)**

Cakes

Cakes entered my consciousness early in life. Sweet, moist, light, pretty, cakes make an occasion of any meal. My Grandmother McLeroy was a cake baker. There was always a cake around during the few times she made the journey from Alvarado, Texas to Oyster Bay, New York. Her specialties were Devil's Food and Banana Nut. Frosted layer cakes fascinated me, and I tried many before arriving at anything quite as beautiful as Granny's.

Market Share I ....

Our original windows created our retail display.

Wholesale bread seemed a more stable market than retail in 1979 when I first started out. The crunchy crowd was returning to the workplace, and whole foods were gaining more wide-spread popularity. In the Burlington marketplace, O'Bread Bakery's wonderful European-style sour dough breads complimented Daily Bread's half whole-grain home-style loaves. We both delivered to Onion River Coop, Origanum Natural Foods and Brothers Two, a local fresh produce market. O'Bread also shipped their breads out via UPS, and Daily Bread delivered to a few local mom and pop markets.

Just about the time customers were urging me to expand the retail line and hours, a third bread supplier from southern Vermont entered the market. Moldy returns mounted. The chickens were happy, but the bakery was losing money. So we plunged into the world of retail and regular shop hours. No more "Gone Fishin'" sign on the door. We got a bigger coffee pot and started to offer pizza, calzones, quiche and potato turnovers on a regular schedule. Granola was the only product we continued to wholesale until the late 1990s when we went back into a little wholesaling in addition to the retail bakery and café.

General cake notes:

Cakes take elbow grease of a different sort than used in yeast baking. Beating air into butter or margarine or egg whites gives cakes loft. The reaction of baking soda to moisture and acid or baking powder to moisture and heat also helps cakes rise. The air requires some structure to hold it up, which is where the proteins of eggs, flour, milk or tofu come in. These reactions are also important to remember when altering a recipe to take out or change an ingredient. You must make some substitution to accomplish the same thing.

Each of these reactions requires your help or that on an electric mixer.

We baked most of our cakes as sheet cakes, serving generous one-layer squares. In the beginning, they were gigantic 4x4 slices. They were really too big. We reduced the size to 3x4, which was still generous. By the 1990s, falling profits and customer concerns over weight and fats reduced the size again to 3x3 1/2. The amounts given are for a 10x14 inch baking pan or for two 9-inch layers.

Chocolate (10"x14" or 2 9-inch layers)

Neighbor Onnie Palmer offered this recipe when I first began collecting for my business, referring to it as "Cheap Chocolate." It is an oil-based specimen, and there is a version in about every cookbook. This is a quick, no-fail cake with a rich chocolatey flavor guaranteed to satisfy any chocolate lover. Abenaki elder Grandmother Doris Minckler requested this cake, with mayonnaise substituted for the oil, for her late October birthday, complete with candy corn and sugar pumpkins on top. This also became the base for the famed Amazon cupcake (see page 83).

2 3/4 cups flour, unbleached or all purpose
1 2/3 cups white sugar
1/3 cup unsweetened cocoa
2 teaspoons baking soda
1/8 teaspoon salt
2 1/4 cups cold water
2/3 cup oil or mayonnaise
2 tablespoons white vinegar
2 teaspoons vanilla

Preheat oven to 350 degrees. Grease and flour baking pan/s. Stir together flour, sugar, cocoa, soda and salt. In a separate bowl, beat together water, oil or mayonnaise, vinegar and vanilla. Add liquid to flour mixture, beating well with wire whisk or spoon to make a smooth loose batter. Pour into prepared baking pan/s. Bake 35 minutes or until a toothpick inserted in the center comes out clean or the center springs back to the touch. Cool. Frost using your favorite choice of icing (pages 79-80).

Maple Chocolate/No Sugar Chocolate (10"x14" or 2 9-inch layers)

This is a variation of the above, sweetened with maple syrup and barley malt for the natural sweetener crowd. Many bakers worked on this one including Lynn E. Alden, Judy Bush and Chris Billis. Ex-counter-person and *WildEarth* magazine editor Tom Butler's favorite nickname for this was "Why Bother?" We finally changed the name from No Sugar to Maple after customers turned up their noses at it, afraid it would be bitter. Far from it, this is sweet and rich!

1/4 pound plus 4 tablespoons margarine/ 1 1/2 sticks
1 cup maple syrup
2/3 cup barley malt
2 teaspoons vanilla
3 3/4 cup unbleached or allpurpose flour
1 cup unsweetened cocoa
2 1/2 teaspoons baking soda
1 pinch salt
2 cups cold water
4 tablespoons vinegar

Preheat oven to 350 degrees. Grease and flour baking pan/s. Cream margarine, syrup, barley malt and vanilla together till light and fluffy. Stir flour, cocoa, soda and salt together. Add water to vinegar in a separate cup or bowl. Alternately add flour, water, flour, water, flour to margarine mixture, beating well after each addition. Spread into prepared pan/s. Bake 35-40 minutes until center springs back to the touch or toothpick comes out clean. Cool and frost.

New Marble (10″x14″ or 2 9-inch layers)

I'm not sure where this one originated. I just know we called it "new" because it replaced the original we had used, which dried out too fast. This is showy, due to the marbling and has lots of flavor, enough even for chocolate lovers.

1/2 pound plus 6 tablespoons butter/ 2 3/4 sticks
1 1/3 cups white sugar
4 eggs
2 2/3 cups unbleached or allpurpose flour
1 tablespoon baking powder
1/4 teaspoon salt
1 cup milk
1 2/3 teaspoons vanilla
1/4 cup unsweetened cocoa
1 2/3 tablespoons butter
3 tablespoons hot water
1/2 teaspoon baking soda

Preheat oven to 350 degrees. Grease and flour pan/s. Cream butter and sugar till light and fluffy. Add eggs and beat to incorporate. Stir together flour, baking powder and salt. Add vanilla to milk. Alternately add flour, milk, flour, milk, flour to butter mix, beating well after each addition. Take out 1/3 of the batter and put aside. Dot the rest in blobs in pan/s. Stir together cocoa, butter, water and soda. Add to the 1/3 set aside and stir well to incorporate. Blob these in between the vanilla blobs. Then take a butter knife and cut back and forth to create a marble effect. Bake 30-35 minutes. Cool and frost. Using a vanilla frosting with chocolate glaze drizzled over it is especially showy (see pages 79-80 for Vanilla Buttercream and Chocolate Goo recipes).

Chocolate Cherry (10″X14″ or 2 9-inch layers)

Andrew Paschetto and Krista Willett joined forces for this variation of chocolate cake. We started buying dried cherries by the 30-pound box, and this is one of the items their presence inspired. The cherry flavor is there but not overwhelming. A cherry-flavored buttercream adds to the cherry experience and gives it a soft pink color.

1 cup dried cherries, check for stray pits!
1/3 cup white sugar
1 1/3 cups hot water
1 cup yogurt
1/4 pound plus 4 tablespoons butter/ 1 1/2 sticks
1 cup white sugar
4 eggs, added one at a time
2/3 cup whole wheat pastry flour
1 1/3 cups unbleached or allpurpose flour
2/3 cup unsweetened cocoa
1 teaspoon baking soda
1 1/2 teaspoons baking powder

Preheat oven to 350 degrees. Grease and flour pan/s. Combine cherries, 1/3 cup white sugar and hot water in a saucepan. Bring to a boil, remove from heat and let stand 10-15 minutes. Pour off the liquid and reserve for frosting. Puree drained cherries in a blender or food processor. Add yogurt and buzz to combine. Cream butter and sugar in an electric mixer or a separate bowl. Add eggs to butter, one at a time, beating after each addition. Stir together flours, cocoa, baking powder and soda. Alternately add flour mix, cherry mix, flour, cherry, flour to butter mixture, beating well after each addition. Spread in prepared pan/s. Bake 35-40 minutes. Cool and frost. For cherry butter cream, heat strained cherry liquid and reduce to syrup. Use this and/or additional pureed cherries for liquid in butter cream (see page 79).

Vegan-Friend of the Devil (10"X14" or 2 9-inch layers)

This is an Andrew Paschetto original. In the mid-1990s, we were getting lots of requests for non-dairy and low fat desserts. Andrew came up with this recipe. You would never know that it is low in fat. It tastes rich and slightly fruity. Notes Andrew, "The absence of much oil means it will stale quickly, so only make what you will eat."

1 1/4 cups prune puree
4 cups unbleached or allpurpose flour
2 1/2 teaspoons baking powder
1 teaspoon baking soda
1/2 teaspoon salt
1 3/4 cup unsweetened cocoa
13 ounces tofu
2/3 cup water
1 1/4 teaspoons vanilla
2 1/2 cups maple syrup
1 cup barley malt

Preheat oven to 350 degrees. Grease and flour pan/s. Prepare prune puree: chop pitted prunes and buzz in a blender or food processor with just enough liquid to make a paste. (This prepared paste may be found on the shelves of many health food or specialty groceries, sometimes called *lekvar*.)   Stir together flour, baking powder, soda, salt and cocoa. Whip tofu, water and vanilla in a blender or food processor till smooth and creamy. Pour into mixing bowl. Add syrup, barley malt and prune puree to tofu mixture and beat with wire whisk to combine well. Beat dry ingredients into the syrup, tofu, prune mixture, working it well 25-30 strokes to develop the proteins to hold the batter up while baking. Spread in greased and floured baking pan/s. Cool and frost with Vegan Goo or the vegan margarine so-called buttercream (see page 79).

Mocha Hazelnut (10"x14" or 2 9-inch layers)

I received the original version of this recipe from Frau Scheiter, the host mother of one of my American Field Service exchange colleagues in Cologne, Germany in 1965. Some of the amounts were difficult to translate, and the original had a tendency to dry out too quickly for our commercial setting. Baker Andrew Paschetto to the rescue! This recipe reflects his alterations.

5 ounces filberts or hazelnuts/ 1 cup plus 2 tablespoons
1/3 cup white sugar
4 tablespoons butter/ 1/2 stick
1/3 cup white sugar
3 eggs, one at a time
1 1/3 cups unbleached or allpurpose flour
2 teaspoons espresso or any finely ground coffee
2 teaspoons baking powder
1/2 cup milk

Glaze:
2/3 cup powdered sugar
1 2/3 tablespoons hot brewed coffee
1 tablespoon butter
1 1/2 teaspoons instant coffee
1/2 cup good quality chocolate syrup or Goo (see page 80)

Preheat oven to 350 degrees. Grease and flour pan/s. Grind together nuts and 1/3 cup sugar in food processor till very fine. Cream butter and second 1/3 cup sugar till light and fluffy. Add eggs, one at a time and beat after each addition. Stir together flour, espresso and baking powder. Alternately add flour, milk, flour, milk, flour to butter mixture. Fold in nut mixture. Spread into prepared baking pan/s. Bake 25 minutes until the center just springs back to the touch. Prepare glaze and spread on cake while still hot. Once glaze has set, drizzle chocolate goo or syrup decoratively over cake; you too can try to paint like Jackson Pollock.

Bet Your Bonnet

Two families sent this rewrite of the old nursery tongue twister: the Sagar and Galligans of Huntington and the Field and Rogers of Waterville.

Molly and Cora Sagar-Galligan

Betsy Bott (sic) bought some butter
"But," she said, "The butter's bitter!
If I put it in my batter
It will make my batter bitter.
But a bit of better butter
That will make my batter better.
So she bought a bit of butter
Better than her bitter butter
And she put it in her batter
And her batter wasn't bitter.
Wasn't it better, Betsy Bott?
Bought a bit of better butter?" (20)

Maple (10"x14" or 2 9-inch layers)

Richmond resident and long-time bakery regular Peg Farr gave me this recipe. She received it from a 1950's cook at the Cambridge Inn in Cambridge, Vermont. Peg's husband, Sumner Farr was a farmer and equipment dealer in Richmond when Daily Bread first opened for business. He was one of the few town "fathers" who took an active interest in the bakery. He especially enjoyed coming in just before noon for a hot loaf of bread for dinner.

Maple cake became Daily Bread's signature cake, oft requested and always baked for Daily Bread special occasions. It served as the base for many wedding cakes and remains my personal favorite. The aroma of this cake baking is unbelievably tantalizing. Frosted with a maple-sweetened cream cheese icing, yum, yum, yum.

1/4 pound plus 4 tablespoons butter/ 1 1/2 sticks
3/4 cup plus 1 tablespoon maple syrup
1/3 cup plus 1 tablespoon white sugar
2 cups plus 2 tablespoons unbleached or allpurpose flour
2 1/2 teaspoons baking powder
1/2 teaspoon salt
3/4 cup plus 1 tablespoon milk
1 teaspoon vanilla
4 eggs, whites only
1/2 cup white sugar

Preheat oven to 350 degrees. Cream together butter, syrup and sugar till light and fluffy. Stir together flour, baking powder and salt. Add vanilla to milk. Alternately add flour, milk, flour, milk, flour to butter mixture, beating well after each addition. Beat egg whites and sugar to form stiff peaks. Gently fold whites into the batter using a rubber spatula or your hands to thoroughly incorporate. Spread into greased and floured pan/s. Bake 35-40 minutes till top is golden brown and center just springy. Cool and frost with maple cream cheese icing (see page 79).

Orange Butter (10"X14" or 2 9-inch layers layers)

No one owns up to bringing in this recipe, and I can't remember where I might have found it. It became a regular offering, with many fans. It has only a light glaze, but don't let that fool you. It is rich, sweet and delicate with lots of orange flavor. Wolfsong was responsible for instituting half brown sugar. His variation became standard. If you want a layer cake, try a vanilla or orange flavored buttercream frosting.

      1/4 pound plus 4 tablespoons butter/ 1 1/2 sticks
      1 cup white sugar
      1 cup brown sugar
      3 eggs
      3 1/4 cups unbleached or allpurpose flour
      1 1/2 tablespoons baking powder
      1/3 teaspoon salt
      1/3 teaspoon nutmeg
      1 1/4 cups orange juice
      Grated zest of 1 orange

      Glaze:
      1 cup powdered sugar
      2 1/2 tablespoons hot water
      1 1/4 tablespoons butter
      1/3 teaspoon almond extract

Preheat oven to 350 degrees. Prepare pan/s. Cream together butter and sugars till light and fluffy. Add eggs and beat to incorporate. Stir together flour, baking powder, salt and nutmeg. Add orange zest to orange juice. Alternately add flour, juice, flour to butter mixture, beating well after each addition. Spread batter into greased and floured pan/s. Bake 35-40 minutes until just golden brown and springy to the touch in the center. Remove from oven. Stir together powdered sugar, water, butter and almond extract to make a smooth, gravy-like consistency. Spread on hot cake.

Yellow (10"x14" or 2 9-inch layers)

There are many versions of basic yellow cake. The original quantities for this particular one came from one of those pamphlets from the 1940s or 1950s called *100 Best Cakes*. It is rich with butter and eggs. It can take any number of frostings depending on your preference. My favorite was chocolate. Andrew Paschetto specialized in fruit *coulis*, made by cooking strained fruit juice down to a syrup, decoratively drizzled over a vanilla buttercream.

      1/2 pound butter/ 2 sticks
      1 2/3 cups white sugar
      5 eggs, separated

3 2/3 cups unbleached or allpurpose flour
1 tablespoon baking powder
1/4 teaspoon salt
2 cups milk
1 1/3 teaspoons vanilla
1/8 teaspoon cream of tartar

Preheat oven to 350 degrees. Cream butter and sugar together till light and fluffy. Separate eggs. Set egg whites aside. Add yolks to butter mixture, one at a time, beating well after each. Stir together flour, baking powder and salt. Stir together milk and vanilla. Alternately add flour, milk, flour, milk, flour to butter mixture. Grease and flour baking pan/s. Add cream of tartar to egg whites and whip to form shiny peaks. Fold whites gently but thoroughly into batter using a rubber spatula or hands. Spread into prepared pans. Bake 25-30 minutes until golden brown and center springs back to the touch or toothpick comes out clean. Cool and frost with your choice of icing.

Spice (10"x14" or 2 9-inch layers)

This is Krista Willett's grandmother's recipe. Krista called Mary Sheridan Cowles her "pastry grandmother." This is a delicious cake, sweet and fragrant with spice. It is especially good with a ginger-flavored buttercream or orange-honey cream cheese frosting (see page 79).

1/2 pound plus 4 tablespoons butter/ 2 1/2 sticks
1 2/3 cups white sugar
1 1/4 cups brown sugar, firmly packed
5 eggs, lightly beaten
3 2/3 cups unbleached or allpurpose flour
1 2/3 teaspoons baking powder
2/3 teaspoon baking soda
2/3 teaspoon salt
1 1/4 teaspoons ground cloves
1 1/4 teaspoons cinnamon
1 pinch black pepper
1 2/3 cups buttermilk
1 1/2 teaspoon vanilla

Preheat oven to 350 degrees. Grease and flour pan/s. Cream together butter and sugars till smooth, but not too fluffy. Add beaten eggs and mix till all incorporated. Stir together flour, baking powder, soda, salt and spices. Add vanilla to buttermilk. Alternately add flour, buttermilk, flour to butter and egg mixture. Spread into prepared pan/s. Bake 30-35 minutes till center springs back to the touch. Cool and frost.

The Towers ....

When asked, why buy locally, I responded that the safety of our food supply is at stake. Most of our food travels on average 1,200 miles from field to table. Many farms in the area went out of dairying, and kept less time-consuming and/ or more lucrative products like maple syrup, hay, firewood and pumpkins.

The 250-acre Towers farm lies in the rich Huntington River valley where the towns of Richmond and Huntington meet. The upper pastures and wood lot rise up into the foothills which stretch towards Camels Hump. Ralph is a fourth-generation farmer who knows every square foot of that land. He and his wife Rachel raised their sons there and milked cows into the 1980s. Their farm-raised turkeys were the tastiest around and graced many Thanksgiving tables. Their front yard is covered with pumpkins and squash every fall. Their giant blue hubbard squash were perfect for our use. We kept them in the cellar and baked them up as needed for pies, cakes, soups or casseroles.

The farm abuts the Green Mountain Audubon Nature Center. The Center's biggest fund-raiser is its annual Haunted Forest. Ralph hays 20 acres of their fields and in turn donates close to 300 pumpkins every year to the cause. Still a kid at heart, Ralph cuts almost that many for his own jack o'lantern display in front of the farm.

Carrot (10"x14" or 2 9-inch layers)

Before I had a place to open shop or knew the name would be Daily Bread, Vermont Women's Health Center colleague Janet Young and her husband-to-be Wes Graf requested I bake their wedding cake. They wanted carrot cake. I tested 4 or 5 different recipes, and chose this one. There are many excellent versions of this, from plain to fancy. This has a strong honey flavor, and we frosted it with a honey sweetened cream cheese icing (see page 79).

2 1/2 cups grated carrots/ 3-4 medium carrots
5 eggs
3/4 cup plus 1 tablespoon oil, sunflower or other light variety
1 2/3 cups honey
Grated zest of 1 orange
2 1/2 cups unbleached or allpurpose flour
2 1/3 teaspoons baking soda
2 1/3 teaspoons cinnamon
1 cup raisins or coarsely chopped walnuts, or both!

Preheat oven to 350 degrees. Grease and flour pan/s. Beat together eggs, oil, honey and zest with a wire whisk. Add grated carrots to this mixture. Stir together flour, soda and cinnamon. Beat flour mix into egg and carrot mixture, giving it a good workout of 25-30 strokes. Fold in raisins or nuts or both. Batter will be on the liquidy side. Pour into prepared pan/s. Bake 35-40 minutes until center springs back to the touch or toothpick comes out clean. Cool. Frost with honey cream cheese icing.

Pumpkin or Squash (10″x14″ or 2 9-inch layers)

Charlotte, Vermont, "hippie" doctor Bunky Bernstein's son Josh got this recipe from the cook at Charlotte Central School. She used mashed sweet potato. Bunky gave it to me when Josh requested it for his birthday cake. Andrew Paschetto fine-tuned it, and was especially fond of adding chocolate chips. Nick Sansone preferred a honey cream cheese icing.

    1 2/3 cups white sugar
    4 eggs
    2 cups pumpkin, yam or squash, cooked, mashed and cooled/ 1 16-ounce can
    1/3 cup oil, sunflower or other light variety
    2/3 cup orange juice
    2 1/3 cups unbleached or allpurpose flour
    2 teaspoons baking soda
    3/4 teaspoon baking powder
    1/2 teaspoon salt
    1/3 teaspoon ground ginger
    3/4 teaspoon cinnamon
    1/3 teaspoon mace
    2/3 cup walnuts or raisins or chocolate chips

Preheat oven to 350 degrees. Grease and flour pan/s. Beat together sugar and eggs with a wire whisk or in an electric mixer till pale yellow and foamy. Whisk in pumpkin, oil and orange juice to just combine. Stir together flour, baking powder, soda, salt and spices in a mixing bowl. Fold egg/pumpkin mixture into the flour mix with a rubber spatula or spoon. Mix well. Stir in walnuts or raisins. If using chocolate chips, wait till batter is in the pan/s. Spread batter into prepared pan/s. Throw (literally) chocolate chips at the batter so they will sink slightly. Bake 45 minutes. Cool. Frost as desired.

Extended Family

Sisters Deandre, Brita and Kate clown on the beach.

Daily Bread was always a family-friendly place. Many members of the same family worked at the Bread over time. Buffy Labelle's crew was one of many.

When I first met Buffy Labelle in 1972 or '73, she was driving an orange VW bug with numerous bumper stickers plastered on its fenders declaring "Sisterhood is Powerful" among other things. She and her toddler daughter Deandre were part of the Ethan Allen Childcare network, where my housemate's children spent some of their days. She was friends with a bunch of University of Vermont medical students who were building a stone house up on Sherman Hollow Road in Huntington. After the others had abandoned the project, she and one of the house partners Herb Klein joined forces and ended up with the beginnings of a house and a beautiful spot on the planet. Their daughter Brita was born. Buffy was pregnant with Kate when Herb died in an accident.

Buffy raised her three girls single-handedly, with help from family and friends. Someone later asked Buffy how she managed the acting out adolescent years. "I sent them to Betsy," was her reply. She later married Jim Hildebran; they added Silas to the family.

Satisfaction from successfully producing food which makes people happy is very powerful. To be trusted with the responsibility to do so is even more powerful. The setting of the bakery was a safe place to meet and interact with a diverse community of co-workers and customers. All three daughters were excellent employees. Buffy worked, too, for a while as a counter person.

We had many brothers and sisters put in their high school weekends at the Bread: Ben, Henry and Chelsie Bush; Chris and Ben Cichoski; Patrick, John and Liz Earle; Deandre Labelle and her sisters Brita and Kate Klein; Pamela and Malcolm Purinton; Nick and Paul Sansone; Katie and Karen Steece; Heather and Donovan Ward; Judd and Martha Yaggy. Ingrid Cichoski joined the staff after her sons Chris and Ben were off to college and beyond. Jeremy and Ali Cohen both spent time at the Bread while at college.

Glo Daley and her grown daughter Kris held down lunch spots. Meg Howard ran Local Legends and her daughter April did counter work and learned to bake.

Italian Cream (10"x14" or 2 9-inch layers)

This cake was Buffy's favorite and very popular with Daily Bread customers. Another contribution from Krista Willett, who got it from Kay Pryor, hostess at Bolton Valley Resort when Krista baked there. It is quite sweet and rich with coconut and pecans, yet light in texture. It comes with its own frosting, a variation on cream cheese and a perfect match.

4 tablespoons butter/ 1/2 stick
1/4 pound plus 2 tablespoons margarine/ 1 1/4 sticks
1 2/3 cups white sugar
5 eggs, separated
1 2/3 cup unbleached or allpurpose flour
1 1/4 teaspoons baking soda
1 1/4 cups buttermilk
1 1/4 teaspoons vanilla
1 1/4 cups coconut
1 1/4 cup coarsely chopped pecans

Frosting:
6 tablespoons butter/ 3/4 stick
1 cup powdered sugar
1 teaspoon vanilla
10 ounces cold cream cheese/ 1 1/4 8-ounce packages
1/2 cup chopped pecans

Preheat oven to 350 degrees. Grease and flour pan/s. Cream butter, margarine and sugar till very light and fluffy. Separate eggs. Set whites aside. Add yolks to butter mixture, one at a time, beating well after each addition. Stir together flour and soda. Add to butter and yolk mixture and beat well. Add buttermilk and beat well. Whip egg whites to stiff peaks. Fold beaten whites, nuts and coconut into batter, gently but thoroughly, with rubber spatula or your hands. Spread into prepared pan/s. Bake 35 minutes only. Cake should feel slightly mushy in the center.

For frosting, beat butter, powdered sugar and vanilla till very light and fluffy. Continue beating while you add small pieces of cold cream cheese. Continue beating till all cream cheese is added and frosting is very fluffy. Fold in pecans. Spread on cooled cake.

Banana (10"x14" or 2 9-inch layers)

I believe this is another from the old l940s *100 best...* pamphlets. There are many banana lovers out there. And of course, there are often "older" bananas looking for a good home. This is a sturdy, full flavored, not-too-sweet cake, good by itself or delicious with buttercream or cream cheese frosting (see page 79).

    1/4 pound plus 2 tablespoons butter/ 1 1/4 sticks
    2 cups sugar
    3 eggs, one at a time
    2 cups mashed banana/ 4-6 bananas
    2 teaspoons vanilla
    4 cups flour, unbleached or allpurpose
    1 teaspoon baking soda
    1/4 teaspoon salt
    1 cup yogurt or buttermilk

Preheat oven to 350 degrees. Grease and flour pan/s. Cream butter and sugar till light and fluffy. Beat in eggs, one at a time, beating well after each addition. Add banana and vanilla. Stir to incorporate. Stir together flour, soda and salt. Add alternately flour, yogurt (or buttermilk), flour, yogurt, flour to butter banana mix, beating well after each addition. Spread into prepared baking pan/s. Bake 35-40 minutes until center springs back to the touch or a toothpick comes out clean. Cool and frost.

Clean Vanilla-Vegan (10"x14" or 2 9-inch layers)

Andrew Paschetto received this from Chef Frank Arcuri, one of Andrew's teachers at Anne Marie Colbin's Natural Gourmet Cooking School in New York City. It was the base to a fancy layered Savannah Cream Cake, but we found it made a light and mapley cake which could take a fruit topping (cook a fruit pie filling on top of the stove) or a margarine-based so-called buttercream frosting. I often describe it as tasting like Graham crackers. It is also the base for a chocolate frosted cupcake we called a "Blacktop" (see page 85).

Andrew notes that maple syrup is essential:
Accept no substitutes. Otherwise, this could be just one more too-heavy-to-call-cake-healthfood-something. In fact, the effect that the maple has is nothing short of miraculous.

2 1/2 cups unbleached or allpurpose flour
2 cups whole wheat pastry flour
2 1/3 teaspoons baking powder
1 2/3 teaspoons baking soda
3/4 cup plus 1 tablespoon oil, sunflower or other light variety
1 3/4 cups maple syrup
2 1/2 tablespoons vanilla
2 1/3 tablespoons cider vinegar .
2 2/3 cups cold water

Preheat oven to 350 degrees. Grease and flour pan/s. Stir together flours, baking powder and soda in mixing bowl. Whisk together oil, syrup, vanilla, vinegar and water in a separate bowl. Fold wet ingredients into flour mixture and then beat well with wire whisk or spoon 35-50 strokes, till very smooth. Pour into prepared pan/s. Bake 20-25 minutes until center of the cake springs back to the touch or a toothpick inserted into the center comes out clean. Cool and frost as desired.

Made From Scratch •

Early on Daily Bread adopted the motto "Every batch made from scratch." It was not original, but it captured the philosophy and reality of our operation.

It certainly characterized the business itself. Other than a ten day stint assisting baker Nora at the late 1970s Burlington bakery, Quiche and Things, I never worked in a commercial kitchen, at a retail counter or waited tables. Self-educated, gleaning as much as I could from those around me, I set out by the seat of my pants.

Most commercial bakeries use mixes for everything. They come in 50-pound bags; just add water or eggs or oil. Or there is the amazing variety of frozen proof-and-bake products. If you wonder why things taste the same in almost any bakery, restaurant or Mom-and-Pop store you visit, wonder no more. They are the same.

We started from scratch with almost everything until we got into the café business. Before the cafe we picked strawberries and raspberries, bought cases of peaches and plums and prepared them for the freezer.   After the cafe we bought IQF (individually quick frozen) fruit, Prosage vegetarian sausage, tofu, tempeh, frozen corn tortillas, canned tomato products, mayonnaise and on and on. We made some of our own mixes for pancakes and hot cereal, and otherwise prepared everything from basic ingredients.

We prided ourselves on using high quality, fresh ingredients. We bought locally as much as possible.

original design by Judy Bush

Frosting and Fillings

Cream Cheese (to cover 10"x14" or 2 9-inch layers)
1/4 pound butter/ 1 stick
1/2 cup honey or maple syrup
3/4 pound cream cheese, cold/ 1 1/2 8-oz. packages

Beat butter till light and fluffy; an electric mixer is handy, but elbow grease works too. Add honey or syrup to butter and continue beating till mixture is fluffy and light. Throw pieces of cold cream cheese into the butter mixture, till all cream cheese is in the mix. Continue beating, beating, beating till all shiny and fluffy. Spread on cooled cake/s.

Buttercream (to cover 10"x14" or 2 9-inch layers)
1/2 pound butter/ 2 sticks (use margarine for vegan variation)
4 cups powdered sugar
1 1/2 teaspoons vanilla
2 to 4 tablespoons yogurt or applesauce or strong coffee and/or cocoa

Beat butter till light and fluffy. Add powdered sugar, a little at a time, and continue beating. Add vanilla and enough yogurt or other liquid to make a spread-able consistency. Continue to beat 5 minutes to a shiny, fluffy mix. Spread on cooled cake/s.

Sugar Chocolate Goo (to cover 2 9-inch layers, 12 cupcakes or 4 pound cakes)
1 cup heavy cream
1/4 pound butter/ 1 stick
2 cups sugar
1 1/2 cups unsweetened baker's cocoa
1 1/2 ounces baker's chocolate
1 teaspoon vanilla

Combine cream, butter, sugar, cocoa and baker's chocolate in the top of a double boiler or heavy saucepan over very low heat. Stir while heating till all well combined and the mixture begins to thicken. Remove from heat. Add vanilla once mixture has cooled to lukewarm. Spread on cake/s. This may be kept for a few weeks in the refrigerator. Reheat, stirring all the time, to a spreadable consistency.

Vegan Goo (to cover 2 9-inch layers, 12 cupcakes or 4 pound cakes)
    1 cup soy milk
    1/4 pound margarine/ 1 stick
    1 cup maple syrup
    1 1/2 cups baker's cocoa
    1 ounce baker's chocolate
    1 teaspoon vanilla

Combine soy milk, margarine, maple syrup, cocoa and baker's chocolate in the top of a double boiler or over a pot of boiling water. Heat, stirring occasionally until mixture is smooth and thickens. Remove from heat and stir in vanilla. Cool to lukewarm. Dip cupcakes or spread with a spatula.

Note: do not substitute rice milk or rice and soy blend; it causes the mixture to harden into a crumbly unspreadable mess.

Lo-fat Vegan Goo for Friend of the Devil (to cover 10"x14" sheet or 2 9-inch layers)
    3/4 cup honey or maple syrup
    1/4 cup water
    1/2 cup unsweetened cocoa
    1/4 cup cornstarch

Combine honey or syrup and water in a small saucepan. Stir cocoa and cornstarch together. Whisk into water mixture. Heat over medium flame, stirring constantly till just boiling. Cool mixture slightly before spreading on cooled cakes.

Tea Cakes

Orange Tea (6 or 12 cakes)

I know you bought the cookbook just for this recipe! This one came from Judy Bush, whose mother baked them in her Minnesota home for special occasions. These delectable little frosted cakes freeze well, and Judy's mother frequently kept some on hand--or so she thought. Judy remembers she and her sisters surreptitiously "sampling" the supply, significantly reducing those left for guests. These became so popular at the bakery that people planned their week to arrive Thursday afternoon to make sure they could get some. The cakes traveled to Europe on special request. And when the new owner's "professional" baker took charge and tossed the recipe, she had to call and plead; there was a near revolt in Richmond when Thursday rolled around and there were no Orange Tea Cakes! I have included amounts for 6 or 12.

We replaced our old windows with a real bakery case, around 1998, tea cakes lower right.

6	**12**
3 tablespoons butter	5 tablespoons
3 tablespoons margarine	5 tablespoons
1/2 cup white sugar	1 cup
1 egg	2 eggs
1/3 cup sour cream	2/3 cup
1 1/2 tablespoons orange juice	3 tablespoons
2 teaspoons orange zest	4 teaspoons

1 1/3 cups unbleached or all purpose flour	2 2/3 cups
1/3 teaspoon baking powder	2/3 teaspoon
1/3 teaspoon baking soda	2/3 teaspoon

Preheat oven to 350 degrees. Cream together butter, margarine and sugar till very light and fluffy. Beat together in a separate container egg/s, sour cream, orange juice and zest. Stir together flour, baking powder and soda. Alternately add flour, sour cream mix, flour to butter till just combined. Too much working of the dough will make them tough. The dough should be stiffer than cake batter and hold its shape when scooped out. Grease and flour a baking sheet. Portion out by the 1/3 cup onto baking sheet, leaving 1 to 2 inches in between. An ice cream scoop works well for this. Bake 20 minutes till golden brown and the center springs back to the touch. Cool and frost.

Frosting:

3 tablespoons butter	6 tablespoons
1 tablespoon orange zest	2 tablespoons
1 cup powdered sugar	2 cups
1 tablespoon orange juice	2 tablespoons

Beat butter and zest till light and fluffy. Add powdered sugar a few tablespoons at a time, and continue beating. Add orange juice and beat till light and creamy. Spread on cooled cakes.

Chocolate Tea (6 or 12 cakes)

I wanted to try a variation on the theme and adapted the orange version to chocolate.

6	**12**
3 tablespoons butter	5 tablespoons
3 tablespoons margarine	5 tablespoons
1 1/2 ounces baker's chocolate, melted and cooled	3 ounces
1/2 cup white sugar	1 cup
1 egg	2 eggs
1/3 cup sour cream	2/3 cup
1/2 teaspoon vanilla	1 teaspoon
1 drop almond extract	1 drop
1 1/4 cups unbleached or all purpose flour	2 1/4 cups
1/4 teaspoon baking soda	1/2 teaspoon
1/4 teaspoon baking powder	1/2 teaspoon
1/4 cup coarsely chopped walnuts	1/2 cup
or 1/4 cup chopped dried cherries	1/2 cup

Preheat oven to 350 degrees. Melt baker's chocolate over a double boiler. Cool to warm. Cream together butter, margarine, baker's chocolate and sugar till light and fluffy. Beat together egg/s, sour cream, vanilla and almond extract to blend. Stir together flour, soda, baking powder and walnuts or cherries. Alternately beat flour, sour cream, flour into butter mixture till just combined. Too much working the dough will make cakes tough. Grease and flour baking sheet. Portion out batter in 1/3 cup amounts, leaving 1 to 2 inches between; use an ice cream scoop if you have one. Bake 20-25 minutes until tops gently spring back to the touch. Cool and frost with your choice of chocolate icing (pages 79-80).

Cupcakes

Amazons (12 large cupcakes)

The original inspiration for these came from Margaret Fox's *Cafe Beaujolais Cookbook*, a gift from baker Alison Forrest's parents when I first started work on this cookbook fifteen years ago! These became another Daily Bread standard, baked every Wednesday afternoon. The cream cheese filling dropped into the cake batter before baking makes them reminiscent of Hostess cupcake sold in my high school cafeteria, but way better.

WildEarth magazine employee Kathleen Fitzgerald immortalized them as:
...a swirled gem of chocolate and cream cheese, replicating the diverse regions of Mt. Kenya. The crunchy top of the cupcake reminds me of my boots walking on the crusty snow, and the warm-gooey middle brings me back to the bog-region of the mountain. Finishing the cupcake is like reaching the summit... you "kick back" in total euphoria. (20)

Filling:
1/2 pound cream cheese/ 1 8-ounce package
1/4 cup white sugar
1 egg
1/3 cup whole walnuts
2/3 cup chocolate chips

Beat together cream cheese, sugar, egg and walnuts till all very smooth; the walnuts will break up as you work this. Stir in chocolate chips to just distribute.

Cake:
2 3/4 cups unbleached or allpurpose flour
1 1/2 cups white sugar
1/2 cup unsweetened cocoa
1 3/4 teaspoons baking soda
1/3 teaspoon salt
2 1/4 cups cold water
2/3 cup oil, sunflower or other light variety
2 tablespoons vinegar, white or cider
1 3/4 teaspoons vanilla

AMAZON CUPCAKE

Preheat oven to 350 degrees. Grease and flour muffin tins or preferably line with paper baking cups. Stir together flour, sugar, cocoa, soda and salt in mixing bowl. Whisk together water, oil, vinegar and vanilla in a separate bowl. Pour water mixture into flour and beat well with spoon or wire whisk, about 25-30 strokes. Batter should be fairly liquidy. Fill muffin tins 2/3 full of batter. Drop between 1/2 and 1 tablespoon filling into each. Bake 35-40 minutes until cake portion just springs back to the touch.

Pumpkin Walnut Crumb (6 or 12)

Jesse Spear started out as a Youth Employment student and ended up working as a regular employee. He apprenticed baking with Andrew and took culinary courses at the local technical center. He later worked as both baker and cook. Jesse found this recipe and thought it would be good. These are moist and spicy with those ever satisfying crumbs on top to make a tasty combo.

6	**12**
Crumbs:	
4 tablespoons butter/ 1/2 stick	1/4 pound/1 stick
1/4 cup unbleached or allpurpose flour	1/2 cup
1/4 cup white sugar	1/2 cup
3/4 teaspoon cinnamon	1 1/2 teaspoons

Cut or rub together butter and flour with pastry blender or hands to make a coarse crumb. Toss sugar and cinnamon into flour mixture to just combine. Set aside.

Cake:	
2 eggs	3 eggs
3/4 cup cooked and mashed pumpkin or winter squash	1 1/2 cups
3/4 cup white sugar	1 1/2 cups
1/3 cup plus 1 tablespoon oil	3/4 cup
3/4 cup unbleached or allpurpose flour	1 1/2 cups
3/4 teaspoon baking powder	1 1/2 teaspoons
1/3 teaspoon baking soda	3/4 teaspoon
3/4 teaspoon cinnamon	1 1/2 teaspoons
1/3 teaspoon nutmeg	3/4 teaspoon
1/8 teaspoon ground cloves	1/3 teaspoon
1/8 teaspoon salt	1/4 teaspoon
3/4 cup coarsely chopped walnuts	1 1/2 cups

Preheat oven to 350 degrees. Prepare crumbs. Grease and flour muffin tins or line with paper baking cups. Beat together eggs, pumpkin, sugar and oil till smooth. Stir together flour, powder, soda, cinnamon, nutmeg, cloves, salt and walnuts in a mixing bowl. Add pumpkin mixture to flour, folding wet into dry until all just combined. Fill muffin tins 2/3 full. Sprinkle crumbs on top. Bake 25-30 minutes until center of cupcake just springs back to the touch.

Blacktops-Vegan (6 or 12)

The cake is mapley and fragrant. The topping is dark chocolate. Baker Andrew Paschetto brought this recipe, and came up with the name. We tried for a while to imitate the look of tire tread in the tops, but no extra gimmicks were necessary. These are yummy just as they are.

6	12
1 1/4 cups unbleached or allpurpose flour	2 1/2 cups
1 cup whole wheat pastry flour	2 cups
1 1/4 teaspoons baking powder	2 1/3 teaspoons
1 teaspoon baking soda	1 2/3 teaspoons
1/3 cup plus 2 tablespoons oil	3/4 cup plus 1 tablespoon
1 cup maple syrup	1 3/4 cups
1 1/2 tablespoons vanilla	2 1/4 tablespoons
1 1/4 tablespoons cider vinegar	2 1/3 tablespoons
1 1/3 cups water	2 2/3 cups

Preheat oven to 350 degrees.   Grease and flour muffin tins or line with paper baking cups. Stir together flours, powder and soda in a mixing bowl. Whisk together oil, syrup, vanilla, vinegar and water in a separate bowl. Fold into flour mixture, beating well 25-30 strokes till very smooth. Fill tins 2/3 full of batter. Bake 20-25 minutes at 350 degrees until center of the cupcake just springs back to the touch. Cool and dip or frost with Vegan Goo (see page 80).

Gary Wills: Everyday Savior

Gary Wills operated under many different titles at Mount Mansfield High School. School doesn't work for all students, and Mr. Wills helped many of those kids navigate both the school system and the real world. Gary and his wife, Janet, also a special educator, brought students to Daily Bread for placements, some to practice communicating with others, some to learn work place skills, some for a job.

We were pleased and surprised in 1996 to receive recognition for our workplace training.

Department of Employment and Training
Dear Linda:
I am writing to nominate employer Betsy Bott...for the Governor's Award for Excellence in Employment and Training. Betsy and her employees have provided EYEP and SYEP (Early Youth Employment Program and Summer...) students with meaningful work experiences for many years. Betsy provides students with opportunities that are designed to meet their specific needs. ...
... (District supervisor) Jim (Clark) found Betsy and the bakery very supportive of students in need of work site accommodations. This support extends into the Richmond community where Betsy opens the door of opportunity for many teenagers who are willing to work.   Betsy's support of JTPA programming within the Richmond, Huntington and Bolton area has been, in large, responsible for the acceptance of students' various backgrounds within the business community. ...
Sincerely,
Gary Wills (21)

Winooski hardware store owner Joe Paskevitch was also honored at the awards ceremony. We hoped to continue to provide jobs for youths in our home communities but without the two jobs programs for teens. Both programs lost their federal funding.

"Employers and students and families were pleased with the results," Wills said, "But the program was cut, so we get along as best we can."

Tortes

Tortes are flourless cakes, raised with beaten egg whites. Ground nuts or cake crumbs generally replace the flour. We didn't have much call for tortes, but occasionally baked them for special orders. They are light, but rich, and an unusual variation on cake.

Almond Torte (2 8-inch layers)

Judy Bush's grandmother had this recipe among her special occasion offerings, and Judy brought it to Daily Bread.

8 eggs, separated
1 2/3 cups powdered sugar
Grated zest of 2 lemons
1 2/3 cups finely ground almonds
3/4 cup finely ground walnuts
1 2/3 teaspoons cornstarch
3/4 teaspoon baking powder

Glaze:
1 cup powdered sugar
1 1/2 teaspoons lemon juice

Filling:
1/2 pint whipping cream/ 1 cup

Preheat oven to 325 degrees. Line bottoms of two 8-inch cake pans with parchment or brown shopping bag paper. Do not grease pans! Separate eggs. Beat together egg yolks, powdered sugar and lemon zest till very light and lemony yellow. Stir together almonds, walnuts, cornstarch and baking powder. Beat egg whites to stiff peaks. Alternately fold nut mixture and beaten whites into yolk mixture, using rubber spatula or hands to just combine all. Spread gently and evenly into prepared pans. Bake 1 to 1 1/2 hours at 325 degrees. Do not open the oven for 20 minutes.

Remove from oven and allow to cool in pans. Use a sharp knife to loosen edges. Loosen with a spatula and lift gently out; peel paper off bottoms. Place one layer on the serving plate. Put the other on the upside down layer pan till you're ready. Combine powdered sugar and lemon juice to make glaze. Brush glaze onto tops of layers. Just before serving, whip cream and spread in between layers.

Coconut Macaroon Torte (1 8-inch cake)

This is a Krista Willett original. Krista taught a State of Vermont chef's apprenticeship program for many years and became active in the Vermont Chef's Association. She developed several torte variations for a Taste of Vermont competition, in which the Chef's Association participated, because tortes were out of the ordinary. This is one which she brought to Daily Bread. Almonds and coconut give the layers body and flavor. With fruit preserves in between and a chocolate glaze over top, what could be finer?

     5 eggs, separated
     1/3 cup plus 1 tablespoon light brown sugar
     1/3 teaspoon salt
     1 cup finely ground almonds
     3/4 cup coconut, lightly toasted and cooled
     1/3 teaspoon grated orange zest

     1/2 cup apricot or raspberry preserves
     1 cup Chocolate Goo (see page 80)

Preheat oven to 325 degrees. Line the bottom of an 8-inch spring form pan with parchment or brown paper. Do not grease pan/s! Separate eggs. Beat egg yolks till light and lemony in color. Gradually add brown sugar and salt to egg yolks and beat 2 minutes. Stir together almonds, coconut and zest. Beat egg whites to firm peaks. Alternately fold whites and nuts into yolk mixture, using rubber spatula or hands to just combine. Spread evenly into prepared spring form pan. Bake 1 to 1 1/2 hours. Do not open oven for at least 20 minutes. Remove and cool completely in pan. Use sharp knife to loosen edges. Remove ring of spring form and, using sharp or serrated knife, slice into two layers. Place bottom layer on serving plate, removing paper. Spread preserves on top of bottom layer. Place top layer on bottom. Cover all with chocolate glaze, allowing it to drip artfully down edges.

A Daily Bread Baker ....

Hello Betsy, and, and, and…
As I'm doing these "thank you" letters to the raffle prize donors, I'm realizing that I have much more to thank you for than a donation to the Apprenticeship Raffle.

Krista, Kris Hulphers and Rosa Warnock look over a new recipe or special order.

I really appreciate being able to work at the bakery. So many people work at places they either can't stand or are totally indifferent about. Your presence, thought, (non)-management style, and ideas about which parts of the business are truly important make being your "employee" a joy.

I don't think I know of...many, any? other folks running a food service business with your consideration of all the tribulations that happen amongst employees. I've heard someone say that you resisted changing the way things are done...--I'm not sure that resistance is bad! Like a rock in the stream with the water rushing around, I find that you are our steadying influence.

Thanks ... for giving a "Bolton Valley Baker" a chance to learn and grow into a Daily Bread Baker.

Krista **(22)**

Coffee Cakes

I have to admit a special love of coffee cake. Dad's arrival with a blue bakery box of Crumb Buns while we were growing up led me on a long search to find their equivalent, our so-called Regular Crumb Cake. You will be a definite hit at a brunch or tea with a pan of any of the following. I offer amounts for an 8"x8" pan for small groups and 10"x14" for larger ones.

Burlington Free Press food columnist Debbie Salomon wrote of coffee cake, "It's more than a muffin, sweeter than a bagel...Bott built a reputation on 17-by-24 inch pans of meltingly delicious coffeecakes that include vegan maple oat crumb and lemon berry walnut demanded by her clientele." **(23)**

Regular Crumb Cake (8"x8" and 10"x14")

Housemate Wendy Weldon found a recipe for upside down cake in a magazine or newspaper which finally seemed to live up to my memory of Crumb Buns. It is light and airy while still up to the task of holding buttery crumbs on top. Add cut apples, berries, rhubarb or even chocolate chips! It also makes an excellent base for upside down cake. And don't forget the favorite Plum Crumb!

8"x8"	**10"x14"**
Crumbs:	
1/3 cup unbleached or all purpose flour	2/3 cup
5 tablespoons cold butter	1/4 pound plus 2 tablespoons/ 1 1/4 sticks
1 teaspoon cinnamon	2 teaspoons
1/3 cup white sugar	2/3 cup
1 cup prepared fruit, etc.	2 cups
Cake:	
3 eggs, separated	5 eggs
2/3 cup white sugar	1 1/4 cups
1/4 cup water	1/2 cup
1 cup unbleached or all purpose flour	2 cups
3/4 teaspoon baking powder	1 1/2 teaspoons
1 pinch salt	1/8 teaspoon

Preheat oven to 375 degrees. Grease and flour baking pan. Prepare crumbs. Cut cold butter into flour and cinnamon to form coarse crumb. Toss sugar into the mixture. Prepare fruit if you are using it.

Prepare the cake. Combine egg yolks, sugar and water in a bowl. Set aside whites. Stir together flour, baking powder and salt. Stir into yolk mix, beating it by hand 15-20 strokes to make smooth batter. Whip egg whites to form stiff peaks. Fold whites into yolk mixture gently but thoroughly, using rubber spatula or hands. Spread batter into prepared pan. If using fruit, sprinkle on top now. Sprinkle crumbs over the whole thing. Bake 30-35 minutes.

Sour Cream Coffee Cake (8"x8" and 10"x14")

This recipe originally came from housemate Terry Bachman's paternal grandmother. It is very easy and always popular. It lends itself to everything from raisins to berries, even coconut and chocolate chips.

8"x8"	**10"x14"**
1/2 cup white sugar	1 cup
6 tablespoons melted butter/ 3/4 stick	1/4 pound plus 2 tablespoons
1 egg	2 eggs
3/4 cup sour cream	1 1/2 cups
3/4 teaspoon vanilla	1 1/2 teaspoons
3/4 cup plus 2 tablespoons flour	1 3/4 cups
1/3 teaspoon baking powder	3/4 teaspoon
1/3 teaspoon baking soda	3/4 teaspoon
3/4 cup raisins, nuts, berries	1 1/2 cups
1 tablespoon white sugar	2 tablespoons
1 pinch cinnamon	1/8 teaspoon

Preheat oven to 325 degrees. Grease and flour pan. Melt butter. Mix together sugar, butter, sour cream and vanilla. Stir well to combine. Stir flour, baking powder and soda together. Add to sour cream mixture and beat well to combine. Fold in fruit. Spread batter into pan. Sprinkle cinnamon sugar on top. Bake 30-35 minutes till top is golden brown and the center springs back to the touch.

Old-Fashioned Crumb (8"x8" and 10"x14")

Who knows what old leaflet this came from originally? Perhaps my early neighbor and seamstress Lael Livack brought it to me. It is called old-fashioned mostly due to the molasses. It lends itself well to the addition of apples, rhubarb or blueberries, and is plenty tasty by itself.

8"x8"	**10"x14"**
Crumbs:	
1/3 cup flour	2/3 cup
5 tablespoons cold butter	1/4 pound plus 2 tablespoons
1/3 cup sugar	2/3 cup
1 teaspoon cinnamon	2 teaspoons
Cake:	
3 tablespoons soft butter	5 tablespoons
1/3 cup plus 2 tablespoons white sugar	3/4 cup
2 tablespoons molasses	1/4 cup
1 egg	2 eggs
1/2 teaspoon vanilla	1 teaspoon

1 cup flour	2 cups plus 2 tablespoons
1 teaspoon baking powder	1 1/2 teaspoons
1/2 teaspoon baking soda	1 teaspoon
1/2 cup yogurt	1 cup
3/4 cup cut fruit, optional	1 1/2 cups

Preheat oven to 350 degrees. Grease and flour pan. Prepare crumbs. Cut or rub cold butter into flour to make a coarse crumb. Toss sugar and cinnamon into crumbs to distribute. Set aside. Prepare batter. Cream together butter, sugar and molasses till light brown and airy. Add egg/s and vanilla and beat to incorporate. Stir together flour, baking powder and soda. Alternately add some flour, some yogurt, more flour, then more yogurt, adding the rest of the flour last to the sugar and egg mixture. Fold in prepared fruit, if using. Spread batter in prepared pan. Sprinkle crumbs on top. Bake 35-40 minutes.

Maple Spice Crumb (8″x8″ and 10″x14″)

This originated in a dog-eared pamphlet of *100 Cakes...* or some such. It is decadently rich and sweet, with a tangy background. It does not keep as well as some others, so eat it up before it dries out.

8″x8″	**10″x14″**
Crumbs:	
1/3 cup flour	2/3 cup
5 tablespoons cold butter	1/4 pound plus 2 tablespoons/ 1 1/4 sticks
1/3 cup sugar	2/3 cup
1 teaspoon cinnamon	2 teaspoons
Cake:	
1/4 pound butter, soft/1 stick	1/2 pound/ 2 sticks
1/2 cup maple syrup	1 cup
1 egg	2 eggs
1/2 cup hot tap water	1 cup
1 2/3 cup flour	3 cups
1/2 teaspoon cinnamon	1 teaspoon
1/2 teaspoon ground ginger	1 teaspoon
1/2 teaspoon ground cloves	1 teaspoon
1/2 teaspoon baking soda	1 teaspoon

Preheat oven to 350 degrees. Prepare crumbs. Cut cold butter into flour to form a coarse crumb. Toss in sugar and cinnamon to just combine. Set aside. Prepare cake. Cream together butter and syrup. Add egg/s and beat. Stir together flour, spices and soda. Alternately add flour, then water, more flour, the rest of the water, the last of the flour to the egg and butter mixture. Grease and flour baking pan. Spread batter into pan. Sprinkle crumbs on top. Bake 30-35 minutes until middle just springs back to the touch.

Brown Sugar Crumble (8"x8" and 10"x14")

The concept for this recipe came from the original *Tassajara Bread Book,* presented there as a special treat for guests. Cindy Bramon substituted buttermilk and came up with this result.

8"x8"	**10"x14"**
Topping:	
1/3 cup plus 1 tablespoon brown sugar	3/4 cup
1 cup walnuts or pecans, chopped	1 1/2 cups
1 tablespoon flour	1 1/2 tablespoons
1 teaspoon cinnamon	1 1/2 teaspoons
2 tablespoons melted butter	4 tablespoons/ 1/2 stick
Cake:	
1 1/4 cups flour	2 1/4 cups
2/3 cup brown sugar	1 1/4 cups
1 1/2 teaspoons baking powder	1 tablespoon
1/3 cup buttermilk	3/4 cup
2 eggs	3 eggs
3 tablespoons melted butter	6 tablespoons/ 3/4 stick

Preheat oven to 350 degrees. Grease and flour pan. For topping, stir together brown sugar, nuts, flour and cinnamon. Melt butter and pour over flour mixture. Toss with a fork to blend. Put aside. Prepare cake. Stir together flour, brown sugar and baking powder. Combine milk, eggs and melted butter and beat with a fork or wire whisk. Beat wet into dry to form a slightly thick batter. Spread into prepared pan. Crumble topping over batter. Bake 30-35 minutes till center of the cake just springs back to the touch.

Maple Oat Crumb-Vegan (8"x8" and 10"x14")

Andrew Paschetto and Heather Ward removed sugar, eggs and dairy from a recipe given to me by former bakery neighbor and seamstress Cherisse Desrossiers. It became a favorite of customers, vegan and non-vegan alike. Because of the lack of eggs to help the cake rise, it is important to really work the batter to develop the proteins to hold it up.

8"x8"	**10"x14"**
Vegan Crumbs:	
1/2 cup flour	2/3 cup
1/2 teaspoon cinnamon	2/3 teaspoon
5 tablespoons soy margarine	1/4 pound plus 2 tablespoons/ 1 1/4 sticks
2 tablespoons maple syrup	3 1/2 tablespoons

Cake:

2/3 cup rolled oats	1 1/4 cups
1/3 cup oil	2/3 cup
3/4 cup maple syrup	1 1/2 cups
1 tablespoon cider vinegar	2 tablespoons
1 ounce tofu	2 ounces
1/3 cup water	2/3 cup
3/4 cup unbleached or all purpose flour	1 1/4 cups
1/3 cup soy flour, lightly toasted	2/3 cup
3/4 teaspoon baking soda	1 2/3 teaspoon
1 pinch salt	1/8 teaspoon

Preheat oven to 350 degrees. Grease and flour pan. To make crumbs, cut margarine into flour and cinnamon to make a coarse crumb. Pour syrup over flour mixture and toss lightly with fork to just wet; otherwise, you may end up with a gooey glob. Set aside. Prepare cake. Stir together oats, oil, syrup and vinegar and let stand to soak. Cream tofu and water in blender or food processor to make creamy smooth. Add to oat mixture. Stir together flours, soda and salt. Add to wet mix and beat well 25-50 strokes. Grease and flour baking pan. Spread batter into pan. Sprinkle crumbs on top. Bake 35 minutes until center just springs back to the touch.

Maple Walnut Coffee Cake (8"x8" and 10"x14")

Many people chose to limit their intake of refined sugar. Baker Lynn E. Alden requested a maple sweetened coffee cake option. This is what we came up with, using the Sour Cream Coffee Cake recipe as guide. Walnuts were by far the favorite addition, and peaches are delicious too.

8"x8"	**10"x14"**
1/2 cup maple syrup	1 cup
1 egg	2 eggs
5 tablespoons melted butter	1/4 pound plus 2 tablespoons/ 1 1/4 stick
2/3 cup sour cream	1 1/3 cups
1/2 teaspoon vanilla	1 teaspoon
1 1/3 cups flour	2 2/3 cups
1/2 teaspoon baking powder	1 teaspoon
1/3 teaspoon baking soda	3/4 teaspoon
2/3 cup walnuts, coarsely chopped	1 1/3 cups
1/8 teaspoon cinnamon	1/4 teaspoon
1 tablespoon maple syrup	2 tablespoons

Preheat oven to 325 degrees. Melt butter. Mix together syrup, egg/s, butter, sour cream and vanilla. Stir together flour, baking powder and soda. Add to syrup mix and beat well to make a smooth batter. Fold in chopped nuts. Grease and flour pan. Spread batter in pan. Sprinkle cinnamon on top. Bake 35-40 minutes at 325 degrees until golden brown and cake springs back to the touch. Remove from oven and drizzle additional maple syrup on top.

Lemon Berry Walnut Coffee Cake-Vegan (8″x8″ and 10″x14″)

This is a reworking of Orange Cranberry Cake, originally from the cookbook *Sweets for Saints and Sinners.* Krista baked the original version for guests at Bolton Valley Resort when she worked there. She substituted honey when she brought it to Daily Bread. Judy Bush and Andrew Paschetto collaborated to come up with this version, not absolutely vegan because it does contain honey, an insect product.

8"x8"	**10"x14"**
1 1/3 cups unbleached or all purpose flour	2 1/2 cups
3 tablespoons soy flour, lightly toasted	1/3 cup
3/4 teaspoons baking powder	1 1/3 teaspoons
1/8 teaspoon baking soda	1/4 teaspoon
1 pinch salt	2 pinches
1/2 coarsely chopped walnuts, lightly toasted	1 cup
2/3 cup water	1 1/4 cups
1 1/2 ounces tofu	3 ounces
1/3 cup honey	2/3 cup
2 teaspoons cider vinegar	1 1/4 tablespoons
1/4 cup oil	1/3 cup oil
1 cup berries	2 cups

Glaze:	
1/2 lemon, grated zest and juice	1 lemon
1 tablespoon honey	2 tablespoons

Preheat oven to 350 degrees. Lightly toast nuts and soy flour. Grease and flour pan. Stir together unbleached flour, soy flour, baking powder, soda, salt and nuts. Whip water and tofu in blender or food processor till smooth and creamy. Combine tofu mixture with honey, vinegar and oil. Add liquid mix to flour mixture and beat well, 25-50 strokes. Fold berries and zest into batter. Grease and flour pan. Spread batter into pan and bake 40 minutes until top lightly browned and springy to the touch in center of cake. Meanwhile, stir together lemon juice and honey to make a glaze. While cake is still hot, poke a number of holes in the top with a tooth-pick. Spread or brush glaze over the whole thing.

Peach Raspberry Lo-fat Coffee Cake (8″x8″ and 10″x14″)

Rose (Rosa) Warnock found this recipe in a *Cooking Light* magazine. Don't be put off by the two toppings. They are both straightforward and quick to prepare.

8"x8"	**10"x14"**
Topping 1:	
2/3 cup diced frozen or canned peaches	1 1/3 cups
1/3 cup fresh or frozen raspberries	2/3 cup
2 tablespoons sugar	4 tablespoons

Topping 2:

2 tablespoons rolled oats	1/4 cup
1 teaspoon raw or toasted wheat germ	2 teaspoons
1/8 teaspoon cinnamon	1/4 teaspoon
2 tablespoons chopped pecans	1/4 cup

Cake:

2/3 cup unbleached or all purpose flour	1 1/3 cups
1 cup whole wheat pastry flour	2 cups
1/2 cup sugar	1 cup
3/4 tablespoon baking powder	1 1/2 tablespoons
2/3 teaspoon cinnamon	1 1/3 teaspoons
1/3 teaspoon salt	2/3 teaspoons
2 eggs, separated	4 eggs
3/4 cup plus 1 tablespoon buttermilk	1 1/2 cups
1 yolk of eggs above	1 yolk of eggs above
2/3 teaspoon vanilla	1 tablespoon

Preheat oven to 350 degrees. Grease and flour pan. Prepare toppings. For topping 1, chop peaches. If using canned, drain all liquid. Toss together peaches, berries and sugar. Set aside. For topping 2, stir together oats, wheat germ, cinnamon and pecans. Set aside.

Prepare cake batter. Stir together unbleached and whole wheat pastry flours, sugar, baking powder, cinnamon and salt in mixing bowl. Separate eggs. Save one yolk. Store remainders for other baking projects. Beat whites to form firm, but not dry, peaks. Beat together buttermilk, yolk and vanilla. Alternately fold whites and buttermilk mixture into dry with rubber spatula or hands till all well incorporated. Spread batter in prepared pan. Distribute Topping 1.over batter. Sprinkle Topping 2. over everything. Bake 35 minutes.

Lo-fat Spice Coffee Cake (8"x8" and 10"x14")

This is an unusual cake, spicy and fruity. It is a nice option to offer friends who are eating light. Prune puree replaces fat in this recipe. Who knows how cooks or food scientists figured this out?!

8"x8"	**10"x14"**
3/4 cup plus 1 tablespoon pitted prunes	1 1/2 cups
1/4 cup hot water	1/2 cup
1/3 cup buttermilk	1 cup
1 egg	1 egg
2 eggs, whites only	3 eggs, whites only
1 1/3 tablespoons sugar	3 2/3 tablespoons
1 pinch cream of tartar	1 pinch

1 cup flour	2 cups
1/2 cup plus 1 tablespoon sugar	1 cup
1 teaspoon baking powder	2 teaspoons
1/8 teaspoon baking soda	1/4 teaspoon
1/8 teaspoon salt	1/4 teaspoon
1 teaspoon cinnamon	2 teaspoons
1/8 teaspoon nutmeg	1/4 teaspoon
1 pinch ground cloves	1/8 teaspoon
1 tablespoon sugar	2 tablespoons

Preheat oven to 350 degrees. Grease and flour pan. Pour hot water over prunes. Combine whole egg and buttermilk in a blender or food processor. Add prunes and water to egg and buttermilk and whiz all to make a smooth creamy liquid. Pour into mixing bowl. Stir together flour, sugar, baking powder, soda, salt and spices. Whip egg whites, sugar and cream of tartar to form stiff, shiny peaks. Alternately fold flour, then egg whites, then the rest of the flour to the prune mixture, working gently with rubber spatula or hands to thoroughly blend. Spread batter into prepared pan. Sprinkle with additional white sugar. Bake 35 minutes.

Alison, Betsy and Lynn E pose in the kitchen BC (before cafe), circa 1984.

Pound cakes

Pound cakes are generally rich and denser than layer cakes or coffee cakes. These cakes freeze well and can easily be made ahead of time and frozen to have on hand for unexpected guests. They derived their name from the original recipes calling for one pound each of butter, sugar, eggs, flour and milk. As a teenager, I baked a pound cake recipe from my grandmother Katherine Helms Bott's early 20th century Gold Medal Cookbook. The book was unfortunately lost during my parents' move from New York to New Mexico. That cake was flavored with rose water and tasted "Victorian" to me. Mollie Katzen's original *Moosewood Cookbook* has an excellent basic recipe with variations. Here are a few we offered at Daily Bread.

General Notes:

Pound cakes rely on plenty of air beaten into the butter, the eggs and the whole mix to make them rise and hold their shape during and after baking. Give them lots of time in the mixer or with your whisk.

Note: Double this recipe to make an 8- or 9-inch tube pan for a large party. Bake at 325 degrees for 1 hour or until the middle springs back to the touch.

Mississippi Mud (2 small loaves / 4"x8"x2 1/2")

When I first began collecting recipes, my neighbor Onnie Palmer gave me this one. She got it from her mother's neighbor in Connecticut. There are others by the same name, but this one tops them in my book. For the chocoholic in your life, this is a sure winner.

2 cups hot brewed coffee
3/4 pound butter/ 3 sticks
1 1/2 cups sugar
1/2 cup unsweetened cocoa
2 cups unbleached or all purpose flour
1 teaspoon baking soda
2 eggs, one at a time
1 1/2 teaspoons vanilla (the original called for bourbon)
Chocolate Goo for frosting (see page 79)

Preheat oven to 275 degrees. Grease and flour two small loaf pans. Combine hot coffee and butter in mixing bowl. Stir to melt butter. Add sugar and cocoa and beat with wire whisk to combine. Stir together flour and soda. Beat into coffee mixture till smooth. Add eggs, one at a time and beat thoroughly after each addition. Stir in vanilla or bourbon. Pour into prepared pans. Bake 1 1/2 hours. Do not peek or open oven until at least 1 hour has elapsed! Center of the cake should spring back to the touch when done. Cool and carefully remove from pans. You may need to loosen edges with a knife or bench scraper. Prepare goo. Pour or spread glaze over cooled cakes.

Poppy Seed Pound Cake (2 small loaves/ 4"x8"x2 1/2")

This recipe came from the Minnesota kitchen of Judy Bush's mother Margaret Burchell. We changed the white sugar to honey. The subtle flavor of cinnamon adds to the overall experience. We also baked this basic recipe as a bar (see page 226).

    1 cup yogurt
    1/2 cup poppy seeds
    1/2 pound butter, soft/ 2 sticks
    1 cup honey
    4 eggs, one at a time
    1 teaspoon vanilla
    2 1/2 cups unbleached or all purpose flour
    2 teaspoons baking powder
    1 teaspoon baking soda
    1/2 teaspoon salt
    2 teaspoons cinnamon

Mix together yogurt and poppy seeds. Let stand at least 1/2 hour or up to overnight. Preheat oven to 350 degrees. Grease and flour pans. Cream butter and honey till light and fluffy. Beat eggs into butter mixture one at a time. Add vanilla. Turn this mixture into a mixing bowl large enough to really work this batter. Stir flour, baking powder, soda and salt together. Alternately add some flour, some yogurt, more flour, the rest of the yogurt, then the rest of the flour into the butter mixture, beating well after each addition. Spoon half of the batter into pans. Sprinkle 1 teaspoon cinnamon on top each half. Add the second half of batter. Bake 1 hour. Do not open oven until at least 45 minutes have elapsed. Cakes are done when the center just springs back to the touch. Remove and cool slightly before taking out of the pans.

Honey Lemon Pound Cake (2 small loaves/ 4"x8"x2 1/2")

Krista Willett did a lot of professional baking besides at Daily Bread. She received the basis for this recipe from Vermont State Representative Val Vincent to serve at Vincent's establishment, 3 Main, in Waterbury. Krista remembers Val's version being an orange. Krista changed the sugar to honey, and this is the result.

    6 ounces butter/ 1 1/2 sticks
    1 cup honey
    4 eggs, one at a time
    4 cups unbleached or all purpose flour
    2 teaspoons baking powder
    Grated zest of 2 lemons
    1 cup milk

Glaze:
6 tablespoons honey
Juice of 2 lemons

Preheat oven to 350 degrees. Grease and flour two small loaf pans. Cream together butter and honey till light and fluffy. Beat in eggs one at a time, beating well after each. Transfer to a mixing bowl. Stir together flour, powder, salt and lemon zest. Add alternately flour, milk, flour, milk, flour to egg mixture, beating well with spoon or wire whisk after each addition. Pour into prepared pans. Bake 1 hour. Do not open the oven until at least 45 minutes have elapsed! Prepare glaze by stirring together honey and lemon juice. Remove cakes from oven and pour glaze over while still hot. Let cool slightly before attempting to remove from pans. Loosen edges with a knife.

Irish Tea Brack (2 small loaves 4"x8"x2 1/2")
Krista Willett found the original of this recipe in "some magazine." It was a low fat recipe, so she gave it a try. The Earl Grey tea and the dried fruits give it a decidedly rich taste. It keeps extremely well.

Note: Double this recipe to make an 8- or 9-inch tube pan for a large party. Bake at 325 degrees for 1 hour or until the middle springs back to the touch.

    1 1/2 cups Earl Grey tea, 3 tea bags brewed strong
    1 1/2 cups brown sugar
    1/2 cup raisins
    1/2 cup pitted and chopped dates
    1/2 cup chopped dried apricots
    1/2 cup dried cherries or your choice of dried fruit
    Grated zest of 2 lemons or oranges
    2 eggs, lightly beaten
    1 1/2 cups unbleached or all purpose flour
    1/2 cup whole wheat pastry flour
    1 1/2 teaspoons baking powder
    1 teaspoon cinnamon
    1/2 teaspoon nutmeg
    1/2 teaspoon salt

Preheat oven to 350 degrees. Brew tea. Mix together sugar, dried fruits and zest. Pour tea over fruits and allow to "plump." When the fruits have cooled to lukewarm, add eggs and stir to combine. Stir together flours, baking powder, cinnamon, nutmeg and salt. Add to fruit mixture and stir well to combine. Grease and flour two small loaf pans. Pour/spoon batter into pans. Bake 45 minutes or until center of loaf springs back to the touch.

Food for People ···

October 20, 1989

Dear Betsy,

I think we all succeeded in doing a remarkable thing today. At around 1 PM a truck loaded with approximately 3500 pounds of locally produced food, some of Vermont's best, set out for Castlewood, Va. (that's in a deep corner of the state near Tennessee, Kentucky and West Virginia)....Really, an imposing outpouring of generosity on the part of our fellow food producers. That generosity was matched by the generosity of two Teamster Union members, who volunteered to drive the donated food 800 miles there and back (not to mention the Teamster's Union itself, and the Vt. Council of Labor, who paid for the rental...and gas...).

To me, it feels a little funny looking for aid for the striking coal miners, when the California earthquake had occurred the same week...But...the Pittston strikers have been struggling for half a year now; and the rest of the country hasn't taken much notice of them....

    Jules Rabin (24)

Upland Baker's Jules Rabin called for donations for a number of cross country projects such as the above. We were happy to contribute.

Granola

What 1970s hippie household didn't bake at least one batch of granola, that sweet and usually rich toasted combo of nuts and grains? So, of course, I wanted to offer a Daily Bread version. Granola has a longer shelf life than bread, and it seemed like a natural to add to our products. After a few miscues (Molasses Sunflower?!), we developed our line.

We started wholesaling granola in 1980, and sold to up to seven coops at one time. In the late '80s, bigger commercial operations started producing "granola" on a large scale. We could not compete. We continued to serve our local coops and bake for individuals, and it became a one afternoon a week shift.

Note: We used thick rolled oats because they could withstand the Hobart mixer's workout. Regular rolled oats will not crumble if mixed by hand. Quick rolled oats should not be substituted.

Maple Cashew (5 pounds, about 1 gallon)

Pat Bates, one of the first bakery employees, offered her special mix, Maple Cashew. It is still my personal favorite. The sweetness of the maple and the richness of the cashews make it almost candy. The aroma of it baking is heavenly. We used it as the base for our Back Country Bar (see page 194).

    11 cups rolled oats, thick if you can find them
    3 3/4 cups wheat flakes
    2 1/4 cups cashews

1 1/2 cups wheat bran
1 1/2 cups coconut
1 cup oil, sunflower or safflower preferably
1 cup maple syrup
1/3 cup barley malt
1 teaspoon vanilla

Preheat oven to 350 degrees. Stir together oats, wheat flakes, cashews, bran and coconut in a large bowl. Stir oil, syrup, barley malt and vanilla in a separate bowl or measuring cup. Add liquids to dry and stir just to moisten. You don't want to break up the oats too much or you will have a powdery end product. Generously oil baking pans, and spread cereal about 1 inch deep. Use as many pans as you need, depending on their size. Bake 10 minutes. Remove from oven and mix cereal. Try to get to all the corners and to get the bottom stirred around. Return to the oven and bake another 10 minutes. Stir again. Return and check after 5 minutes. Take out when all is light brown and feels just slightly damp to the touch. Cool completely, stirring every once in a while. Store in a tightly lidded container. If you don't go through it quickly, a portion may be frozen.

Almost Hatch's (5 pounds/ about 1 gallon)

Food coop members Russ and Connie Ireland approached me in 1980 to custom bake granola for them. "We have David Hatch's original recipe," they beamed. The late David Hatch was the first health food wholesaler and store owner in Vermont, and had developed a following. His St. Johnsbury store served customers from Lake Champlain to the mountains of Maine. Jack Cook wrote in a 1976 *Country Journal* article:

> "They don't advertise, their phone is not listed in the local directory, but they have the largest stock of natural foods north of Boston…Hatch's is not in business for its health. It's in business for everybody's health." **(25)**

Unfortunately, the Interstate right of way demanded his building, and illness took his life shortly after he had relocated to Virginia.

We left out the flax seeds, apricots and dates. Otherwise this is pretty close to the original. Hatch baked his in 55 gallon drums turned over a propane burner.

This is a real meal. It will stick with you for many a mile. It makes excellent and nutritious trail food, and has nourished many hikers along the Appalachian Trail.

9 cups rolled oats, thick if you can get them
1 cup wheat flakes
2 cups coconut
1 1/2 cups unsalted roasted soy nuts

1 cup sunflower seeds
3/4 cup almonds
2/3 cup sesame seeds
3/4 cup oil, sunflower or safflower
2/3 cup honey
2 cups raisins

Preheat oven to 350 degrees. Combine oats, wheat flakes, coconut, soy nuts, sunflower and sesame seeds and almonds in a large bowl. In a separate bowl or cup, mix oil and honey. Pour over the dry ingredients and stir till just combined. Generously oil baking pans. Spread cereal about 1 inch deep. Use as many pans as you need. Bake 10 minutes. Remove from oven and stir, getting into all corners and into the bottom to prevent sticking. Return to the oven and bake another 10 minutes. Remove and stir. Return to oven for 5 minutes, and repeat until cereal is lightly browned and slightly damp to the touch. Remove for the last time. Add raisins. Cool completely, stirring occasionally. Store in a tightly lidded container. Or freeze some, if it will not be eaten within a week.

Unsweetened Hatch's (5 pounds/ about 1 gallon)
For many, granola was too sweet for their taste or constitution. We came up with this variation. The apple juice (or cider) and cinnamon provide enough flavor to make this a satisfying alternative.

9 cups rolled oats, thick if you can get them
1 cup wheat flakes
2 cups coconut
1 1/2 cups roasted unsalted soy nuts
1 cup sunflower seeds
3/4 cup almonds
2/3 cup sesame seeds
1/2 cup plus 1 tablespoon apple juice or cider
3/4 cup oil
1/4 teaspoon cinnamon
2 cups raisins

Mix dry ingredients in a large bowl. Combine apple juice, oil and cinnamon. Pour over the dry mix and stir quickly to prevent clumps (juice soaks in more readily than honey). Proceed as above. Add the 2 cups of raisins after baking is complete. Note: this mix should feel dry when done.

Fat Free (1 gallon)

My sister's friend Joe brought me a sample of a fat-free granola he liked. This is our attempt at duplication. It is both fat-free and wheat free. It makes a nice gift to people who are wheat sensitive. It is on the sweet side.

9 cups rolled oats, thick if you can find them
3 2/3 cups barley flakes
2 3/4 cups rye flakes
1 1/3 cups honey
1/3 cup maple syrup
1 tablespoon vanilla
2 cups raisins
1/2 6-ounce bag puffed rice, added after baking

Combine oats, barley flakes and rye flakes in a large bowl. Combine honey, syrup and vanilla in a separate bowl or cup. Pour over dry mix. Proceed to bake the same as other granola. After baking is complete, add raisins and puffed rice.

Keep the Wheels Turning

I wasn't able to attend Bread and Puppet's Resurrection Circus every year; someone had to keep the home fires burning, feeding all those hungry pilgrims making their annual Daily Bread stop on their way north. We usually sent a bag of granola up a week or two before the performance.

Lynn E breaks up lumps before bagginig baked cereal.

20 August 1984
Dear Betsy,
Thank you for the delivery of granola. It was a generous donation and a very wise one. There were scores of puppeteers crowding into the kitchen for breakfast that last week and your gift was a great treat to us....
Thanks again for helping to keep the wheels turning.
Sincerely,
Linda Elbow
Bread and Puppet Theater **(26)**

Crusts and Wrappers

We sold many more turnovers than pies over the years, more often savory than sweet. We made Potato Smokers every Tuesday, Quesadillas on Wednesday, a special savory once or twice a week, fruit turnovers every Friday and Quiche of some sort on Sunday. Pizza and Calzones filled in the other days, based on a yeasted crust. At Thanksgiving and other holidays people wanted full pies, otherwise they preferred the fully wrapped one or two person turnover.

The following are recipes for the pastry portion of pies and turnovers, sweet and savory, pizza, calzones, quesadillas and burritos. The instructions for assembling and recipes for fillings and toppings follow.

General notes:

Pie crusts and tortillas are made by cutting or rubbing shortening into flour and then adding just enough liquid to make rollable dough.

We used King Arthur special bread flour for everything at Daily Bread. Purpose all or pastry flour will give a slightly more tender result.

Shortening and liquid need to be cold. This keeps the shortening from actually combining with the flour. It wants to maintain its individuality to create the little pockets that make pastry flaky. We used a combination of butter and soy margarine. We used lard at the beginning, but discontinued due to customer and staff preferences. Lard makes a very flaky product. Vegetable shortening makes a crumblier crust. Butter makes crust crisp.

Work quickly. Toss the flour rather than stir. Use your hands only enough to bring it together for rolling. The dough wants to be just slightly damp. Too dry and it will fall apart. Too sticky, you will have to add flour on the board.

Wrapped tightly, pastry dough will keep for up to a week in the refrigerator. Make double batches and surprise the household with pie for dessert!

To roll, divide in half or six. Sprinkle the rolling surface with a little flour; here is a good place for your flour shaker (see page 20). Flatten the piece gently with your palm. Begin rolling, rolling it in one direction, then the opposite. Turn the piece over. Continue rolling creating as round a piece as you can, at least an inch larger than the pan you are using. Lift the edges gently and fold in half to transfer to you pan.

Bake pastries at a high temperature, usually 425 degrees, for the first five minutes to seal the crust from the liquid. Reduce the heat to 350 or 375 degrees and finish baking; see individual recipes for total times.

Pat Quinn •

The 1960s back-to-the-land movement looked to the old ways for guidance. The self-sufficient home-stead depended on what could be produced on the farm or traded with neighbors. Lard and butter had their seasons.

Both of these were produced locally. It seemed a good decision to purchase local products. The Richmond Coop Creamery in the village sold 5 pound boxes of whey butter as a by-product of their mozzarella operation. Jonesville meat-cutter and honorary mayor Bernard "Pat" Quinn sold me lard. We used it for crusts and cookies the first three years.

Quinn's Store in Jonesville was a local landmark. Not only did the low-ceilinged, labyrinthine store sell the best meat around, it was also the local liquor store and game-reporting station. With employees and with such a wide variety of products, Pat Quinn knew all about quarterly tax reports and state inspectors.

"We have to do a lot of work for the federal and state governments for no pay," Pat told a *Burlington Free Press Sunday* reporter in 1983. Then he rattled off all the inspectors: boiler, meat, cigarettes, ice cream, ammunition, drugs, liquor and on and on. "I am not polite to them, no. I don't call them sir," he continued. (27)

After making it through numerous Winooski River floods, Pat Quinn's original store burned. He reopened across Route 2, but it was never quite the same. He retired a few times from the Jonesville store only to reappear at the Richmond Corner Market in the late 1990s, enjoying and entertaining customers and still offering the best meats around.

Basic Pie Dough (2 crusts, 6 turnover wrappers)

This is the recipe we used for the first 15 years for all pies and turnovers, sweet and savory. The combination of half butter and half margarine gives it flake without being brittle, as sometimes happens with all butter. For the first few years, we used butter and lard. Dietary concerns for heart health and an ever increasing number of vegetarian customers led us to substitute margarine. In the later years, we offered an all margarine version for those who were lactose intolerant or vegan. Despite the instructions of grandmothers and home economics teachers, this is a slightly damp version. It is easy to roll out, and you can always add flour as you work.

> 2 cups unbleached flour
> 6 tablespoons cold butter/ 3/4 stick
> 6 tablespoons cold margarine/ 3/4 stick
> 1/2 cup cold water, added one tablespoon at a time

Cut or rub butter and margarine into flour with pastry blender or hands to a medium crumb resembling corn meal. Toss with a fork from the bottom of your bowl as you add water one table-spoon at a time until all is damp and will just hold together. Form a ball, discarding stray bits of flour. Wrap tightly and refrigerate until you are ready to use it. It will keep, refrigerated, up to one week.

New Pie Dough (2 crusts, 6 turnover wrappers)

Andrew Paschetto felt we could do better, and got this one from baker and artist Chris Billis, whose mother used this alternate version. The egg and vinegar make it more tender and even easier to roll. Brush with an egg and water glaze just before baking for a showy and delightfully crunchy result.

    1 3/4 cup unbleached flour
    1/4 teaspoon salt
    6 tablespoons cold butter
    4 tablespoons cold margarine
    1 egg, slightly beaten
    1 1/4 teaspoons vinegar, white or cider
    Cold water to make 1/2 cup liquid total when added to egg and vinegar

Cut or rub butter and margarine into flour and salt with pastry blender or hands to a medium crumb resembling cornmeal. Combine egg and vinegar in a measuring cup. Add enough cold water to make 1/2 cup liquid altogether. Toss with a fork from the bottom of the bowl as you add the liquid, one tablespoon at a time till all ingredients are damp. Form a ball, discarding stray crumbs of flour. Wrap tightly and refrigerate until you are ready to use it. This will keep up to one week, refrigerated.

Tart Pastry (6 3-inch or 2 8-inch shells)

We rarely baked tarts, and I include this just because it is an excellent recipe for pre-baked shells. Nora, a baker at the short-lived Quiche and Things, gave this to me during my 10-day apprenticeship with her. One of these sweet, crunchy shells filled with a little softened cream cheese or custard and topped with fresh berries in season makes an elegant dessert.

    2 cups all purpose or unbleached flour
    1 tablespoon sugar
    1 pinch salt
    4 tablespoons cold margarine
    6 tablespoons cold butter
    1 cold egg
    1/3 cup cold water

Chris Billis measuring ingredients at the bake table.

Stir together flour, sugar and salt in a mixing bowl. Cut or rub margarine and butter into the flour mixture with a pastry blender or your hands to a medium crumb resembling cornmeal. Beat the egg lightly. Toss it into the flour with a fork. Then add the cold water and toss until dough will just stick together into a ball. Wrap or seal in a tight container and refrigerate till you need it.

To make shells, divide dough into two or six pieces depending on the size. Preheat oven to 400 degrees. Sprinkle your rolling surface and dough with flour. Roll each into a circle an inch to an inch and a half larger than your pans. Roll edge under to stand up and pinch to make a scallop design. Prick all over the bottom with a fork, emphasis on the all. Bake 15-20 minutes till lightly browned. Cool and fill.

Syrup Crust (8″x8″ crust)

The saga of syrup crust began with Alison Forrest. She brought a cheesecake bar recipe from the *Tassajara Bread Book* which used honey as the sweetener for the crust. Baker Lynn E. Alden wanted a maple version, so substituted syrup. We increased the butter; too greasy. The final version was just right. This crust is used for many of our bars. See specific recipes beginning on page 177. Or try out your own filling. The aroma of this baking is especially mouth watering.

1 1/3 cups whole wheat pastry flour
6 tablespoons melted butter or margarine
3 tablespoons maple syrup

Preheat oven to 350 degrees. Stir syrup into melted butter or margarine. Pour over flour and toss lightly with fork to moisten. Press into an ungreased baking pan. Bake 12 minutes. Top with filling of choice.

Coffee Break Counter. . . . .

How did we start serving coffee and offering lunch specials? Our services grew because Richmond had a vital village center, pedestrian and family friendly. People volunteered for many ambitious community projects from creating a new park to renovating the former elementary school buildings into Richmond Free Library's new home, town offices, school district offices and the local post office, to purchasing playground equipment and developing ball fields. These efforts kept community resources in the center of town. People usually get hungry sooner or later.

Moose Creek carpenters, who worked on phase 3 of the renovation of the Round Church, urged me to sell hot beverages; there was no heat in the church, and they frequently sought a haven in the hallway of the bakery. The local telephone company and school district offices were across the street. The local bank branch was right next door. The creamery and the hardware store employed people within walking distance. The elementary school was just down the block. People asked for something they could grab for lunch. I began a rotation of lunch pastries and leased a "real" coffee pot from a local coffee service.

Soon we had a shelf to lean on out in the hallway.

Daily Bakery Lunches

In keeping with our name, we developed lunch specials based on or in bread. Over time a schedule of daily specials evolved.

Monday and Thursday

Pizza (12"x16" sheet or 2 9-inch rounds)

This version came about through trial and error, with influences from *Diet for a Small Planet* (addition of soy) to add nutritive value. Judy Bush offered major inspiration, serving tempting steaming pans at her home table. Pizza was the first savory I sold before we even had a shelf to lean on. It was a standard lunch offering at the Bread, which we served twice a week. It was the first step in the urge for a place to sit down. It is yeast dough, so remember to plan ahead, at least 2 hours.

Dough:
1 1/2 cups warm water
1 1/2 tablespoons yeast
1/2 teaspoon black pepper
1/2 teaspoon dried oregano /1 teaspoon fresh
1/2 teaspoon salt
1/4 cup olive oil
1/2 cup soy flour
3 to 3 1/2 cups unbleached flour

The leaning counter was the first step.

Proof yeast in warm water till foamy. Add pepper, oregano, salt, olive oil and soy flour. Add half the unbleached flour and stir 25-50 strokes. Add additional flour to make a soft dough. Turn onto a floured surface and knead well till smooth and springy to the touch. Place in a greased bowl and let rise till doubled.

Meanwhile prepare sauce, gather toppings and grate cheese/s.

Sauce: (2 cups, enough to cover 2 12"x16" or 4 9-inch rounds)
2 tablespoons olive oil
1 1/2 teaspoons minced or pressed garlic/ 3 cloves
1 1/2 teaspoons dried basil/ 1 tablespoon fresh
1 1/2 teaspoons dried oregano/ 1 tablespoon fresh
1/2 teaspoon black pepper
1 14-ounce can tomato sauce

Heat garlic and herbs in oil. Add tomato sauce and simmer 15 minutes or more.

Toppings:
2 cups vegetables, cut in bite sized pieces and sautéed as necessary:
Steamed broccoli, cauliflower, sweet corn
Raw sugar snap peas, spinach, fresh tomato
Sauteed onions, garlic, peppers, mushrooms
Marinated artichoke hearts, black or green olives

Or 1 pound vegetarian or meat sausage, browned

Plus:
1/4 cup grated parmesan cheese
 2 1/4 cups grated mozzarella cheese/ 10 ounces

Or

Dwayne's Vegan Topping (to cover a 12"x16" or 2 9-inch rounds)

The 1990s brought requests for non-dairy options to many bakery favorites, including pizza. Cook Dwayne Doner concocted this mixture to produce a "vegan" white pizza.

1 1/4 pounds tofu
1/2 cup olive oil
4 cloves minced or pressed garlic
2 tablespoons dried basil/ 4 tablespoons fresh
1/2 teaspoon dried thyme/ 1 teaspoon fresh
1/2 teaspoon dried marjoram
1 tablespoon tamari
2 cups vegetables, diced, sliced and sautéed, as necessary

Crumble tofu into bowl of a food processor. Add olive oil, garlic, herbs and tamari and buzz till smooth and homogenous. Spread topping on partially baked crust. Top with vegetables. See baking instructions below.

To assemble:

Grease and lightly cornmeal baking pan/s. Turn dough onto floured surface. Roll large enough to fit pan/s. Place in pan/s and let rise till doubled, 15 to 30 minutes. Preheat the oven to 450 degrees. After rising in the pan/s, bake 10 minutes. It should look dry.

Take out and spread 1 cup sauce on each 12"x16" pan, 1/2 cup on each 9-inch round.

For plain, sprinkle cheese on now. For fancy, arrange vegetables or other choice of extra on top of sauce. Sprinkle parmesan over vegetables and mozzarella over all. Return to oven and continue to bake another 10-20 minutes until cheese bubbles and begins to brown.

Pizza Genie

Jean and Judy clown around in front of a tray of perfectly formed pretzels.

Out in the Mountains reporter Chris Tebbets asked me what people could do to support Daily Bread other than buying its products. I replied that individuals could start their own business, taking an idea and turning it into a livelihood benefitting both worker and customer, bank account and neighborhood. I used the example of Jean Kelly who started a small, home pizza business after working at the Bread.

Jean arrived at Daily Bread in the mid-1990s. She, her son Elden and her husband Lee Rosen were renting in Richmond while Lee finished his degree at the University of Vermont. Jean had worked at COTS (Committee for Temporary Shelter) in Burlington, and needed a break. She picked up a few shifts at Daily Bread and enjoyed it.

She wanted even more time at home, so experimented with her version of Pizza. Her crust is crisp and garlicy. Lots of vegetables. Plenty of sauce and cheese. She started at the Richmond Farmer's Market and sold out the first day. *Burlington Free Press's* food columnist Debbie Salomon called Jean's the "second best of my lifetime"! (28)

Jean mixed her dough in our big Hobart during our off hours, enough for a few days at a time. She soon had stores in Shelburne, Charlotte, Huntington and Richmond taking her product.

Tuesday

Potato Smokers (6 turnovers)

I worked one college summer at radio station WNEW in downtown Manhattan. One of my favorite lunches was a potato knish purchased from a street vendor or deli. They were an orange-sized portion of mashed potato or kasha spiced with onions and black pepper, wrapped in a thin flaky pastry. When I started baking professionally, I wanted to make something similar. I came up with this version but they didn't catch on at first.

Knish sounded too strange to 1979 Richmond ears. Kenny Dunbar stopped in one day and asked for "one of those potato patties." He returned in less than 5 minutes to buy another one, proclaiming the first "the smokin'est potato patty" he had ever eaten. The name stuck, and we baked them every Tuesday as our bakery lunch special. Leftover mashed potatoes can be used, but the best are prepared from fresh, hot ones.

1 recipe pie dough (see page 105-6)

Filling:
2 large white potatoes, peeled, boiled and mashed/ about 2 cups
8 ounces cream cheese
1 egg
1 medium onion, peeled and diced fine
1 clove minced or pressed garlic
1/3 teaspoon salt
1/8 teaspoon black pepper
1 1/2 cups vegetable of choice, diced and sautéed/ optional
1 egg and water for glaze

Prepare pie dough. Chill while you prepare filling. Cook and mash potatoes. While still hot, add cream cheese. Use potato masher, fork or hands to thoroughly mix. Add egg, onion, garlic, salt and pepper. Stir to combine. If additional vegetables are desired, prepare and add to the potato mixture.

To assemble: preheat oven to 450 degrees. Divide pie dough into 6 pieces. Roll out into 6 inch circles. Divide filling onto circles. Fold over, turnover style. Fold edges together to seal. Place on lightly greased baking sheet. Whisk together egg and a little water. Brush onto turnovers. Bake 15-20 minutes.

All My Relations..

Kenny Dunbar, who named the Potato Smoker, was one of the many people who came to Richmond because of the Sunray Meditation Society's five year residence in nearby Huntington before it found its permanent home in Lincoln.

Louise Lindner Sunfeather Diamond was well known in Vermont for her work helping groups to communicate and successfully govern themselves by consensus. She was an early advocate for seniors and alternative healing, and has dedicated her life to help bring peace to the planet. While living in Washington, D.C. and caring for her elderly parents, she co-founded with retired Diplomat John McDonald, the Institute for Multi-Track Diplomacy.

Louise was responsible for bringing Sunray's teacher Dhyani Ywahoo to Vermont. Dhyani is a Native American Cherokee lineage holder and also empowered to share Buddhist teachings.

I met Dhyani and many students on their way to and from teachings and retreats. They ordered bread and granola from the bakery, and I got to know the shoppers.

When I was looking for an employee, one of the kitchen folks applied. I hired Lynn E. Alden. Her experiences of Cherokee principles and Buddhist teachings began to weave their way into our few hours of time together. These cosmologies offered principles I could believe in and practice every day. I studied and practiced with the Sunray sangha for seven years. The teachings strongly influenced how Daily Bread operated and how I continue to view the world:

We are all one. What happens here affects what happens everywhere else. We need to consider how our actions affect seven generations forward.

All places around the circle are equal; there is no "head" to a circle. We held our staff meetings in a circle, always beginning with one round for each person to have the opportunity to speak. Each one in turn had the floor completely.

The elements--fire, water, earth, air and metal--are our allies and teachers. We set up a small shrine holding examples of each element. Krista always said the bread rose better when the candle was lit.

The children are our future. We always welcomed children. We had a milk crate out in the hallway by the old retail window so the short folks could be part of the transaction. Customers felt comfortable bringing in their whole families. In the 1999 refit, we had enough room to designate the front room for kids. Customers generously donated outgrown toys.

These principles informed life at the Bread. They helped us all to accommodate the special needs of customers and coworkers. We had a lot of coworkers in transition, recovering from serious illness, considering a career change, returning to work after a baby; we could be flexible.

Summer staff at the Sunray Peace Village in front of the office in Lincoln, Vermont.

Wednesday
Flour Tortillas (6)

My parents became frequent customers at Santa Fe's Tecolote Cafe. Owner Bill Jenison gave me this recipe when I raved about their tortillas and found out that they made them on premises. The authentic New Mexico tortilla uses lard for shortening. We substituted margarine. These are delicious by themselves or as the basis for Quesadillas and Burritos (see separate recipes).

3 3/4 cups unbleached flour
1/2 cup whole wheat bread flour
1 teaspoon baking powder
6 tablespoons cold margarine
1 to 1 1/2 cups cold water

Stir together unbleached, whole wheat flour and baking powder. Cut margarine in with a pastry blender or your hands to resemble coarse meal. Toss in cold water, a little at a time to dampen. Gather into a ball and knead gently 3 or 4 rounds. Let dough rest 1/2 hour. Turn out onto a lightly floured surface and roll into a snake about 2 inches in diameter. Divide into 6 equal pieces. Roll each piece into a 6 or 8 inch diameter circle. Bake, grill or fill depending on the particular recipe you are preparing.

Quesadillas (6 turnovers)

My family moved west in 1970. Numerous visits to Santa Fe, New Mexico and the arrival of cook Mare Kuhlman, fresh from a stint at the Cowboy Cafe in Arizona brought the elements of our Quesadillas together. Bakery-made flour tortillas wrapped lettuce, tomato, onion, pinto beans, cheese and either pizza or red chili sauce.

Filling:
 3 cups grated cheddar or Monterey Jack cheese/ 12 ounces
3 cups shredded lettuce/ 3/4 head
3/4 cup sliced onion/ 1 medium onion
2 medium tomatoes, diced
3/4 cup canned pinto, shell or kidney beans, drained/ 1/2 14-ounce can

Toss cheese, lettuce, onion and tomatoes together. Add drained beans just before filling tortillas.

Sauces:
1/2 cup pizza sauce (see page 108)
1/2 cup red chili sauce (see page 216)

To assemble:

Preheat oven to 425 degrees. Divide dough into 6 and roll out to 8-inch circles. It is helpful, if you have the counter space, to roll out all 6; you can then evenly portion out filling without having any left over. Add a generous tablespoon of either pizza sauce or red chili sauce. Fold tortilla over and roll edges to seal. Place on greased and lightly cornmealed baking sheet. Bake 20-30 minutes until tops are lightly browned.

Friday

Calzone (6 turnovers)

I first encountered calzones when I lived in the Bronx, New York from 1968-72. The Pizza store around the corner served immense, deep fried cheese-filled pastries called "calzones." Theirs were enough for two people and reminded you all afternoon of your indulgence. I searched around for recipes, and eventually arrived at the old recipes we served for years at Daily Bread. We later changed to *Moosewood Cookbook*'s filling and French bread dough for the wrapper. Here are the original versions. This is a "weaker" wrapper and has a tendency to burst open in the oven. Either way, they are filling and delicious.

Wrapper:
1 cup warm water
1 tablespoon yeast
1/3 teaspoon black pepper
1/3 teaspoon salt
3 tablespoons olive oil
1/3 cup cornmeal
1 1/2-2 cups unbleached flour

Proof yeast in warm water till foamy. Add pepper, salt, oil, cornmeal and half the flour. Stir well, 25-50 strokes. Add enough additional flour to make soft dough. Turn out onto floured surface and knead until springy. Place in greased bowl to rise till double.

Filling:
2 cups ricotta cheese/ 1 pound
1 egg
3 cloves minced or pressed garlic
1/8 teaspoon black pepper
1/8 teaspoon dried basil/ 1/4 teaspoon fresh
1/8 teaspoon salt
1 tablespoon flour
2 cups grated mozzarella cheese/ 1/2 pound

Combine ricotta, egg, herbs, spices and flour together and stir till well mixed. Fold in grated mozzarella. Vegetables or Prosage may be folded in at this point, if desired.

Optional additions:
2 cups sautéed vegetables
2 cups Prosage or other vegetarian sausage, diced and pre-baked/ 1 pound
1 cup pizza sauce (see page 108)

To assemble:
Turn dough out onto a floured surface. Preheat oven to 450 degrees. Divide dough into six pieces. Knead each into a round. Let rest 15 minutes. Roll out to 6-inch circles. Put 1/3-1/2 cup filling on wrapper. Add generous tablespoon pizza sauce, if desired. Fold wrappers over to form half moons. Fold edges under. Place on greased and lightly cornmealed baking sheet. Bake 20 minutes until tops are golden brown.

Sunday

We made quiche for brunch and lunch before we had a dining room. We sold whole pies and slices. When we opened the café and began serving brunch, a cheese pie of some sort was a natural for Sunday's savory offering from the oven. Here are some of the favorites from the rotation.

Cheddar Pie/ Quiche (9- or 10-inch pie)
1/2 recipe pie dough (p. 105-6)/ 1 unbaked crust

Filling:
4 eggs
1 12-ounce can evaporated milk or 1 1/2 cups coffee cream
1/8 teaspoon salt
1 pinch black pepper
1 pinch nutmeg
2 cups grated cheddar cheese/ 1/2 pound
1 to 2 cups prepared vegetables, optional

Prepare vegetables, if desired as addition. Preheat oven to 450 degrees. Roll out pie dough about 1 1/2 inches larger than pie tin. Gently press into tin, draping extra over edge. Roll full amount of extra under, all the way around, to sit on top of lip of pan. Pinch together to form a decorative edge. Beat together eggs, milk or cream, salt, pepper and nutmeg. Distribute cheese in bottom of prepared crust. Add vegetables on top of cheese, if using them. Pour egg mixture over all immediately before baking to prevent a soggy bottom crust. Bake 10 minutes. Reduce heat to 350 and continue baking another 20-30 minutes until center is set and firm to the touch.

Yankee Soul Pie (9- or 10-inch pie)
Richmond farmer George Safford had a knack for growing cabbage, which he stored all winter in his cellar and delivered to us from August through April. This is one of the recipes we found to use it up. The inspiration came from a *Moosewood Cookbook* recipe called Solyanka, thus the play on words in the title. What is more Yankee than the combination of cabbage, potatoes

and onions? While cabbage was the first, we found that snow peas and snap peas worked too.

1/2 recipe pie dough (p. 105)/ 1 crust

Filling:
1 cup hot mashed potato/ 1 large potato
1 cup ricotta cheese/ 1/2 pound
1 egg
1/4 cup sour cream
1 tablespoon flour
2 1/2 cups green cabbage, sliced, or 2 cups pea pods or sugar snaps
2 tablespoons butter
1 large onion, sliced
3/4 teaspoons caraway seed
1 teaspoon salt
1/2 teaspoon black pepper

Prepare crust. Line pie tin, gently pressing crust into pan, leaving generous edge. Roll edge under all the way around to sit on pan lip. Pinch to make decorative edge. Preheat oven to 450 degrees. Combine mashed potato, ricotta, egg, sour cream and flour. Stir well, and set aside. Sauté cabbage or snow peas (leave sugar snaps raw; they will keep their crunch), onion, caraway, salt and pepper in a medium skillet till vegetables wilt. Add vegetable mixture to potato and cheese. Pour into prepared pie crust. Bake 10 minutes. Reduce heat to 350 and continue baking another 25-35 minutes until filling is set and firm to the touch.

Zucchini Pie (9- or 10-inch pie)

You just can't have too many ways to use zucchini.

1/2 recipe pie dough (p.126)/ 1 crust

Filling:

4 cups thinly sliced zucchini/ 2-3 small
2 cups ricotta cheese/ 1 pound
1/2 pound grated cheddar cheese/ 1/2 pound
3 eggs
1/4 teaspoon salt
1/2 teaspoon black pepper
1 clove minced or pressed garlic
3 tablespoons flour

Prepare pie dough. Roll out 1 1/2 inches larger than pie tin. Gently press into pan leaving generous edge. Roll under full amount of edge to sit on top of pan lip. Pinch to make decorative edge. Preheat oven to 450 degrees. Steam zucchini lightly over boiling water. Set aside. Combine ricotta, cheddar, eggs, salt, pepper, garlic and flour. Stir well to combine. Fold zucchini into cheese mixture. Spread into prepared crust. Bake 10 minutes at 450 degrees. Reduce heat to 350 and continue baking another 25-30 minutes until filling set and lightly browned.

The Richmond Times

Back in 1983 and 1984, Richmond was debating zoning regulations. As I told *Vermont Times* reporter Matt Sutkoski in 1991, "There were a lot of nasty political 'fact sheets' appearing around town, ...

At the Daily Bread, some people mentioned how horrible these rumors were. Facts needed to be presented as facts…rather than innuendo." (29)

Talk in the hallway led to possibly starting a newspaper. I called on my father the newspaper man for guidance. He suggested an excellent "how to" book, and we discussed many details. He died the following spring before we printed our first edition. Graphic artist Irene Horbar's studio was next door, where Lael Livack's Sewing Saloon had been.

A number of local citizens joined forces to become reporters, ad salespeople, typists, photographers and transporters. We gathered a few hundred dollars from family and friends and went to press. This is how we introduced ourselves in November:

It is with a great deal of enthusiasm that we begin publication of "The Richmond Times." We hope to utilize this newspaper to foster a stronger sense of community among our residents by providing a means of communication that will objectively inform the residents of Richmond on those subjects which are important to our town's vitality….

The early *Times* staff stand behind Daily Bread's entry into the Round Church Art show sponsored by the newspaper and the Historical Society.

We have a genuine regard for the adage that "an informed citizen is a responsible citizen."…

Betsy Bott	Randy Gillett
Gary Bressor	Irene Horbar
Paula Casey-Bellerose	Corine McHugh
Art Cernosia	Tom McHugh
Jennie Cernosia	Mary Ann McMaster
Carol Feierabend	Karen Yaggy (30)

Daily Bread staff became adjunct newspaper help. We had a notebook for *Times* messages. Irene shared our phone. Her studios served as the *Times* offices until she moved to Charlotte. Irene graciously moved forward in the building to make way for the 1986 dining room and café kitchen.

The newspaper took up residence in a succession of rooms upstairs, usually sharing space with another non-profit. We joined forces with *The Huntingtonian,* for a while with Bolton, becoming *The Times Ink!* Heidi Racht took over design and production after Irene moved.

We gathered once a month to do our rough layout, stick down columns of type and advertisements, write headlines and keep up to date with each others' families and careers. Once the typesetting and layout bacame computerized, our convivial monthly sessions lost their reason to be. Then Editor Heidi Racht moved the office to her Huntington home.

Wolfsong

Wolfsong was born Eric Provencher in Addison, Vermont, a Native American of mixed ancestry-- Abenaki-Mohawk; Cherokee; Scotch-Irish, English, and French. He grew up in a big family and left a big family when he died suddenly in 2001.

Wolfsong worked as a carpenter, a baker and most happily as a story teller. His publicity brochure read:

> He brings a message of the oneness of All that is-- the Earth is made of our Bones; our Bones are made of the Earth.
> They express the ideas of cooperation, trust, courage, healing, and humor--people to people, people to animals; people to plants; etc.
> In these stories you will meet Old Man Coyote, the trickster; Gluscabe, a helper of man in times of need; Buffalo Calf Road Woman, a Brave Heart woman of the Cheyenne People; the Friendly Wolf and many others. (31)

He worked with Vermont's own first people the Abenaki and introduced many co-workers and customers to the legacy of the land they now called home.

Wolfsong passing his granola crown on to Jean Palmer. Poster for his cassette of stories in the background.

Other crusted savories

Prosage Onion Turnovers (6)

Daily Bread baker and late storyteller Wolfsong came from French Canadian as well as Native American stock, and he wanted to recreate Quebecois *tourtiere* or meat pie. He and then wife Myra Timmins experimented. Rose Warnock fine-tuned it, and this became a staff and customer favorite. The flaky crust around the sweet onion and greasy "meat" is one of those comfort food tastes which gives the eater a satisfied stomach and mind.

1 recipe pie dough (see page 105-6)

Filling:
2 to 3 tablespoons butter
2 cups chopped onions/ 2-3 medium onions
12 ounces Prosage vegetarian sausage (or any other meat or veggie brand)
1 teaspoon ground cumin
1/4 teaspoon dried basil
1/2 pinch curry powder
1/2 tablespoon flour

Prepare pie dough. Refrigerate while preparing the filling. Sauté onions and Prosage in butter till onions are translucent. A heavy bottomed fry pan works well for this. Add cumin, basil and curry powder to the onion mixture and cook for 3 minutes. Sprinkle flour over the mix and cook another 3 minutes. Remove from heat.

Preheat oven to 425 degrees. Divide pie dough into six equal pieces and roll each piece into a 6-inch circle. Portion the filling onto the center of each wrapper. Fold in half. Press edges together and roll them under. Place on a lightly greased baking sheet. Bake 20-25 minutes until golden brown.

Becca's Samosas (6)

One time bakery counter person and silk artist Becca Cunningham spent time in India during her 20s. She maintained a fondness for the foods she encountered there. While she used many other recipes, she developed this particular Samosa filling herself. We were into potatoes and spice, so these were a natural. The green peas, garbanzos and green chili give them texture and color. The full range of curry spices make them delightfully aromatic and delicious. Compared to the appetizer variety found in many Indian restaurants, these are full-sized and a meal in themselves.

1 recipe pie dough (see page 105-6)

Chris Billis and Becca share a laugh on Chris' way out the door after a morning bake shift.

Filling:
2 2/3 cups fresh hot mashed potatoes
6 ounces cream cheese/ 3/4 of 8-ounce package
2 tablespoons sunflower or other light oil
2/3 cup minced onion
1/2 to 2/3 cup fresh, frozen or canned and drained green peas
1/3 cup cooked and drained garbanzo beans
1/2 jalapeno pepper
2 teaspoons grated fresh ginger root
1/2 teaspoon salt
2 teaspoons ground coriander
1 pinch cayenne
2 teaspoons ground cumin

2/3 teaspoon Garam Masala curry blend
1 1/3 tablespoons water
1 teaspoon lemon juice

Prepare pie dough. Cook and mash potatoes. While potatoes are hot, add the cream cheese and beat it with a spoon or use the masher to thoroughly combine. Set aside. Heat oil in a large fry pan. Sauté onion, peas, garbanzos and jalapeno with ginger, salt, coriander, cayenne and cumin. Cook 2 minutes. Add to potato mixture and stir well to distribute vegetables throughout. Preheat oven to 450 degrees. Divide pie dough into six equal pieces. Roll each into a 6-inch circle. Portion filling onto wrappers. Fold each in half to form a half moon. Pinch the edges and turn them under. Place on a lightly greased baking sheet. Bake 20-25 minutes at until the tops are golden brown.

Dwayne's Yam Burritos (6)
Daily Bread customers had become accustomed to good New Mexico food by the time Dwayne Doner arrived on the scene in 1998. When Dwayne suggested these, they were a natural. These became one of my personal favorites. The flavorful peppers and onions next to the spiced yam give your mouth lots to think about. A homemade flour tortilla makes this out of the ordinary. Store-bought tortillas will do.

1 recipe flour tortillas (see page 113)

Filling:
3 pounds yams or sweet potatoes, roasted till soft
2 stalks celery, diced
3 diced scallions
1/4 cup minced cilantro
1 tablespoon ground cumin
1/4 teaspoon crushed red pepper
1/4 teaspoon black pepper
1 1/2 tablespoons lemon juice
2 tablespoons olive oil
1 1/2 green peppers, sliced into thin strips
1 1/2 red peppers, sliced into thin strips
1 onion, thinly sliced

Toppings:
Red Chili sauce (see page 216)
Heidi's Fresh Ginger Salsa (see page 217)
Sour cream

Preheat oven to 375 degrees. Use a fork to make a few steam holes in the yams. Bake about an hour or until quite soft. Cool slightly, then peel and mash. Prepare flour tortilla dough and set it aside to rest.

Prepare filling. Sauté celery, scallions, cilantro, cumin, crushed red pepper and black pepper in 1 tablespoon olive oil in a large fry pan until mixture is aromatic and vegetables just beginning to wilt. Add lemon juice and remove from heat. Add this to prepared mashed yam and stir to combine. Set aside. Heat second tablespoon of olive oil and sauté green pepper, red pepper and onion till peppers begin to brown. Set aside.

To assemble:
Divide tortilla dough into six equal pieces. Roll each into an 8-inch circle. Heat a heavy fry pan or griddle and lightly grill tortillas till bubbles appear and they are turning golden. Turn over and grill the second side. You are going to roll these around your filling, so keep them on the soft side.

Lay 1/6 of the pepper and onion mixture down the middle of each grilled tortilla. Portion yam mixture on top of peppers. Roll tortilla around filling. Tuck in the ends and roll to even out the filling. Place seam side down on a serving platter. Serve with your choice of red chili sauce and/or salsa and sour cream (or yogurt).

These can be eaten hot or cold.

Curried Tempeh Flatbread (for 4 ounces tempeh/ 4 servings)

Dwayne Doner strikes again. He worked a long time to perfect the flatbread portion of this dish. The tempeh, veggies and flatbread are all spicy with curry. Plain yogurt or cucmber raita makes a nice accompaniment. These can also be rolled and baked for a dinner dish.

Tempeh:
4 ounces tempeh cut into 16 triangles (cut each triangle below in half)
1/2 cup sunflower or other light oil
1/2 cup tamari
1/2 cup water
1 tablespoon curry powder
1 tablespoon dried parsley
4 to 5 cloves garlic, minced or pressed
1/4 teaspoon crushed red pepper
1/4 teaspoon turmeric

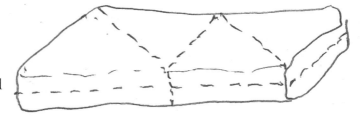

Slice the tempeh in half horizontally. Cut each half into 8 triangles. In a bowl big enough to hold tempeh and marinade, whisk together oil, tamari, water, curry powder, parsley, garlic, red pepper and turmeric. Add tempeh and stir lightly to coat. Cover and refrigerate overnight.

Flatbread:
4 cups unbleached allpurpose flour
1/2 cup whole wheat pastry flour
2 teaspoons baking powder
1/2 tablespoon curry powder
2/3 cup olive oil
2 cups cold water

A few hours before you want to eat, prepare the flatbread. Whisk together the unbleached flour, whole wheat pastry flour, baking powder and curry. Stir oil and water together lightly and toss into the flour mix till dry ingredients are just damp. Knead a few times lightly. Dough will be fairly stiff. Divide into 8 balls. Roll each ball into an 8-inch circle. Heat a heavy fry pan or griddle to medium high. Brown flatbreads lightly on each side. Set aside. Reheat in a warm oven or serve room temperature.

Vegetables:
2 cups shredded bok choy/ 1/2 pound
2 cups slice cauliflower/ 1/2 head
1 cup sliced celery/ 2 stalks
1/2 cup sliced scallions
1 sweet red pepper in strips
4 to 5 cloves garlic minced or pressed
1/2 tablespoon curry powder

Prepare the vegetables. Toss together and cover until ready to cook.

To assemble:
Heat fry pan or griddle again and grill vegetables till they begin to caramelize. Set vegetables aside. Repeat to grill tempeh.
1. Serve two flatbreads, four triangles tempeh and a pile of vegetables for each person.
2. Or roll tempeh and vegetables into flatbread and heat 10 minutes in the oven.

Garlic Gateau (12"x16" sheet or 2 9-inch rounds)
Williston garlic grower Hope Yandell gave us a recipe to try out. It had a complicated crust, calling for only russet potatoes and other onlies. We tried it once that way, but found that our Brioche dough pleased our taste buds even better. We added the cheeses, scallions and olive oil. While it seems like a lot of garlic, the butter and eggs in the dough sweeten the garlic in the baking. Serve as an accompaniment to soup or salad or as a showy hors d'oeuvre.

1 recipe Brioche dough (see page 60)

Topping:
1/4 cup peeled and slivered garlic/ 8 to 12 cloves
2 to 3 tablespoons olive oil
1 1/2 teaspoons dried oregano/ 1 tablespoon fresh
1 1/2 teaspoons dried basil/ 1 tablespoon fresh
3 tablespoons coarsely chopped fresh parsley
4 to 6 scallions, coarsely chopped
1 cup grated mozzarella cheese/ 1/4 pound
1 tablespoon grated parmesan cheese

Prepare Brioche dough. Set to rise about 1 hour. Peel and slice garlic, and get other herbs, scallions and cheeses ready. After the dough has risen once, turn out onto a floured surface and roll out into a rectangle or two rounds to fit the pan/s you are using. Grease pan/s and lightly dust with cornmeal. Place dough in pan/s and press to the edges. Use a sharp knife to slit dough and insert sliced garlic into each slit. Get as much into the dough as possible. Preheat oven to 350 degrees. Let gateau rise till doubled. Drizzle olive oil over. Sprinkle herbs and scallions, mozzarella and parmesan on, distributing evenly. Bake 25 minutes until golden brown. Cut and serve.

French Shrimp Rolls (1 filled loaf or 6 generous spiral rolls)
I am not sure of the origins of this recipe. We began trying filled bread in the early days of the cafe, post 1986, as a lunch special. Both this version and the following one, using Prosage vegetarian sausage as its base, became popular. There was always the doughy end piece of the filled bread that did not sell as well. The rolls sold better at Daily Bread. You may like the loaf variety better.
1/2 recipe un-baked Sourdough French dough (see page 36)

Filling:
12 ounces peeled shrimp, steamed and chopped
1/2 small onion, minced fine
1 tablespoon olive oil
2 cloves minced or pressed garlic
2 tablespoon coarsely chopped fresh parsley
1 pinch black pepper
6 ounces grated mozzarella cheese
1 1/2 tablespoons grated parmesan cheese
1 egg and water for glaze

Prepare dough. While it is rising, prepare filling. Sauté onion and garlic in olive oil till onion begins to become transparent. Add shrimp, parsley and black pepper. Continue to sauté to warm shrimp. Remove from heat. Add cheeses and toss just to combine.

1. For filled bread, press dough out into an oval. Pile filling down the center. Bring edges around and pinch to seal. Place seam side down on greased baking sheet. Let rise. Preheat oven

to 350 degrees. Beat together egg and a few drops of water. Brush this glaze onto loaf. Bake 45-50 minutes.

2. To make spiral rolls, use rolling pin to flatten dough into a rectangle about 8 inches long, long side toward you (see drawing on page 64). Spread filling on dough, leaving 1 1/2 inches at top for sealing edge. Roll up like a jelly roll, keeping filling well distributed all the way to the ends. Pinch to seal. Using a sharp or serrated knife, slice into six equal pieces. Place cut side down on greased baking sheet. Preheat oven to 350 degrees. Let rolls rise till doubled. Brush with egg glaze. Bake 25-35 minutes till golden brown.

French Prosage Rolls (1 filled loaf or 6 generous spiral rolls)

There are many ethnic variations on the filled bread theme. This one takes its flavors from the Italian style. Any vegetarian or meat sausage will do.

1/2 recipe unbaked Sourdough French dough (see page 36)

Filling:
6 ounces Prosage chopped small (or use your favorite sausage)
6 ounces mushrooms, sliced
1/3 cup finely minced onion
1 tablespoon olive oil
2 cloves minced or pressed garlic
2 tablespoons fresh parsley, coarsely chopped
1 pinch black pepper
1 1/3 cups grated mozzarella cheese/ 1/3 pound
1 1/2 tablespoons grated parmesan cheese
1 egg and water for glaze

Follow method for Shrimp Roll/s above, substituting Prosage and mushrooms for shrimp.

From other sources:
Moosewood Cookbook:
Broccoli-Cheese Strudel as filling for Broccoli Turnover
Mushroom Strudel as filling for Mushroom Turnover
Spanikopita as filling for Spinach Turnover

Vegetarian Epicure:
Kasha Knish filling

A Place to Sit Down

Daily Bread existed as a bakery for its first 7 years "before providing more than a shelf for groupies to lean on while they ate her fabulous--there is no other word--bread, cinnamon rolls, scones and cookies," as Debbie Salomon of the *Burlington Free Press* put it. (32) We were open five days a week with two people on each day, overlapping at the noon hour.

By 1985, my three parttime employees and the customers convinced me to add a kitchen and dining room. "Just a place to sit down," they kept assuring me.

The place to sit down became a full-time job, a $20,000 bank loan to repay, a staff and payroll, grey hair and restless sleep. It was only the confidence of the bank manager next door that got me the loan: "The numbers don't add up, but if anyone can do it, you can." We started out trying to incorporate dinners three nights a week. That so over-taxed our space and patience that we abandoned that for fulltime breakfast and lunch, open seven days a week!

The staff was always heavy on artistic types, and we approached the new configuration very much like a stage set. We hadn't heard of feng shui yet. Lynn E. led us toward bright colors. We fell into the southwestern look with a turquoise trim, white walls and deep red floors. We kept the kitchens public with many windows in the plan. No secrets, no mysteries. We cooks and bakers were entertained by the parade which passed before us. We followed pregnancies as profiles changed. A shared smile or energetic nod at just the right sweet roll could brighten your whole day or even start a friendship. It was its own stage, with a constant exchange of audience and players.

Jeb Bush fabricated the steel bases for the cafe tables, and

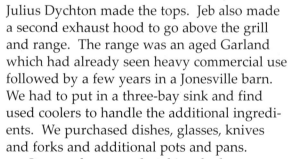

Julius Dychton made the tops. Jeb also made a second exhaust hood to go above the grill and range. The range was an aged Garland which had already seen heavy commercial use followed by a few years in a Jonesville barn. We had to put in a three-bay sink and find used coolers to handle the additional ingredients. We purchased dishes, glasses, knives and forks and additional pots and pans.

It was a larger undertaking, had many more personalities involved, and greater responsibility for profit right away. I could eat the same soup night after night, but employees expect to be paid cash for their labor on a regular basis.

Pies and Turnovers

Fruit pies and turnovers are truly earthly delights. I personally request birthday pie when offered a choice. Vermonters are known for serving pie at breakfast. While full pies were not a big seller at the Bread, we baked turnovers every Friday afternoon with many avid regulars. The late maple syrup scientist Sumner Williams made it a point to stop by Friday afternoons and was known to me as "turnover man" for years.

For special occasions and holidays we took orders for pies, baked in large 10-12 inch returnable tins. The amounts given for a 10 inch pie will fill six turnovers. Since many households only have the smaller 8-9 inch pie plate, I have included those quantities too.

Turnover Basics

1 recipe filling for 10-inch pie (see pages 128-30)
1 recipe pie dough for a 2-crust pie (see pages 105-6)
1 egg and water for glaze

We prepared turnover fillings, with the exception of apple, on top of the stove and cooled them before use. The thickened filling is less messy. Heat the fruit to boiling over a low flame in a heavy saucepan, stirring often to prevent sticking. Combine the sugar or syrup, spices and cornstarch in a cup or small bowl, stirring well to combine. Add to hot fruit all at once, stirring constantly until mixture thickens. Cool to room temperature.

To assemble:
Preheat oven to 450 degrees. Divide pie dough into six equal pieces. Roll each into a 6-inch circle. Portion filling onto wrappers. Turn over (?!) and fold edges under to create half moon shapes. Brush with egg glaze. Place on lightly greased baking sheet. Prick tops with a fork or knife to allow steam to vent. Bake about 15 minutes until golden brown.

Pie Basics

1 recipe filling (see pages 128-30)
1 recipe crust for a 2-crust pie/
    1/2 recipe for single crust (see pages 105-6)
1 egg and water for glaze if desired

Pie filling is not usually pre-cooked, though bakers Heather Ward and Nick Sansone preferred cooking the filling first.

Prepare fruit, unless otherwise noted. Fresh is always better, but we primarily used IQF (individually quick frozen).

Combine sugar or syrup, spices or flavorings, and cornstarch together in a cup or bowl. Add to fruit and stir gently but thoroughly to combine. Preheat oven to 450 degrees.

Roll. Divide pie dough into two pieces, one slightly larger than the other. Roll out the larger one on a floured surface to at least 1 1/2 inches larger than the pan you are using. Fold in half and transfer to pan. Gently press crust into the pan with a minimum of stretching. Stretching the dough will lead to shrinking in the oven. Leave the extra hanging over the edge.

1. If baking a one crust pie, roll the edge under so it just sits on top of the lip of the pie pan. Pinch decoratively all the way around. Fill and bake 10 minutes. Reduce to 375 and continue baking an additional 40-50 minutes.

2. For a 2-crust pie, roll out the second half of dough into a circle 1/2 to 1 inch larger than your pan. Pour prepared filling into lined pan. Place second crust over filling. Roll the two crusts together all around and pinch to seal. Use a sharp knife to cut slits in the top to allow steam to escape; be creative, cut the shape of the fruit or someone's initials or the name of the fruit! Brush with egg glaze, if desired. Bake 10 minutes. Reduce heat to 375 degrees and continue baking another 40-50 minutes until top is golden brown and you can see evidence of thickened filling bubbling out through the steam holes.

3. To prepare a pre-baked crust: Preheat oven to 375 degrees. Roll out half of dough, leaving a generous amount to roll under for the edge. Be extra careful not to stretch dough while putting it in the pan. Roll and pinch the edge. Begin at the center and prick the bottom and sides up to the edges all over with a fork. Bake about 20 minutes until golden brown. Cool before filling.

Fruit Fillings
10-inch   8-inch
Apple

10-inch	8-inch
8 cups peeled, pared and sliced apples	5 to 6 cups
1/2 cup sugar or 4 tablespoons syrup	1/3 cup or 3 1/3 tablespoons
1/4 teaspoon cinnamon	1/8 teaspoon
1/8 teaspoon ground ginger	1 pinch
4 tablespoons flour	2 1/2 tablespoons
1/2 teaspoon lemon juice	1/4 teaspoon

Blueberry

6 cups blueberries   4 cups
1 1/2 cups sugar   1 cup
6 tablespoons cornstarch   4 tablespoons
1 tablespoon lemon juice   2 teaspoons
1/8 teaspoon ground ginger   1 pinch

BLUEBERRY PIE

Straight method Strawberry

6 cups hulled and halved strawberries   4 cups
1 1/4 cups sugar or 3/4 maple syrup   1 cup or 1/2 cup
6 tablespoons cornstarch   4 tablespoons
1/8 teaspoon cinnamon, optional   1 pinch

Peach

6 cups peeled and sliced peaches   4 cups
1 cup sugar   2/3 cup
6 tablespoons cornstarch   4 tablespoons
1/3 teaspoon ground ginger   1/8 teaspoon

FRESH LOCAL PLUM PIE

Plum

6 cups pitted and quartered prune plums   4 cups
1 1/4 cups sugar   3/4 cup
6 tablespoons cornstarch   4 tablespoons
2 tablespoons lemon juice   4 teaspoons

Rhubarb

6 cups sliced rhubarb   4 cups
1 1/4 cups sugar or 1 cup maple syrup   3/4 cup or 2/3 cup
5 tablespoons cornstarch   3 tablespoons
1 egg, lightly beaten   1 egg

Strawberry Rhubarb

3 cups sliced rhubarb   2 cups
3 cups hulled and halved strawberries   2 cups
1 1/2 cups sugar or 1 cup maple syrup   1 cup or 2/3 cup
6 tablespoons cornstarch   4 tablespoons

Use general instructions on page 127 with any of the above fillings.

Fresh Strawberry/ Strawberry Glace

This is my favorite strawberry pie. It also works well with fresh blueberries. The full flavor of the berries comes through delightfully in this variation on a theme. The cream cheese keeps the filling from making the crust soggy and offsets the sweetness of the fruit. It requires a pre-baked shell (see page 127).

1 10-inch baked crust	1 8-inch crust
5 ounces cream cheese, softened	3 ounces
6 cups hulled and halved fresh strawberries	4 cups
3/4 cup water	1/2 cup
1/2 cup maple syrup	1/3 cup
3 tablespoons cornstarch	4 teaspoons

Measure out 1 1/4 cups berries (1 cup for smaller pie) into a small saucepan. Add water and bring to a boil. Reduce heat and simmer for 3 minutes. Combine syrup and cornstarch, stirring well to prevent lumps. Add this to the simmering fruit. Continue to cook another minute, stirring constantly. Remove from heat. Spread softened cream cheese over the bottom of the baked crust. Arrange uncooked berries on top of cream cheese, and pour cooked mixture over. Make sure all uncooked berries are covered. Refrigerate before serving.

Betsy Boss

An insurance company letter once slipped up and addressed me as "Ms. Boss." I became a reluctant boss. Business partnership and cooperative proposals tempted me a few times, but by the end of the first seven years, I felt I had invested too much to risk losing it. It seems that the only way to dissolve a partnership would dissolve the business too.

Before the 1986 expansion to include the café kitchen and dining room, we were a staff of four at the most. We shared twelve shifts over six days. We could easily communicate and keep current. Our shifts overlapped in the middle of the day. Otherwise each person was his or her own boss.

Once the staff increased to from thirteen to twenty parttime workers, communication became more important and more difficult. We kept a notebook and we had three to four paid staff meetings per year to discuss challenge areas, to design changes together and fine tune kitchen rules. Everyone was invited to contribute items for the agenda. Here's a sample of recurring topics:

Dishes:
How can we keep soot from the bottom of the cook pots from getting on everything?
Muffin tin technique
Proper silverware etiquette
The dishwasher is just a sanitizer; wash them first!
How do you define "few" as in: "It's okay to leave a few dishes...?"

Record keeping:
Proper math when figuring paycheck totals
Oops, how can I fix a cash register mistake?
"Saves" and keeping track thereof
Remember to update shopping lists
Special orders
IOU's and tabs
Rotate stock: first in, first out

Communication:
Check with coworkers for break times
Put tapes/ CD's back in their cases
Compost etiquette (we separated for chickens and straight compost)
Bakers need to write down what they make
When do we mark things down to 1/2 price?

I encouraged coworkers to learn as many positions as they wanted to. Judy Bush, Alison Forest, Rose Warnock, Betsy Field, Rose Lovett, Andrew Paschetto, Krista Willett, Dwayne Doner and Tod Sagar took major administrative weight off my shoulders which allowed me to travel, to see family, to study, to garden, to dance, to have a life other than work.

We had an open sub policy. Your position had to be covered by a person who knew your shift.

It was the combined effort of all 160 hard-working, warm-hearted individuals who worked there that made Daily Bread what it was.

- DO ALL REMAINING LUNCH DISHES (ANY!)
- BRING ALL SAMANTHA BOTTLES AND OTHER RECYCLED CONTAINER INTO KITCHEN & RINSE. PUT CLEAN BOTTLE INTO RECYLING CAN (DEPOSIT BOTTLES GO IN THEIR OWN BINS)
- TURN OFF GRILL & CLEAN WITH GRILL PADS & WATER. BE CAREFUL IF IT IS STILL HOT.
  * BE PREPARED TO COOK THINGS IN PANS IF YOU TRY THIS BEFORE 4 o'clock.
- SWEEP KITCHEN FLOOR (UNDER THINGS ALSO.)
- AT 4 o'clock (OR BEFORE IF YOU'RE DARING.) PUT SOUPS & LUNCH ITEMS (COVERED & LABELED) INTO LUNCH SIDE (RIGHT HAND SIDE) OF COOLER.
- CONSOLIDATE ALL GARBAGE (2 BATHROOMS, COFFEE STATION, DINING ROOM, BAKERY & KITCHEN) INTO **1** BAG.
- DUMP WATER CAN UNDER DOUBLE DOOR COOLER.
- COVER COMPOST PAILS (REPLACE IF FULL)
- TURN OFF GRILL LIGHT AND HOOD FA

Other Sweet Pies

Pumpkin (10-inch or 8-9-inch pie)

This is dark with molasses and spices, which many customers liked. If you prefer a lighter filling, increase the sugars by a few tablespoons or substitute honey for the molasses. We offered this recipe as a holiday special. The day before Thanksgiving was our busiest baking day of the year.

1 unbaked 10-inch crust (see page 105-6)	1 unbaked 8- or 9-inch
Filling:	
2 cups cooked and mashed pumpkin/ winter squash	1 1/3 cups
1 cup evaporated milk	2/3 cup
1/2 cup brown sugar	1/3 cup
1/4 cup white sugar	2 tablespoons
2 tablespoons molasses	1 tablespoon
1/2 teaspoon salt	1/3 teaspoon
1 1/2 teaspoons cinnamon	1 teaspoon
1/2 teaspoon ground ginger	1/3 teaspoon
1 teaspoon mace	2/3 teaspoon
3 eggs, lightly beaten	2 eggs

Prepare crust. Preheat oven to 450 degrees. Combine all filling ingredients and whisk together till there are no lumps and it appears velvety smooth. Pour into your unbaked pie shell. Bake 10 minutes. Reduce heat to 350 degrees and continue baking another 40-50 minutes until the middle of the pie gently springs back to the touch, or a knife inserted into the middle comes out clean.

Pecan or Walnut-Sugar Method (1 8- or 9-inch pie)

Nut pies are not quite as sweet as Quebecois sugar pie, but close. Rich nuts and sweet custard are cradled in crispy pie pastry. The combination melts in your mouth and worries the heart specialist. We sold most of these at the holidays.

1 unbaked 8- or 9-inch pie crust (see page 105-6)
Filling:
1 1/2 cups coarsely chopped walnuts or pecans
3 eggs, lightly beaten
3/4 cup brown sugar
1/2 cup white sugar
3/4 cup evaporated milk or 1/2 and 1/2
1 teaspoon vanilla extract
1/8 teaspoon salt
3 tablespoons melted butter

Preheat oven to 425 degrees. Prepare pie crust. Spread nuts over crust. Beat eggs. Add the brown and white sugars, evaporated milk, vanilla, salt and butter. Whisk the mixture well. Pour over nuts. Bake 10 minutes. Reduce heat to 325 degrees and continue baking another 20-30 minutes until filling is set. The classic test is when a silver knife inserted into the center comes out clean.

Maple Walnut or Pecan (1 8- or 9-inch pie)
This maple sweetened version of the classic is even more candy-like.

1 unbaked 8- or 9-inch pie crust (see page 105-6)

2 cups coarsely chopped walnuts or pecans
3 eggs, lightly beaten
1 cup maple syrup
1 teaspoon vanilla
4 tablespoons melted butter

Preheat oven to 425 degrees. Prepare pie crust. Spread nuts over crust. Beat eggs. Add syrup, vanilla and butter. Whisk the mixture well. Pour over nuts. Bake 10 minutes. Reduce heat to 325 degrees and continue baking another 20-30 minutes until filling is set.

Benefits . . . .
Daily Bread did not give traditional job benefits like health insurance or retirement plans, but offered other contributions to long life and happiness.

The kitchens were spacious with lots of natural light. Cooks, bakers and counter folks conversed freely with each other and customers in the open plan.

We listened to each others' music and were generally tolerant.

Co-workers were engaging people, young and old, with many interests and talents other than food and cooking.

Workers could trade shifts, allowing time for family, workshops, classes, illness or travel.

Workers could get their paychecks on whatever one's personal "last" day of the week was. We always had enough check signers that someone was available every day. I insisted that employees figure the math on their pay each week. I felt they should know how much of their pay went to which withheld tax, week after week. There are software programs and payroll services now which distance both employer and employee from the realities of deductions. It made for extra bookkeeping for me and a line of bookkeepers. It seemed worth the cost and effort. Many old employees have told me that having that trust given to them was one of the most empowering experiences of their lives. Workers became more conscious taxpayers as a result.

John Earle relaxes for a minutes' reflection between customers.

Workers could purchase bulk food at wholesale prices, received 1/2 price café food while working and could deduct 10% off bakery goods at any time.

The Bread provided the mandated Worker's Risk insurance to cover work related injuries and unemployment insurance, state and federal. Small businesses are charged these insurances based on the experience records of the big guys.

Many workers had health insurance through spouses' jobs. Some chose to have none. A few paid their own. Vermont introduced the Vermont Health Plan in the 1990s for low income Vermonters. Many physicians charged reduced fees to the uninsured. If you were in need of care in Vermont, you were not turned away.

Then there were the moans of ecstasy as customers dug in to their plate of perfect home fries or luscious slice of maple cake. How can you put a price on that?

Cheesecakes and Cheese Pies

Here we enter the most decadent pie group: cheesecakes! Their unbelievably rich ingredients somehow comfort the taste buds. As folk singer Steve Goodman put it: "Fat is where it's at." These are a treat for any special meal or occasion. From the full-sized "Lindy's" and Christina's "Quark" cake to the smaller pie-sized "Berta's," they are worth the effort and ingredients.

Note: It is important to take the time to beat filling until velvety smooth to eliminate any lumps.

Lindy's (1 9-inch spring form)
I grew up a "press brat" near New York City during the '50's and '60's. My parents were the grateful recipients of many complimentary tickets to Broadway shows, and thus ate out at many restaurants, including Lindy's. One evening, Mom asked for, and was given, their cheesecake recipe. It went through a few changes, but closely resembles the original. We used our pie dough to line the spring form, but you may substitute your favorite graham cracker crust, lining just the bottom.

3/4 recipe pie dough (see pages 105-6) or your choice of crust

Filling:
2 1/2 pounds cream cheese/ 5 8-ounce packages!
1 1/4 cups sugar
1/4 cup sour cream
Grated zest of 1 lemon
1 teaspoon vanilla
6 eggs, added one at a time
3 tablespoons flour

Prepare pie dough or crust and line spring form. If using pastry, allow it to extend over the top edge of the pan. It can be trimmed later, you don't want the crust to slide down into the pan while baking. Preheat oven to 500 degrees. Beat cream cheese and sugar till light and fluffy. An electric mixer works well, though with enough elbow grease, you can do it by hand. Add the sour cream, lemon zest and vanilla and continue beating till well combined. Beat in eggs one at a time. Reduce mixer speed and add flour.

Pour filling into the lined spring form. Place in the middle of hot oven and bake 8 minutes. Reduce oven to 200 degrees and continue baking another 45 minutes until the middle of the cake is set. At this point, it may be poofed up; not to worry. Turn off the oven and leave the cake in the oven with the door slightly propped open until the cake is completely cooled. This will let the cake relax slowly rather than collapse. Take the cooled cake out and trim off excess pastry. Refrigerate before slicing.

Chocolate Lindy's (1 9-inch spring form)
Chocolate can always make something better!

3/4 recipe pie dough (see pages 105-6) or crust of your choice

Filling:
2 1/2 pounds cream cheese/ 5 8-ounce packages!
1 1/2 cups sugar
4 tablespoons butter
1/4 cup sour cream
1 teaspoon vanilla
1/4 teaspoon almond extract
6 eggs, added one at a time
3 tablespoons flour
3/4 cup unsweetened cocoa

Prepare pie dough or crust and line spring form, leaving some dough draped over the top edge. You can trim this off later. Preheat oven to 500 degrees. In the bowl of an electric mixer, beat cream cheese, sugar and butter till light and fluffy. Add sour cream and flavorings and continue beating to combine. Add eggs, one at a time and beat till all velvety smooth. Reduce speed and add flour and cocoa. Mix till a consistent color. Pour into the lined spring form. Bake 8 minutes. Reduce heat to 200 degrees and continue baking another 45 minutes until the middle is set. Turn off heat and leave oven door propped slightly open until completely cooled. Remove from oven and trim off excess pastry. Refrigerate before slicing.

Quark Cake (1 9-inch spring form)

"Bargain" Bob was a bakery regular for many years before he met his wife Christina, who had grown up in Germany. She and I often compared notes on our favorite German desserts, which I had encountered as an exchange student. She offered this cheesecake recipe, which is lighter than and not as sweet as many others. It requires preparing Quark, a simple cheese made by draining liquid out of yogurt overnight. Quark has finally made its appearance in specialty dairy cases, so you may use commercial if you can find it. This cake is especially tasty served with fresh fruit in season.

Day One: Quark
4 cups plain yogurt/ 2 pounds

Line a colander or large strainer with cheesecloth. Place colander over a pan or bowl to catch the liquid. Pour yogurt into the lined colander and let it stand overnight. It will resemble a curdless, dry cottage cheese. Discard liquid.

Day Two:
Crust:
2 1/2 cups flour
3 tablespoons sugar
8 tablespoons butter/ 1 stick
1 egg, yolk only, save white for filling
2 tablespoons water

Combine flour and sugar. Cut or rub butter into flour and sugar to resemble a coarse meal using a pastry blender or your hands. Separate egg. Save the white for filling. Add water to yolk and whisk to combine. Add to the flour mixture, tossing with a fork to dampen. This will be crumbly. Press into your spring form, bringing it up the edges as high as it gracefully extends, usually an inch. Refrigerate while preparing filling.

Filling:
Quark from 4 cups yogurt (see above)
3 eggs, separated, plus egg white from crust
1 1/4 cups sugar
1/2 cup oil
1/4 cup milk
1 tablespoon vanilla
4 tablespoons cornstarch

Preheat oven to 350 degrees. Separate eggs. Add whites to the one you saved from crust. Set aside. Combine Quark, egg yolks, sugar, oil, milk and vanilla in the bowl of an electric mixer. Beat together until very smooth. Reduce speed and sprinkle cornstarch on top and mix till just combined. Remove bowl from mixer. If you only have one mixer bowl, turn cheese mixture into another bowl. Wash and thoroughly dry bowl before beating whites. Whip egg whites to firm but not dry peaks. Fold beaten whites into the cheese mixture using a rubber spatula or hands, working gently but thoroughly. Turn filling into lined pan. Bake 50-60 minutes, until the middle is set. Remove from oven and cool to room temperature. Refrigerate before serving.

Pumpkin Cheesecake (1 9-inch spring form)

This is an unusual variation on the cheesecake theme, but a nice change of pace for a turkey dinner dessert. Wendy Weldon found the original in some now-forgotten magazine or newspaper. This is close. For an extra zip, use gingersnaps as a base for a crumb crust (see your favorite basic cookbook).

3/4 recipe pie dough (see pages 105-6) or graham cracker or gingersnap crumb crust

Filling:
2 pounds cream cheese/ 4 8-ounce packages
1 1/4 cups sugar
5 eggs, added one at a time
2 teaspoons mace
2 teaspoons ground ginger
1 tablespoon vanilla
1/4 cup flour
2 cups cooked and mashed pumpkin or winter squash/ 1 16-ounce can

Prepare crust. Line spring form, allowing crust to drape over the top edge to keep from sliding down while baking. Or press crumb crust into the bottom, bringing the edges up the side an inch. Preheat oven to 500 degrees. In the bowl of an electric mixer, beat cream cheese and sugar till light and fluffy. Beat in eggs, one at a time. Add spices, vanilla and flour and turn down mixer to slow speed. Add pumpkin and mix till all combined and very smooth. Pour filling into lined spring form. Bake 8 minutes. Reduce heat to 200 degrees and continue baking another 50 minutes until the center is set. Turn off heat and leave in the oven, door propped slightly open, till all completely cooled. Remove from oven and refrigerate before slicing.

Berta's Cheese Pie (1 10-inch pie)

Longtime friend Berta Geller gave us this simple variation on cheesecake. Don't let its simplicity fool you: there's plenty to wrap your taste buds around.

1/2 recipe pie dough (see pages 105-6)/ 1 unbaked crust

Filling:
1 1/2 pounds cream cheese/ 3 8-ounce packages
1/2 cup sugar
1 1/2 teaspoons lemon juice
2 eggs, one at a time

Topping:
1 1/2 cups sour cream
3 tablespoons sugar
1 teaspoon vanilla

Roll out crust and line pie tin. Preheat oven to 450 degrees. Prepare filling. Beat together cream cheese, sugar and lemon juice in an electric mixer till light and fluffy. Beat in eggs, one at a time. The mixture should be velvety smooth. Pour into unbaked pie shell. Bake 10 minutes. Reduce heat to 350 degrees and continue baking another 30-35 minutes. Meanwhile, stir together sour cream, sugar and vanilla for topping. Remove pie from the oven and carefully spread topping over the baked filling. Return to the oven and bake another 5 minutes. Cool to room temperature and then refrigerate before serving.

Chocolate Almond Cheese Pie (1 10-inch)

The original inspiration for this recipe came from a late 1970s issue of *Gourmet* magazine. We tweaked it over time to fit our tastes and ingredients. It is a rich, not-too-sweet, chocolate dessert, impressive enough in appearance and flavor to complement a special dinner.

1/2 recipe pie dough (see pages 105-6)/ 1 unbaked crust

Filling:
3/4 pound cream cheese / 1 1/2 8-ounce packages
1/2 cup sugar
1/3 cup unsweetened cocoa
3 tablespoons sour cream
1/2 teaspoon vanilla
1 teaspoon almond extract
2 eggs, added one at a time

Topping:
1 1/2 cups sour cream
1 tablespoon sugar
1/2 teaspoon vanilla
1/3 cup chopped almonds

Prepare pie dough. Roll out and line pie tin. Preheat oven to 450 degrees. Beat cream cheese, sugar and cocoa in the bowl of an electric mixer. Add sour cream, vanilla and almond extract and beat to combine. Add eggs, one at a time and continue beating till all light and fluffy. Pour filling into prepared crust. Bake 10 minutes. Reduce heat to 350 degrees and continue baking another 30-35 minutes. Meanwhile, stir together sour cream, sugar and vanilla. Remove pie from oven and spread topping gently over the filling. Sprinkle almonds over the topping. Return to the oven and bake another 5 minutes. Remove and cool to room temperature. Chill before serving.

Apple Bavarian Torte (1 10-inch pie)

The Champlain Valley of Vermont is apple country, and we were always on the lookout for ways to use more of them. Richmond's George Safford and Peter Whitaker, Monkton's Boyer's Orchard, Shelburne Orchard's Nick Cowles, Addison's Will and Judy Stevens grew numerous varieties, each with its special qualities and season.

A recipe in the very beautiful *Joy of Cheesecake* book my brother once sent me inspired this combination. This is a fruity, honey sweetened variation on the theme.

1/2 recipe pie dough (see pages 105-6)/ 1 unbaked crust

Filling:
1 pound cream cheese/ 2 8-ounce packages
1/4 cup honey
1 teaspoon vanilla
2 eggs, added one at a time

Topping:
2 cups peeled, pared and diced apples
3 tablespoons honey
1/2 teaspoon cinnamon
1/4 teaspoon vanilla
1/4 cups coarsely chopped walnuts

Roll out crust and line pie pan. Preheat oven to 450 degrees. Prepare filling. Beat cream cheese, honey and vanilla together in an electric mixer till light and fluffy. Beat in eggs one at a time till all smooth. Set aside. Combine apples, honey, cinnamon, vanilla and walnuts for topping. Pour filling into prepared crust. Spoon apple topping over the filling. Bake 10 minutes. Reduce heat to 350 and continue baking another 30-35 minutes. Cool to room temperature. Refrigerate before serving.

Hiring and Firing

Many employees commented that Daily Bread was the most collective hierarchy they had ever experienced. A reluctant employer, I told *Out in the Mountains* reporter Chris Tebbets in a 1999 interview, I felt it necessary to provide:

a humanitarian workplace for people, where people's politics and personhood is (sic) respected no matter what their beliefs are, or dress, or sexual orientation. ...you don't have to have an adversarial relationship with people who are your employees. I very much value the opinion of my employees whether they're sixteen or sixty. (33)

Hiring was the easy part. Until the late 1990s when McDonald's offered $8/hour starting salary, people seemed to present themselves at just the right time. There were a few full-time folks, but most were part-time. Having many part-time workers added to the bookkeeping necessary for the government, but it allowed workers to have more life than work. We kept a file of self-styled notes of application. We contacted those people first. Many of the high school students recommended their younger friends or siblings.

In 21 years, with over 160 employees, I only had to ask five to leave. Those were the most difficult decisions I had to make as a boss. I considered long and hard before and after why these people, friends before and sometimes after, did not work out, why we as a staff community were not able to accommodate them. They were all competent, warm hearted individuals, who contributed a great deal to Daily Bread. Firing wasn't always the right thing to do. I have since sworn never to become a boss again.

Cookies

Cookies are small sweet pastries, high in sugar, high in fat. We used half butter and half soy margarine for our basic line. Others are as noted. We never did develop naturally sweetened cookies. Our experiments did not meet our customers' satisfaction.

General instructions:

Cream sugar and shortening until light and fluffy. You can do this by hand or with an electric mixer. This is how you get air into your mix.

Stir together eggs, liquids, vanilla or other flavoring.

Combine flour with salt and leavening (soda or powder).

Alternately add flour, liquid, flour, liquid, flour, working only enough to combine. You don't want them to be tough.

Chill to make easier to handle. Freeze some for later or portion and bake. Each basic recipe makes 24 large cookies. You can make them any size.

Bake on a lightly greased baking sheet about 13 minutes at 350 degrees, longer for crunchy cookies.

Chocolate Chocolate Chip (24 large cookies)

Ben Bush came up with this recipe through trial and error after enjoying a cellophane wrapped version in the Mount Mansfield Union High School cafeteria. For those wishing for more chocolate from their chocolate chip cookie, this is it.

1/4 pound butter/ 1 stick
1/4 pound margarine/ 1 stick
1 cup brown sugar
1 cup white sugar
2 eggs, lightly beaten
1 teaspoon vanilla
2 1/3 cups unbleached or allpurpose flour
1/3 cup unsweetened cocoa
1 teaspoon baking soda
1 cup chocolate chips

Cream together butter, margarine, brown and white sugars till light and fluffy. Use a mixer or work by hand. Add vanilla to beaten eggs. Whisk together flour, cocoa and soda. Alternately add flour, egg, flour, egg, flour to creamed butter mixture, beating well in between each addition. Fold chocolate chips into batter. Refrigerate, freeze or bake right away. Preheat oven to 350 degrees. Drop 1 1/2 tablespoon portions onto a lightly greased baking sheet. Bake 11 to 14 minutes depending on whether you like chewy or crunchy cookies.

Oatmeal Coconut (24 large cookies)

This variation on a theme came about when I discovered toasted coconut chips at our local food coop in the early 1980s. As one who doesn't care for raisins in baked goods, these seemed like a tasty alternative. The toasted chips disappeared from my suppliers' catalogues after a number of years, and so we used unsweetened "dessicated" coconut. If you should see the toasted variety, it is definitely worth buying for this recipe.

    1/4 pound butter/ 1 stick
    1/4 pound margarine/ 1 stick
    1 cup brown sugar
    1/2 cup white sugar
    2 eggs, lightly beaten
    1 tablespoons water
    1 teaspoon vanilla
    1 1/2 cups unbleached or allpurpose flour
    3/4 teaspoon baking soda
    2 2/3 cups rolled oats, not quick cooking
    1 3/4 cups unsweetened coconut flakes or toasted chips, if you can find them

Cream together butter, margarine, brown and white sugars till light and fluffy. Stir water and vanilla into eggs. Stir soda into flour. Alternately add flour, egg, flour, egg, flour to creamed butter mixture, beating well between each addition. Fold oats and coconut into dough. Bake, freeze or refrigerate. Preheat oven to 350 degrees. Drop 1 1/2 tablespoon portions onto a lightly greased baking sheet. Bake 11-14 minutes, depending on whether you like crunchy or chewy cookies.

Oatmeal Peanut Butter (24 large cookies)

Krista Willett was a teacher before moving to full time baking. This recipe came from "Farin Seiferth's Mom, one of my kids when I was teaching." And yes, there really is no flour.

    1/4 pound butter/ 1 stick
    1/2 cup brown sugar
    1/3 cup white sugar
    1 1/2 cups peanut butter
    3/4 teaspoon vanilla
    3 eggs, added one at a time
    4 2/3 cups rolled oats, not quick cooking
    1 3/4 teaspoons baking soda

Cream together butter, brown and white sugars till light and fluffy. Add peanut butter and vanilla to this mix and beat to thoroughly incorporate. Add eggs, one at a time, beating thoroughly after each one is added. Stir baking soda into oats. Fold oats into butter, peanut butter and egg mix. Bake, freeze or refrigerate. Preheat oven to 350 degrees. Drop 1 1/2 tablespoon portions onto a lightly greased baking sheet. Bake 13 minutes.

Molasses Ginger (24 large cookies)

Heidi Champney contributed this recipe, which came from her mom, Peggy Champney of Yellow Springs, Ohio. These are soft in the middle, crunchy on the outside and full of flavor. They fill the kitchen with a delicious aroma while baking.

1/4 pound butter/ 1 stick
1/4 pound margarine/ 1 stick
1 1/3 cup white sugar
1/3 cup molasses
2 eggs, lightly beaten
3 cups unbleached or allpurpose flour
1 2/3 teaspoon baking soda
1 teaspoon cinnamon
1/2 teaspoon ground ginger
1/2 teaspoon ground cloves
1/2 teaspoon salt
1/2 to 2/3 cup additional white sugar to roll in before baking

Cream together butter, margarine and white sugar till light and fluffy. Add molasses and beat. Stir together flour, soda, cinnamon, ginger, cloves and salt. Alternately add flour, eggs, flour, eggs, flour to the creamed butter mixture. Bake, freeze or refrigerate. Preheat oven to 350 degrees. Put white sugar for rolling in a small bowl. Portion dough into 1 1/2 tablespoon amounts. Roll into balls. Roll each ball in white sugar before placing on a lightly greased baking sheet. Bake 13-15 minutes. Note: some people leave balls as such, others flatten them on the baking sheet. The ball method gives a chewier end result.

Snicker doodles (24 large cookies)

Jean Palmer wanted more cookie options. Krista came through with yet another family recipe, this one from her paternal side, a Cowles family favorite. This is a sugar cookie rolled in cinnamon sugar before baking. Toddlers seemed to love these.

1/2 pound plus 4 tablespoons butter/ 2 1/2 sticks
2 cups white sugar
3 eggs, one at a time
3 2/3 cups unbleached or allpurpose flour
2 1/2 teaspoons cream of tartar
1 tablespoon baking soda
1 pinch salt
1/2 to 3/4 cup white sugar plus 2 teaspoons cinnamon for rolling

Cream butter and sugar together till light and fluffy. Add eggs, one at a time, beating well after each addition. Stir together flour, cream of tartar, soda and salt. Fold into butter and egg mixture until all well combined. Refrigerate at least 1/2 hour before portioning out to ease handling. Or freeze for another time. Preheat oven to 350 degrees. Stir cinnamon and sugar together. Portion out dough into 1 1/2 tablespoon amounts. Roll each into a ball. Roll each ball in cinnamon sugar and place balls (do not flatten) on a lightly greased baking sheet. Bake 13-15 minutes.

From other sources:

Chocolate Chip from the basic Nestle's Toll House Chip bag
Oatmeal Raisin from the Quaker Oats box

Holiday Cookies

In the dark of the year they remembered the light and celebrated each in their own way. Christmas is where it all began for me as a young baker. First, decorating the cookies. Then I made the dough. Eventually, I tried my hand at fruitcake, baking them well ahead and soaking them with rum! All of these were my gifts to family, friends and neighbors.

Every winter solstice, Christmas, Chanukah season, I am driven to bake goodies to give away. Daily Bread was very much an extension of my own kitchen, and I delivered many bags and boxes of goodies to our village neighbors, store owners, the bank, the post office, the highway garage, the delivery people --all those people who helped to make life a little easier day to day.

You can see the German influence in many of these goodies, though many of the recipes came from friends and employees. These are neither lo-fat nor heart healthy, but worth the indulgence.

Oat Shortbread (36 cookies)

Pat Bates introduced me to these. In her childhood home, these were made into the shape of candy canes and glazed with alternating red and white stripes. This was a little labor intensive for us. These are wonderfully rich, not too sweet. And the oats make you feel a little less guilt.

Shortbread:
1/2 pound butter/ 2 sticks
1/2 cup powdered sugar
2 2/3 tablespoons water
2 teaspoons vanilla
2 1/2 cups unbleached or allpurpose flour
1 1/4 cups rolled oats

Glaze:
1 cup powdered sugar
2 tablespoons water
1/4 teaspoon vanilla

Cream butter and sugar till light. A mixer works well, but it can be done by hand. Add water and vanilla and continue beating till light and fluffy. Stir together flour and oats. Fold into butter mixture to make a stiff dough. Form a 3 inch wide, 1 inch thick block on wax paper. Wrap tightly and refrigerate. It can wait up to a week before baking.

When ready, preheat oven to 325 degrees. Take dough out of refrigerator. Use a sharp knife to cut 1/4-inch slices. Place, cut side down on an ungreased baking sheet. Bake 20 minutes until light brown. Mix powdered sugar, water and vanilla to make glaze. Brush or drizzle onto cookies while still hot. Cool and store in a tight container.

Vienna Crescents (36 cookies)

This was developed by combining recipes found in the big blue *New York Times Cookbook* and *Mimi Sheraton's German Cookbook*. These melt in your mouth. Make sure the nuts are very finely chopped.

1/2 pound butter/ 2 sticks
3/4 cup white sugar
2 1/2 cups flour, unbleached or allpurpose
1 cup very finely ground walnuts

For sprinkling on after baking:
2 cups powdered sugar
1 teaspoon vanilla

Grind walnuts to a fine meal in a food processor or blender. Cream butter and white sugar till very light and fluffy. Stir flour and nuts together, and fold into butter mixture. Form into a block 1 1/2 inches wide and 1 inch thick on wax paper. Wrap tightly and chill at least 1 hour or up to a week.

Preheat oven to 350 degrees. Use a sharp knife to slice dough about 1/4 inch thick. Use fingers to pinch ends to create crescent shapes. Place on ungreased baking sheet, leaving an inch in between cookies. Bake 15-18 minutes until light brown. Meanwhile sprinkle vanilla over powdered sugar. Cool cookies 1 minute. Sift flavored powdered sugar over cookies. Cool and store in a tight container.

We had big outdoor celebrations every 5 years, inviting the community to the park

Longtrail Lanny (Schnipa) . . . .

The following note appeared written on a piece of birch bark. Many hikers made the pilgrimage into the village for a boost from Daily Bread to get them over the next ridge.

Thank you Daily Bread
You have awesome food and a homey atmosphere. Cool mobiles too! I wish I could take one on the trail with me. You provided a dry & warm place on a rainy day and nourishment for body & soul to sustain us on the rest of our trip North.
May the Goddess Bless You All
Lanny (Schnipa') & Alan (34)

Lebkuchen (32 to 36 cookies)

There are many different versions of this cookie. They are all spicy and sweet. Some are cakey, some crunchier. This is a crunchy one which came from Judy Bush who lovingly recalls her grandmother baking these every Christmas. Her grandmother baked them well ahead of time and aged them.

3/4 cup honey
1/4 cup molasses
1/2 cup white sugar
6 tablespoons butter/ 3/4 stick
2 teaspoons lemon juice
Grated zest of 1 lemon
2 eggs, one at a time
3 1/2 cup unbleached flour
3/4 teaspoon soda
1/4 teaspoon salt
1 teaspoon cinnamon
1 teaspoon ground cloves
1 teaspoon mace
1/4 teaspoon ground cardamom
1/2 cups almonds, thinly sliced or finely chopped
Glaze:
1 1/2 cup powdered sugar
2 tablespoons boiling water
1/4 teaspoon almond extract
or try some with Chocolate Goo (see page 80)

Will Rossi, Silas Hildebrand, Betsy, Paulo Rossi and Krista playing with icing and sprinkles.

Heat together honey, molasses and sugar till mixture reaches a soft boil. Remove from heat. Add butter and stir until butter is melted. Pour into a bowl and cool to room temperature. Beat in lemon juice and zest. Beat in eggs one at a time, beating well after each. Stir together flour, soda, salt, spices and almonds. Stir flour mixture into egg and sweetener mixture to form a medium stiff dough. Cover and chill. This dough can also wait up to a week, tightly covered, before baking.

Preheat oven to 400 degrees. Roll dough out to 1/4-inch thick. Cut into rectangles or shapes of your choice. Place on lightly greased baking sheet. Bake 10 minutes. Meanwhile stir together powdered sugar, water and extract to make glaze. Or warm Chocolate Goo (see page 79) over heat to a spreadable consistency. While cookies are still hot, brush tops with glaze or Goo. Cool and then store in a tight container.

Pfeffernusse (36 cookies)

These are spicy (yes, pfeffer translates to pepper!) and sweet; chewy on the inside, crunchy on the outside. Don't be dissuaded by what pass for Pfeffernuss commercially in this country: rocks drenched in powdered sugar. These take a little extra attention, and they are well worth it. They need to dry overnight before baking, so plan ahead. The basis for this version is derived from *Mimi Sheraton's German Cookbook,* a farewell gift from my German host family's neighbors, the Cuhlmanns.

5 eggs
1 1/2 cups brown sugar
1 1/2 cups white sugar
1/4 cup grated lemon zest
1/2 cup finely chopped walnuts or almonds
5 cups unbleached flour
1 1/2 teaspoons cinnamon
1/2 teaspoon ground cloves
1 teaspoon ground cardamom
1/2 teaspoon black pepper
1/2 teaspoon baking soda
1 cup powdered sugar for dusting

Beat together eggs, brown and white sugars until foamy, thick and lemon colored. A mixer works best, but a wire whisk and elbow grease will do. Add lemon zest and nuts. Stir together flour, cinnamon, cloves, cardamom, pepper and soda. Add to egg mixture bit by bit and stir well after each addition. It will be a fairly stiff and sticky dough. If you have parchment paper, line baking sheets with it and sprinkle with a little white sugar before portioning out cookies. Otherwise lightly grease your baking sheets and sprinkle with a little white sugar. Scoop out by the tablespoon onto prepared sheets. Leave rounded tops up. And leave an inch between cookies. Let dry overnight.

In the morning, preheat oven to 300 degrees. Bake 20 minutes. Do not over bake. While still hot, sift powdered sugar over cookies. Cool, then store in a tight container.

Gingerbread (48 small cutouts)

We used this recipe for decorated cut-out cookies for all occasions. It is loosely based on the original from the big blue *New York Times Cookbook.* It is mild and sweet enough for kids, and it is easy to work with. We accumulated an eclectic array of cutters over the years from the standard stars, moons, boys, girls and hearts to cows, pigs, hens, roosters, pick up trucks and maple leaves. We invited local children to a decorating party around Christmas every year and delighted in their creations.

1/2 pound plus 4 tablespoons butter or margarine/ 2 1/2 sticks
1 cup brown sugar, packed
1 tablespoon ground ginger
2 teaspoons cinnamon
1/2 teaspoon ground cloves
1 teaspoon salt
2 eggs
1 1/2 cups molasses
6 cups unbleached or allpurpose flour
2 teaspoons baking soda
1 teaspoon baking powder

Cream together butter (or margarine), brown sugar, ginger, cinnamon, cloves and salt till light and fluffy. Add eggs and molasses to the creamed butter mixture and continue beating till incorporated and foamy. Stir together flour, soda and baking powder. Fold into the butter and molasses mix to make fairly stiff dough. Cover tightly or wrap in wax paper and refrigerate at least 1 hour before rolling out to bake.

Preheat oven to 400 degrees. Lightly grease a few baking sheets. Divide dough in half. Roll out one piece on a lightly floured surface to 1/4 inch thick. Cut into shapes, trying to leave as few scraps in between as possible. Transfer cookies to your prepared baking sheets. Bake 10 minutes.

Collect scraps and knead together. Set aside. Repeat rolling, cutting, and baking procedure with second half of dough and then scraps. Spread or brush with your favorite frosting or use a powdered sugar glaze and decorate with choice of sprinkles, raisins, coconut, chopped nuts, whatever.

Cutter Butter (48 small cut-out cookies)

For a light and non-spiced cookie for cutting out, try this tasty sugar cookie. It also derived from the big blue *New York Times Cookbook*. These lend themselves to a simpler decorating approach: sprinkle with colored sugars before baking, and they're done! Or get as fancy as you like with frosting or glazes afterwards. We sold uncooked dough too.

1/2 pound butter or margarine/ 2 sticks
1 cup brown sugar
1/2 cup white sugar
2 eggs, added one at a time
2 teaspoons vanilla
4 cups unbleached or allpurpose flour
1/2 teaspoon salt
1 teaspoon baking powder
1/2 teaspoon baking soda
2 tablespoons milk

Cream butter (or margarine), brown and white sugars together till light and fluffy. Beat in eggs, one at a time, and then vanilla, beating well after each addition. Stir together flour, salt, baking powder and soda. Alternately add flour, milk, flour, milk, flour to the butter and egg mix to make a firm dough. Cover tightly or wrap in wax paper and chill thoroughly, 1 hour or up to a week.

Preheat oven to 400 degrees. Lightly grease baking sheets. Divide dough into two pieces. Roll out one on a floured surface to 1/4 inch thick. Cut out with your favorite cutters, leaving as few scraps in between as possible. Transfer cookies to prepared baking sheets. Bake 10 minutes. Collect scraps and knead lightly. Repeat rolling, cutting, baking with second half of dough and then scraps. Decorate as you please.

Biscochitos (about 30 1-inch cookies)

From Germany to Mexico! My parents moved to Santa Fe, New Mexico in 1971. Biscochitos are a favorite Mexican holiday cookie. Mom got this recipe from her friend Trinidad Baca. They are traditionally made using lard or vegetable shortening. We found margarine worked fine. The characteristic combination of anise seed and cinnamon sugar on top gives these their authentic taste.

1/2 pound margarine, lard, vegetable shortening or combination/ 2 sticks
3/4 cups sugar
1 egg
3 cups unbleached or allpurpose flour
1 tablespoon crushed anise seed
2/3 teaspoon baking powder
1/2 teaspoon salt
1/3 cup wine or brandy

For tops:
1/4 cup white sugar
3/4 teaspoon cinnamon

Cream together margarine (or shortening of choice) and sugar till light and fluffy. Beat in egg. Stir together flour, anise seed, baking powder and salt. Alternately stir in flour, wine (or brandy), flour, wine, flour to form soft but workable dough. Knead lightly. This can be chilled, but can also be rolled out immediately.

Preheat oven to 350 degrees. Divide dough into two pieces. Roll out on a floured surface to 1/4-inch thick. Cut into small circles, squares or stars. Transfer to a lightly greased baking sheet. Sprinkle with cinnamon sugar. Bake 10 minutes until just brown. Knead together scraps. Repeat rolling, cutting and baking with rest of dough.

Nick's Grandma Masini's Anise (about 30 1-inch cookies)

Nick Sansone came from a family of cooks and bakers. He suggested we try these because they tasted good and were pretty, topped with pink frosting and sprinkles. Customers agreed, and these joined the ranks of regular holiday offerings.

6 eggs
3/4 cup oil, sunflower or other light variety
1 cup white sugar
1 tablespoon crushed anise seed
4 cups unbleached or allpurpose flour
2 teaspoons baking powder

Frosting:
2 cups powdered sugar
2 1/2 to 3 tablespoons water
A few drops red food coloring
3/4 cup red sprinkles

Beat eggs till light and lemon colored. Slowly beat in oil. Stir together sugar and anise. Add to egg and oil mixture, continuing to beat. Stir together flour and baking powder, and fold into egg, sugar, oil mix. Turn out onto a floured surface and lightly knead into a smooth ball.

Preheat oven to 350 degrees. Tear off walnut sized pieces and roll each into a smooth ball. Place on lightly greased baking sheet. Bake 10 minutes. Let cookies cool slightly. Combine powdered sugar and water and enough food coloring to make a nice pink. Spread frosting on each cookie, sprinkles on top. Let frosting dry completely before storing in a tight container.

Weissli (30 small meringues)

I found this and the next recipe in an early 1980s *Gardens for All* newspaper (precursor to *National Gardening Magazine*). They seemed like an unusual and tasty addition to standard holiday fare. The nuts make them rich, the egg whites and self-frosting make them chewy, and the cinnamon gives them a flavor reminiscent of "red hots."

    4 eggs, whites only
    1 teaspoon cream of tartar
    1/2 tablespoon rum
    2 cups white sugar
    3 cups finely ground walnuts
    3 tablespoons cinnamon
    Additional white sugar for baking
    Parchment paper for baking is very helpful

Beat together egg whites, cream of tartar, rum and sugar in an electric mixer to form stiff peaks. Put aside 1/4 cup of this for frosting! Stir cinnamon and walnuts together and gently fold into the remaining beaten egg whites. Preheat oven to 200 degrees. Line baking sheet/s with parchment paper if you have it. Sprinkle sheet/s lightly with sugar. Portion out onto prepared sheets. Spread reserved meringue mixture on top of cookies. Bake 30 minutes.

Brunsli (30 small meringues)

We were seriously lacking in anything chocolate for our holiday assortments. These seemed like a tasty addition. The original came from the same *Gardens for All* newspaper as the Weissli above. These do not keep as well as many other of the holiday specials, so bake these close to when they will be eaten.

    3/4 cup chocolate chips
    1/2 cup white sugar
    3 cups finely ground almonds
    3 eggs, whites only
    1/2 teaspoon cream of tartar
    1 tablespoon rum
    1 1/2 cup white sugar
    Parchment paper for baking
    Additional sugar for baking sheet/s

Melt together chocolate chips and sugar in a small sauce pan. Grind almonds to a fine meal in a food processor. Pour chocolate over ground almonds, stirring occasionally till cool. Beat egg whites, cream of tartar and rum together in an electric mixer to form firm peaks. Add 1 1/2 cups sugar gradually to the beating whites till stiff peaks are formed. Fold whites mixture gently into chocolate and nuts. Preheat oven to 200 degrees. Cut parchment paper, if you have it, to fit your baking sheet/s. Otherwise grease lightly. Sprinkle lightly with sugar. Drop meringue by the tablespoon-full onto prepared sheet/s. Bake 30 minutes. Let cool and store in a tight container.

Serving the Community: Camp! ·

One of the many service groups which employees supported and continue to support is Camp! Judy Bush inspired numerous Bread employees and others to offer a residential summer camp experience to many Vermont children who otherwise would have never had the opportunity.

In 1991, funding fell through for a camp program for migrant workers' children staffed partly by residents of Richmond and Huntington. The Vermont Migrant Education Program had administered the camp. Without federal dollars, the State decided to discontinue the camp. Judy and past director David Young gathered with other former camp workers to found Camp!, Inc. to continue the program without the federal funding.

Young didn't want the camp to dissolve because it served a large population of kids who would otherwise not have the opportunity to go to camp.

A smiling head cook Alison Forrest on far left with a crew of happy Camp! cooks.

Judy wanted to continue the program which provided a safe environment for taking risks in activities from swimming to arts to computers.

Early Camp! workers included Linda Young, Ben Bush, Chris Cichoski, Wolf Song, Alison Forrest, Patty Griffiths, Grace Freeman, Michelle Jenness, Shea Soule, and Matthew Witten.

As of summer 2003, Judy continued to direct Camp! Numerous local residents and Daily Bread workers have given up their last week of summer to work at Camp! and have given many kids successes to remember.

Heidi Racht, standing far right, another Daily Bread baker spending time in the Camp! kitchens.

Muffins

I don't really know why, but Daily Bread did not get into the muffin business until we expanded to become a bakery cafe in 1986! I suppose it was because we didn't have muffin tins!? Alison Forrest and Lynn E. Alden convinced me that we should invest in some tins when we purchased other equipment we needed for the cafe. Muffins were, and continued to be, popular morning fare. Alison was responsible for bringing in the first recipes, and we collected the rest along the way, with many undergoing changes to accommodate changing customer preferences.

Muffins fall somewhere between biscuits and cake. They usually have plenty of shortening and eggs or soy but not too much sweetener. They use baking powder and/ or soda for rising. To stay tender use only a minimum of mixing once the wet is added to the dry; a few lumps are fine.

Note: to save time in the morning, muffins are easy to prepare ahead of time. Mix up your dry ingredients and cover. Mix up wet ingredients and refrigerate. In the morning, heat oven, prepare your tins, and combine the wet and dry. Voila! Fresh baked muffins in less than 30 minutes! If you have an ice cream scoop or disher, this makes portioning the batter easy and gives a uniform round top to all your muffins.

Blueberry/ Any-berry (12 medium muffins)

Alison used the *New York Times Natural Foods Cookbook* for the original amounts for these. With a number of small changes, we used this with berries of all varieties; it also worked beautifully with dried apricots.

        2 cups unbleached or allpurpose flour
        2 teaspoons baking powder
        3/4 cup milk
        1/4 cup orange juice
        1/3 cup honey
        2 eggs
        4 tablespoons melted butter/ 1/2 stick
        1/2 teaspoon grated orange or lemon zest
        3/4 cups berries or 1/2 cup diced dried apricots

Preheat oven to 400 degrees. Grease and liberally flour muffin tins. In a mixing bowl, stir together flour and baking powder. In a separate bowl or large measuring cup, combine milk, juice, honey, eggs, melted butter and zest. Beat with a wire whisk to thoroughly combine. Fold wet mixture into flour with a large spoon or rubber spatula to just combine into a slightly lumpy batter. Fold in fruit to evenly distribute. Portion into prepared muffin tins, about 2/3 to 3/4 full. Bake 15-20 minutes until tops are nicely browned and the center springy to the touch.

Apple Spice (12 medium muffins)

This is another Alison contribution, which she derived from an original in the *New York Times Natural Foods Cook Book*. These are especially good in the autumn when there are lots of tasty apples around. These are light, a little spicy and loaded with apples.

    1 3/4 cups peeled, pared and diced apples/ 2 to 3 apples
    1 cup whole wheat pastry flour
    3/4 cup unbleached or all purpose flour
    1/2 cup bran
    1 1/2 teaspoons baking soda
    3/4 teaspoon cinnamon
    1/8 teaspoon nutmeg
    1 pinch ground ginger
    1 pinch salt
    1 1/4 cups yogurt
    1/4 cup honey
    1 egg
    4 tablespoons melted butter/ 1/2 stick

Preheat oven to 400 degrees. Grease and flour muffin tins. Prepare apples. Stir together flour, bran, soda, cinnamon, nutmeg, ginger and salt in mixing bowl. Combine yogurt, honey, eggs and melted butter in a separate bowl. Beat with a wire whisk until all thoroughly mixed. Fold liquids into flour mix with a rubber spatula or large spoon to dampen all. Fold in apples to evenly distribute. Fill muffin tins 2/3 to 3/4 full. Bake 15-20 minutes till tops begin to brown and the center springs back to the touch.

Wheat germ (12 medium muffins)

Here is the third in the Alison/*N.Y. Times Natural Foods* collection. We found that a combination of wheat germ and coconut or wheat germ and sesame seeds suited customer and staff tastes better than straight wheat germ. We used maple syrup to sweeten.

    1 cup less 1 tablespoon unbleached or allpurpose flour
    2 1/2 teaspoons baking powder
    1/8 teaspoon salt
    1 cup milk
    3 tablespoons maple syrup
    1 egg
    5 tablespoons melted butter
    1 1/4 cups wheat germ
    Or 1 cup wheat germ plus 1/2 cup coconut
    Or 1 cup wheat germ plus 1/2 cup sesame seeds

Preheat oven to 425 degrees. Grease and flour muffin tins. Stir together flour, baking powder and salt in mixing bowl. Combine milk, syrup, eggs and melted butter in a separate bowl. Beat well with wire whisk to thoroughly mix. Fold liquid into flour mix with a large spoon or rubber spatula to just damp, lumps are OK. Fold wheat germ or wheat germ/ coconut or sesame combo into batter to thoroughly distribute. Portion into muffin tins, 2/3 to 3/4 full. Bake 15-20 minutes till tops are lightly browned and the center springs back to the touch.

Bran (12 medium muffins)

This is the fourth in the *New York Times Natural Foods* quintet from Alison. Bran muffins had a large following in the 1980s and early 1990s, but were overshadowed by fruitier offerings (and scones) in the late '90's. This is a very good version of the bran muffin, and lends itself to a number of different additions. Raisins were the expected, dates not unusual, pecans nice, cranberries excellent, but my own favorites were Cran' Bran Pecan, for the taste combination and because they were fun to say.

1 cup plus 2 tablespoons buttermilk
1 cup plus 2 tablespoons bran
2 tablespoons molasses
1/2 cup honey
1 egg
2 1/2 tablespoons melted butter
1 1/4 cups unbleached or allpurpose flour
3/4 teaspoon baking soda
1/2 cup raisins
Or dates
Or cranberries
Or pecans or a combination of your choice

Preheat oven to 400 degrees. Grease and flour muffin tins. Stir together buttermilk and bran in a mixing bowl. Let sit 15 minutes to 1/2 hour. Add molasses, honey, eggs and melted butter to bran mix and beat well. Stir together soda and flour. Fold into bran mixture to just moisten. Fold in fruit or nuts of your choice to evenly distribute. Fill muffin tins 2/3 to 3/4 full. Bake 15 to 20 minutes.

Local Legends

When local musicians Lausanne Allen and Tim Jennings approached me to use the newly opened dining room for an acoustic "kitchen cabaret," I gladly agreed. Tim and Lausanne thought once a month would be good to start out with, but soon expanded to weekly shows due to popular demand. Musician, story teller and state senator Dick McCormack performed at Daily Bread and wrote in his 1987 *Vermont Vanguard* Press column:

Local Legends is located in Daily Bread Café in Richmond, and is operated on a nearly volunteer basis by Tim Jennings (Vermont's pre-eminent storyteller, who resembles a lumberjack gnome) and Lausanne Allen (the hippie rural beauty who plays fiddle with the Northern Lights String Band). It started last spring as a monthly event and is now weekly. Featured artists have included ...Michael Hurley, Dan O'Connell, Mary Ann Samuels and Karen Downy, myself, Jon Gailmore and Nancy Beaven, among others.

Folk music and storytelling...thrive in what Allen calls an 'intimate, homelike, unintimidating setting like their own kitchen.'

Contemporary folk music generally has been removed not only from its original setting and economics (or lack thereof) but from its essential spirit as well. Real folk music has nothing to do with profit. Farmers, loggers, farm wives and sailors traditionally sang for the pure joy of it. Local Legends has revived the tradition, providing a conducive setting for music and tales and a reassertion, too, of the animating principle of folk as a labor of love. (35)

Summer nights were too warm for comfortable listening, so we took off July and August. I helped organize a number of summer concert series at the bandshell in Volunteers Green. Local Legends continued for nine years, featuring the best local acoustic musicians. And it continued to be a labor of love. Lausanne worked Thursdays for years. Rick Klein took over after Tim Jennings' story telling schedule became too busy. Meg Howard and Carlee Geer teamed up as hosts for another four or five years.

Some shows were so packed that all spare 5-gallon pails and milk crates were in use and there were still folks willing to stand in the hall. Audiences dwindled in the mid-1990s after every other bakery and bar had added a "coffee house," and I discontinued the series. We revived it in the '99 expanded dining room, but it was never quite the same.

Whole Wheat (12 medium muffins)

Jericho neighbor and original University of Vermont food service vegetarian "Garbanzo Chef" Stephen Holtz recommended this recipe, originally presented in the *Tassajara Bread Book* as "Somethin' Missin' Muffins." Some customers loved the grainy, wholesome crunch of these muffins, though they did not sell as well as others. Cindy Bramon gave them an extra special touch with the addition of raspberries and dates. Any berry or fruit will work fine.

1 2/3 cups whole wheat pastry flour
2 teaspoons baking powder
1/3 cup powdered milk
2 eggs
1/4 cup oil
1/4 cup maple syrup
1 cup water
3/4 cup fruit (your choice!)

Preheat oven to 400 degrees. Grease and flour muffin tins. Combine flour, baking powder and powdered milk in mixing bowl. Mix eggs, oil, syrup and water in a separate bowl. Beat with a wire whisk to thoroughly combine. Fold liquids into flour mixture to just combine. Fold in fruit to evenly distribute. Fill muffin tins 2/3 to 3/4 full. Bake 20 minutes till tops begin to brown and center springs back to the touch.

Lee Baughman, John Hadden, JB Bryan and Betsy as "The Sweet Buns."

Lemon or Orange Walnut (12 medium muffins)

The idea for these came from Molly Katzen's *The Enchanted Broccoli Forest*. She called the recipe "Lemon Yogurt Muffins." We made some changes, and this is the result. They are light and tangy. The customer favorite was Orange Cranberry, with a combination of walnuts and cranberries added to the orange version.

    1 cup unbleached or allpurpose flour
    1 cup whole wheat pastry flour
    1/8 teaspoon nutmeg
    1 teaspoon baking soda
    1 cup yogurt
    1/2 cup honey
    4 tablespoons melted butter/ 1/2 stick
    1 egg
    3 tablespoons lemon or orange juice
    3/4 teaspoons grated lemon or orange zest
    1/2 cup coarsely chopped walnuts
    Or 2/3 cup whole, sliced or chopped cranberries
    Or 1/2 cup mixed nuts and berries

Preheat oven to 400 degrees. Grease and flour muffin tins. Stir together flours, nutmeg and soda in mixing bowl. Combine yogurt, honey, melted butter, eggs, juice and grated zest in a separate bowl. Beat thoroughly with a wire whisk. Fold liquids into flour to just combine. Fold nuts and/or berries into batter. Fill muffin tins 2/3 to 3/4 full. Bake 15-20 minutes until tops lightly browned and center springs back to the touch.

Orange Chocolate Chip (12 medium muffins)

The original concept and quantities came from a mid-1980s issue of *Harrowsmith* magazine. Doug Perkins refined the recipe to become one of Daily Bread customers' favorite weekend offerings. Self-described chocoholic Krista Willett made them every other week during her Saturday morning bakes. The tangy orange flavor, rich chocolate chips and light texture melt in your mouth.

    1 cup unbleached or allpurpose flour
    1 cup whole wheat pastry flour
    3/4 teaspoon baking powder
    1/4 teaspoon baking soda
    6 tablespoons melted butter/ 3/4stick
    1/2 cup maple syrup
    1 1/2 teaspoons grated orange zest
    2 eggs
    1/2 cup yogurt
    1/3 cup orange juice
    1/2 cup chocolate chips

Preheat oven to 400 degrees. Grease and flour muffin tins. Stir together flours, powder and soda in mixing bowl. Combine melted butter, syrup, zest, eggs, yogurt and juice in separate bowl or a large measuring cup. Beat thoroughly with a wire whisk to combine. Fold wet mix into flours with a rubber spatula or large spoon to just moisten all; a few lumps are allowed. Fold in chocolate chips. Note that this batter is a little more liquid than most other muffin batter. Fill muffin tins 2/3 to 3/4 full. Bake 15-20 minutes at 400 degrees until tops are lightly browned and center springs back to the touch.

Matron of the Arts

I grew up in a household full of music, books and art. Dad's press privileges got us in to many New York City clubs, theaters and concert halls. Mom took us to all of New York City's many and varied museums. I didn't realize what a gift it was to see all that classic art up close and personal. Those experiences led me to a deep enjoyment and appreciation of art and artists.

I also believe that three or four days a week of working out for a wage should be enough, that a person is entitled to pursue his or her own life needs and projects, their avocations. Many Bread employees were also parents, artists, nurses, social workers, students or healers. There is little support in the every day T.V. world for the individual. We were able to give that support to each other, to provide an alternative model.

Here are two of the musicians who gained time and courage to pursue their muses.

Doug Perkins

...I want to make sure you are thanked for providing such a delightful hub for the community...Not to mention all the great food, and interest in so many people's lives, and the little performance space that got me going again....
Perk **(36)**

Doug with his trusty sidekick
Blackberry Blossom.

Matthew Witten

You have hired the wayward and the idealist and given us a home. You have created the hub of the Richmond/ Huntington area--more than a place for wholesome, reasonably priced food, but a warm atmosphere for people to meet and exchange feelings and ideas. You have brought spirituality to us all through your various works and practices. You have engendered an atmosphere for workers where they are respected, paid as best you can, and included in a democratic and decision-making process.

That has been empowering for many of us! You have opened your doors to musicians and music lovers, and put a great deal of effort into Local Legends, which gave many people joy and gave musicians like me a chance to perform and be heard. You have put blood, sweat and tears into the Times Ink! which is yet another civic service that testifies to your dedication to creating a communicative , informed community. You have supported local and local organic agriculture, which is perhaps one of the most important keys to preserving a beautiful, rural way of life....
Matthew **(37)**

Oatmeal Raisin (12 medium muffins)

No one claimed this as his or her own, and I have no recollection either. They are a simple muffin, and still satisfyingly rich. And there is that something about oats and raisins enjoying each others' company...

1 1/2 cups unbleached or allpurpose flour
1/2 cup regular rolled oats
2 teaspoons baking powder
3/4 cup milk
2 eggs
1/4 cup honey
6 tablespoons melted butter/ 3/4stick
1/2 cup raisins

Preheat oven to 450 degrees. Grease and flour muffin tins. Stir together flour, oats and baking powder in mixing bowl. Combine milk, eggs, honey and melted butter in separate bowl. Beat thoroughly with a wire whisk. Fold liquids into flour and oat mix to just moisten all. Fold in raisins. Fill muffin tins 2/3 to 3/4 full. Bake 10-15 minutes degrees till tops are lightly browned and center springs back to the touch.

French Doughnuts (12 medium muffins)

These are simple muffins made special by rolling them in butter and cinnamon sugar after baking, to resemble a sugar doughnut. Richmond resident and frequent bakery customer Paul Letourneau brought us this recipe. It was a hit with staff and customers alike.

1 1/2 cups unbleached or allpurpose flour
1 scant tablespoon baking powder
1/4 teaspoon nutmeg
1/2 cup milk
1/2 cup light oil such as sunflower or canola
1/4 cup honey
1 egg

Topping:
3 tablespoons melted butter
1/2 cup sugar
1 1/2 teaspoons cinnamon

Preheat oven to 375 degrees. Grease and flour muffin tins. Stir together flour, baking powder and nutmeg in mixing bowl. Combine milk, oil, honey and eggs in a separate bowl. Beat thoroughly with a wire whisk. Fold liquids into flour to just moisten all. Fill muffin tins 2/3 to 3/4 full. Stir together cinnamon and sugar in a small bowl. Bake 20-25 minutes. Let cool 5 to 10 minutes. Remove from tins and dip tops in melted butter. Then roll in cinnamon sugar.

Coconut Pecan (12 medium muffins)

Another unclaimed recipe. I believe it was an adaptation of the basic Blueberry muffin, thought up by one of the numerous early morning Daily Bread bakers. They are chewy and moist, not too sweet.

2 cups unbleached or allpurpose flour
2 1/2 teaspoons baking powder
3/4 cup coconut, lightly toasted
1/4 cup coarsely chopped pecans
3/4 cup milk
1/4 cup orange juice
1/3 cup honey
2 eggs
4 tablespoons melted butter/ 1/2 stick
1/2 teaspoon vanilla

Preheat oven to 400 degrees. Grease and flour muffin tins. While oven is heating, spread coconut on a baking sheet and lightly toast, about 10 minutes. Stir together flour, baking powder, coconut and pecans in a mixing bowl. Combine milk, juice, honey, eggs, melted butter and vanilla in a separate bowl. Beat thoroughly with a wire whisk. Fold liquid into flour mixture with a rubber spatula or large spoon to just moisten all. Fill muffin tins 2/3 to 3/4 full. Bake 15-20 minutes.

Coconut Chocolate Bit (12 medium muffins)

One early morning, 4:30 or so, Krista Willett thought, "Chocolate is a fruit, and Mounds bars are good...," and arrived at this adaptation of the Blueberry recipe. For whatever reason, it really does make a difference to chop the chocolate chips into bits. These developed a real following, with staff and customers alike. They are especially tasty split and grilled.

2 cups unbleached or allpurpose flour
2 1/2 teaspoons baking powder
3/4 cup coconut, lightly toasted
1/2 cup chocolate chips, chopped into bits
3/4 cup milk
1/3 cup yogurt
1/4 cup honey
2 eggs
1 teaspoon vanilla
4 tablespoons melted butter/ 1/2 stick

Preheat oven to 400 degrees. Spread coconut on baking sheet and put in oven to toast 10 minutes while you assemble the rest of ingredients. Grease and flour muffin tins. Chop chips with a chef's knife or a very short buzz in a food processor. Stir together flour, baking powder, coconut and chocolate in mixing bowl. Combine milk, yogurt, honey, eggs, vanilla and melted butter in a separate bowl. Beat thoroughly with a wire whisk. Fold liquids into flour mixture with a rubber spatula or large spoon to just combine. Fill muffin tins 2/3 to 3/4 full. Bake 20 minutes till tops begin to brown and centers spring back to the touch.

Cherry Almond (12 medium muffins)

Muffin queen Krista Willett found the concept for these in "some woman's magazine" in the 1990s. Another recipe inspired by having lots of dried cherries on hand.

And, of course, if almonds are good, chocolate and almonds are better.

1/2 cup dried cherries, check for stray pits
1/4 cup hot tap water
2 1/4 cups unbleached or allpurpose flour
3/4 tablespoons baking powder
1/4 teaspoon allspice
1/3 cup coarsely chopped almonds

Or 1/2 cup chocolate chips
1 cup milk
1/4 cup sour cream
2 eggs
1/4 cup honey
1 teaspoon vanilla
1/4 teaspoon almond extract
4 tablespoons melted butter/ 1/2 stick

Preheat oven to 400 degrees. Pour hot water over cherries to plump while assembling other ingredients. Grease and flour muffin tins. Stir together flour, baking powder, allspice and almonds or chocolate chips. Combine milk, sour cream, honey, eggs, vanilla, almond extract and melted butter in a separate bowl. Beat thoroughly with a wire whisk. Fold liquid mixture into flour to just moisten. Fold plumped cherries with any remaining liquid into the batter. Fill muffin tins 2/3 to 3/4 full. Bake 20 minutes until tops are lightly browned and centers spring back to the touch.

Pina Colada (12 medium muffins)

Heather Ward made up this combo. This is another adaptation of the basic Blueberry recipe. Using coconut milk (the canned variety) in place of dairy milk gives them an even stronger coconut flavor. No rum, but....

2 cups unbleached or allpurpose flour
2 1/2 teaspoons baking powder
3/4 cup coconut, lightly toasted
3/4 cup milk, dairy or coconut
2 eggs
1/4 cup honey
1/4 cup mashed banana/ 1 ripe banana
1/4 cup drained crushed pineapple
1 teaspoon vanilla
4 tablespoons melted butter/ 1/2 stick

Preheat oven to 400 degrees. Spread coconut on a baking sheet and lightly toast while oven is heating. Grease and flour muffin tins. Stir together flour, baking powder and coconut. Combine milk, eggs, honey, banana, pineapple, vanilla and melted butter. Beat thoroughly with a wire whisk. Fold liquid mixture into flour to just moisten all. Fill muffin tins 2/3 to 3/4 full. Bake 20 minutes until tops lightly browned and the centers spring back to the touch.

Heather

Heather Ward made her first bakery appearance at about age 10 when she won the privilege to build her original design gingerbread house with Judy Bush and Krista Willett. She worked the weekend counter and then learned both baking and cooking when she was in high school. Heather sent the following with the birth announcement of her daughter Salvadora Prajna Ward November 9, 2002:

I just made some oat cranberry scones. I am dancing around my kitchen wildly eating one and my thoughts turned to you. I was thinking of all the baking mistakes you let me make without judging me. I was thinking of how that job gave me so many gifts at such a young age....Bets, you weren't just running a bakery, you were supporting folks, the community, feeding our souls and our lives with your ability to help us deal with and celebrate reality.... **(38)**

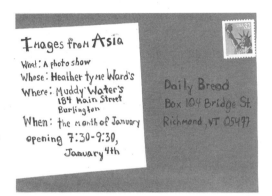

Heather with newborn Salvadora and invitation to her Burlington exhibit of photos from an Asian independent study tour.

Apple Cheddar (12 medium muffins)

I found the original recipe in a mid-1980s copy of the *Christian Science Monitor*. They are spicy, tender and sweet. The sharper the cheddar, the more the flavor will come through.

1 cup pared and diced apples/ 1-2 apples
1 cup grated sharp cheddar cheese/ 1/4 pound
1/3 cup coarsely chopped walnuts or pecans
1 cup unbleached or allpurpose flour
2/3 cup whole wheat pastry flour
1/2 teaspoon baking soda
2/3 teaspoon baking powder
1 pinch nutmeg
1 pinch cinnamon
1 pinch allspice
1/2 cup milk
2 eggs
1/4 cup maple syrup
6 tablespoons melted butter/ 3/4 stick

Preheat oven to 400 degrees. Grease and flour muffin tins. Prepare apples. Grate cheese. Stir together flours, soda, baking powder and spices in mixing bowl. Combine milk, eggs, syrup and melted butter in a separate bowl. Beat thoroughly with a wire whisk. Fold liquid mixture into flours to moisten. Fold apples, cheese and nuts into batter. Fill muffin tins 2/3 to 3/4 full. Bake 20 minutes until tops begin to brown and centers spring back to the touch.

Maple Nut (12 medium muffins)

The original quantities for these came from a mid-1980s copy of *Harrowsmith* magazine. These are very sweet with maple syrup, and tend to dry out more quickly than most other muffins. This served as the basis for the vegan Hazelnut muffin below.

2 cups unbleached or allpurpose flour
1/2 cup rolled oats, buzzed to a coarse meal in a blender or food processor
2 1/2 teaspoons baking powder
1 cup coarsely chopped walnuts or pecans
1/3 cup milk
1 egg
1 cup maple syrup
1 1/2 teaspoons vanilla
4 tablespoons melted butter/ 1/2 stick

Preheat oven to 400 degrees. Grease and flour muffin tins. Stir together flour, buzzed oats, baking powder and nuts in mixing bowl. Combine milk, eggs, syrup, vanilla and melted butter in a separate bowl. Beat thoroughly with a wire whisk. Fold liquid mixture into flour with a rubber spatula or large spoon to just moisten all ingredients. Fill muffin tins 2/3 to 3/4 full. Bake 20 minutes till tops golden brown and centers spring back to the touch.

Vegan Collection

We classified food as vegan if it was naturally sweetened, contained no dairy products and no eggs. Soy flour and/or tofu provide protein for structure. Vinegar, lemon juice and cider substitute for lactic acid usually derived from dairy products. Oil, soy margarine, sesame tahini, mashed banana and apples take the place of butter to smooth out end result. Unlike most muffins, you must work these more like cake batter to ensure protein development.

Hazel Nut -Vegan (12 medium muffins)

Andrew Paschetto adapted the above Maple Nut recipe to take out the dairy and eggs for our many vegan customers. The addition of sesame tahini adds to their richness. And they are just as sweet as their "parent" muffin. They also have a fairly short shelf life. I don't think they'll hang around long enough to find out. These were very popular.

2 cups unbleached or allpurpose flour
1/2 cup rolled oats, buzzed to a coarse meal in blender or food processor
2 teaspoons baking powder
3 tablespoons soy flour, preferably toasted
1 cup finely chopped hazelnuts or filberts
2/3 cup water
1 cup maple syrup
3 tablespoons sesame tahini
4 tablespoons melted margarine/ 1/2 stick

Preheat oven to 400 degrees. Grease and flour muffin tins. Stir together flour, buzzed oats, baking powder, soy flour and nuts in mixing bowl. Combine water, syrup, tahini and melted margarine in a separate bowl. Beat thoroughly with a wire whisk. Fold liquids into flour mixture using a rubber spatula or large spoon. Give the batter 20-30 strokes to develop the proteins so they don't fall. Fill muffin tins 2/3 to 3/4 full. Bake 20-25 minutes till tops golden brown and centers spring back to the touch.

Sunny Banana-Vegan (12 medium muffins)

This muffin began with a recipe from the cookbook *Sweets for Saints and Sinners.* Krista brought it in because it was a honey sweetened recipe. When we began experimenting with veganizing recipes, this one adapted well. Andrew Paschetto is responsible for the fine tuning. These are full of banana flavor, moist and chewy, and plenty sweet enough for any palate.

1 1/2 cups whole wheat pastry flour
1/2 cup whole wheat bread flour
1 tablespoon soy flour, preferably toasted
2/3 teaspoon baking soda
1/2 teaspoon salt
1/2 cup sunflower seeds, lightly toasted
3/4 cups mashed banana/ 2 ripe bananas
6 tablespoons honey
2 tablespoons maple syrup
1/4 cup water
1 1/2 teaspoons cider vinegar
1/2 teaspoon vanilla
1/8 teaspoon almond extract
4 tablespoons melted margarine/ 1/2 stick

Preheat oven to 400 degrees. Grease and flour muffin tins. Stir together flours, soda, salt and sunflower seeds in a mixing bowl. Combine bananas, honey, syrup, water, vinegar, vanilla, almond extract and melted margarine in a separate bowl. Beat thoroughly with a wire whisk. Fold liquids into flour mixture with rubber spatula or large spoon. Give the batter 20-30 strokes to develop proteins. Fill muffin tins 2/3 to 3/4 full. Bake 20-25 minutes until tops lightly browned and centers spring back to the touch.

Honey Apple-Vegan (12 medium muffins)

This recipe has undergone a number of incarnations since I first made its acquaintance. Wendy Weldon noticed it in a late 1970s *Burlington Free Press* as Apple Knob Cake. It was sweetened with brown sugar and full of apples. We made it that way until we had more calling for honey sweetened cakes. We changed the recipe to accommodate honey. Then, around 1990, we began getting the first requests for vegan confections. So, Andrew Paschetto worked with the recipe to take out the eggs. Somehow, it didn't translate that well as a cake. But one early morning, I thought of trying it as a muffin, and it worked beautifully. They are full of apples and sweet honey goodness.

2 cups pared and diced apples/ 2-3 apples
1/2 cup honey
3 tablespoons water
1/2 tablespoon vanilla
1 cup unbleached or allpurpose flour
1/3 cup whole wheat pastry flour
1 1/2 teaspoons cornstarch
1 teaspoon baking soda
1/2 teaspoon nutmeg
1/4 teaspoon cinnamon
4 tablespoons melted margarine/ 1/2 stick
1/4 cup coarsely chopped almonds

Preheat oven to 350 degrees. Grease and flour muffin tins. Prepare apples. Cream together margarine and honey. Add water and vanilla and continue to beat until incorporated. Add apples and set aside. If you think ahead, prepare this part a few hours or the evening before to let the apples soak, though this is not essential. Stir together flours, cornstarch, soda, nutmeg and cinnamon. Fold creamed mixture into flours and beat 15-20 strokes to develop proteins. Fold in prepared apples. Fill muffin tins 2/3 to 3/4 full. Sprinkle chopped almonds on top. Bake 30 minutes until tops golden brown and centers spring back to the touch.

Apple Carrot-Vegan (12 medium muffins)

Here is the last of the *New York Times Natural Foods* inspired muffins, this time brought in by Andrew Paschetto. They sound a little healthy for most tastes, but don't let the name fool you. These are sweet, moist and spicy.

2/3 cup grated carrot/ 1-2 carrots
2/3 cup grated apple/ 1 apple
1 cup plus 1 tablespoon whole wheat bread flour
1 cup whole wheat pastry flour
2 teaspoons baking powder
1/4 teaspoon salt
1/2 teaspoon cinnamon
1/4 teaspoon ground cloves
1/2 teaspoon nutmeg
1/2 cup soy milk
1/2 cup oil, sunflower or other light variety
1/3 cup honey
1/4 teaspoon vanilla

Preheat oven to 400 degrees. Grease and flour muffin tins. Prepare apples and carrots. Stir together flours, baking powder, salt, cinnamon, cloves and nutmeg in a mixing bowl. Combine soy milk, oil, honey and vanilla in a separate bowl. Beat thoroughly with a wire whisk. Fold liquids into flour, beating 20-30 strokes. Fold in apples and carrots till evenly distributed. Fill muffin tins 2/3 to 3/4 full. Bake 25-30 minutes until tops begin to brown and centers spring back to the touch.

Lemon Ginger-Vegan (12 medium muffins)

I first found the original in a 1980s *Christian Science Monitor.* They sounded good, and were popular with staff and customers. Again, vegan requests brought alterations. These are sweet, moist and loaded with lemon and fresh ginger for a tangy taste treat.

1 1/2 cups whole wheat pastry flour
1/2 cup unbleached or allpurpose flour
3/4 teaspoon baking soda
3 tablespoons soy flour, toasted preferably
1/2 cup honey
3/4 cup plus 1 tablespoon water
1 tablespoon cider vinegar
6 tablespoons melted margarine/ 3/4 stick
1 1/2 tablespoons fresh ginger, grated or blended with some of above liquids
2 teaspoons grated lemon zest

Glaze:
1/2 tablespoon honey
1/2 lemon's juice

One incarnation of the Daily Bread Bakery Blues Band playing for the judges during Richmond's July Fourth parade.

Preheat oven to 400 degrees. Grease and flour muffin tins. Stir together flours and soda in a mixing bowl. Combine honey, water, vinegar, melted margarine, ginger root and zest in a separate bowl. Beat thoroughly with a wire whisk. Fold liquids into flour and beat 20-30 strokes to develop proteins. Fill muffin tins 2/3 to 3/4 full. Bake 20-25 minutes until tops are golden brown and centers spring back to the touch. Stir together honey and lemon juice. Brush on hot muffins.

Pumpkin Pecan-Vegan (12 medium muffins)

This began with a mid-1980s *Harrowsmith* magazine recipe. First we substituted honey for sugar. Then Andrew Paschetto veganized it. These are light, moist with the flavor of pumpkin pie, and a little added crunch from the pecans.

    3/4 cup whole wheat pastry flour
    2/3 cup unbleached or allpurpose flour
    1/2 teaspoon nutmeg
    1/2 teaspoon cinnamon
    1 teaspoon baking powder
    1/4 teaspoon baking soda
    2 tablespoons soy flour, preferably toasted
    1/3 cup coarsely chopped pecans
    1 ounce tofu
    1/2 cup water
    1/2 cup cooked and mashed pumpkin or winter squash
    4 tablespoons orange juice
    4 tablespoons maple syrup
    3 tablespoons honey
    3/4 teaspoon cider vinegar
    1/4 cup oil, sunflower or other light variety

Preheat oven to 400 degrees. Grease and flour muffin tins. Stir together flours, nutmeg, cinnamon, baking powder, soda and pecans in a mixing bowl. Buzz tofu with water in a blender or food processor till creamy and smooth. Combine pumpkin, orange juice, syrup, honey, vinegar and oil in a separate bowl. Add creamed tofu to pumpkin mixture. Fold liquids into flour. Beat 20-30 strokes to develop the proteins. Fill muffin tins 2/3 to 3/4 full. Bake 25 minutes until tops start to brown and centers spring back to the touch.

Oat Apricot-Vegan (12 medium muffins)

Some restless morning bakers flipped through the cookbooks to see if anything new jumped out to try. Krista Willett was leafing through *Uprisings* and found the basis for this recipe. It looked like it would fit in with our other offerings: chewy, moist, sweet and vegan.

1 cup coarsely chopped dried apricots
1/2 cup hot tap water
1 1/2 ounces tofu
1/4 cup oil, sunflower or other light variety
1/3 cup plus 1 tablespoon honey
2/3 cup water
1/2 cup coarsely chopped walnuts
1 3/4 cups whole wheat pastry flour
1/4 cup regular rolled oats
2 teaspoons baking powder
1/8 teaspoon baking soda
3 tablespoons soy flour, preferably toasted
1 teaspoon cinnamon

Preheat oven to 400 degrees. Pour hot water over apricots to plump. Grease and flour muffin tins. Buzz tofu, oil, honey and water in a blender or food processor till smooth and creamy. Stir together walnuts, flours, oats, baking powder, soda and cinnamon in mixing bowl. Fold apricots, including their water, and creamed tofu into flour. Beat 20-30 strokes to develop proteins. Fill muffin tins 2/3 to 3/4 full. Bake 20-25 minutes until tops begin to brown and centers spring back to the touch.

Bakery, cafe & gallery

original watercolor by Gardiner Lane

The walls of the dining room became gallery space, featuring a different artist each month. April became staff month featuring a single staff artist or often a group show.

One of the favorites was Gardiner Lane's fall water color show. In his 80s, Gardiner with the help of other "Old Goats," created many of Bolton's favorite cross country touring trails. Gardiner loved to paint the surrounding mountains and woodland streams.

Brownies

Bars and brownies are denser than cake and more concentrated in sweet and shortening. They are just about candy. Bars keep well, if you can refrain from gobbling them up. Kids and adults will be happy when you show up with any of these at a potluck, bake sale or party. Many of the Daily Bread collection had their origins in *The Brownie Book*, which my sister Patti, another confirmed chocoholic, sent me in the early 1980s when she was baking goodies for Judy and Bill Hill's City Lights movie theater in Santa Fe, New Mexico.

Brownies are by far the most popular. Most are chocolate-based. There are also equally decadent 'blonde' brownies: Congo Bars, Blondies and Mandarin Orange Brownies. Some recipes call for baking powder, some do not. Eggs often provide the only loft, so it is important to take the time to beat in the eggs one at a time.

Unlike cakes and breads, brownies do not like to be overworked, especially after the flour has been added. Most home kitchens are equipped with a few square brownie pans, usually 8"x8" or 9"x9". Amounts are given for both sizes.

Double Fudge (8"x8" and 9"x9")

This became our standard brownie offering. They are sweet, moist, fudge-y and definitely chocolate.

8"x8"	9"x9"
7 tablespoons soft butter	1/4 pound/ 1 stick
5 tablespoons soft margarine	7 tablespoons
1/2 cup white sugar	3/4 cup
1/4 cup barley malt (can substitute maple)	1/3 cup
2 eggs, one at a time	3 eggs
1 teaspoon vanilla	1 1/2 teaspoons
1/2 cup unsweetened cocoa	3/4 cup
3/4 cup plus 1 tablespoon flour	1 cup
3/4 cup chocolate chips	1 cup
1/3 cup chopped walnuts	1/2 cup

Preheat oven to 350 degrees. Grease and flour baking pan. Cream together butter, margarine, sugar and barley malt or syrup till light. Add vanilla and eggs, one at a time, beating well in between each addition. Stir together cocoa, flour, chocolate chips and nuts. Fold flour mixture into butter mix till all are well combined. Spread evenly in your prepared pan. Bake 25-30 minutes. The center may still feel slightly mushy. A toothpick inserted 1 inch from the edge of the pan should come out clean.

Espresso Brownies (8"x8" and 9"x9")

Lynn E. Alden discovered the original in *The Brownie Book*, which she adapted to natural sweeteners. They are more cakelike than others, and will stick to your teeth. We found that a fine ground coffee substituted well for espresso powder, which you may or may not find on the shelf of your local market.

8"x8"
3 1/2 tablespoons butter, soft
6 tablespoons margarine, soft/ 3/4 stick
2/3 cup maple syrup
2 2/3 tablespoons barley malt
2 eggs, one at a time
2/3 cup flour
2/3 cup unsweetened cocoa
2 teaspoons espresso powder or coffee
1/3 teaspoon baking powder
1/3 cup chopped walnuts or pecans

9"x9"
4 tablespoons/ 1/2 stick
7 tablespoons
3/4 cup plus 1 tablespoon
3 1/3 tablespoons
3 eggs
1 cup
3/4 cup plus 1 tablespoon
1 tablespoon
1/2 teaspoon
1/2 cup

Preheat oven to 350 degrees. Grease and flour pan. Cream together butter, margarine, syrup and barley malt till light and fluffy. Beat eggs into the butter mixture, one at a time. Stir together flour, cocoa, espresso and baking powder. Stir flour mixture into butter and eggs until all are well combined. Fold in nuts. Spread into your prepared pan. Bake 25-30 minutes or until a toothpick inserted 1 inch from the edge comes out clean.

Roasted Almond Brownie (8"x8" or 9"x9")

Baker Krista Willett was a confirmed chocoholic and thought these would be a little different. She started with a recipe in *The Brownie Book*, and perfected them over the years with this mouth-watering result.

8"x8"
1 cup coarsely chopped almonds, roasted
3 1/2 ounces unsweetened baker's chocolate
1/3 cup chocolate chips/ 2 ounces
4 tablespoons margarine/ 1/2 stick
7 tablespoons butter
1 cup white sugar
2 1/2 tablespoons barley malt
1 teaspoon vanilla
2 eggs, one at a time
1 1/4 cups flour

9"x9"
1 1/4 cups
4 ounces
1/2 cup/ 3 ounces
6 tablespoons/ 3/4 stick
1/4 pound/ 1 stick
1 1/4 cups
3 tablespoons
1 1/4 teaspoons
3 eggs
1 1/2 cups

Preheat oven to 325 degrees. Spread almonds on your baking pan and put it in the oven while you prepare the rest. Melt the baker's chocolate and chips together over low heat. Remove from heat and cool 5 minutes. Cream together margarine, butter, sugar, barley malt and vanilla till light. Stir in melted chocolate. Check toasting nuts; they want to be aromatic and only lightly browned. Add eggs, one at a time, beating well after each addition. Stir roasted nuts into the flour. Grease and flour baking pan. Fold flour and roasted nuts into butter mixture to just combine. Spread evenly into prepared pan. Bake 30-35 minutes. A toothpick inserted 1 inch from the edge should come out clean. The middle may still feel a little mushy, and that is okay.

Peanut Butter Fudge Swirl Brownie (8"x8" and 9"x9")

Another Krista Willett find, adapted from *The Brownie Book*, and a Daily Bread favorite. In the late 90's, Nick Sansone decided to see how long he could keep them in the window without them selling out. He gave up trying. These are light in texture with a mild peanut buttery background for the fudgey chocolate swirls.

8"x8"	**9"x9"**
1/3 cup chocolate chips/ 2 ounces	1/2 cup/ 3 ounces
1 ounce unsweetened baker's chocolate	1 ounce/ 1 square
6 tablespoons soft butter/ 3/4 stick	1/4 pound/ 1 stick
1 cup plus 2 tablespoons white sugar	1 1/2 cups
1 teaspoon vanilla	1 1/4 teaspoons
2 eggs, one at a time	3 eggs
1 cup flour	1 1/4 cups
1/2 teaspoon baking powder	3/4 teaspoon
1 pinch salt	1 pinch
2 tablespoons half and half	2 tablespoons
1/2 cup peanut butter	2/3 cup

Preheat oven to 350 degrees. Grease and flour pan. Melt chocolate chips and baker's chocolate together over low heat. Set aside. Cream together butter, sugar and vanilla till light. Beat in eggs, one at a time, and then cream, beating well after each addition. Stir together flour, powder and salt. Fold into butter mixture until all well combined. Remove 1/3 of batter into a separate bowl. Stir melted chocolate into this and set aside. Stir peanut butter into the original 2/3 and blob this into your prepared pan. Blob chocolate mixture over the peanut butter layer. Draw through the batter with a table knife to create a marble effect (see illustration). Bake 25-30 minutes until a toothpick inserted 1 inch from the edge comes out clean.

Baker and cook Nick Sansone.

Peanut Butter Chocolate Chip Brownie (8"x8" and 9"x9")

I started baking these early in Daily Bread history, unsure of the exact origins. I enjoyed the tang provided by the touch of molasses. Peanut butter and chocolate are often seen together, so that is no surprise.

8"x8"	9"x9"
4 tablespoons soft butter/ 1/2 stick	6 tablespoons/ 3/4 stick
4 tablespoons soft margarine/ 1 stick	6 tablespoons/ 3/4 stick
1/4 cup packed brown sugar	1/3 cup
3 tablespoons barley malt	1/4 cup
2 tablespoons molasses	3 tablespoons
2 eggs, one at a time	3 eggs
1/2 teaspoon vanilla extract	3/4 teaspoon
3 tablespoons peanut butter	1/4 cup
1 cup flour	1 1/2 cups
1 teaspoon baking powder	1 1/3 teaspoon
1 pinch salt	1/8 teaspoon
3/4 cup chocolate chips	1 cup

Preheat oven to 350 degrees. Grease and flour pan. Cream together butter, margarine, brown sugar, barley malt and molasses till light and fluffy. Add eggs to the batter one at a time, beating well after each. Add vanilla and peanut butter and continue beating to blend. Stir together flour, baking powder, salt and chips. Fold flour mixture into butter mix till just combined. Spread into prepared pan. Bake 25-30 minutes until a toothpick inserted 1 inch from the edge comes out clean.

Milk Chocolate Cherry Brownie (8"x8" and 9"x9")

These came about through serendipity. I picked up the wrong bag of chips from the food coop; they were sweet milk chocolate. I wanted brownies at home, so used them anyway. I had some dried cherries. The resulting brownies were delicious, sweeter than most, with a chewy rich back ground of cherry. We made them for customers, and they liked them too! The recipe is loosely based on "Rosie's Award Winning" from a cookbook put out by Rosie's chocolate shop in the Boston area.

8"X8"	**9"X9"**
7 tablespoons butter	1/4 pound plus 2 tablespoons
1/2 cup milk chocolate chips/ 3 1/2 ounces	2/3 cup/ 4 1/2 ounces
3/4 cup plus 1 tablespoon packed brown sugar	1 cup, packed
1/8 teaspoon almond extract	1/4 teaspoon
1/8 teaspoon vanilla extract	1/4 teaspoon
2 eggs, one at a time	3 eggs
3/4 cup plus 1 tablespoon flour	1 cup
1/2 cup chopped dried cherries (check for pits)	2/3 cup

Preheat oven to 325 degrees. Melt butter and chocolate chips in a small saucepan over low heat till chips just melt. Grease and flour your baking pan. Pour melted butter mix into a medium mixing bowl. Add sugar, almond extract and vanilla to butter and beat to a smooth consistency, a little lighter in color. Beat in eggs one at a time, beating well after each. Add flour and cherries all at once and stir only till combined; this will ensure a fudgey end result. Spread into your prepared pan. Bake 30-35 minutes.

From other sources:

Maida Heatter's Book of Chocolate Desserts   *Rosie's...*
Rich and Beautiful Brownies   Rosie's Award-winning Brownies
Chocolate Vienna Walnut Bars

Low Overhead: Chop Wood, Carry Water •

I would not have been able to run Daily Bread and the *Times Ink!* the way I did without having low home and business rents. I lucked into a little place in Hinesburg in 1980, a tenant house built in 1820 on 30 acres of mostly perpendicular hillside. The owners were in the diplomatic service, had spent their boyhood summers there and held onto the place for sentimental reasons. I only had running cold water until 1989, the highest profit year at Daily Bread. I got hot water and a bathtub that year. Even so, the shallow well ran dry for three to five months every summer and fall. My motto was: have towels, will travel. Many people, especially Irene Horbar, were generous with their showers and water. I kept the outhouse, a composting set up using 55 gallon barrels and lots of wood chips.

I had to pay the next higher tax bracket in 1989, and decided to keep the profit down by sharing more with the employees. It felt better to share with employees and local organizations than to send it to the government, whose spending choices I seriously questioned. I was able to do that because I did not have a mortgage or car payment or health insurance premium to pay every month. Mind you, our pay was still low; this culture does not value food preparation very highly.

I heated primarily with wood. I had up to 1/4 acre of vegetables under cultivation, space I shared with friends who needed a little extra room. We served the produce at the bakery. I kept laying hens, whose eggs we sold to bakery customers. We collected compost for the chickens and for the garden. The chickens made the compost into fertilizer, which grew more vegetables. The circle went around and around.

When I gave up the chickens due to an influx of rodents, compost went to Heidi Racht's chickens and sheep.

Rent at the Old Shirt Factory was also low by Chittenden County commercial standards. When I sold in 2000, I was paying $1,000/month for 2,700 square feet plus storage space in the cellar. The furnace was an ancient coal-fired beast which had been converted to oil, and the building had ostensibly no insulation, so heat was expensive in cold years. It was still less expensive than most other commercial options, especially with an adjoining municipal parking lot.

Leisure is what we are supposedly trying to purchase with automation and higher paying jobs. There is also the other option of lowering your cash needs so you have more of your own time to take care of your own needs and to consider how best to use what resources you have.

Blondies

Congo Bars (8"x8" and 9"x9")

This version of a blonde brownie with chocolate chips came from Krista's Cowles relatives, "a family tradition." Andrew Paschetto added the apple juice and altered them slightly in other proportions to improve their shelf life. I don't think they will hang around long enough to be a concern.

8"x8"	**9"x9"**
6 tablespoons soft butter/ 3/4 stick	1/4 pound/ 1 stick
1 cup packed brown sugar	1 1/4 cups
2 eggs, one at a time	3 eggs
3 tablespoons apple cider or juice	3 1/2 tablespoons
1 1/3 cups flour	1 2/3 cups
1 teaspoon baking powder	1 1/2 teaspoons
1 pinch salt	1/8 teaspoon
1/2 cup chocolate chips/ 3 ounces	2/3 cup/ 4 ounces
1/2 cup coarsely chopped walnuts	2/3 cup

Preheat oven to 350 degrees. Grease and flour baking pan. Melt together butter and brown sugar in a small saucepan over low heat. Remove from heat, transfer to a medium mixing bowl and cool to just warm. Beat in eggs, one at a time, and then apple juice, beating well after each addition. Stir together flour, baking powder and salt. Fold flour mix into batter, stirring just enough to incorporate. Fold in chips and walnuts. Spread into prepared pan. Bake 30-35 minutes until top is crusty and a toothpick inserted 1 inch from the edge comes out clean.

Mandarin Orange Brownies (8"x8" and 9"x9")

The Brownie Book provided inspiration for this brownie-with-a-difference. Andrew Paschetto and Krista Willett tweaked the recipe before arriving at the following variation. They are slightly crumbly, and chock full of orange and chocolate flavors with a surprise visit from almonds.

8"x8"
1/4 pound soft butter/ 1 stick
1/2 cup white sugar
1/3 cup plus 1 tablespoon brown sugar
1 teaspoon vanilla
4 teaspoons grated orange zest
2 2/3 tablespoons orange juice
2 eggs, one at a time
1 cup plus 2 tablespoons flour
1 teaspoon baking powder
1/2 cup coarsely chopped almonds
2/3 chocolate chips/ 4 ounces

9"x9"
1/4 pound plus 4 tablespoons/ 1 1/2 sticks
2/3 cup
1/2 cup
1 1/4 teaspoon
1 1/3 tablespoons
3 1/3 tablespoons
2 eggs
1 1/4 cups
1 1/4 teaspoons
2/3 cup
3/4 cup/ 5 ounces

Preheat oven to 350 degrees. Grease and flour baking pan. Cream together butter, white and brown sugars till light. Add vanilla, zest and juice to batter. Beat in eggs, one at a time, beating well after each. Stir together flour and baking powder. Fold into butter mixture to blend. Fold in chips and almonds. Spread into prepared pan. Bake 35 minutes at 350 degrees until the top is light brown and a toothpick inserted 1 inch from the edge comes out clean.

Blondies (8"x8" and 9"x9")

Baker Jean Palmer brought Daily Bread this recipe. Among blonde brownie fanciers, these win hands down. They are incredibly rich with butter, butterscotch-reminiscent with brown sugar and full of walnuts. What could be finer? Do not overbake.

1/2 pound butter, soft/ 2 sticks
1 1/3 cups packed brown sugar
1 teaspoon vanilla
2 eggs, one at a time
1 1/2 cups flour
1/2 teaspoon baking powder
1 2/3 cups coarsely chopped walnuts

1/2 pound plus 4 tablespoons/ 2 1/2 sticks
1 2/3 cups
1 1/4 teaspoons
3 eggs
2 cups minus 1 tablespoon
2/3 teaspoon
2 cups

Preheat oven to 350 degrees. Grease and flour baking pan. Cream together butter, brown sugar and vanilla till light and fluffy. Beat in eggs, one at a time, mixing well after each addition. Stir together flour and powder. Fold into butter mixture just enough to incorporate all ingredients into batter. Fold in walnuts. Spread into prepared pan. Bake 30 minutes at 350 degrees till a toothpick inserted 1 inch from the edge comes out clean. Top should look a little crackle-y.

Cheesecake Bars

When you have a yen for cheesecake, but don't have all the time or ingredients to go the whole route, these are delicious and satisfying. They make a showy dessert or welcome offering to a potluck or bake sale. The original idea for these came through baker Alison Forrest and local hand-spinner Jamie Harmon (who also cleaned the bakery for at least 16 years) from the *Tassajara Bread Book*. We substituted maple syrup in the crust and then substituted Krista Willett's lighter and taller filling.

Cheesecake Bars (8"x8" and 9"x9")

These are the basic variety, lemony and delicious.

8"x8"	9"x9"
Crust:	
2/3 cup whole wheat pastry flour	3/4 cup plus 1 tablespoon
4 tablespoons melted butter/ 1/2 stick	6 tablespoons/ 3/4 stick
3 tablespoons maple syrup	1/4 cup
Filling:	
8 ounces cream cheese/ 1 8-ounce package	10 ounces/ 1 1/4 packages
1 1/3 tablespoons soft butter	1 2/3 tablespoons
2/3 cup sour cream	1 cup
1/4 cup honey	1/3 cup
1 egg	2 eggs, one at a time
1 teaspoon grated lemon zest	1 1/4 teaspoons
1 teaspoon vanilla	1 1/4 teaspoons

Preheat oven to 350 degrees. Prepare crust. Melt butter in a small saucepan. Remove from heat. Add flour and syrup and stir to combine with a fork. Press into your baking pan. Wax paper or plastic wrap works well to distribute the crust evenly without getting your hands sticky. Bake crust 12-15 minutes until aromatic and just beginning to dry out.

Prepare filling. Whip cream cheese and butter till light and fluffy. This is easier with an electric mixer, but plenty of elbow grease and a heavy spoon or wire whip will do the same. Take time to scrape down the sides to work away any lumps. Add sour cream, honey, egg/s (one at a time for 9"x9"), zest and vanilla, continuing to beat to make a very smooth creamy texture. Pour over baked crust; it is all right if the crust is hot. Smooth out filling to distribute evenly. Bake 30-35 minutes until filling is just set. The top will not be brown and will be just a little wiggly. Cool and refrigerate before cutting.

Chocolate Cheesecake Bars (8"x8" and 9"x9")

There are many people who prefer anything chocolate! We played with the above cheesecake bar recipe to come up with this one that we liked.

8"x8"	**9"x9"**
Crust:	
2/3 cup whole wheat pastry flour	3/4 cup plus 1 tablespoon
4 tablespoons melted butter/ 1/2 stick	6 tablespoons/ 3/4 stick
3 tablespoons maple syrup	1/4 cup
Filling:	
1 8-ounce package cream cheese	1 1/4 8-ounce packages cream cheese
3 tablespoons soft butter	4 tablespoons/ 1/2 stick
1/4 cup honey	1/3 cup
1 tablespoon maple syrup	1 1/2 tablespoons
1 egg	2 eggs, one at a time
2/3 cup sour cream	1 cup
3 tablespoons unsweetened cocoa	1/4 cup
1 drop almond extract	1/8 teaspoon
2/3 teaspoon vanilla extract	1 teaspoon

Preheat oven to 350 degrees. Prepare crust. Melt butter in a small sauce pan. Remove from heat. Stir flour and maple syrup into the melted butter. Toss lightly with a fork to combine. Press into your baking pan, using wax paper or plastic wrap to smooth out the crust. Bake crust 12-15 minutes until aromatic and just beginning to brown.

Prepare filling. Whip cream cheese and butter till light and fluffy. An electric mixer makes this easier. Scrape down the sides of the bowl to work away any lumps. Add honey, syrup, egg/s (one at a time) and sour cream. Continue to beat till very smooth and velvety. Add cocoa, almond and vanilla extracts and beat till incorporated. Pour filling over the pre-baked crust. Smooth filling evenly with a spoon or rubber spatula. Bake another 30-35 minutes until just set. The center may still wiggle a little. Cool and refrigerate before cutting.

Marbled Cheesecake Bars

(8"x8" and 9"x9")

Here we have the best of both worlds. These are creamy and full of flavor. Impress family and friends with these showy bars. Andrew Paschetto contributed this recipe, origin unknown. He notes:

The chocolate mix has to have the same consistency as the blonde filling or it will crack and taste dry. The ratio of blonde to chocolate should be about 2 to 1. Bake this slower than usual, 325 degrees, to keep the filling tender.

8"x8"

Crust:
4 tablespoons melted butter/ 1/2 stick
2/3 cup whole wheat pastry flour
3 tablespoons maple syrup

Filling:
10 ounces cream cheese/ 1 1/4 packages
1 1/3 tablespoons soft butter
1/4 cup honey
1 egg
1/3 cup sour cream
1 teaspoon vanilla extract

For chocolate:
1/3 cup unsweetened cocoa
1 egg
1/3 cup maple syrup
1/2 tablespoon sour cream

9"x9"

6 tablespoons/ 3/4 stick
3/4 cup plus 1 tablespoon
1/4 cup

14 ounces/ 1 3/4 8-ounce packages
1 2/3 tablespoons
1/3 cup
1 egg
1/2 cup
1 teaspoon

1/3 cup plus 1 tablespoon
1 egg
1/3 cup plus 1 tablespoon
1 tablespoon

Preheat oven to 350 degrees. Prepare crust. Melt butter in a small saucepan. Remove from heat and stir in flour and maple syrup till just combined. Press crust into pan using wax paper or plastic wrap to press evenly into all corners. Bake 12-15 minutes at 350 degrees.

Prepare filling. Beat cream cheese and butter till fluffy. An electric mixer makes this easier. Scrape down the bowl to avoid lumps. Beat honey, first egg, sour cream and vanilla into the cream cheese mixture till smooth and velvety. Turn oven down to 325 degrees. Pour 2/3 of this mixture onto the prepared crust. Add cocoa, second egg, syrup and sour cream to the remaining 1/3, and beat to fully incorporate. Blob the chocolate mixture over the vanilla. Use a table knife to draw lightly through the filling to create a marble effect (see illustration on page 173). Bake 40 minutes till filling is just set. The top should not really brown, but begin to appear dry. The center may still feel a little mushy. Cool and refrigerate before cutting.

Richmond in Business

In 1987, there were seventy-five businesses in Richmond, many occupying space in the village center. The Old Shirt Factory, which housed Daily Bread, was just one of many incubator spaces providing affordable space to small businesses. Some people had outgrown space at home. Others enjoyed the convenience of the village and accessiblity to Interstate 89. Wilson Ring wrote in a 1987 *Vermont Times* article:

> The numerous ... businesses tucked away in the village have bolstered the local tax base, provided jobs for residents and allowed enterprising Richmondites to keep their work close to home. (39)

The businesses covered a wide range, including a computer software firm, a pharmacy, law offices, a deli, a bank, magazine publishers and the bakery.

Fruit Bars

Original Johnny Bars (8"x8" and 9"x9")

I visited my brother Robert in his Old Chelsea, Quebec home in the summer of 1971 with my then husband Dan and a few New York City friends. Robert took us to spend a few days with his friends Douf and Rachel up north, who were living on an abandoned farmstead. They had a large garden full of late summer bounty. The old apple trees produced lots of tasty fruit. They had a primitive set up (screens, cheesecloth and cardboard served as windows) with an outhouse and wood cook stove. I felt I had arrived at a long lost "home."

Rachel baked a luscious dessert from freshly ground flour, farm apples and moist Turbinado sugar. She called them Johnny Apple Seed Bars.

8"x8"	9"x9"
2 1/2 cups pared and sliced apples/ 3	3 cups/ 3-4 apples
1 cup flour	1 1/4 cups
1 1/3 cups regular rolled oats	1 2/3 cups
1 cup packed brown sugar	1 1/4 cups
3 tablespoons wheat bran	1/4 cup
1 pinch salt	1/8 teaspoon
1/2 teaspoon baking soda	2/3 teaspoon
1/3 teaspoon cinnamon	1/2 teaspoon
2 eggs	2 eggs
2/3 cup oil, sunflower or other light	3/4 cup

Preheat oven to 350 degrees. Prepare apples. Set aside. Grease and flour baking pan. Stir together flour, oats, sugar, bran, salt, soda and cinnamon in small mixing bowl. Beat eggs and oil in a separate bowl. Pour egg mixture over the flour mixture and toss lightly with a fork to moisten. Press 2/3 of this into the prepared pan. Arrange sliced apples over crust, and then crumble remaining 1/3 over the apples. Bake 30-35 minutes degrees until lightly browned. These are wonderful hot out of the oven!

Vegan Johnny Bars (8"x8" and 9"x9")

Judy Bush and Andrew Paschetto played with the above recipe over the years and arrived at this no-egg, naturally sweetened alternative.

8"x8"	9"x9"
1 1/2 cups coarsely chopped dates or apricots	2 cups
1 cup hot water for soaking	1 cup
1 cup flour	1 1/4 cups
1 1/3 cups regular rolled oats	1 2/3 cups
3 tablespoons bran	1/4 cup
1 pinch salt	1/8 teaspoon
1/2 teaspoon baking soda	2/3 teaspoon
1/3 teaspoon cinnamon	1/2 teaspoon

1 ounce tofu	1 1/2 ounces
1/3 cup apple juice or cider	1/2 cup
1/3 cup oil	1/2 cup
1/3 cup honey or maple syrup	1/2 cup

Preheat oven to 350 degrees. Chop dates or apricots and pour hot water over them in a small bowl to plump. You may puree the soaked fruit, though this is not necessary. Grease and flour your baking pan. Combine flour, oats, bran, salt, soda and cinnamon in a mixing bowl. Cream tofu in a blender or food processor with some of the apple juice/ cider. Beat the creamed tofu with the rest of the juice, oil and honey or syrup. Pour over the flour mixture and toss with a fork till moistened. It may be sticky. Press 2/3 of this mixture into your pan. Spread the prepared fruit over the crust. Crumble or drop remaining 1/3 of the batter over the fruit. Bake 30 minutes until top lightly browned.

Nutty Applesauce Bars-Vegan (8"x8" and 9"x9")

The basic recipe and the concept originated in Frances Moore Lappe's *Diet for a Small Planet*. They are vegan, though the term had not been invented yet. They are good, sweet snacks that stick to your ribs. The proteins from wheat, soy and peanuts combine to pack a good wallop of nutrition. Don't let that turn you away; they taste good too. They remind me of the apples and peanut butter my Mom served us for an after school snack.

8"x8"	**9"x9"**
1/2 cup honey	2/3 cup
1/4 cup oil, sunflower or other light variety	1/3 cup
1/3 cup peanut butter	1/2 cup
2/3 cup applesauce	1 cup
1 cup flour	1 1/4 cups
1/4 cup soy flour, toasted preferably	1/3 cup
2/3 teaspoon baking soda	1 teaspoon
1/8 teaspoon salt	1/8 teaspoon
1/3 teaspoon cinnamon	1/2 teaspoon
1/3 teaspoon ground ginger	1/2 teaspoon
2/3 cup raisins, dates or nuts	1 cup

Preheat oven to 350 degrees. Grease and flour baking pan. Beat together honey, oil, peanut butter and applesauce in a mixing bowl until smooth. You can use either an electric mixer or a heavy wire whisk. Stir flours, soda, salt, cinnamon and ginger in a separate bowl. Stir flour mixture into applesauce mix, beating 25-30 strokes. Fold in raisins, dates or nuts. Spread into prepared pan and bake 30 minutes until the center springs back to the touch or a toothpick comes out clean.

Nutty Banana Bars-Vegan (8"x8" and 9"x9")

This is a slight variation of the above, adapted for bananas.

8"X8"	9"X9"
3/4 cups plus 1 tablespoon mashed ripe banana/2 bananas	1 cup/ 2 1/2 to 3
1/2 cup honey	2/3 cup
1/3 cup peanut butter or sesame tahini	1/2 cup
1/4 cup oil, sunflower or other light variety	1/3 cup
3/4 cup plus 1 tablespoon flour	1 cup
1/4 cup soy flour, preferably toasted	1/3 cup
2/3 teaspoon baking soda	1 teaspoon
1/3 teaspoon salt	1/3 teaspoon
1/3 teaspoon nutmeg	1/2 teaspoon
1/3 teaspoon ground ginger	1/2 teaspoon
1/3 cup raisins, dates or nuts	1/2 cup

Preheat oven to 350 degrees. Grease and flour baking pan. Beat together mashed banana, honey, peanut butter or tahini and oil in a small mixing bowl. Stir together flours, soda, salt, nutmeg and ginger in a separate bowl. Stir flour mixture into the banana mix, beating well 25-30 strokes. Fold in raisins, dates or nuts. Spread into your prepared pan. Bake 30 minutes until the center springs back to the touch or a toothpick comes out clean.

Hermits-Vegan (8"x8" and 9"x9")

Local artist and bakery grandmother Marcia Rhodes asked for these. Andrew Paschetto took the best from Ken Haedrich's *Maple Syrup Baking and Dessert Cook Book* version and the *Joy of Cooking*'s to arrive at these. They are rich, sweet and fruity, with all the old-fashioned goodness I remember from the Hermits of my childhood. Andrew cautions against heavy-handing the spices.

Marcia at her mid-life celebration.

8"X8"	9"X9"
4 tablespoons margarine/ 1/2 stick	5 tablespoons
1/2 cup plus 1 tablespoon honey or rice syrup	3/4 cup
2 teaspoons molasses	1 tablespoon
1 1/2 tablespoons apple juice or cider	1 2/3 tablespoons
3/4 cups coarsely chopped walnuts or pecans	1 cup
1 cup chopped raisins	1 1/4 cup
1/2 cup plus 1 tablespoon whole wheat bread flour	3/4 cup
2/3 cup whole wheat pastry flour	3/4 cup

1/2 teaspoon baking soda	2/3 teaspoon
3/4 teaspoon cinnamon	1 teaspoon
1/3 teaspoon ground cloves	1/2 teaspoon
1/3 teaspoon nutmeg	1/2 teaspoon
1 pinch salt	1/8 teaspoon

Preheat oven to 325 degrees. Grease and flour baking pan. Cream together margarine, honey and molasses till light and fluffy. Add apple juice and continue beating to incorporate. Add raisins and nuts and beat enough to distribute throughout the batter. Stir together flours, soda, cinnamon, cloves, nutmeg and salt. Fold flour mixture into margarine mixture with a rubber spatula or large spoon to just combine all ingredients. Spread evenly into your prepared pan. Bake 25-30 minutes until the top begins to brown. These are supposed to be chewy. They usually fall some after they come out of the oven, and that is OK.

Blueberry Crumble Bars (8"x8" and 9"x9")

The original recipe which inspired these came from a little gem of a cookbook called *Super Natural Desserts*, a gift to the bakery from customer Karen Alpert. That book called it Crumble Berry Pie. Some of the crumb crust is reserved to be sprinkled over the sour cream and berry filling. These are creamy and mapley, almost a custard, with lots of berry goodness. Raspberries work beautifully too.

8"x8"	**9"x9"**
Crust and crumbs:	
1/4 pound cold butter/ 1 stick	1/4 pound plus 2 tablespoons
2 cups whole wheat pastry flour	2 1/3 cups
1/4 cup maple syrup	1/3 cup
Filling:	
1 cup sour cream	1 1/4 cups
1/2 cup maple syrup	2/3 cup
1 egg	2 eggs
2/3 teaspoon vanilla extract	3/4 teaspoon
2/3 teaspoon cinnamon	3/4 teaspoon
1 pinch ground mace	1/8 teaspoon
1 1/3 cups blueberries or raspberries	1 2/3 cups

Preheat oven to 350 degrees. Prepare crust. Cut or rub butter into flour with pastry blender or hands to make a coarse crumb. Pour maple syrup over crumbs and toss with a fork to moisten. Put aside 1/3-1/2. Press the rest into your baking pan.

Prepare filling. Combine sour cream, syrup, egg/s, vanilla, cinnamon and mace in mixing bowl and beat till very smooth and creamy. Stir in berries just enough to evenly distribute, or berries will "bleed" into the filling and turn it a less appetizing gray color. Pour filling over the crust, distributing it evenly. Sprinkle the reserved 1/3-1/2 crumbs on top. Bake 45-50 minutes until the center is springy to the touch and crumbs are lightly browned. Cool before cutting.

Apple Cheddar Bars (8"x8" and 9"x9")

Besides teaching blind campers to ski, teaching elementary school in Marshfield, selling Carvel and waitressing at Howard Johnson's, Krista Willett worked for the Dairy Council of Vermont. This recipe is one she prepared for them, originally as a tart, with apples "artfully arranged" over top with the cheddar under the apples. We found it worked better for us to bake the apples in the middle. These are apple pie with a slice of cheddar all together in one bar! These had many fans.

8"x8"	9"x9"
Crust:	
1/4 pound cold butter/ 1 stick	1/4 pound plus 2 tablespoons/ 1 1/4 sticks
1/4 cup sugar	1/3 cup
1 cup flour	1 1/4 cups
1/8 teaspoon vanilla	1/4 teaspoon
Middle:	
2 1/2 cups pared and diced apples /3 + apples	3 1/3 cups /4+ apples
Topping:	
1 1/4 cups grated sharp cheddar/ 5 ounces	3/4 cups/ 7 ounces
1 3/4 tablespoons sugar	2 1/4 tablespoons
1 egg	1 egg
1/3 teaspoon vanilla extract	1/2 teaspoons vanilla
2 tablespoons finely chopped walnuts	2 1/2 tablespoons
Syrup:	
1/3 cup honey	1/2 cup
1/3 teaspoon cinnamon	1/2 teaspoon

Preheat oven to 400 degrees. Prepare crust. Stir together sugar and flour. Cut butter into this with a pastry blender or your hands to make a coarse crumb. Drizzle vanilla over crumbs. Press this mixture into your baking pan and chill while assembling the rest.

Prepare apples. Layer them on top of chilled crust. Stir together cheddar, sugar, egg, vanilla and nuts to just combine. Spread evenly over apples. Heat honey and cinnamon to liquefy and pour over the top. Bake 10 minutes. Reduce heat to 350 and continue to bake another 25-30 minutes until top is lightly brown, apples are bubbling and you can't wait any longer.

Fruit Crunch--Vegan (8"x8" and 9"x9")

Andrew Paschetto encountered the original at Anne Marie Colbin's Natural Gourmet Cookery School in New York City. Heather Ward popularized it. It is a maple sweetened fruit filling between two layers of almost granola. It helps to bake the "crunch" in two pans to keep it crunchy. Eat these up, as the moisture from the filling will turn them soggy.

8"x8"	**9"x9"**
Crust:	
2 cups rolled oats	2 1/2 cups
2/3 cup whole wheat pastry flour	3/4 cup
2/3 cup chopped almonds	3/4 cup
1/4 teaspoon salt	1/3 teaspoon
1/3 cup oil, sunflower or other light oil	1/2 cup
1/4 cup maple syrup	1/3 cup
Filling:	
1 2/3-2 cups berries or diced fruit	2-2 1/2 cups
1/4 cup maple syrup	1/3 cup
1 2/3 tablespoon cornstarch	2 tablespoons
3/4 cup cold water	1 cup less 1 tablespoon

Preheat oven to 350 degrees. Have two pans of equal size. Prepare crust. Stir together oats, flour, almonds and salt in mixing bowl. Stir together oil and syrup in a separate bowl. Pour over dry ingredients and toss lightly with a fork to combine. Spread 1/2 the mixture into each pan. Bake 20 minutes or till the mixture has dried out but not scorched.

Meanwhile, mix fruit, syrup and 1/2 the water in a saucepan till mixture boils. Stir frequently. Mix cornstarch with other 1/2 of water and add to the boiling fruit. Continue to stir until mixture thickens, about 5 minutes. Pour hot fruit mixture over one crust. Crumble the second crust over the top of the fruit. Cool and cut.

Lemon Bars (8"x8" and 9"x9")

This is a honey-sweetened version of the classic pastry often served with English tea: a sweet crust with a sweet and tart lemon curd type topping. This recipe went through many versions at Daily Bread. I believe this particular one can be attributed to Jean Palmer.

8"x8"	**9"x9"**
Crust:	
1/4 pound plus 2 tablespoons butter/1 1/4 sticks	1/4 pound plus 6 tablespoons
1/3 cup powdered sugar	1/3 cup plus 1 tablespoon
1 1/3 cups unbleached or allpurpose flour	1 2/3 cups
Filling:	
3 eggs	4 eggs
1/3 cup lemon juice/ 2 juicy lemons	1/3 cup plus 1 tablespoon/ 2-3 lemons
1 1/3 teaspoon grated lemon zest	1 2/3 teaspoons
1/2 cup honey	2/3 cup honey
1 1/3 tablespoons flour	1 2/3 tablespoons
1 pinch baking powder	1 pinch
1 pinch salt	1 pinch

Preheat oven to 350 degrees. Prepare crust. Cream together butter and powdered sugar till light. Stir flour into creamed mixture. Press into pan and bake 15-20 minutes till just beginning to brown.

Prepare filling. Whisk together eggs, lemon juice, zest and honey in the top of a double boiler. Stir together flour, baking powder and salt. Whisk flour mixture into egg mixture to make a smooth consistency. Heat mixture over hot water, whisking all the while to avoid lumps until mixture thickens. Pour hot custard over baked crust. Return to the oven and bake 6-8 minutes until filling just begins to set. Do not over-bake or it will dry out.

Cranberry Pecan Bars (8"x8" and 9"x9")

Colleagues from the Vermont Womens Health Center got together every few years for potluck dinner and conversation. Janet Young brought these to one, and I thought they were delicious and different. I especially liked the juxtaposition of sweet and tart.

8"x8"	9"x9"
Crust:	
1/2 cup plus 1 tablespoon flour	3/4 cup
1 tablespoon white sugar	1 1/3 tablespoons
2 tablespoons cold butter	3 1/2 tablespoons
2 tablespoons finely chopped pecans	3 1/2 tablespoons
Topping:	
3/4 cup white sugar	1 cup
1 tablespoon flour	1 1/4 tablespoons
1 egg	2 eggs
1 tablespoon milk	1 1/3 tablespoon
1/2 tablespoon grated orange zest	3/4 tablespoon
1/2 teaspoon vanilla	3/4 teaspoon
1/2 cup plus 1 tablespoon chopped cranberries	3/4 cup
1/4 cup coconut	1/3 cup
2 tablespoons finely chopped pecans	3 1/2 tablespoons

Preheat oven to 350 degrees. Prepare crust. Stir together flour, sugar and pecans in mixing bowl. Cut butter into flour mixture with a pastry blender or your hands to make a coarse crumb. Press into your pan and bake 12-15 minutes till crust just begins to brown.

Prepare topping. Stir together flour and sugar in a mixing bowl. Beat together egg/s, milk, zest and vanilla in a separate bowl or cup. Fold this into the flour mixture, scraping bowl to combine all. Fold berries, coconut and pecans into this mixture to combine. Spread on baked crust and return to the oven. Bake another 25 minutes. Note: we sometimes prepared this in a round pan and cut wedges; it is showy for a fancy occasion.

Betsy, Judy , Emma, Sue Burton, Sue Wiseheart, Janet and Berta at the Cafe.

From other Sources:
The Enchanted Broccoli Forest
Cashew Shortbread

Miscellaneous Other Bars

Rose's Brown Sugar Bars (8"x8" or 9"x9")
Rose Lovett brought in this recipe as a quick and easy treat. They are like a chocolate chip cookie in a bar, and customers loved them.

8"x8"	**9"x9"**
2/3 cup packed brown sugar	3/4 cup
1 egg	1 egg
1/3 cup oil, sunflower or other light oil	1/2 cup less 1 tablespoon
1/3 teaspoon vanilla extract	1/2 teaspoon
1 cup flour	1 1/4 cups
1/3 teaspoon salt	1/2 teaspoon
1/3 teaspoon baking soda	1/2 teaspoon
1/3 cup warm coffee	1/2 cup
2/3 cup chocolate chips	3/4 cup

Preheat oven to 350 degrees. Grease and flour baking pan. Mix brown sugar and egg in mixing bowl to combine. Add oil and vanilla and mix. Stir together flour, salt and soda in a separate bowl. Have warm, not hot, coffee ready. Alternately add flour, coffee, flour, coffee, flour to the brown sugar mixture. Spread into prepared pan. Sprinkle chips on top. Bake 25-30 minutes till toothpick inserted 1 inch from the edge comes out clean.

Caramelitas (8"x8" and 9"x9")
These are by far the richest, densest bar we made. Staff and customers loved them. Cindy Bramon worked in Burlington at the Gourmet Food Exchange for a while, and used this recipe there. When she returned to Daily Bread, she brought it with her. From the sound of the directions, you may not think it will turn out, but it really does work as written. Honey, half and half, chocolate chips, nuts, and rolled oats--all your basic food groups!

Crust:	
1/4 pound plus 4 tablespoons butter/ 1 1/2 sticks	1/2 pound / 2 sticks
1/3 cup honey	1/2 cup
1 cup flour	1 1/4 cups
1 cup rolled oats	1 1/4 cups

Caramel:	
2/3 cup honey	3/4 cup
2/3 cup half and half, 1/3 cup at a time	1 cup, 1/2 cup at a time

Sprinkle:

1 cup chocolate chips	1 1/4 cups
1/2 cups chopped walnuts or pecans	2/3 cup

Preheat oven to 350 degrees. Prepare crust. Beat together butter and honey till light. Fold flour and oats into creamed mixture till just combined. Set aside 1/3 for top. Press 2/3 into pan. Bake 15 minutes at 350 degrees.

Meanwhile, prepare caramel. Combine honey and half of the cream in a saucepan. Bring to a soft boil over medium heat. Pour in second half of cream and bring mixture to a second boil. Remove from heat; this will be liquidy. Sprinkle chocolate chips and nuts onto baked crust. Pour caramel over that. Blob the reserved one third of the crust over the whole thing. Bake 25-30 minutes. Cool and cut.

Almond Nirvana (8"x8" and 9"x9")

Always on the lookout for new recipes, I spied the original in Ken Haedrich's *Maple Syrup Baking and Dessert Cook Book.* These are full of almonds, rich with butter and cream and sweet with "all your sugar groups," as we used to joke to customers.

8"x8"	**9"x9"**
Crust:	
7 tablespoons soft butter	1/4 pound/ 1 stick
1/4 cup brown sugar	1/3 cup
1 egg	1 egg
1 cup flour	1 cup
1/3 cup almonds, ground to a fine meal	1/2 cup
Topping:	
3 tablespoons butter	4 tablespoons/ 1/2 stick
1/3 cup maple syrup	1/2 cup less 1 tablespoon
1/4 cup brown sugar	1/3 cup
1 3/4 tablespoons honey	2 1/4 tablespoons
1 3/4 tablespoons half and half	2 1/4 tablespoons
1 cup coarsely chopped almonds	1 1/4 cup
1/3 teaspoon vanilla extract	1/2 teaspoon

Preheat oven to 375 degrees. Prepare crust. Cream butter and brown sugar till light. Add egg and beat to combine. Fold in flour and almond meal to just moisten. Press into pan. Bake 15 minutes. Prepare topping. Combine butter, syrup, brown sugar and honey in a saucepan, and heat to boiling. Add half and half. Bring to a second boil and continue boiling 2 minutes. Remove from heat. Fold almonds and vanilla into the hot mixture. Spread over hot, baked crust. Return to oven and bake 20 minutes. Cool and cut.

Maple Pecan Bars (8"x8" and 9"x9")

These yummy items are like pecan pie in a bar. Betsy Field spied these at the annual Vermont Farm Show held in Barre every January. They were entered by Ann Clark of Graniteville. We altered them a little, but not much. Thank you, Ann Clark!

8"x8"	**9"x9"**
Crust:	
1/2 cup flour	2/3 cup
1/2 cup whole wheat pastry flour	2/3 cup
3 tablespoons brown sugar	3 tablespoons
5 tablespoons cold butter	7 tablespoons
1 1/3 cups coarsely chopped pecans	1 2/3 cups
Topping:	
1/3 cup brown sugar	1/3 cup plus 1 tablespoon
7 tablespoons maple syrup	1/2 cup
1 egg	2 eggs
1/3 teaspoon vanilla extract	1/2 teaspoon
1 tablespoon flour	1 2/3 tablespoons
1 pinch salt	1/8 teaspoon

Preheat oven to 350 degrees. Prepare crust. Stir together flours and brown sugar. Cut cold butter into mixture to make a coarse crumb. Press into your baking pan. Bake 12-15 minutes.

Prepare filling. Combine brown sugar and maple syrup in a small saucepan, and heat to boiling. Reduce heat and simmer 5 minutes. Cool to warm. Beat egg/s in a mixing bowl. Pour cooled syrup into eggs, whisking constantly till well combined. Stir vanilla, flour and salt into egg mixture. Sprinkle pecans on baked crust. Pour egg mixture over nuts and crust. Return to oven and bake 20-25 minutes.

Inspiration Bars (8"x8" and 9"x9")

These are another bakery favorite derived from an original in Ken Haedrich's *Maple Syrup Baking and Dessert Cook Book*. He called them "Killer Bars." We just couldn't bring ourselves to do so. This is another crusted bar topped with the inspiring mixture of nuts, dates, chocolate chips and coconut with a maple custard to hold it all together. These are guaranteed to satisfy even the most intense sweet tooth.

8"x8"	**9"x9"**
Crust:	
1 1/3 cups whole wheat pastry flour	1 2/3 cups
5 tablespoon melted butter	7 tablespoons
2 1/2 tablespoons maple syrup	3 1/2 tablespoons

Custard:

1 egg	2 eggs
1/2 cup maple syrup	2/3 cup
2/3 teaspoon vanilla	1 teaspoon
1 3/4 tablespoons flour	2 1/4 tablespoons
1/4 teaspoon baking powder	1/3 teaspoon

Topping:

1/2 cup chopped nuts	2/3 cup
1/2 cup pitted dates, chopped	2/3 cup
1/2 cup chocolate chips	2/3 cup
1/3 cup coconut	1/2 cup

Preheat oven to 350 degrees. Prepare crust. Pour melted butter and maple syrup over flour, tossing lightly with a fork to moisten. Press into your pan. Bake 12 minutes.

Prepare custard. Combine egg/s, syrup and vanilla in mixing bowl. Beat together till light and foamy. Sprinkle flour and baking powder onto egg mixture and beat to thoroughly mix. Stir together nuts, dates, chips and coconut and spread evenly on top of baked crust. Pour custard over the whole thing. Return to the oven and bake 25-30 minutes until topping is just set.

Turkish Coffee Bars (8"x8" and 9"x9")

This recipe originated in the *Tassajara Bread Book,* and underwent some changes to suit our tastes and portions. Coffee and chocolate make another appearance with the added interest of walnuts, cinnamon, nutmeg and a hint of coriander (the Turkish touch). These are sweet and surprisingly light.

8"x8"	**9"x9"**
6 tablespoons butter, cold/ 3/4 stick	1/4 pound plus 2 tablespoons/ 1 1/4 stick
2/3 cup packed brown sugar	1 cup
1 1/4 cups whole wheat pastry flour	1 3/4 cups
2/3 tablespoon espresso powder	1 tablespoon
1 teaspoon cinnamon	1 1/2 teaspoons
1/3 teaspoon nutmeg	1/2 teaspoon
1/8 teaspoon ground coriander	1/4 teaspoon
1/3 cup chocolate chips	1/2 cup
3/4 cup sour cream	1 cup
1/2 teaspoon baking soda	3/4 teaspoon
1 egg	1 egg
1/3 cup chopped walnuts	1/2 cup

Preheat oven to 350 degrees. Grease and flour baking pan. Stir together brown sugar, flour, espresso, cinnamon, nutmeg and coriander in mixing bowl. Cut or rub butter into this mixture with a pastry blender or your hands to make a coarse crumb. Take 1 cup (8x8) or 1 1/2 cups (9x9) of this mixture and press it into your prepared pan. Sprinkle chocolate chips on top.

Add the sour cream, soda, egg and walnuts to the remaining crumb mixture. Beat to combine well. Spread over crust and chips, being careful not to pull crust off the bottom of the pan. Bake 25-30 minutes until the center springs back to the touch.

Honey Gingerbread Bars (8"x8" and 9"x9")

This is a moist and rich version of classic gingerbread. I found the recipe somewhere in the early days of Daily Bread, but have no idea now where that was. Numerous bakers have left their mark, altering the recipe or varying the topping. Cream cheese icing is nice (see p. 79). Or add extra grated fresh or candied ginger. Plain or fancy, these are full of ginger flavor.

8"x8"	9"x9"
4 tablespoons butter, soft/ 1/2 stick	6 tablespoons / 3/4 stick
3 tablespoons molasses	3 1/2 tablespoons
1/3 cup honey	1/2 cup
1 egg	2 eggs
2/3 cup flour	3/4 cup
1 cup whole wheat pastry flour	1 1/4 cups
1/2 teaspoon baking soda	2/3 teaspoon
1/2 teaspoon baking powder	2/3 teaspoon
1 pinch salt	1/8 teaspoon
1/2 teaspoon ground ginger	2/3 teaspoon
1 teaspoon cinnamon	1 1/2 teaspoons
2/3 cup yogurt	3/4 cup
1/2 cup raisins or crystalized ginger	2/3 cup
Honey Cream Cheese Frosting, optional (see page 79)	

Preheat oven to 350 degrees. Grease and flour baking pan. Combine butter, molasses and honey in mixing bowl. Cream together till fluffy. Add egg/s and continue to beat till light. Stir together flours, soda, baking powder, salt, ginger and cinnamon. Alternately add flour, yogurt, flour, yogurt, flour to the creamed butter, stirring well after each addition. Fold in choice of raisins, additional ginger or nuts. Spread evenly into your prepared pan. Bake 30-35 minutes until center just springs back to the touch.

Cool and frost as desired.

Poppy Seed Bars (8"x8" and 9"x9")

This is the same basic recipe as Judy Bush's mother's Poppy Seed Pound cake on page 98. We found that people preferred the bar form in the 1990s. Go figure!

8"x8"	9"x9"
1/3 cup yogurt	1/2 cup
1/4 cup poppy seeds	1/3 cup

7 tablespoons soft butter	1/4 pound/ 1 stick
1/3 cup plus 1 tablespoon honey	1/2 cup
2 eggs, one at a time	2 eggs
1/3 teaspoon vanilla	1/3 teaspoon
1 cup plus 1 tablespoon flour	1 1/3 cups
3/4 teaspoon baking powder	1 teaspoon
1 pinch baking soda	1/8 teaspoon
1 pinch salt	1/8 teaspoon

Glaze:

2 1/2 tablespoon lemon juice	3 tablespoons
2 1/2 tablespoons honey	3 tablespoons

Mix yogurt and poppy seeds and let rest 1 hour or overnight. Preheat oven to 350 degrees. Grease and flour baking pan. Cream butter and honey till light and fluffy. Add eggs, one at a time and beat well after each. Stir in vanilla. Alternately add flour, yogurt mixture, flour, yogurt, flour to creamed butter, beating well after each addition. Spread into prepared pan. Bake 25-30 minutes till center gently springs back to the touch. Heat honey and lemon juice and brush on hot bars.

Maple Macaroons--Vegan and Wheat-free (6 and 12)

This delightful variation on a theme, vegan and wheat-free, came through the kitchen of Origanum Natural Foods, a long time purveyor of good food in the Burlington area. I finally got the nerve up to request the recipe to make for a special Jamaican dinner. They were a hit (so was the dinner!). They are very simple to prepare. Portioned out with an ice cream scoop, they are beautiful golden mounds of sweet, nutty goodness.

6	**12**
2 1/3 cups coconut	4 1/2 cups
1/2 cup chopped almonds	1 cup
1/3 cup barley flour	3/4 cup
1/3 teaspoon salt	1/2 teaspoon
3/4 cup maple syrup	1 1/2 cups
1 teaspoon almond extract	2 1/4 teaspoons

Preheat oven to 350 degrees. Grease and flour baking sheet or line with parchment paper or flattened paper muffin cups. Stir together coconut, almonds, barley flour and salt in a mixing bowl. Stir almond extract into maple syrup and pour over coconut mixture. Stir to just moisten. It is a little crumbly at this stage. Use an ice cream scoop or 1/3 cup measure to portion out onto prepared pan. Bake 20 minutes or till light brown.

Back Country Bars (12 3-ounce patties)

Granola bars started to appear on health food store shelves in the early 1980s, and it seemed we could fashion one of our own. These have their fans and their detractors. They are definitely high energy food, great for hikes, skiing and camping. We always cautioned customers to keep them close to their bodies in the cold weather. They do become quite brittle, and we didn't want anyone to break a tooth on one of our products. No one else claims the credit for these. I think I must have worked out the original mix. We called them Granola Chews at first, but Back Country Bar and its accompanying logo, designed by the young Ben Bush, sounded and looked much more appetizing.

1 pound maple cashew granola (see page 100)/ about 4 cups
1 cup tahini or peanut butter
1 cup barley malt
1 cup carob or chocolate chips

Melt barley malt and tahini together over low heat in a saucepan, watching and stirring to prevent scorching until the mixture is smooth and hot, but not boiling. Stir together granola and chips in a mixing bowl. Pour hot mixture over granola mixture and stir or work with your hands to thoroughly combine. We portioned them out with an ice cream scoop and wrapped them individually. You may shape any way you like. Cool and eat.

Italian Shortbread (15 pieces)

Either Andrew Paschetto or Heidi Racht brought in this biscotti-like recipe. These are more like shortbread than biscotti: slightly crumbly, rich with butter, sweet with sugar and a light touch of anise.

1/4 pound butter at room temperature/ 1 stick
1/2 cup white sugar
2 eggs
1/2 teaspoon vanilla
2 1/4 cups flour
2 teaspoons baking powder
1/4 teaspoon salt
2 teaspoons crushed anise seed
Or 1 teaspoon almond extract

Glaze options:
1 egg and water plus sesame seeds to coat

Or 1 cup powdered sugar
2 tablespoons hot water
1 drop vanilla or other flavoring, if desired

Preheat oven to 350 degrees. Grease and flour a baking sheet. Combine butter and sugar and cream till light and fluffy. Add eggs and vanilla and beat to incorporate. Stir together flour, powder and salt. Fold gently into the butter and egg mixture to make soft dough. Add anise, almond extract or nothing. Form into a log, 3 inches wide, 1 inch tall, rounded on the top on your prepared pan. Bake 20 minutes. Remove from oven. Cool 20 minutes. Then slice into 15 pieces, crescent shaped or like biscotti. Turn cut side down. If making sesame variety, brush now with egg and water glaze and sprinkle with sesame seeds. Return to oven and bake another 15-20 minutes till golden brown. Frost with the powdered sugar glaze for extra sweetness or leave as they are.

Robin's Collection

Huntington rural mail carrier Robin Hadden was once a baker at the Mammoth Bakery in Billings, Montana. That bakery specialized in naturally sweetened goodies, and she passed along her collection of favorites. The next three were inspired by this collection, though they have undergone a few changes.

Janet Coles ·

Waddya mean ex-bread-head? I'll have you know that the smile I'm wearing in the enclosed photo is largely due to my having just consumed a Dugway Road Bar, home baked to Daily Bread specs!...
Janet Coles, ecologist with the Colorado Natural Areas Program, 1999(40)

Dugway Road Bars -Vegan (8"x8" and 9"x9")

Mammoth called these Rocky Road Bars, but somehow with carob instead of chocolate and without the marshmallows, the name didn't work for us. Playing on the popularity of the Huntington Gorge and the often bumpy condition of the gorge road, Dugway Road came to mind. The name stuck. These were immensely popular.

Janet Coles and smile somewhere in Colorado.

8"x8"	9"x9"
Crust:	
1/4 pound plus 2 tablespoons margarine/1 1/4 sticks	1/4 pound plus 4 T/ 1 1/2 sticks
1/3 cup honey	1/2 cup
2/3 cup whole wheat pastry flour	1 cup
2/3 cup rolled oats	1 cup
Topping:	
1/3 cup cashews	1/2 cup
1/3 cup walnuts	1/2 cup
1/3 cup pecans	1/2 cup
1/3 cup almonds	1/2 cup
2/3 cup carob chips	1 cup
1/4 cup honey	1/3 cup
1/4 cup barley malt	1/3 cup

Preheat oven to 350 degrees. Grease and flour baking pan. Prepare crust. Beat together margarine and honey till light. Add flour and oats and continue beating till thoroughly combined. Press/spread into prepared baking pan. Bake 25-30 minutes till golden brown. Remove from oven.

Prepare topping. Stir together nuts and carob chips. Sprinkle evenly over baked crust. Heat honey and barley malt in a small saucepan till liquid and easily pour-able. Remove from heat and pour over nuts and chips. Return to the oven just long enough to begin to melt the chips, 5-10 minutes. Cool and cut.

Carob Marvels (8"x8" and 9"x9")

Carob has a bad reputation, which was difficult to overcome. Cindy Bramon made these look so tempting that customers tried them! I am convinced that the baker's enjoyment of the product was contagious. These are a moist and rich carob brownie-like base marbled with a sweetened cream cheese topping.

8"x8"	9"x9"
Bottom:	
4 tablespoons butter	5 tablespoons
1/3 cup carob chips/ 2 ounces	1/3 cup/2 ounces
1/3 cup honey	1/2 cup
2 tablespoons barley malt	3 1/2 tablespoons
2 eggs	3 eggs
2/3 teaspoon vanilla	1 teaspoon
1 cup flour	1 1/4 cups
1/2 teaspoon baking powder	2/3 teaspoons
1/2 cup coarsely chopped walnuts	2/3 cup
1/3 cup carob chips	1/3 cup

Top:

6 ounces cream cheese/ 3/4 8-ounce pkg.	8 ounces/1 package
2 tablespoons honey	3 tablespoons
1 egg	1 egg
1 tablespoon milk to thin	1 tablespoon more or less

Preheat oven to 350 degrees. Grease and flour baking pan. Melt butter and carob chips in a saucepan or in the heating oven. Transfer to a mixing bowl. Add honey, barley malt, eggs and vanilla to melted carob. Beat well to a light and creamy consistency. Stir together in a separate bowl flour, baking powder, walnuts and carob chips. Fold into egg mixture and beat to just combine. Reserve 1/3 cup for 8"x8" or 1/2 cup for 9"x9" for topping. Spread the rest in your prepared pan.

Beat together cream cheese, honey and egg. Thin with milk to the consistency of custard. Pour this over the carob batter. Dot the reserved carob batter on top of cream cheese layer. Using a butter knife or rubber spatula, cut through all three layers to swirl into a marble design. Bake 25-30 minutes until the top springs back to the touch, but is not browned, or they may be dry.

Coffee Toffee Bars-Vegan (8"x8" and 9"x9")

It took Heather Ward to gain a following for these. Another case of contagious enjoyment: if the baker is enthusiastic about the item, it will turn out taller, tastier and chewier. Check for dairy-free chocolate chips. Rice syrup may be substituted for the honey to make them truly vegan. These are a mocha shortbread with chocolate chips and almonds, a definitely 1990s combo.

8"x8"	**9"x9"**
1/4 pound margarine, soft/1 stick	1/4 pound plus 4 tablespoons/ 1 1/2 sticks
1/3 cup honey	1/2 cup
2 tablespoons strong brewed coffee	2 1/2 tablespoons
1 1/3 tablespoons instant coffee	1 2/3 tablespoons
2/3 teaspoon almond extract	1 teaspoon
1/2 teaspoon vanilla	2/3 teaspoon
2/3 cup flour	1 cup
1/2 cup whole wheat pastry flour	3/4 cup
1/3 teaspoon baking powder	1/3 teaspoon
1 pinch salt	1 pinch
2/3 cup chocolate chips	1 cup
1/3 cup coarsely chopped almonds	1/2 cup

Preheat oven to 350 degrees. Grease and flour baking pan. Cream together margarine and honey till light and fluffy. Add brewed and instant coffees, almond extract and vanilla to the creamed margarine and beat till well incorporated. Stir together flours, baking powder and salt in a separate bowl. Fold into the butter mixture and beat just to combine. Fold chips and almonds into the batter to evenly distribute. Spread in prepared pan. Bake 25-30 minutes until top begins to brown and feel set.

Scones

Scones gained popularity shortly after the croissant craze of the 1980s. They remained a close runner up to sweet rolls in sales, and we baked them every morning.

Scones are a sweet, rich biscuit. Traditional Scots scones are dry and crumbly. We found we preferred a moister version. They need more work than pastry crust, less than bread. Knead the dough a few turns before rolling and cutting.

Nationally known ice cream aficionado Ben Cohen ate often at Daily Bread. When asked what he ate for breakfast in a "Scoop shop magnates answer weird food questions" article in the *San Francisco Examiner*, Ben replied, "I usually don't eat breakfast, but occasionally I like bagels with lox and cream cheese or pastry and coffee from the Daily Bread Bakery in Richmond, Vt."**(41)** The pastry was most likely a scone or a sweet roll.

Note: These are easy to prepare ahead. Prepare the wet ingredients. Cover and refrigerate. Prepare the dry ingredients and cut in the shortening. Cover. In the morning, preheat the oven. Prepare your baking pan. Stir wet into dry. Roll and bake!

Patty's (6)

This became the Bread's standard scone. Wolfsong returned from a visit with Patty, his wife Myra Timmins' sister, raving about her scones. We tried them, and found the public to be enthusiastic about them too. These are rich and buttery and lend themselves to any number of additions: currants, raisins, apricots, dates or berries.

2 cups unbleached or allpurpose flour
1 scant tablespoon baking powder
4 tablespoons cold butter
1/2 cup half and half
1 egg
2 tablespoons maple syrup
1/2 cup dried fruit of choice or 2/3 cup fresh or frozen fruit
1 egg and additional half and half for glaze

Myra Timmins.

Stir baking powder into flour. Use pastry blender or hands to cut or rub butter into flour. Refrigerate or continue. Preheat oven to 350 degrees. Whisk half and half, egg and syrup together to combine. Add to dry ingredients and stir lightly, just till all ingredients are moist. Stir in fruit. Turn out onto a lightly floured surface. Flour hands and knead lightly a few turns. Pat out into an approximate rectangle. If you use a rolling pin, cover the dough with a piece of wax paper or plastic wrap to keep from sticking. Cut into three rectangles (see next page). Cut each rectangle into two triangles. Place on greased baking sheet, leaving space in between. Brush tops with egg and half and half glaze. Bake 25 minutes until lightly browned and springy to the touch.

Nina's (6)

Customer Nina Jaffe brought in this recipe when a special diet kept her from eating eggs. These are a little crumbly and still satisfyingly rich.

2 cups unbleached or allpurpose flour
1 teaspoon cream of tartar
1/2 teaspoon baking soda
1/2 teaspoon salt
4 tablespoons cold butter
1/4 cup coffee half and half
5 tablespoons milk
3 tablespoons maple syrup
1/2 cup dried fruit or 2/3 cup fresh or frozen fruit
Half and half for glaze

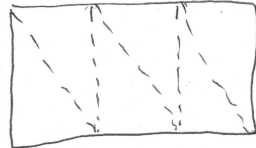

Make rectangle. Divide into three. Divide each third in half to make two. Separate and place on the prepared baking sheet.

Preheat oven to 350 degrees. Grease and flour a baking sheet. Stir together flour, cream of tartar, soda and salt in a small mixing bowl. Cut or rub cold butter into the flour mixture, to the consistency of a coarse meal, using your hands or pastry blender. Whisk half and half, milk and syrup together in a separate bowl. Pour milk and cream mixture into dry. Add fruit. Toss lightly and quickly with a fork to moisten all. Knead lightly. Turn out onto a floured surface. Form into a rectangle. Cut into three. Cut each rectangle into 2 triangles, making six all together. Brush with cream. Bake 25 minutes until golden brown and springy to the touch.

Honey Oatmeal (6)

Krista Willett's cousin Pat Gavula, a baker in her own right, passed this recipe along. These are even richer than our other scones, with a hint of orange and extra texture from the oats. Note: use only regular rolled oats, not quick cooking or instant. This is a good one for preparing ahead; the oats soak up more of the flavors.

1 cup rolled oats
2/3 cup milk
3 tablespoons honey
1 1/2 cups unbleached or allpurpose flour
2 teaspoons baking powder
1 pinch salt
Grated zest of 1/2 orange
8 tablespoons butter, cold/1 stick
2/3 cup chopped raisins or diced apples, optional
2 tablespoons honey plus 1 tablespoon melted butter for glaze

Pour milk over oats. Stir in honey. Let stand at least 1/2 hour (this mixture is fine to prepare the day before). Preheat oven to 350 degrees. Combine dry ingredients and use a pastry blender or hands to cut or rub butter into dry mix. Stir wet oat mix into the dry, using a fork to stir until all ingredients moistened. Fold in fruit, if desired. Grease and flour a baking sheet. Turn out dough onto sheet and pat into a circle. Brush with honey and butter glaze. Use sharp knife to cut into six wedges, like the spokes of a wheel. If you prefer crisp edges, separate the wedges. Or leave as is and break apart after baking. Bake 25 minutes at 350 degrees.

Whole Wheat Honey or Jam-filled (6)

Scone queen Krista Willett was responsible for this one too. She found the original in "some magazine." We changed it to fit our ingredients and customer preferences. I came to prefer the plain version of this. The jam-filled had to be high priced, so they were not as popular as others. But for a special brunch or tea, they are a lovely treat.

1 cup unbleached or allpurpose flour
1 cup whole wheat pastry flour
2 1/2 teaspoons baking powder
1 pinch salt
1/4 to 1/2 teaspoon each: nutmeg, cinnamon, cloves, allspice, ginger
6 tablespoons soft butter
3 tablespoons honey
2/3 cup half and half
2/3 cup chopped raisins, dates or currants
3/4 cup jam for jam-filled version

Preheat oven to 350 degrees. Stir together dry ingredients. Beat together butter and honey till light and fluffy in a mixer or by hand. Cut or rub butter mix into dry mix with a pastry blender or hands to make coarse crumb. Stir half and half and fruit into the dry mix to just combine.

For plain version, roll and cut as for Patty's or Nina's (pages 199-200). Bake 25-30 minutes.

To make the jam-filled variety, divide into two equal pieces. Grease and flour a 9-10 inch round layer pan. Pat one piece of dough into the pan. Spread jam onto this, leaving room at the edge to seal top. Pat or roll the second piece on a floured surface to the size of your pan. Carefully place over jam and pinch the edges all around. Use sharp knife to make a number of slits in the top to let steam escape. Bake 45-55 minutes.

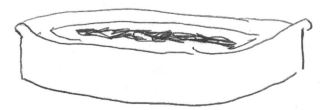

Pat first half into pan. Spread jam, leaving an inch empty of jam all the way around. Roll out second half. Place carefully on top, pinching edges to seal.

Apple Tea Scones (6)

Krista Willett strikes again. Bakers like variety as much as customers do, and Krista found this variation in a magazine. This is a drop rather than a rolled variety. We used an ice cream scoop to portion these out. A 1/3 cup measure will do. Apples, nuts and cinnamon predominate. Try them some autumn or winter morning.

Tony Palmer preps for the next day's scones.

3/4 cup rolled oats, buzzed to a fine meal
1 cup unbleached flour
1 teaspoon baking powder
1 teaspoon cinnamon
4 tablespoons cold butter
1 egg, beaten
2 1/3 tablespoons maple syrup
Sour cream to make 2/3 cup liquid altogether with the above 2 ingredients
1/3 cup peeled and diced apple/ 1/2 apple
1/2 cup chopped walnuts

Preheat oven to 375 degrees. Stir together oats, flour, baking powder and cinnamon. Cut or rub butter into dry ingredients with pastry blender or hands to make a coarse meal. In a 1-cup or larger measure, beat egg and syrup. Add enough sour cream to make 2/3 cup. Peel and chop apple. Add wet mixture, apples and nuts to dry mix. Stir to moisten all ingredients. Use 1/3 cup measure to portion out onto a greased and floured baking sheet. Leave room in between so they will not run into each other. Bake 15-20 minutes until they spring back to the touch.

Corny Oat (6)

An early customer, BC (before cafe), brought in the original of this recipe, called Ham and Cheese Scones. Krista reworked the recipe to handle fruit or savory additions. We served the savory variety, with crumbled Prosage (a vegetarian sausage) and cheddar cheese, as a brunch option. Cranberries seemed to be the preferred fruit.

1 cup rolled oats
1 cup unbleached or allpurpose flour
1/4 cup cornmeal
1 teaspoon baking powder
1 pinch salt
4 tablespoons cold butter
1 egg
2 tablespoons maple syrup
2/3 cup frozen or fresh fruit

Or 1/2 cup grated cheddar cheese/ 2 ounces
1/2 cup Prosage or other vegetarian or meat sausage

Preheat oven to 350 degrees. For savory version, cook Prosage or other sausage in a fry pan or in the oven till lightly browned. Stir together oats, flour, cornmeal, baking powder and salt. Cut butter into dry ingredients with pastry blender or hands to make a coarse crumb. Whisk egg and syrup together. Add to dry mix and stir just to moisten all ingredients. Fold in fruit or cheddar and Prosage combo. The dough will be rather wet. Flour hands and turn dough out onto a floured surface. Pat into a circle, 1/2 inch thick. Cut into six wedges. Use spatula to transfer to a greased and floured baking sheet. Bake 20-25 minutes.

Lo-fat Lemon Ginger (6)

Rose Warnock wanted us to offer a low fat scone option. She found the basis for this recipe in a magazine. The full flavors of lemon and lots of pureed fresh ginger made these a satisfying breakfast treat.

2 cups unbleached or allpurpose flours
1 1/4 teaspoons baking soda
1 teaspoon cream of tartar
1/8 teaspoon salt
3/4 cup buttermilk
1/4 cup honey
1 tablespoon oil
Grated zest of 1 lemon
1 1/2 tablespoons grated fresh ginger root, pureed with a little of the buttermilk

Preheat oven to 400 degrees. Grease and flour a baking sheet. Stir together flour, soda, cream of tartar and salt. Prepare ginger root. Combine buttermilk, honey, oil, zest and ginger. Stir wet into dry to just moisten all ingredients. The dough is sticky. Turn onto a well-floured surface. Pat into a rectangle. Cut into three rectangles/squares. Cut each square into two triangles. Transfer to your prepared baking sheet. Bake 20 minutes, or until light brown.

First Words . . . .

Many moms and dads with young kids walked around the village with their infants on their backs or toddlers in strollers. The Bread was one of many regular stops for them as they made their rounds of park, post office, market, bakery. Rita Murphy brought young Liam in with her, and reported one day that his first full sentence was, "I want a scone."

A number of years later, I ran into Rita and husband Ed with a much taller Liam. They wrote in a note:

Thank you, Betsy for creating such a wonderful place. When we were young parents, we knew we could always go to the Daily Bread, and have something nutritious to eat at an inexpensive price and be met with such a great 'vibe' with a welcoming atmosphere.**(42)**

The funkiest ongoing bakery-restaurant in New England.............

Opening up the menu to serve more than a baked lunch pastry brought us to breakfast and lunch. We experimented a few times with dinners, but they never really took hold. The cafe enabled us to network with additional local farmers for vegetables and dairy products. We even found local producers of tempeh and seitan.

We had a lot of regulars from the contractors, the creamery, Harrington's fine foods, the bank, all the small village businesses. And neighbors met over breakfast or lunch.

One of my favorite reviews is from the second edition of the *Intersate Gourmet, a guide to good eating along Intersate 89*:

There are a few tables and chairs now, some art on the walls, and specials like shrimp rolls and cashew-chicken pasta, but this is still the funkiest ongoing bakery-restaurant in New England, still occupying

the back room of a former shirt factory, still full of oddball baked goods (try Amazon cupcake, for example), and still run by Betsy Bott....
Everything is made from scratch. The Amazon cupcake is an organically chocolaty thing, suggestively rich and moist, but it is the shrimp roll that merits praise without limit....Drop in, drop out, and return to a world hardly seen beyond the borders of Vermont since Henry Kissinger retired and "plastic" ceased to be a dirty word.(43)

Breakfast

When envisioning and planning the café, we all agreed that breakfast was our own favorite meal to eat out. Alison lobbied that the economics made good sense. "Keep it simple." Potatoes were a must. Mare had "the best home fry recipe." Our breads made excellent toast and we could grill English muffins on the new grill top. Weekday breakfasts were a natural. Saturday and Sunday brunches became the café's most popular and lucrative meals. I always say, do what you love, and the people will follow.

Toast from the Postman

Postman and poet Arthur Ezra "Art" Tishman lived and worked in Richmond for a few years in the late 1980s with his wife Marsha Lambreau and their son Charley. Art continued to visit even after leaving the area. He read the following piece at a Local Legends poetry evening and then gave it to me and the bakery.

B: It's taken over a year of reading this poem aloud to finally discover whom this poem is for! Arthur Ezra

Toaster
To the Sunbeam we offer our sacred bread. Gleaming stainless,
Its two slots the great equal sign of the universe, accept,
Without judgment these slices of wheat. By this ritual we
Give over, then receive back the grain of our earth, and by
This aroma we come to know something of Home, overflowing with
Radiance and grace. Yes, I, eater, belong! These
Bricks of our day escort us across that groggy bridge from
Night past, into the fully awakened Sun. We draw the toast
To our lips, strike the holy spark, fortified by the electric
Eye of God's own "man." We have done nothing, if not that
For which we can, fulfilling our destiny, slot by slot, slice
By slice, in the image of, yes, the ONE. By this bread we
Mark our time. From this manna we shall build our house
Of days. This toast in our mouths that talks to us of time and
Sweat and loss and finally of our own fruits, ripened to
Sweetness, at last.

Ezra Tishman
Re-vised 2/94 (44)
Used with the author's permission

Potatoes

Marinated Home fries

These potatoes became a legend at Daily Bread. Mare Kuhlman first encountered them when she worked at Nearly Normal's in Corvallis, Oregon. Nearly Normal's called their style or cooking "Gonzo Cuisine." They agreed to let us use their recipe if we would not give it out.

I reached the folks at Nearly Normal's, still cookin' in 2004, and they agreed to let me share it. The marinade makes the potatoes spicy and salty, and they brown up beautifully. Marinated potatoes will keep up to a week in the fridge, the marinade a few weeks.

Judy Bush gifted the cafe one of her full-size woodcut prints.

Home Fry Marinade (enough to marinate 4 batches of 6 cups each of home fries)

10 to 12 cloves garlic, minced or pressed
2 tablespoons Spike or other seasoned salt
1 teaspoon black pepper
1/3 cup tamari
1/3 cup sunflower or other light oil

Mix all together in a pint jar or container with a tight fitting lid. Refrigerate until ready to use. Shake well before pouring over potatoes.

Home fries (6 cups)

We did have the occasional angry customer who did not like these potatoes--too spicy. More often we had people who would drive miles out of their way for a plate of steaming, crispy Daily Bread fries.

6 cups pared and diced red potatoes/ about 2 pounds
1/2 cup diced onion
3 1/2 tablespoons marinade, see above

Boil potatoes till just fork tender, about 20 minutes. Drain and save the cooking water for stock or for baking. Add onion to the cooked potatoes. Shake marinade well. Pour 3 1/2 table-spoons marinade over potatoes. Mix to coat everything. Allow to cool to room temperature before covering. Refrigerate until ready to use. Heat a griddle or large fry pan to medium hot. Grill potatoes till brown and crunchy, turning once or twice.

Potato Specials

We built a number of special dishes around the home fries. Most were in response to customer requests, thus the names.

D&L Supreme (one serving)

This combination of home fries, mixed vegetables and cheese originated with David and Linda Young who used to order their home fries with cheese, thus the "D&L." We added vegetables to the "D&L Special" to make the "Supreme." We sold a lot of this dish.

1 cup marinated home fries (see above)
1/2 cup mixed vegetables (red and green peppers, red onion, zucchini or your choice)
1/2 cup grated cheddar/ 2 ounces

Grill the potatoes and vegetables together over medium heat in a heavy fry pan or griddle. When potatoes are almost crisp enough, 5 to 10 minutes, sprinkle cheese on top and continue cooking till the cheese is melted and bubbly. Serve right away.

Cindie's Special (one serving)

Grill cook and neighbor Cindie Scherr requested this combination of home fries, Prosage vegetarian sausage and marinated tofu for some protein without the dairy. Other customers saw her plate and asked for "what she has." This dish is filling. We used Prosage vegetarian sausage, but you may use whatever sausage you like, meat or veggie.

1 cup home fries
1 slice marinated tofu, crumbled (see page 267)
2 slices Prosage vegetarian sausage, or sausage of your choice
Pinch nutritional yeast, optional
Pinch granulated garlic, optional

Heat griddle or heavy fry pan over medium heat. Start potatoes grilling. Crumble tofu and Prosage into potatoes. Sprinkle with nutritional yeast and garlic, if you are using. Continue to grill, turning once or twice to brown everything. Serve immediately.

Tempeh Taters (one serving)

Cook, musician and long-time vegetarian George Abele suggested we offer a tempeh breakfast dish. He came up with this combination which was especially popular with vegans who ate no animal products (there is egg white in Prosage): sweet and sour Reuben marinated tempeh, mixed vegetables and home fries grilled together.

1 cup home fries
2 ounces Reuben marinated tempeh (see page 269)
1/2 cup mixed vegetables

Heat griddle or heavy fry pan over medium heat. Start potatoes grilling. Add tempeh, cut, broken or crumbled into bite sized pieces, and vegetables. Continue to grill, turning once or twice, until potatoes and tempeh are browned. Serve right away.

Homey with a Health Food Twist

In a review of area brunch offerings, *Burlington Free Press* reporter Amy Killinger called the Bread's food "homey with a health food twist,"(45) and I think that was very apt. We served hefty 3-egg omelets and pancakes that fell off the plate. There was nothing artificial in our maple syrup. We garnished our Huevos Rancheros with a generous handful of alfalfa sprouts. We offered a variety of scrambled tofu options and made up deliciously decadent sweet roll specials. It was the food, the memorable tastes and textures that brought customers back again and again.

Cereal and 'Cakes

Hot Cereal (mix to prepare 16 servings)

Though Alison Forrest does not take credit for this, my memory is of her going around the bakery taking a cup here, a cup there and ending up with a few sliced almonds to make it something extra-ordinary. This is dressed up oatmeal, with interest added from the wheat flakes, cornmeal and almonds. We had many regulars at the Bread, who ordered this day after day, sometimes with raisins, sometimes without, or maybe banana or some other fruit. It's very filling.

The mix will keep for weeks, even unrefrigerated, so don't hesitate to make the whole batch.

Mix:
4 cups rolled oats
4 cups wheat flakes
1 cup bran
1 cup cornmeal
1 cup sliced or coarsely chopped almonds

Toss all together in a medium mixing bowl. Store in an airtight, lidded container.

Cereal (one generous serving):
2/3 cup mix
1 1/3 cup water
Raisins, bananas, apples or nuts

Heat mix and water in a small saucepan. Bring to a boil over medium heat. Reduce the heat, stirring frequently, and simmer until cereal is thickened, about 5 minutes. Serve with sweetener, milk (dairy, soy or rice) or yogurt, and fruit if you wish.

Pancakes

These were legendary: light and so big they fell off the plate. We offered three varieties: wheat, buckwheat and blue corn. On the weekends, we added a fruit option, and occasionally chocolate chips. Judy Bush brought the original concept for these pancakes to me. She called them "Steak cakes" because one serving offered as much protein as a piece of steak. Judy recalls taking the idea from Frances Moore Lappe's *Diet for a Small Planet*. Whipping the egg whites separately creates extra light cakes, though we discontinued this practice at the Bread once we moved the grill around the corner, too far away to share the baker's mixer.

Dry mix for @18 pancakes:
Whole Wheat

2 cups whole wheat pastry flour
1 cup soy flour
1 tablespoon baking powder

Amounts to make 3 large pancakes:

1/2 cup dry mix
1/2 cup milk
2 teaspoons oil
2 eggs, separated

Dry mix for 18 pancakes:
Blue Corn

    1 cup blue corn meal
    1 cup whole wheat pastry flour
    1 cup soy flour
    1 tablespoon baking powder

Buckwheat

    1 cup buckwheat flour
    1 cup whole wheat pastry flour
    1 cup soy flour
    1 tablespoon baking powder

Amount to make 3 large pancakes:

    1/2 cup dry mix
    1/3 cup milk
    2 teaspoons oil
    2 eggs, separated

    1/3 cup dry mix
    1/2 cup milk
    2 teaspoons oil
    2 eggs, separated

To prepare mixes, stir together the flours and baking powder. Store in an airtight container until ready to use.

To prepare pancakes, measure out mix, milk and oil into a small mixing bowl. Heat griddle or large fry pan to medium hot while you prepare the batter. Separate eggs, adding yolks to your mix and putting whites in a beater bowl for an electric mixer. Stir mix, milk, oil and yolks together. Whip the whites to stiff, but not dry, peaks. Fold into the mix to incorporate but not fully deflate. Portion onto hot griddle. Cook till bubbles form all over the tops and the bottoms are nicely browned. Flip and continue cooking until other side is browned. Serve with butter or margarine and maple syrup. To make fruited cakes, add 1/4 to 1/3 cup fruit to batter before grilling.

Fat Content . . . .

A short-lived Vermont mountain biking magazine called *Fat Content* published a humorous review of Daily Bread breakfast in its July/ August 1995 issue:

Journeying to the Eastern Cup and in search of the ultimate pre-race feed, our intrepid reporter and his support crew (Penny) descended upon a small eatery in the village of Richmond, Vt., known as The Daily Bread Bakery and Café. And soon their orders are ready, appearing majestically at the pick up window, hot and fresh and prepared with pride by the smiling boy who, recognizing a distinguished reviewer when he sees one, places extra tomato slices and sprouts gently upon the steaming mound of homefries and slides another pat of butter between the second and third cakes in the stack….The pancakes measure nine inches in diameter and the stack sits 1.5 inches off the plate…. "These are some damn fine blue corn peach pancakes," …

Excited about the upcoming event, our reporter has ample opportunity to explore the lavatory, which is clean and well equipped and affords a relaxing atmosphere in which to conduct business….In fact, it occurs to him that the whole place is relaxing, a very laid back operation providing a casual, almost rustic dining experience.

In anticipation of multiple hours of punishment, our young friend returns to the table to explore his home fries. Perfectly cheesy and crisp, with chunks of

Brunch cook Chelsie Bush

veggies scattered throughout. But after finishing half of Penny's cakes, he has no room for the full serving, and saves most for his post-punishment nourishment....

Later, on lap three, our reporter smiles, remembering the doggie bag of homefries that await his finish. He stands on his pedals and heads for home. **(46)**

Eggs, Tofu and Friends

Omelet Herbs (1 cup)

There are some little things that make eating out special. An herb mix to sprinkle on your omelet before flipping is one of those. Mare Kuhlman suggested this blend when she set up our original breakfast menu, and it stuck. Save a commercial spice bottle with sprinkle top to have your own on hand to impress your family or guests.

1/3 cup dried parsley
1/3 cup dried basil
1/3 cup dried marjoram

Combine in a small dish. Toss with a fork to evenly distribute. Fill an empty spice jar. Replace the sprinkle top. Label container and store with your other spices.

Scrambled Tofu Herbs (about 3/4 cup)

When we first discussed the breakfast menu, Lynn E. Alden waxed rhapsodic about the "incredible scrambled tofu" she used to order at a café in Saint Louis, Missouri. She and Mare Kuhlman played with different combinations before arriving at the following. It is curryish in nature, slightly spicy and turns the tofu yellow. We had a few customers complain it was too spicy, so we offered a choice, using the omelet herb combo for our herby variety. Add this spicyer mix to scrambled eggs for a little extra zip!

1 tablespoon curry powder
2 tablespoons granulated garlic
1/2 teaspoon cayenne
1 tablespoon turmeric
1 tablespoon dried marjoram
2 tablespoons dried basil
2 tablespoons Spike or other seasoned salt
2 tablespoons dried parsley
1 tablespoon ground cumin

Mix all together in a small mixing bowl. Toss to combine. Store in a covered jar. Decant some into a used spice jar with sprinkle top to have next to the stove. Label container and store with your other spices.

Basic 3-egg Omelet

This is the style omelet we adopted at Daily Bread, a fluffed and folded 3-egg omelet done in an 8-inch pan. It was very generous, looked good on the plate and left customers well satisfied and fortified. We had a few who chose a 2-egg version, not quite as fluffy. And we had "whites only" requests as lower fat, heart healthier habits took hold in the 1990s. A few grill cooks preferred the instantly cooked poured variety done on the grill top, and served them that style if requested.

    3 eggs
    1 teaspoon water
    1 teaspoon butter for the pan
    1/4 cup grated cheddar cheese, if desired/ 1 ounce
    1/4 cup lightly sautéed vegetables, as desired
    Omelet herbs or your own mix

Break the eggs into a small bowl. Add water. Beat well with a whisk or fork. Meanwhile, heat an 8-inch sauté pan over medium-high heat. Throw in the butter. When it sizzles, pour in your beaten eggs. Use a spatula to lift the edges to let the liquid egg run under. Keep it moving. When the top surface begins to set up, sprinkle with omelet herbs and flip over. Put cheese, vegetables, or both on omelet. Turn down heat. Fold omelet in half. Cover and continue to cook until cheese is melted. Turn out onto a plate and eat.

A few suggested fillings:

    Herbed cream cheese (scallions, garlic, pepper, herbs) with home fries
    Indonesian veggies and sauce (see below)
    Wilted spinach, Kalamata olives and feta cheese
    Chopped fresh tomatoes, green chilies and sour cream inside a cheese omelet
    Cream cheese and jam, using a light cinnamon dusting in place of herbs

Indonesian Vegetable Filling (for 3 omelets or scrambled tofu)

Brunch specials at Daily Bread ran the gamut from simple fruit pancakes and Huevos Rancheros to elaborate combinations such as this. Dwayne Doner's recipe of a crunchy mixture of vegetables with the spicy rich peanut sauce was popular with the brunch crowd both as an omelet and scrambled tofu. Leftovers found an occasional home as a pizza topping or as a roll-up filling at the Bread.

    2 tablespoons sunflower or other light oil
    2 tablespoons toasted sesame oil
    3-4 cloves garlic, minced or pressed
    3/4 teaspoons grated fresh ginger root
    1/2 cup sliced onion
    1/2 cup sliced carrots, crinkle cut if you have a crinkle cutter
    1/2 cup diagonally sliced celery
    1/2 cup sliced mushrooms

1/2 cup cauliflower florets, in small pieces
1/2 cup finely sliced Bok Choy or other Chinese Cabbage
1/4 to 1/2 cup green peas, fresh or frozen
1 tablespoon sesame seeds
1 teaspoon turmeric
2 tablespoons tamari

Heat sunflower and sesame oils in a large fry pan. Add garlic and ginger and sauté until aromatic. Add onion, carrot, celery and mushrooms and continue to sauté another 5 minutes, stirring frequently. Add cauliflower, Bok Choy, peas, sesame seeds, turmeric and tamari and cook another 5 minutes. Remove from heat and use immediately or cover and chill until ready to use. Heat per serving for omelets or tofu.

Indonesian Omelet Sauce (1 to 1 1/2 cups)

This is one of Dwayne's many peanut sauce variations. Poured over the veggies, it makes a flavorful crunchy, spicy, rich omelet or scrambled tofu which will keep you going all the way up the mountain.

2 tablespoons sunflower or other light oil
2 to 3 cloves garlic, minced or pressed
3/4 teaspoons grated fresh ginger root/ about one inch of root
Pinch crushed red pepper
2 tablespoons tamari
1/3 cup peanut butter
1/2 cup cold water
1 teaspoons minced fresh parsley

Heat the sunflower oil in a medium fry pan. Sauté the garlic, ginger and red pepper in the oil 2-3 minutes. Lower the heat to a simmer and whisk in the tamari and peanut butter. Cook 2-3 minutes, stirring constantly. Gradually whisk in the cold water and parsley. Bring to a boil. Remove from heat or keep warm in the top of a double boiler. Spoon over the vegetables inside the omelet before you fold it over or add to scrambled tofu just before serving it. Spoon a little bit more on top for those who like it hot (some do!).

Scrambled Supreme (one serving)

This became a regular brunch offering. It was easy and used our standard prepared ingredients to make something new. Lightly sautéed vegetables were seasoned with either omelet herbs or scrambled tofu herbs with 2 eggs and cheddar scrambled into them. Thick buttered toast on the side…yum, yum.

1 teaspoon cooking oil or butter
1/3 cup diced raw vegetables (red and green peppers, zucchini, mushrooms and red onion)

1/2 teaspoon omelet herbs, tofu herbs or your choice of spices
2 eggs, lightly beaten
1/4 cup grated cheddar cheese/ 1 ounce
2 slices toast

Heat a small sauté pan over medium heat. Add oil or butter and allow to sizzle. Add vegetables and herbs. Sauté until onions begin to wilt. Add beaten eggs and cheese. Scramble, using a spatula or metal spoon and continue cooking till eggs are done to your taste. Serve with buttered toast, English muffin or whatever you please.

Cheese Dreams (1 to 1 1/2 servings)

There are many dishes by this name. We used it to describe a French toasted cheddar cheese sandwich. The batter was either flavored with nutmeg, cinnamon and vanilla for a sweet taste or with omelet herbs or tofu herbs for a savory experience. My own personal favorite was only possible during high garden tomato season. Use garlic French bread for the base. Season the batter with omelet herbs. Tuck a thick slice of fresh picked tomato inside along with the cheddar. Serve with sour cream and fresh salsa. That is my idea of heaven!

2 or 3 slices bread
About 1 ounce sliced or 1/4 cup grated cheddar (sliced is not as messy)
1/2 to 2/3 cup milk
1 egg
1/8 teaspoon vanilla, dash nutmeg, dash cinnamon
Or 1/4 teaspoon omelet herbs
1 teaspoon butter or oil for frying
Maple syrup, butter, sour cream, salsa, red chili sauce, your choice

Make a sandwich of your bread and cheese. Beat together milk, egg and spices or herbs of choice. Heat a heavy fry pan or griddle on a medium heat. Dunk the whole sandwich into the batter, turning it over once to coat both outsides. Place on hot pan or griddle and grill until lightly browned, batter fully cooked and cheese melted. Serve with butter and either maple syrup or sour cream and salsa or red chili sauce.

Daily Bread Special (one serving)

Some staff and customers wanted us to call this the "Egg McBott," parodying the golden arches version. We substituted our bakery made English muffin and vegetarian Prosage sausage. If you eat meat sausage, it can be used. For brunch specials, we sometimes added spinach and sautéed red onions or sautéed mushrooms and alfalfa sprouts. Use your imagination; there are endless options.

1 English muffin, split
1 tablespoon butter

2 slices Prosage or other vegetarian or meat sausage
2 eggs
1/4 cup grated cheddar cheese/ 1 ounce

Toast the English muffin, butter it and keep warm while sausage cooks. Heat heavy fry pan or griddle over medium heat and fry Prosage until browned on both sides. Place on English muffin. Fry eggs as desired. Place on top of Prosage. Turn heat to lowest setting. Sprinkle cheese on top. Cover and continue to cook until cheese melts. If using optional extras, add after the Prosage, before the eggs.

Scrambled Tofu (one serving)

The dish is sautéed and seasoned tofu and mixed vegetables with tamari and toasted sesame oil which looks like scrambled eggs. It is filling, especially accompanied with two slices of bakery toast. This recipe can be easily multiplied; start with a larger pan.

1/2 cup mixed diced vegetables (peppers, zucchini, red onion and mushrooms)
1/2 teaspoon light oil for sauté
4-6 ounces tofu, extra firm works best, pressed and crumbled
1/2 to 3/4 teaspoon herb mixture (Tofu or Omelet, see page 210)
1/4 to 1/2 teaspoon toasted sesame oil
1/4 to 1/2 teaspoon tamari or other soy sauce

Prepare vegetables. Press the cube of tofu between your palms to get rid of some of the water. Set it aside. Heat a small sauté pan over a medium flame. Add vegetables and light oil. Sauté until onions just begin to wilt. Crumble tofu into pan. Add herb mixture and sesame oil; stir to mix. Saute until tofu just begins to brown. Add tamari. Check seasonings. Turn off the heat. Serve.

Egg-less Benedict (enough for 4 servings)

Vegetarians still crave old classics.   Rose Warnock found the basis for this in an *Eating Well* or *Cooking Light* magazine. She and Andrew Paschetto worked on it. We served this over marinated and grilled tofu, sliced fresh tomato and spinach on a bakery maple wheat English muffin.

Sauce:
2 1/4 tablespoons sunflower or other light oil
1 1/2 tablespoons finely minced onion
7 ounces tofu
2 1/4 teaspoons fresh lemon juice
1/8 teaspoon turmeric
1 1/2 tablespoons Marsala or cooking sherry
1/2 teaspoon Spike or other seasoned salt
Pinch black pepper
Smidgeon ground red chili

Sauté onion in oil in a small sauce pan till onion is soft. Puree tofu and lemon juice in a food processor or blender until very smooth. Add tofu, turmeric, Marsala, Spike, black pepper and ground red chili to cooked onion. Warm gently in a small saucepan to serve. Or cover and refrigerate until ready.

The dish:
8 slices TLT marinated tofu (see page 267)
2 fresh tomatoes, sliced
1/2 pound fresh spinach
4 English muffins
1 recipe Egg-less Benedict Sauce (above)

Sauté tofu over medium heat till lightly browned. Meanwhile, slice tomatoes and shred spinach. Toast English muffins. Heat sauce over low heat. On each muffin half, place one slice tofu. Top with a tomato slice and handful of shredded spinach. Top with heated sauce. Serve immediately.

New Mexico Trio and Friends

Our New Mexico connections led to having Huevos Rancheros as a brunch regular, and we developed other specials with a decidedly southwestern flavor. Customers familiar with real New Mexico red chili would nearly swoon when they walked in the door to that unmistakable aroma. Our in-house prepared refried beans and sauces made these dishes memorable. Try our combinations or create your own.

Refried Beans (about 4 cups)

Mare Kuhlman contributed this basic recipe for refries. We used canned beans at first, which are fine. We found we preferred cooking our own from dry beans; this takes prior planning. Andrew Paschetto offers these words of wisdom concerning beans:

I have learned that when it comes to beans, there is no substitute for fat. The most flavorful, satisfying, and memorable refries I have had positively reek of browned pork fat. This is the exact opposite extreme from healthful cooking, but it is good to know this when you're standing over a pot of beautifully seasoned and slow-cooked beans wondering why they still taste thin.

So, here is the basic rule for vegetarian refries, calling for oil, but be adventurous if you are a meat eater and experiment.

2 cups dry pinto beans/ 2 16-ounce cans cooked beans
1/4 cup minced onion

1/2 cup diced celery/ 1 stalk
1 inch Kombu sea vegetable
1/4 cup sunflower or olive oil
1 cup diced onion
1 whole green chili or jalapeno, chopped
3 cloves garlic, minced or pressed
2 teaspoons ground cumin
Salt and black pepper

Sort beans for any stray stones. Cover with 4 cups of cold water to soak overnight. The next day, drain the soaking water. Combine beans, 1/4 cup onion, celery and Kombu with a fresh 4 cups water in a medium saucepan. Bring to a boil. Reduce heat and simmer until beans are soft, up to 2 hours. Drain the cooking liquid from the pot, but save some in case the refries are not wet enough. In a large fry pan, sauté the onion, green chili, garlic and cumin until onion is translucent. Add the sauté to the cooked beans. Mash with a potato masher or in an electric mixer to break up most of the beans; you don't want paste. If this mixture is too dry, add a little of the cooking liquid. Grill on a hot griddle or fry pan for a side dish or use in your favorite burrito, quesadilla or casserole.

Red Chili Sauce (2 to 3 cups)

I learned to love this spicy gravy, served on about everything in New Mexico, after I first visited my parents in Santa Fe in 1971. Judy Humphries and Andrea Escher, coop housemates in Vermont, were New Mexico natives, and taught me how to prepare "red sauce," enchiladas and burritos. Having real ground red chili or chili pods (now available in most health food stores) makes a big difference. If the chili is too hot, substitute paprika for up to 2 tablespoons of the ground red chili.

1/2 cup sunflower or other light oil
4-5 cloves garlic, minced or pressed
1/3 cup ground red chili
1 tablespoon ground cumin
2 teaspoons dried basil
2 teaspoons oregano
1/3 cup plus 1 tablespoon flour
1 1/2-2 cups water

Housemates Andrea, Betsy, Judy and Carol ham it up for the camera at Roz Payne's first annual "Fancy Dress Ladies' Party" circa 1974.

Heat oil and garlic in a medium to large fry pan until garlic is aromatic. Add the ground red chili, cumin, basil and oregano and continue cooking 2-3 minutes, stirring frequently. Add the flour. Cook and stir another 2-3 minutes. Whisk water into this roux to make medium gravy. Reduce heat and simmer 10-15 minutes to blend flavors. Use right away or cover and refrigerate. It will keep up to 2 weeks refrigerated.

Heidi's Fresh Ginger Salsa (about 2 cups)

Heidi Champney made this one up. Daily Bread had the only written copy. The grated fresh ginger root adds a delightful lilt to the otherwise fairly standard salsa fresca combo of tomatoes, scallions, garlic and spices. When we had extra, the staff liked this on yam burritos.

2 to 3 fresh tomatoes, diced
3 minced scallions
2 1/2 tablespoons tamari
2 1/2 tablespoons olive oil
2 1/2 tablespoons vinegar
4 to 5 cloves garlic, minced or pressed
1 3-inch piece of fresh ginger root, finely grated or chopped
1 tablespoon ground cumin
2/3 teaspoon black pepper
1/4 teaspoon ground red chili

Combine all ingredients in a small mixing bowl. Puree some, if you like, but leave at least some chunky. Cover and chill.

Guacamole

This spicy side dish accompanies any of these dishes beautifully. We served it with the Eggs Ole and a few other specials. This is a very basic version. Add your own touches.

2 ripe pear avocados, save the pits
1 large roasted green chili, minced
2 to 3 cloves garlic, minced or pressed
1 teaspoon ground cumin
Juice of half a lemon

Halve the avocadoes and scrape the ripe fruit out into a small mixing bowl. Add chili, garlic, cumin and lemon juice. Mash with a fork or potato masher, leaving it slightly chunky. Push pit into the mixture and cover; the pit helps the guacamole stay fresh and green.

Huevos Rancheros (one serving)

This was a Daily Bread signature dish. It is very simple to prepare. If you eat Mexican style food, you will likely have all the ingredients on hand. Mare Kuhlman brought this particular version to us. The classic Rancheros calls for poaching the eggs in the salsa and serves the rest on the side. We cook the eggs right on top of the tortilla, a one pot meal.

1 corn tortilla
2 eggs
1/2 cup grated cheddar cheese/ 2 ounces
1/2 cup refried beans, warm (see page 215)
2 to 4 tablespoons salsa or red chili sauce (see pages 216-17)
2 tomato slices
Handful of alfalfa or clover sprouts
1 tablespoon or more sour cream, optional

Heat a small fry pan over medium heat. Drizzle a little oil in it and swirl it around to coat the bottom. Put the corn tortilla in it and turn it right over. Break the eggs on top of the tortilla. Sprinkle the cheese on top of the eggs. Put a cover over it and turn the heat down. Wait about 3 minutes; take a peek. When the cheese is melted and the eggs cooked, slide out of the pan onto your plate. Spoon refries over half. Smother the other half with salsa or red chili sauce. Garnish with tomato slices, sprouts and sour cream if desired.

Eggs Ole (one serving)

We used Margaret Fox's variation on chilequiles in her *Café Beaujolais Cookbook* for this brunch dish. The crisped corn tortilla strips give the eggs an unexpected crunch, nicely complimented by the guacamole and refried beans.

1 corn tortilla, folded in half and cut into thin strips
1 teaspoon oil
2 lightly beaten eggs
1/4 cup grated cheddar cheese/1 ounce
1/3 cup hot refried beans
1/4 cup guacamole (see preceding page)
1 tablespoon or more salsa or red chili sauce
Tomato slices and sprouts for garnish, optional

Prepare tortilla. Heat small sauté pan. Add oil and tortilla strips. Shake and turn till strips begin to brown and crisp. Pour in eggs and cheddar. Scramble until eggs are cooked to desired consistency. Serve with refries, guacamole and salsa or red chili sauce.

Santa Fe Morning (one serving)

I tried to sample breads and café food whenever I traveled. One of my favorite Santa Fe stops was Cloudcliff Bakery. They served eggs, chili and cheese on grilled polenta (cooked and cooled cornmeal mush). Cooks Gemma Rinn and Mare Kuhlman.

I returned to Vermont, raving about it. We named it Santa Fe Morning and added a side of refried beans. This is an excellent way to use leftover polenta or slices of the prepared polenta now available in most food stores.

1 teaspoon oil
2 slices of cooked and cooled polenta
2 eggs
1/4 cup grated cheddar cheese/ 1 ounce
1 or 2 tablespoons salsa or red chili sauce
1/3 cup heated refried beans
Tomato slices and sprouts, optional garnish

Heat a small sauté pan or griddle. Add oil and wait till it sizzles. Grill polenta slices till nicely browned on both sides. Fry eggs to your liking. Place on top of the polenta. Sprinkle cheese on top. Serve with refried beans and salsa or red chili.

Honoring the Harvest

Just about every culture marks the harvest. In many cosmologies, each succeeding harvest had its day. For Native Americans living in New England the maple syrup flow in the spring was followed by wild strawberries, green corn and dry corn. The trout and the salmon, the deer and the rabbit all had their seasons. Annual autumn chicken pie suppers still found in every small Vermont town take advantage of bumper crops of potatoes, squash and apples. And they bring folks together after the busy spring and summer seasons.

For a week in September, Jewish people celebrate Sukkoth by eating harvest foods in an outdoor lean-to. I was surprised to learn that Jews in New York City built their Huppas on apartment building roofs.

The Cherokee seasonal cycle, which I learned about from Dhyani Ywahoo, revolves around the agricultural calendar. I tested a Cherokee planting practice of dedicating one plot as an offering to the wild things. This seemed to satisfy the woodchucks and rabbits, but the pesky raccoons still got my cantaloupes and sweet corn.

Balancing my disappointment was unexpected bounty. Squash stored in my root cellar froze. I dumped it on my compost pile, which exploded into a giant squash patch.

Blue hubbard squash giants which grew from out of the compost pile.

DAILY Breakfast 6 –11
WEEKEND BRUNCH 8 –1, *Plus Specials*

..farm fresh eggs, bakery fresh breads & pastries,
"world famous" homefries, plus many vegan options...

EGGS

Eggs any style with toast*
        $2.50 for one **$2.75** for two
Cheddar Omelette with toast*   **$4.50**
Veggie Omelette with toast*   **$4.95**
Cheddar & veggie omelette with toast*
                         $5.25
Daily Bread Special   **$4.88**/full
                         $3.60/half

Pancakes ❤   French Toast ❤

Wheat,   on fresh
Blue Corn or   bakery bread
Buckwheat
$2.95 for 1 • **$3.25** for 2 • **$3.50** for 3

TOFU

Scrambled tofu with toast*
herby or spicy
$5.82 • **$3.05**/half

CEREAL

Our Blend Hot Cereal $3.65
Bakery Granola $4.17
with milk, yogurt or soy milk

*Your choice of toast, sweet roll, muffin,
scone or English muffin

DAILY TOAST CHOICE

Monday	Honey Oat
Tuesday	Maple Wheat
Wednesday	Oatmeal
Thursday	Maple Bran
Friday	Molasses Bran
Saturday	Maple Wheat
Sunday	Corn Molasses or Portuguese White

POTATOES

Our Famous Marinated Homefries
Small $1.59 or $1.25 with order
Large $2.43 or $2.25 with order

D&L (Fries, Veggies & Cheese)
Small $2.65 • Large $5.25

Cindie's Special (Fries, Tofu & Prosage)
Small $2.85 • Large $5.50

Tempeh Taters (Fries, Tempeh & Veggies)
Small $3.05 • Large $5.95

SIDES

Toast 2 for $1.59 • 1 for .96
English Muffin $1.26
Prosage (vegetarian sausage)
2 for $1.38 • 3 for $1.98

Additions

...extra cheese .30 ...extra veggies .50
...extra egg .50

SOURCES

Eggs from Shadow Cross Farm
Cheddar is Cabot Mild
Wheat is from Ben Gleason
Blue corn is New Mexico native-grown
❤ Syrup from Tafts Milk & Maple
Yogurt from Butterworks Farm
Milk from Booth Bros.
Seitan from Sheffield Seitan
Tempeh is from Vermont Soy
Salsa is Green Mountain Salsa

☆ CAFE SPECIALS ☆

will be posted on the blackboard
for Saturday & Sunday

Add 9% for Vermont Rooms & Meals Tax • Eat In or Take Out

Soups and Stews

When customers wanted a place to sit down soup was the first dish we thought of. It goes well with bread. It is relatively inexpensive. It is filling "people's" food. We could use lots of local produce, fresh or from storage. Over the years, we developed quite a collection. Many of them were borrowed from other cookbooks. I have listed those for reference at the end of each section.

In the early 1970s The Fresh Ground Coffee House, a quasi-collective with goals much like Daily Bread, served the Beggar's Banquet, a bowl of soup or chili, a hunk of bread, a piece of cheese and an apple for $1.00! We maintained a reasonable price through the 1990s, charging $1.95 per bowl.

All our soups were prepared from fresh ingredients. We made our own stocks, vegetable and chicken. We saved celery ends, parsley trimmings, carrot tops, onion skins, an odd mushroom or two and cooked them up as needed or as time allowed.

Most of the following recipes yield 8 cups, enough for 4-6 average servings. Soups can easily be increased to feed more people or to fill the freezer with some backup meals.

Lentils and legumes

Alison's Lentil (4-6 servings)

Alison Forrest remembers that she made this up on the spot as the "quickest, easiest way to get those ingredients into a soup!" She now adds 2 tablespoons miso at the end to make a richer broth.

1 1/2 cups green lentils
5 cups water
3/4 cup diced onion/ 1 medium onion
1 tablespoon oil for sauté
1 14-ounce can whole peeled tomatoes in juice/ 1 3/4-2 cups
1 1/2 teaspoons minced or pressed garlic / 3 cloves
Salt and pepper to taste
2 tablespoons miso (optional)

Soak the lentils in water overnight, if possible. Drain and toss the soaking water. Put drained lentils in a soup pot and add a fresh 5 cups of water. Bring to a boil. Reduce the heat and simmer, stirring often, until lentils are tender (45 minutes to 1 hour.) Sauté onion and garlic in oil till translucent. Add to lentils. Smush tomatoes with your hands or a masher to make smaller pieces and add them to the lentils. Simmer 45 minutes or more. (Thin miso with some of the cooking liquid before adding to soup; do not boil after adding miso.) Add salt and pepper.

Alison takes a few minutes out for paperwork.

Curried Yam and Lentil (4-6 servings)

Gemma Rinn doesn't remember bringing this recipe; maybe it came from Rosemary Dennis. Whatever its origin, it is a delicious variation of lentil soup. The yams add a rich sweet taste to juxtapose the curry spices. It warms body and soul!

3/4 cup green lentils
3 1/3 cups water
1 bay leaf
1/3 cup diced onion
1 1/3 cups peeled and diced yam/ can substitute sweet potato or winter squash
2 to 3 cloves minced or pressed garlic
1 1/4 teaspoons toasted sesame oil
2/3 teaspoon ground cumin
1 pinch cayenne pepper
2/3 teaspoon ground coriander
2/3 teaspoon ground cardamom
1/2 teaspoons turmeric
Salt and pepper

Combine lentils, water and bay leaf in your soup pot. Bring to a boil. Reduce heat and simmer at least 30 minutes till lentils are tender. Sauté onions, yam and garlic in oil till onions are translucent. Add spices to onion mixture. Continue to cook another 3 minutes, stirring constantly. Add sauté mixture to lentils. Simmer till yams tender. Add salt and pepper to taste.

Mushroom Lentil Stew (4-6 servings)

I believe this recipe came from Sunray cook Rika Henderson. She focalized the kitchen for many Sunray Meditation Society retreats in the late 1980s. This is a simple, yet flavorful stew, with lots of other vegetables for color and texture.

2 1/2 cups vegetable stock, potato water or plain water
1/4 cup green lentils
1/2 cup minced onion/ 1/2 medium onion
1 stalk celery, chopped
1 large carrot, peeled and sliced
1 cup sliced mushrooms/ 4 ounces
1 14-ounce can tomatoes in juice
1 tablespoon cider vinegar
1/2 teaspoon basil
1 clove minced or pressed garlic
Salt

Put all ingredients except the salt in your soup pot. Bring to a boil. Reduce heat and simmer 2-3 hours until lentils are tender. Put a heat diffuser under the pot to lower the potential for sticking. Stir frequently to prevent sticking. Add salt to taste once lentils are fully cooked.

Sherry's Veggie Stew (4-6 servings)

Sherry Pachman brought us this recipe. It was from a friend of hers named Betsy. Calling it "Betsy's" would be too confusing, thus the name. Rose Warnock improved the original to suit staff and customer tastes. This is a very flavorful soup, not as beany as many others of this type.

1 cup mixed legumes and grains (your choice or combination of any of the following:
lentils, bulgur, barley, great northern beans, pinto beans)
3 cups cold water for soaking
4 cups water or vegetable stock for stew
1/3 cup minced onion/ 1/2 medium onion
1/3 cup shredded cabbage
1/3 cup sliced celery/ 1/2 stalk
1/3 cup peeled and sliced carrot/ 1/2 medium carrot
1/3 cup frozen spinach or 1 cup fresh
1 4-ounce can tomato sauce/ 1/3 cup
1 fresh tomato, diced
1/2 bay leaf
2 to 3 cloves minced or pressed garlic
1 teaspoon honey
1 teaspoon dried dill weed
1/2 teaspoon curry powder
1 teaspoon tamari
2 drops Umeboshi vinegar
Salt and pepper

Soak mixed grains and legumes (1 cup total) in 3 cups water overnight. Drain. Put drained grains and all the rest into your soup pot. Bring to a boil. Reduce heat to simmer 2-3 hours until beans and grains tender; stir frequently. Add salt and pepper to taste.

Alison & Michele serve up more than lunch . . . .

Alison Forrest only worked at Daily Bread for three pivotal years. She made an impression on me at the original Ben and Jerry's gas station scoop shop and then I met her at the Onion River Food Coop and asked if she was looking for additional part-time work. Her influence continued through the many recipes she contributed and the many cooks she trained both at Huntington's Brewster-Pierce Memorial School and at Camp Exclamation Point.

Her innovative approach to institutional cooking has brought her national recognition. She is also an accomplished weaver with a studio in Huntington village where she weaves and offers instruction. She is mother to Sam, partner to Bart. She was instrumental in the formation of Huntington Valley Arts, and is a beautiful dancer of styles as varied as Contra, swing, Afro-Caribbean and clogging.

Alison in her Brewster Pierce school kitchen, pizza waiting to go in the oven for its final bake.

Michele Jenness cooked up Saturday brunch at the Bread for many years. She delighted customers and co-workers with her excellent food and wacky sense of humor. She also volunteered to assist refugees making their way through our immigration bureaucracy and now works full-time as a legal assistant to refugees. She also grows beautiful gardens, the mother of Miles and Eric and Kevin's wife.

Neighbor and baker Heidi Racht's children all attended Brewster Pierce school, and Heidi often helped out in the kitchen. She wrote the following guest commentary for the *Burlington Free Press* in 1998:

School staff members, as well as students, are enthusiastic about the lunch program created by cooks Michele Jenness and Alison Forrest.

Every six weeks or so, there is a theme lunch. A Vermont lunch featured lamb raised in Huntington, apple cobbler made from locally grown fruit, milk from Booth Brothers and potatoes dug from town soil....

How is this done? Well, both cooks are talented and experienced. They are veterans of the Daily Bread Bakery kitchen in Richmond. Forest was one of the original ice cream makers for Ben & Jerry's; Jenness has worked in many restaurants. They have a variety of interests and both are very resourceful.

All the breads, except on Friday, are made from scratch. This is a considerable savings over purchased products or mixes. It's not that difficult, really, and the result is a school filled with the mouth-watering scent of fresh bread. A fresh homemade bun makes a hamburger a special meal.

Commodities--federal food provided for school lunch programs--are incorporated in a creative way. Ground turkey is used in spaghetti sauce. Canned salmon was used successfully in pasta salad. Many ingredients are purchased inexpensively through a food cooperative; many are organic

...The ever popular pizza is served weekly, and soup and sandwiches are featured every Friday, but that's not where it ends. The soup is hearty, homemade fare. Commonplace comfort foods like maca-roni and cheese or turkey and biscuits are all made from scratch too...Fresh fruits and vegetables are a must. A vegetarian alternative is always available.

This (sic) is no microwave, or frying machine, in this kitchen. Each child gets to say "nay" or "yea" to choices...Manners are encouraged. Respect is given in both directions. Names are used. It is obvious that the cooks like working with children.

Nutrition education is part of the program....In the class about lettuce, they learned about vitamin content...the different types of lettuce, the farm workers unions and seasonal growing.

For the lesson on rice, they got a whole sampling of rice products from organic whole grain brown rice to puffed rice. Often, the lunch that day has some form of the lesson high-lighted on the menu.

The kitchen is the hub of the school. Community members drop in to help serve lunch. The kettle is going strong at 10:15 for the kindergarten teacher to make a cup of tea after she puts the early kinder-garteners on the bus. Kids who forget their morning snack can get a piece of fruit or yesterday's pizza or cake.

Administrators often time their visits at the school around lunch. Parents regularly come in and have a mid-day meal with their kids. Pre-schoolers are a common sight in the lunchroom....

Remarked Vermont songwriter Jon Gailmor at the concert ending his two week residency at the school last spring, "The food here is legendary!"

Heidi Racht **(47)**

Other Beans

Zuni Stew (4-6 servings)

This is another Rika Henderson recipe. We sometimes called it "three sisters' stew" for the traditional sustaining indigenous staple foods of corn, beans and squash which many Native Americans referred to as the three sisters. Bountiful crops of winter squash were another George Safford specialty. We used his golden delicious (a red Kuri variety) for everything from pumpkin pie to this Zuni stew. Butternut was the easiest to pare and cube. We were one of the only places to take on Ralph Towers' giant blue or green Hubbards. They kept beautifully in the bakery basement.

The unusual spices and the sweet squash give this a different taste.

  2 tablespoons sunflower or other light oil
  3/4 teaspoon ground cumin
  3/4 teaspoon dried oregano
  1/2 teaspoon salt
  1/8 teaspoon cinnamon
  1 pinch ground cloves
  2 teaspoons paprika
  2 2/3 cups peeled and cubed winter squash
  1 1/3 cups vegetable stock or water
  1 14-ounce can pinto or garbanzo beans and juice
  1 14-ounce can tomatoes in juice
  1 1/3 cups fresh or frozen kernel corn

Sauté spices in oil in the bottom of soup pot. Add squash and stock (or water) and cook till squash is tender. Add beans, tomatoes and corn to pot. Simmer at least 1/2 hour, stirring frequently, to blend flavors.

Garbanzo Stew (4-6 servings)

The base for this came from *Tassajara Recipes,* one in a series of books from the California Buddhist retreat center of the same name. Andrew Paschetto and Rose Warnock worked to fine tune it for our customers. This is a hearty stew, a meal in itself; with steamed rice and/or a green salad, this makes a nice dinner.

  1/2 cup diced onion/ 1/2 medium onion
  2 cloves minced or pressed garlic
  1/2 tablespoon olive oil
  1/2 tablespoon nutritional yeast
  1/4 teaspoon ground cumin
  1 14-ounce can garbanzos, drained/ 1 3/4 to 2 cups cooked beans
  1 1/2 cups vegetable stock

1/2 cup peeled and cubed potato/ 2 small
1/2 cup peeled and cubed turnip or rutabaga
1/3 teaspoon curry powder
1/3 teaspoon paprika
1 pinch ground or rubbed sage
1/2 stalk celery, diced
1/4 green pepper, diced
1/2 cup sliced mushrooms
1/2 tablespoon olive oil
1/2 14-ounce can tomatoes in juice/ about 1 cup
1 teaspoon wine vinegar
1/3 teaspoon dried basil
1/3 teaspoon dried marjoram
Salt and pepper

Sauté onion and garlic till translucent in the bottom of your soup pot. Add yeast and cumin. Sauté mixture another 2 minutes. Add garbanzos and stock. Cook 5 minutes. Add potatoes, turnip, curry, paprika and sage to beans and simmer over low heat 40 minutes. Sauté celery, green pepper and mushrooms in olive oil for 5 minutes in a separate pan. Add tomatoes, vinegar, basil and marjoram to sauté and cook 5 more minutes. Add sauté to soup pot. Heat to thoroughly blend all ingredients. Add salt and pepper.

Pesto Vegetable (4-6 servings)

I believe that the inspiration for this came from *Jane Brody's Good Food Book.* Soup genius Rose Warnock played with it to please our tastes and to use available ingredients. Lots of basil and garlic pesto offsets the blend of vegetables, beans and pasta: green minestrone.

1 tablespoon olive oil
1/2 cup diced onion/ 1/2 medium onion
1/2 cup diced carrots/ 1 small carrot
1/2 cup scrubbed or peeled and diced potatoes/ 1-2 small potatoes
2 1/2 cups water or vegetable stock
1/3 cup frozen spinach
1/3 cup frozen or fresh peas
1 fresh tomato, diced
1/2 cup diced zucchini/ 1/2 small squash
1/2 14-ounce can garbanzos or pinto beans and juice/ 3/4 to 1 cup
1/3 cup prepared pesto (see below or use your favorite recipe)
1 cup uncooked pasta
Water for cooking pasta

Salt and pepper to taste
Parmesan cheese for garnish

Sauté onion and carrots in olive oil in soup pot. Add potatoes and water (or stock) and bring to a boil Reduce heat and simmer 30 minutes. Add the spinach, peas, tomato, zucchini and beans. Prepare pesto or thaw frozen. Simmer soup till vegetables are just tender. Cook pasta separately. Add to soup. (If you will not be serving at once, keep the pasta separate so it does not become soggy and fall apart.) Stir prepared pesto into soup. Adjust seasonings with salt and pepper. Do not boil after adding pesto. Serve and garnish with parmesan cheese.

Pesto (about 2 cups)

This intense sauce can be used all by itself with pasta or as a seasoning in soups, stews or casseroles. This is a basic basil variety.

Note: The basil and oil may be prepared in season and frozen for later use. My friend Miriam froze hers in ice cube trays. The garlic, cheese and nuts can be added when you are ready to serve.

2 packed cups fresh basil leaves
1/2 cup olive oil
6 to 8 cloves garlic, minced or pressed
2 tablespoons pine nuts or walnuts
6 tablespoons grated parmesan or romano cheese

Prepare basil. Chop fine in a blender, food processor or mortar and pestle with olive oil. Add garlic and nuts and continue to puree. Stir in cheese just to combine

Egyptian Red Stew (4-6 servings)

We purchased many of our staples from Associated Buyers, a New Hampshire natural foods wholesaler. Associated started in the late 1960s or early 1970s as a buying coop in Franconia, New Hampshire. Over the years, the company grew and moved first to Somersworth and then Barrington. We developed friendships with Bela and Rachel, long-time phone salespeople, and John and John the truck drivers.

Their catalogues grew to include recipes and serving suggestions. This recipe caught my eye. Again, Rose Warnock did much to bring this up to our standards. Tomatoes and sweet red pepper account for the "red" in the title. The curry spices, garbanzos, green chili and eggplant account for the "Egyptian," all common Middle Eastern staples.

Associated Buyers sales person Rachel Leah.

1/4 cup water
3/4 tablespoon olive oil
1/2 sweet red pepper, diced
1/3 cup diced onion/ 1/2 medium onion
4 tablespoons olive oil
1 1/2 cups peeled, diced and salted eggplant/ 1/2 medium eggplant
1 green chili, diced
1 1/2 cups cauliflower florets/ 1/2 medium cauliflower
3/4 teaspoon ground coriander
3/4 teaspoon ground cardamom
1/3 teaspoon curry powder
1/3 teaspoon dried basil/ 1 teaspoon fresh
1 14-ounce can whole tomatoes and juice/ 1 3/4 to 2 cups
1/2 14-ounce can garbanzos, drained/ 3/4 to 1 cup
1 cup water
3 cloves minced or pressed garlic
Salt

Heat water and oil in your soup pot. Add red pepper and onion. Heat 5 minutes. In a large fry pan, sauté eggplant, green chili, cauliflower, coriander, cardamom, curry and basil 5-10 minutes. Add to the soup pot. Add tomatoes, garbanzos, water and garlic. Bring to a boil. Reduce heat and simmer 20-30 minutes, minimum, till flavors are well-blended. Salt to taste.

Dwayne ....

Dwayne Doner is a genius with food. Many soups, sandwiches and casseroles have his signature. He had been a vegetarian and vegan for many years. He grew up in Enosburg Falls, Vermont, a small town in Franklin County near the Canadian border. He had worked at a ski resort, a Burlington hotel and restaurants in St. Albans, Enosburg and Johnson. How could I resist a letter of application like the following? And when I called for a reference to Johnson's Plum and Main, they told me I was crazy if I passed him up.

I graduated Enosburg Falls High School in 1986. I am currently seeking to further my education in the field of Midwifery. Cooking has always been a passion for me. Your menu appeals to me as I have been a vegetarian for the past 10 years.

My wife is a school teacher who just accepted a job in Hinesburg, Vt.

Special Interests: Reading, Drumming, Harmonica playing, Tarot reading, Sculpting and Drawing.

I am diligent, punctual, caring, and hardworking.

P.S. I have no police record and have not served in the military. **(48)**

Roasted Corn Red Bean Chili (4-6 servings)

Dwayne cooked with spice and comfort. This particular version of chili is his original. The roasted corn gives a wonderful background to a kidney bean chili. With a hunk of corn bread on the side, this is a complete meal.

   3/4 cup kidney beans
   2 to 3 cups cold water
   1/2 sweet red pepper, diced
   1/2 green pepper, diced
   1/3 cup diced onion
   1/3 cup carrots, peeled and diced/ 1/2 carrot
   1/4 cup sliced mushrooms
   1 tablespoon olive oil
   1/3 cup fresh or frozen kernel corn
   1 14-ounce can peeled tomatoes in juice
   1/4 cup water
   1 teaspoon ground cumin
   1 teaspoon paprika
   1/4 teaspoon ground red chili
   1 clove minced or pressed garlic
   1 teaspoon black pepper
   1 pinch cinnamon
   1 pinch nutmeg
   Salt

   Soak kidney beans overnight. Drain. Cook soaked beans in 2-3 cups water till tender, about 1 hour. Sauté peppers, onion, carrots and mushrooms in oil. Add to beans. Roast corn in a 350 degree oven on a baking sheet till it just begins to brown. Add to the beans and vegetables. Add can of tomatoes. Reduce heat to simmer. Stir spices into 1/4 cup water and let soak at least 1/2 hour. Add to the cooking soup and continue to simmer at least 1/2 hour till all tender and flavors well blended. Salt to taste.

Dwayne's 8-Bean Stew (4-6 servings)

This is a hearty and flavorful mélange, full of colors, rich broth, big protein and very filling. This is another Dwayne Doner original, perfect for a chilly autumn or winter meal.

   1/3 cup dry kidney beans
   1/3 cup dry black beans
   1/3 cup dry pinto beans
   1/3 cup dry Great Northern beans
   3 to 4 cups cold water for soaking

3 tablespoons dry green lentils
3 tablespoons dry red lentils
3 tablespoons dry green split peas
2 cups cold water for soaking
1/3 cup cooked and drained garbanzos
2/3 teaspoon salt
2 cups pared and diced red potatoes/ 4 to 6 small potatoes
2/3 cup diced onion/ 1 small onion
1 sweet red pepper, diced
3 cloves minced or pressed garlic
2 teaspoons olive oil
1 teaspoon dried parsley/ 2 to 3 teaspoons fresh
1 teaspoon dried thyme
2 teaspoons flour
1 1/2 teaspoons paprika .
1/3 teaspoon black pepper
1/3 teaspoon "Liquid Smoke", optional

Soak kidney, black, pinto and Great Northern beans in 3-4 cups water overnight. Drain. Soak green and red lentils with green split peas in 2 cups water overnight. Drain. Combine soaked beans and lentils in your soup pot. Add 4 cups fresh water. Bring to a boil. Reduce heat and simmer till beans are tender. Add garbanzos and salt. Meanwhile, boil potatoes in another pot till just tender. Drain and set aside. In a large fry pan, sauté onion, red pepper and garlic in olive oil till onions become translucent. Add parsley, thyme, flour, paprika and pepper to sauté and cook at least 3 minutes, stirring all the while. Add this roux to the soup. Add potatoes. Simmer till flavors well blended, at least fifteen minutes.

Vegetable Bean Stew (4-6 servings)

I came upon the orignal version of this in a *National Gardening Magazine.* I was preparing for a weekend of cooking for a Sunray Meditation Society gathering, and it looked filling and relatively inexpensive for feeding a big group. We played with it to bring out the full flavors and found that Great Northern beans made the creamiest and most delicious broth.

12 ounces dry beans (sort for any stray stones or less than perfect beans)
3/4 cup chopped onion
2 teaspoons light oil
6 cups vegetable stock
2 cups tomatoes and juice/ 1 16-ounce can
1 stalk celery, diced
1 medium carrot, diced
1 medium potato, pared and diced
1/8 teaspoon ground red chili
1 teaspoon paprika

10 ounces firm tofu, cubed
1/2 teaspoon toasted sesame oil
1 teaspoon sesame seeds
Pinch black pepper
Salt

Sort and soak beans in water to cover overnight. Drain. Saute onion in oil in the bottom of your soup pot until it begins to brown. Add drained beans, stock, tomatoes, celery, carrot, potato, chili and paprika to the onions. Bring to a boil over medium to high heat. Reduce to a simmer. This is a good time to use a heat diffuser. Heat sesame oil in a heavy fry pan. Toss tofu, sesame seeds and black pepper in and brown quickly over high heat; keep it moving. Add the toasted tofu to the soup pot. Simmer on a very low heat, stirring frequently, two to three hours until beans are tender. Add salt.

Foodshed

The concept of "foodshed" (as in watershed) refers to a geographic area from which a human population may feed itself. Cornell University's *Northeast Regional Food Guide* considers all of the New England states plus Pennsylvania as one foodshed. We could provide most of our food needs from that area other than exotics like coffee, chocolate, spices and citrus.

Food activist and biochemist Joan Dye Gussow led a fascinating discussion I attended at Northeast Organic Farmer's Association's 1996 winter conference. The theme that year was, "Is organics enough?" Gussow polled the room to make a list of foods they would be "unhappy" to live without. Here is the resulting list:

Artichokes*	Avocados	Chocolate
Coffee	Lemons/ Citrus	Olive oil
Spices	Rice*	Peanut butter*
Raisins*	Salmon	Shrimp
Wine*		

The starred items are already being grown in more temperate Addison County and the Hudson River Valley. In 1996, 15 per cent of Vermont's food was grown in the state, while the balance, 85% traveled on average 1,200 miles from field to table.

"Local" and "sustainable" agriculture may be more beneficial to the planet than organic food produced on the other side of the country--or the world!

See Appendix 1. (page 301) for seasonal eating suggestions.

Judy Bush encouraged me to work out a design on my own.
This became our second T-shirt graphic, which we called the
Circle of Plenty.

Just Vegetables

Betsy's Beet Borscht (4-6 servings)

There are those who enjoy beets, and those who don't. I am one who does. I made this soup at home and thought it would be a good one for the cafe. Richmond farmer George Safford grew the most gorgeous Detroit Dark Red beets, which he stored all winter in his basement. He would show up some winter's day with a bag (or bags) full. We rarely had to purchase any. *Burlington Free Press* food writer Debbie Salomon was very fond of this one: "Bott's specialties are legend. Borscht, if you're lucky." **(49)**

Most Bread employees were avid readers, and often shared titles. Beets played prominent roles in two staff favorites: Tom Robbins' *Jitterbug Perfume* and Louise Erdrich's *Beet Queen*.

1 1/2 cups peeled and diced beets/ 1 George-sized or 3 medium beets
3/4 cup pared and diced potatoes/ 1 medium potato
2 1/2 cups water
2 tablespoons olive or sunflower oil
1/2 peeled and diced carrot/ 1 small
1/2 cup diced celery/ 1/2 stalk
3/4 cup diced onion/ 1 medium
2 cups vegetable stock
1/2 teaspoon dried basil
2 teaspoons cider vinegar
2 teaspoons honey
1/2 14-ounce can whole tomatoes in juice
1 tablespoon miso

Boil beets and potatoes in your soup pot till just fork tender, about 30 minutes. In a separate pan, sauté carrots, celery and onion till onion is translucent. Add to the cooked beets. Add stock, basil, vinegar, honey and tomatoes and simmer at least 30 minutes. Make a paste by adding a little of the soup liquid to the miso. Add to the pot. Do not boil after this point or you will destroy the miso's nutritional contribution.

Potato Kale (4-6 servings)

There is something very Fallish about this soup. The potatoes are fresh out of the ground. The kale has been sweetened by a frost or two. And the touch of red chili adds warmth. Rika Henderson served this at meditation retreats and shared the recipe with Daily Bread. Various cooks played with it to fine tune the textures and flavors for staff and customer preferences. Farmer George Safford also grew abundant crops of kale, which he generously provided for the local eating public.

1 teaspoon olive oil
1/3 cup diced onions/ 1/2 medium onion
1 pinch ground red chili
1/2 bay leaf
2 1/2 cups peeled and diced potatoes/ 3 large potatoes
2 1/2 cups kale, ribs removed, chopped small/ 1 bunch
3 1/2 cups vegetable stock
1/4 teaspoon curry powder
1 clove minced or pressed garlic
1 pinch dried basil
1 pinch dried dill weed
1 pinch Spike or other seasoned salt
1 tablespoon tamari
Salt and pepper

Sauté onion, chili and bay leaf in your soup pot till onions are translucent. Add potatoes, kale, stock, curry, garlic, basil, dill, Spike and tamari. Bring all to a boil. Reduce heat and simmer till potatoes are tender. Use a potato masher or heavy wire whisk to break up some of the potatoes to thicken the broth. Simmer another 5-10 minutes. Add salt and pepper.

Curried Carrot (4-6 servings)

Nick Sansone attended a meditation retreat in northern Massachusetts and brought his memory of this soup back with him. He worked to recreate it for us. It far surpassed all our other attempts at carrot soup. This is loaded with carrots, a beautiful orange color, and aromatic with curry spices. This became a staff favorite. Full of good earth energy, this will ground you if you're feeling a little up in the air.

4 1/2 cups carrots, peeled and chunked/ 6 carrots
3/4 cup water
1 1/2 cups diced onions/ 1 large
3 cloves minced or pressed garlic
1 1/4 teaspoons grated fresh ginger root
1 1/2 teaspoons ground turmeric
1 1/4 teaspoons mustard seed
1 1/4 teaspoons ground cumin
1 2/3 teaspoons ground coriander
3/4 teaspoon fenugreek seed
1 1/2 tablespoons sunflower oil or other light variety
1 1/2 teaspoons salt
1 2/3 teaspoons lemon juice, preferably fresh

Steam prepared carrots over water till carrots are tender, about 15 minutes. Remove from heat. Sauté onion, garlic, ginger, turmeric, mustard, cumin, coriander, and fenugreek in oil till onions become translucent and spices fragrant. Mix carrots with spices and puree in small batches in a blender or food processor. Return pureed mixture to your soup pot. Add salt and lemon juice and warm on a very low flame to heat through and blend flavors. Stir often to prevent scorching. Adjust seasonings if necessary.

Wedding Stew (4-6 servings)

When Judd Yaggy, a bakery regular since childhood and high school counter help, was planning his wedding feast, he and his fiancé Keara McElroy, who later baked at the Bread, asked us to prepare a medieval-style stew. Judd became interested in the medieval historical period and attended reenactments throughout his college years. Bride and groom dressed in period clothing, as did many of the attendees, and they wanted food to match. This is my adaptation of *Moosewood Cookbook's* Russian Cabbage Borscht. We baked bread bowls, large crusty rolls, in which the stew was served.

    3 tablespoons butter
    1/2 cup peeled and diced white turnip or rutabaga
    1/3 cup halved and sliced leeks/ 1-2 leeks
    1/2 cup pared and diced potatoes/ 2 small
    1/2 cup peeled and diced carrot/ 1 small
    1/3 cup sliced celery/ 1/2 stalk
    2 cups shredded green cabbage/ 1/3-1/2 head
    1 teaspoon caraway seed
    1/3 teaspoon dried dill weed
    2 tablespoons rolled oats or bread crumbs
    3 cups water or vegetable stock
    1 tablespoon cider vinegar
    1 tablespoon honey
    Salt and pepper

Sauté turnip, leeks, potatoes, carrot, celery, cabbage, caraway and dill weed in butter in your soup pot, till cabbage wilts. Add the oats or bread crumbs, stock, vinegar and honey to the vegetables. Bring to a boil. Reduce heat and simmer at least 30 minutes, stirring frequently so soup doesn't stick. Add salt and pepper. Serve in regular or bread bowls.

Judd Yaggy during his time working the counter at Daily Bread.

Potato Tomato (4-6 servings)

A bakery employee recommended that we try this recipe, originally out of *Jane Brody's Good Food Book.* Brody's recipe called for milk. We found that our customers preferred it without.

2 tablespoons sunflower or other light oil
1 cup thinly sliced onion/ 1 medium to large onion
2 1/4 cups pared and sliced white potatoes/ 2-2 1/2 large potatoes
2 1/4 teaspoons caraway seeds
2 1/4 cup vegetable stock or water
2 14-ounce cans whole peeled tomatoes in juice, crushed
1/3 teaspoon paprika
2 to 3 cloves minced or pressed garlic
1 1/2 teaspoon honey
Salt and pepper

Sauté onion in your soup pot till golden brown. Add potatoes, caraway and stock or water. Bring to a boil. Reduce heat, cover, and simmer 30 minutes. Add tomatoes, paprika, garlic and honey. Simmer another 30 minutes. Use a potato masher or heavy wire whisk to mash some of the potatoes to thicken the broth (do not puree). Add salt and pepper.

Japanese Vegetable with miso (4-6 servings)

We tried more versions of this soup than I care to remember. Many customers on special diets, often macrobiotic, requested a miso soup. We never did get a simple version together. Our kitchen and warming set ups didn't seem to work. This version will be excellent made at home and eaten right away. Reheated, the vegetables tend to get mushy and unappetizing. The flavors are delicious, and this is a warming, nourishing soup.

3 ounces firm tofu, cubed
1 teaspoon toasted sesame oil
2 to 3 cloves minced or pressed garlic
1 tablespoon toasted sesame oil
1/4 cup thinly sliced onion, thinly sliced/ 1/2 small
1/3 cup diagonally sliced celery / 1/2 rib
3 ounces mushrooms, sliced
2 to 3 cloves minced or pressed garlic
1 1/4 cups pared and thinly sliced carrots/ 3-4 medium carrots
1/4 teaspoon grated fresh ginger root
1 teaspoon tamari
3 cups vegetable stock
1/4 cup thinly sliced green cabbage or Bok Choy
1/4 cup peeled and thinly sliced daikon radish
1/4 cup fresh spinach or other leafy greens (chard, collards, mustard greens)
1/4 cup pea pods/ 6-8

2 tablespoons miso
3 thinly sliced scallions for garnish
Tamari for garnish
Toasted sesame oil for garnish

Pan- or oven-toast tofu with oil and garlic till golden. Use a heavy fry pan over medium heat or a 375 degree oven. Set aside. Sauté onion, celery, mushrooms, garlic, carrots, ginger root and tamari in soup pot. Add stock and simmer over medium heat 20 minutes. Add cabbage, daikon, spinach and snow peas and simmer another 10 minutes. Add toasted tofu. Make a paste with miso and a little broth. Add to the pot and stir to combine. Do not boil after adding miso. Serve with scallions, tamari and sesame oil as garnish.

Zen Stew (4-6 servings)

Baker and cook Andrew Paschetto introduced this describing it:
> ...as mild as a Gregorian chant and as warm as a child asleep in your lap. A picture of this stuff should be in the dictionary next to "soothe." It is creamy with no dairy, and sweet with no sweetener. The barley, onions, carrots, ginger and miso are the whole show. Cook it slowly, and long.

This recipe came originally from Kripalu retreat center, where Andrew once worked. Bright orange carrots peek through its lovely golden base. The ginger gives it a nice lilt. It is a warming soup, not generally prepared during the summer months.

3 1/2 cups strained kombu vegetable stock, save the Kombu (see below)
1/4 cup pearled barley
3/4 cup diced onion
1/2 cup peeled and diced carrot/ 1 small carrot
1/2 cup sliced mushrooms/2 ounces
3 to 4 ounces extra firm tofu, cubed
1 teaspoon toasted sesame oil
2 teaspoon light miso
1 inch piece of fresh ginger root, grated and pressed for juice

Prepare vegetable stock with a 3 inch piece of Kombu (a type of sea vegetable sometimes called kelp). Dice the Kombu after straining the stock and return it to the pot. Cook barley in vegetable stock till tender, 45 minutes to one hour. Sauté onion, carrot and mushrooms in a separate pan, till onions become translucent (save the pan for sautéing the tofu). Add to the soup. Reduce heat and simmer 20-30 minutes. Sauté tofu in oil till lightly browned. Add to soup. Make a paste of miso with some of soup stock. Add it to the soup pot. Do not boil after miso is added. Press grated ginger to extract juice. Add the juice to soup to your taste.

Seitan Stew (4-6 servings)

Leo Denby has made and sold seitan, sometimes called "wheat meat," from his Lyndon home for years; we were glad to have this excellent local product. This is a hearty stew that tastes like your mom's or grandmother's beef variety. Meat and potatoes without the meat! The secret is the duplication of traditional herbs and spices. Heather and Donovan Ward's mom Jean contributed this recipe.

1 1/4 cups pared and diced red potatoes
3 cups water
3 tablespoons soy margarine
1/4 cup minced onion
1/4 cup diced celery/ 1/3 stalk
1/4 cup peeled and diced carrots/ 1/2 small
2 cloves minced or pressed garlic
1/3 teaspoon thyme
1/3 teaspoon dried rosemary/ 1 teaspoon fresh
1/8 teaspoon black pepper
1/8 teaspoon salt
1/4 cup flour
4 ounces seitan, cubed
1/2 cup fresh or frozen green peas
1 1/4 teaspoon dried parsley/ 1 tablespoons fresh

Donovan Ward working on another of his perfect omelets.

Boil potatoes till just tender in 3 cups of water. Drain and reserve stock. Set potatoes aside. In your soup pot, melt margarine and sauté onion, celery, carrot, garlic, thyme, rosemary, pepper and salt till onions become translucent. Reduce heat and add flour. Continue to cook and stir for 5 minutes. Slowly add potato water, stirring the whole time to make gravy. Add the potatoes, seitan, peas and parsley. Simmer on as low a heat as you can get for 20 minutes to heat through and blend flavors. This is a good time to use a heat diffuser if you have one to prevent scorching.

Greens Gumbo (4-6 servings)

This is another from the recipes of cook Andrew Paschetto. This is thick and spicy like gumbo should be, without meat or seafood. The red and green pepper and the greens show through the light base. The secret to its flavor is taking time with the roux. Here are Andrew's notes:

My southern-stock Afro-American wife has taught me that there are three things about which southern cooks are fearless: fat, salt and time. Cook it slowly. This soup really has to get to know itself. Cajun rouxs are defined in negative terms: not actually burnt, not really black. Pay attention to get your roux medium brown, so it is just before being veggies and gravy. Cook the onions a good long time; till you have a goopy weird mess and something magical happens. You know it when it happens.

3 cups water
2 inch piece of Kombu
1/2 bay leaf
3 tablespoons olive oil
1/2 cup minced onion
1/3 cup whole wheat pastry flour
1/2 sweet red pepper, diced
1/2 green pepper, diced
1/2 stalk celery, sliced thin
2 cups chopped, packed, mixed greens:
collards, mustard, chard, beet greens or kale
1 pinch ground red chili
3 to 4 cloves minced or pressed garlic
3 tablespoons tomato salsa
1/2 teaspoon Umeboshi vinegar
1/2 teaspoon gumbo *file*
1/4 teaspoon ground thyme
1/4 teaspoon dried sage
1/4 teaspoon dried basil
1 drop Liquid Smoke, optional
1/2 cup cooked brown rice
Salt and pepper

Betsy congratulates newlyweds Deirdre and Andrew following their Winooski wedding

Simmer water, Kombu and bay leaf 30 minutes. Discard the bay leaf. Dice the Kombu and return it to stock. Toast onion and flour in the olive oil (this is your roux) over medium heat in a heavy skillet. Stir constantly. After 5-10 minutes, add peppers and celery. Reduce the heat. Continue toasting and stirring until roux is light brown. Combine roux, greens and stock in the pot. Simmer 10 minutes. Add chili, garlic, salsa, vinegar, *file*, thyme, sage, basil and cooked rice to soup. Put on a heat diffuser. Simmer 10 minutes. Add salt and pepper.

George Safford

More than any other grower, Jonesville farmer George Safford's vegetable bounty inspired searches for new and delicious ways to use carrots, squash, beets, cabbage, kale and onions. He also inspired his friends and neighbors to greater self-reliance.

My story of "getting started with poultry" was not uncommon. As soon as the potential for poultry became evident (how could I not find space for a few laying hens on thirty acres?) George asked, "How many would you like?" "How many what, George?" And I joined the list of spring baby chick deliveries. The post office resounded with the peeping of hundreds. George made the rounds delivering a few more than you asked for. My first summer was a busy one for me. The hen house was not yet racoon safe come Labor Day, and the babies had become awkward adolescents. My sister's inlaws paid an unannounced visit, and their telling of it is legend in the Loomis household.

George stocked many freezers with delicious raspberries; he had hedges! He provided vegetables for various church suppers. He shared his knowledge of bees, poultry, trees, vegetable gardening and dairy farming. Trees planted as whips in the park and at the old post office are huge shade trees now. And many a home sported one of George's Christmas trees. He had a system of keeping the tree alive by cutting the top only. He would show up the second week of December at the bakery entrance with a pick-up load of trees, free for the taking.

George died suddenly in 2001, leaving a big empty spot in the hearts of his many friends and neighbors. His immediate neighbor Mary Bowen Houle's tribute, printed in the *Times Ink!* says beautifully how George touched us all. What better place to remember George than here between vegetables and chicken?

How do you pay tribute to someone who has been a treasure as a teacher, trainer, student, neighbor and friend?

A mere thank you is not enough, yet appeared to suffice for George Safford.

He was visibly satisfied if what he taught you, you were able to demonstrate to him that you had mastered the lesson or had in some way come close to duplicating the same…if he gave you chickens and all the gear to help with the start up, he was grateful when you let him know the hens had started laying…if you planted one of the trees he gave you the information "water frequently and deeply."

In the event you forgot anything, you were likely to also have a photocopy from George, dated and source credited for reading later on.

If you showed him the tree growing in your yard, he was happy for your success. Passing the information on to someone else meant George had reached another garden-and-land-loving person and another and another.

Growing up as a kid next to George Safford was special in so many ways. In brief, it meant Christmas trees, pumpkins. He gave nickels away to trick-or-treaters. That was when a nickel was worth a buck. When George was your neighbor, you always had winter squash, carrots, garlic, rhubarb, flowers, live Christmas trees and zucchini too.

George Safford introduced Swiss chard and zucchini to me as a gardener and Copra onions, and Provider green beans from Johnny's Seeds. This year, George planted what he had decided was the last installment of the Jade green beans and the first of pole beans called Freedom, again from Johnny's seeds. The last planting of beans was on the 4th of July. I just finished picking them. George said I'd be able to pick into September and I did.

I am now a tree farmer as over the last three years I was given 84 spruce trees. Minus the one I mowed over, 83 survive. George was surprised at how I could "bear down" and get each of the plantings done in good time. So was I. Now I know why his gladiolas were so beautiful and mine did not make it through the winter-over process. Glads must not be stored in air tight containers.

Recently, I learned of a person who offered some jealousy over just having met George Safford this season. She marveled at George's ability to gently extract information from you and introduce you to another person, and give you their brief history right there in his garden. She noted that we all had so much of his time and she had so little. I confess I did not remember all the names of the folks I met in George's gardens but I remember where I met them.

I knew George as a neighbor and so many more of the people around the state knew George from running and exercise, a volunteer driver in the early days of the Food Coop. (Can you guess how heavy 5 gallons of peanut butter is?). I knew George as a farmer. He raised dairy cows and chickens. He planted practically all the trees on his farm. This year, he was pleased to point out American Chestnuts he planted and a couple of apple trees he and his Dad, George Safford Sr., had planted. This year, the apples were especially good due to recent pruning.

After years of patient waiting, the bluebirds finally arrived at George's this year. I was treated to the spectacle of bird watching as I quietly picked peas in the evenings of June and July as the parent bluebirds laid and hatched three wee ones. I delighted in seeing George acting quite like an expectant parent.

This quiet and generous and unselfish man was our gift for the 40-plus years he lived with us in Richmond.

As his brother, Nick Safford said at George's orchard during the service to celebrate his life, each of us who knew George has a personal relationship with him. When I was speaking with George I had 100% of his attention, as you did in the same situation.

We are all richer and healthier because of George Safford. The air you breathe is cleaner because of the trees we planted. And that is sweet!

Thank you, George.

With love,

Mary Bowen Houle **(50)**

Chicken and Fish

Chicken Vegetable (4-6 servings)

Rose Lovett started making this particular version of chicken vegetable soup in the early café days. The comfort thing is really true about chicken soup. Even many mostly vegetarians would go for a simple bowl of chicken soup on a chilly fall or winter day.

1 whole chicken breast or small chicken with bones
5 cups water
1/4 onion, in large chunks
1/2 stalk celery, in large chunks
1/2 small carrot in chunks
3 1/2 cups mixed vegetables: choice of onions, celery, carrots, zucchini, peppers…
1 tablespoon minced fresh parsley/ 1 1/2 teaspoons dried
Salt and pepper

Cook chicken until fork tender along with the chunks of onion, celery and carrot in water to make your stock. Discard the vegetables. Take the chicken out to cool enough to pick the meat off the bones. Add the mixed vegetables and parsley to the stock and cook till fork tender. Take meat off the bones and cut into bite sized pieces. Add to the broth and vegetables. Add salt and pepper to taste. You may add rice or noodles if you like; add to the broth along with the raw vegetables.

Fish Chowder, Manhattan-style (4-6 servings)

This is one I can take credit for. I started making this style of chowder as a teenager in Oyster Bay, Long Island, a hop, skip and jump from Manhattan Island. While many New Englanders shudder at the thought of red chowder, customers enjoyed this soup and often requested it.

6 to 8 ounces firm fish (pollock, haddock, your choice)
1/4 cup coarsely chopped onion
1/2 bay leaf
1 teaspoon dried parsley
2 cups water
1/2 cup minced onion
1 to 2 cloves diced or minced garlic
1 stalk celery, diced
1 1/2 cups pared and diced potatoes/ 2 potatoes
1 14-ounce can tomatoes in juice/ 1 3/4 to 2 cups
Salt and pepper

Combine, fish, coarsely diced onion, bay leaf, parsley and water in your soup pot. Cook till the fish flakes. Strain the stock and return it to your soup pot. Set the fish aside, watching out for bones. Add the minced onion, garlic, celery, potatoes and tomatoes to the stock and bring to a boil. Reduce heat and simmer until potatoes are tender. Add fish to the rest, and bring to a boil. Add salt and pepper.

Chicken Potato (4-6 servings)

This is another Dwayne Doner original. It is more like a stew than a soup, thick and creamy. It has lots of flavor. With biscuits or fresh bread on the side, this makes a fine meal.

Stock:
1 pound chicken, with bones
2 cups water
1/2 bay leaf

Stew:
2 cups pared and diced potatoes/ 3 to 4 medium potatoes
1/3 cup diced onion
1/3 cup diced celery/ 1/2 stalk
1/3 sweet red pepper, diced
1 1/2 tablespoons dried parsley/ 3 tablespoons fresh
1/3 teaspoon dried thyme
Pinch sage
1/2 teaspoon tamari
1 to 2 cloves minced or pressed garlic
3 tablespoons margarine

1/4 cup flour
1/3 cup half and half
1/3 cup milk

Make stock. Cook the chicken and bay leaf in the water until the chicken is just tender. Strain and return the stock to your soup pot. Allow chicken to cool. Remove meat from the bones and cut into bite-sized pieces.

For stew, add the potatoes to the stock and cook till just tender, taking care not to overcook. In a large fry pan, sauté onion, celery, red pepper, parsley, thyme, sage, tamari and garlic in the margarine. Cook and stir until the onions are soft. Add flour to the sauté. Continue to cook and stir over a medium heat another 5-10 minutes. Whisk the stock into the sauté to make a thick gravy-like mass. If your sauté pan is big enough, you can continue in it. If not, transfer back to your soup pot. Add the half and half and milk, and stir or whisk to avoid any lumps. Add the chicken and potatoes and bring all up to temperature. Do not boil once the milk is added to avoid separation.

Chicken Barley Corn (4-6 servings)

This became one of our most popular soups. It has lots of chicken flavor complemented by the vegetables. The barley thickens the stock to help this one really stick to your ribs. We got the idea for this from *Jane Brody's Good Food Book*'s recipe for Brunswick stew.

Stock:
1 full chicken breast with bones
2 1/4 cups water
1 bay leaf
Few chunks of vegetables for stock

Stew:
1/4 cup pearled barley
1/4 teaspoon dried basil
1/4 teaspoon dried thyme
2/3 cup pared and diced carrots/ 1-2 carrots
1/2 cup diced celery/ 1/2 stalk
1 1/4 cups fresh, frozen or canned kernel corn/ 1 16-ounce can
1/4 cup chopped scallions/ 4-6 scallions
1 tablespoon minced fresh parsley/ 1 1/2 teaspoons dried
1/4 teaspoon ground cumin
Salt and pepper

Combine chicken, bay leaf, and vegetable chunks with water in your soup pot. Cook till chicken is just tender. Strain and return the stock to the pot. Allow chicken to cool enough to pick off the bones. Meanwhile, add barley, basil and thyme to stock. Bring to a boil. Reduce heat and simmer about 45 minutes. Add carrots, celery and corn to barley and simmer 10 minutes. Add chicken pieces, scallions and parsley to the soup and simmer another 10 minutes to heat everything through. Add salt and pepper.

South of the Border Chicken (4-6 servings)

Rose Warnock found the beginning of this soup in the *Low Fat Thermometer Cookbook*. There are many people who have to avoid fat. Some folks are predisposed to high cholesterol levels. Our low fat customers especially enjoyed this hearty and spicy version of chicken soup.

Stock:
1 small onion
2 whole cloves
1 full chicken breast with bones/ about 1 pound
1 bay leaf
3 2/3 cups water

Soup:
1 14-ounce can cooked kidney beans/ 1 3/4 to 2 cups beans with juice
1/2 cup salsa
1/2 4-ounce can chopped green chilies
3/4 cup kernel corn, fresh frozen or canned/ 1 8-ounce can
1/3 cups uncooked rice
2/3 teaspoon Umeboshi vinegar (red wine vinegar will do)
1 1/2 teaspoons ground red chili
2/3 teaspoon dried basil
2/3 teaspoon ground cumin
2/3 teaspoon paprika
Salt and pepper

Make stock. Poke whole cloves into the peeled onion. Combine chicken, prepared onion, bay leaf and water in your soup pot. Bring to a boil. Reduce to a medium heat. Cook together about 45 minutes. Strain broth and return it to the pot. Remove cloves from the onion. Chop the onion. Allow the broth to cool if you want to remove the fat. Skim off fat and discard.

Add the chopped onion back to the broth. Add kidney beans, salsa, chilies, corn, rice, vinegar, red chili, basil, cumin and paprika to the broth. Bring to a boil and then reduce to a simmer, stirring frequently to prevent scorching, until rice is cooked, about 45 minutes. Meanwhile, remove chicken from the bones and cut into bite-sized pieces. Add back to the soup and continue to simmer until all is heated through. Add salt and pepper.

Yanique's Caribbean Codfish Stew (4-6 servings)

We occasionally invited friends to be guest chefs at Daily Bread. Yanique Hume, a native of the island of Jamaica, introduced me to Caribbean dance and Afro-Caribbean cosmologies. Besides being a gifted dancer and teacher, she was well-known as an outstanding cook. So she prepared a Jamaican feast at Daily Bread one steamy summer day. I found time to write down this recipe while assisting her with other dishes: channa dhal, rice and peas and fried plantains with coconut sweets for dessert.

Cod is an endangered species now, but for centuries, it was plentiful and inexpensive.

1/2 pound salt cod
Water for soaking
2 cups fresh water
1/2 bay leaf
Pinch black pepper
1/2 green pepper, diced
1/3 cup minced onion/ 1/2 small onion
3 to 4 cloves minced or pressed garlic
3 tablespoons olive oil
1 14-ounce can tomatoes in juice
1/4 cup green olives
2 teaspoons capers
1/2 pound fresh or frozen okra (use canned as a last resort)

Yanique Hume

Soak cod in water overnight. Drain. Cover again with water. Drain. Combine fish, fresh water, bay leaf and black pepper in your soup pot. Bring to a boil. Reduce heat and simmer until fish flakes apart. Remove from heat and discard the bay leaf. In a separate pan, sauté green pepper, onion and garlic in the olive oil until onions become translucent. Add to the fish. Add the tomatoes and return to the heat. Just before serving, add olives, capers and okra. Stir frequently until okra has thickened the stew. Serve immediately.

Ancient Rhythms.

My old friend Onnie Palmer phoned, desperate to find a few more people to sign up for a 6-week series of Afro-Caribbean dance classes in Huntington. She described the teacher, Yanique Hume, as a young Jamaican woman who had danced with the Alvin Ailey dance company. Alvin Ailey's performances had moved me as a teenager. I always loved to dance, and Huntington was close enough to home to justify the splurge. I could carpool with my neighbor Alison, even ride my bike to her house and back to save on a car trip.

After one class, I could not stay away. It struck a very deep and resonant chord in me. Yanique patiently taught our group of mostly middle-aged white women. I wrote the poem below remembering our first class when a rainbow appeared to come right in the window, lighting up the whole valley with its radiance.

Richard Gonzales

A wonderful community came together around the Afro-Caribbean and West African dance and rhythms. Yanique left to study and perform in Jamaica before she returned for another year to complete her bachelor's degree at the University of Vermont. Padma Gordon took over the class schedule, teaching West African dance. Anna Consalvo continued Yanique's classes. Richard Gonzales spent a few years in Burlington bringing his Cuban and Haitian dances and rhythms. Carla Kavorkian carried on Caribbean classes. Padma and the Jeh Kulu company she helped found brought Guinean artisits Sidiki Sylla, Ismael Bangoura and Mohammed Souma to Burlington. Other West African artists have since made Burlington home. Jeh Kulu continues to do school residencies, local performances and sponsor an annual Fall conference. Carla and guest teachers still hold regular classes in Burlington.

I find these rhytms to resonate with the pulse of the planet, with the elements, with the seasons, with the complex ways we relate as human beings. Other Bread folks joined the dancing and drumming off and on, and we added a new genre to our vast collection of CD's and tapes.

Hot Huntington night
Sweetgrass offerings
Your drums, our dance
Called the rainbow.

Sacred sound, creation spirit
Spiral of life, sacred sound

Drums sing Wisdom's song.
Medicine calls Deity dancers
To be what is. **(51)**

Cream Soups

Caldo con Queso (4-6 servings)

Here is a potato soup with a touch of spice. You can serve it either with (*con*) or without (*sine*) the cheese. This recipe came from Mare Kuhlman's extensive repertoire. It is quick and easy and calls for items you are likely to have on hand.

3 1/3 cups diced potatoes/ 4 potatoes
3 1/3 cups water
1/4 cup chopped green chilies/ 1 4-ounce can
1/4 cup salsa
1/4 teaspoon ground red chili
1/3 teaspoon ground cumin
Pinch black pepper
1 cup grated Monterey Jack, cheddar or mozzarella cheese, if desired/ 4 ounces

Combine potatoes and water. Bring to a boil and cook 10 minutes. Add the green chilies, salsa, red chili, cumin and black pepper. Reduce to a medium heat. Continue cooking until potatoes are cooked but not mushy. If everyone who will be eating the soup wants cheese, add it now and stir until the cheese melts. If some do and some don't, you can portion the cheese into each individual bowl and ladle soup over it. Or you can skip the cheese altogether.

Creamy Onion (4-6 servings)

Heidi Champney arrived at Daily Bread after having cooked at Oberlin College's student-run co-op dining halls. This recipe came with her. It is a rich and almost sweet soup, with the carrots adding the extra sweetness and color. Heidi notes that a bouillon cube may be substituted for vegetable stock.

2 to 3 cups minced Spanish onions/ 1 1/2 large onions
1/4 pound butter/ 1 stick
1/2 cup flour
1 cup vegetable stock (or 1 cup water plus 1 bouillon cube)
2 tablespoons grated carrot
1 1/2 teaspoons Spike or your choice of other seasoned salt
1/2 teaspoon dried thyme
2 cups milk
1 1/2 teaspoons tamari
Salt and pepper

Combine onions and butter in the bottom of your soup pot. Sauté slowly in butter until onions are golden and translucent. Add the flour and continue cooking at least 1 minute. Add the stock, carrot, Spike and thyme to the onion mixture, stirring to combine. Continue to simmer while you warm the milk in a separate pan. Whisk warmed milk and tamari into the hot soup and continue to stir until warmed. Add salt and pepper. Serve immediately. If you reheat this soup, be careful not to overheat as it will "break" or separate and appear to have curdled. It will still taste all right, but does not look very appetizing.

Judy's Creamy Tomato (4-6 servings)

This recipe originated in Judy Bush's kitchen. She said she was trying to imitate the "store bought" variety. This is quick to prepare and uses ingredients that you are very likely to have on hand. It is full of vegetable flavor and thicker than most. To my mind, and those of customers, it has "store bought" beat hands down.

2 14-ounce cans tomatoes in juice/ 3 1/2 to 4 cups (or your own home-canned)
1/3 cup grated carrot/ 1/2-1 carrot
1/3 cup minced celery/ 1/2 stalk
1/3 cup minced onion
1/4 teaspoon black pepper

1 1/2 teaspoons dried basil
3 tablespoons butter
3 tablespoons flour
1/3 cup milk

Combine tomatoes, carrot, celery, onion, pepper and basil in your soup pot. Cook over medium heat until vegetables are tender. Cool slightly. Puree in a blender or food processor and return to the pot. Combine butter and flour in a sauté pan and cook 3 minutes over medium heat. Whisk milk into this to make a smooth white sauce. Whisk sauce into the pureed tomato mixture. Heat over a low flame till warm. If you reheat this, do not boil as it may "break" or separate.

Cream of Mushroom (4-6 servings)

This is Dwayne Doner's version of the classic. With the addition of other vegetables, it has a fuller flavor than most.

1 cup finely chopped mushrooms/ 5 ounces
1/2 cup sliced mushrooms/ 3 ounces
1/2 to 3/4 cup chopped onion
1/2 cup chopped celery/ 1/2 stalk
1/4 cup chopped carrot/ 1/2 carrot
1 to 2 cloves minced or pressed garlic
1 teaspoon dried thyme
4 tablespoons butter/ 1/2 stick
1/3 cup flour
1 cup water or stock, vegetable or chicken
1 1/2 cups milk
1/2 cup half and half
Salt and pepper

Doug, Myra, Krista and Rosa work around the big bake table. Chris Billis and Bill Peters chat by the grill.

Combine mushrooms, onion, celery, carrot, garlic, thyme and butter in your soup pot. Sauté over medium heat till vegetables are tender. Reduce to a simmer. Sprinkle the flour over the vegetables and stir for 2-3 minutes.

In a separate pan, heat milk and half and half. Slowly whisk into the vegetable mixture to avoid lumps. Add salt and pepper and serve immediately. Do not boil once milk has been added to avoid separation.

Mexican Cream of Zucchini (4-6 servings)

I remember this recipe coming originally from *Jane Brody's Good Food Book,* but was unable to find it there. Otie Filkorn tested recipes for me and liked this one very much. It had its fans and detractors among bakery staff. You can never have too many recipes for zucchini, so this stayed in the rotation.

1/3 cup chopped onion
1 1/2 tablespoons butter
1 clove minced or pressed garlic
2 1/2 cups vegetable or chicken stock
1 2/3 cups diced zucchini/ 1/2 pound
1 cup fresh or frozen kernel corn, roasting will add flavor
1 1/2 chopped green chilies or jalapeno
Pinch Spike or Cajun seasoned salt
Pinch black pepper
1 1/2 tablespoons flour
1 1/2 tablespoon butter
1 cup milk

Sauté onion and garlic in butter in the bottom of your soup pot. Add stock, zucchini, corn and chili and bring to a boil. Reduce heat and simmer 5 minutes. In a separate pan, cook flour in butter for 2-3 minutes over medium heat. Slowly whisk milk into the butter and flour till smooth and thickened. Add to the vegetable mixture and stir to combine. Add Spike and pepper. Do not boil after you have added the milk.

Judy's Mom's Wild Rice (4-6 servings)

This mild and comforting soup came from Judy Bush's mother who lives in Minnesota. Wild rice is harvested in that neck of the woods and she thought our customers might enjoy this. Dwayne Doner veganized it after we served it the dairy way for many years. I have included both versions.

Original:	Vegan:
1/3 cup wild rice	1/3 cup
4 cups chicken broth	4 cups potato water
	1/2 cube vegetable bouillon
2 tablespoons butter	2 tablespoons margarine or oil
1/2 cup chopped carrot/ 1 carrot	1/2 cup
1/2 cup chopped celery/ 1 stalk	1/2 cup
1/2 green pepper, diced	1/2 pepper
1/4 cup flour	1/4 cup flour
4 tablespoons butter/ 1/2 stick	1/3 cup oil
1 pinch ground coriander	1 pinch
1 pinch dried thyme	1 pinch
2 cups milk or light cream	2 cups water

Cook wild rice in liquid (chicken or potato) until rice is tender, about 35 minutes. Meanwhile, sauté carrot, celery and pepper in butter or oil till they wilt. Add vegetables to rice when rice is done and simmer while preparing the rest. Cook flour and spices in butter or oil 2-3 minutes over medium heat. Whisk cream or water into the roux till it is smooth and slightly thickened. Whisk into the rice and vegetable mixture. Add salt and pepper. If you reheat, do not allow it to come to a boil or it may separate.

Creamy Garlic (4-6 servings)

When I first tasted the Garlic soup served at Mary's Restaurant (now Mary's at Baldwin Creek, both in Bristol), I thought I had died and gone to heaven. How could anything so garlicky be so smooth and almost sweet? I tried a number of other versions of garlic soup, and none held up. When we offered a Garlic Galore summer Sunday dinner special, one of my bakers brought in her version of what she remembered from waitressing at Mary's.

    1 1/4 cups freshly mashed potatoes
    1 1/4 cups potato water saved from cooking the mashed potatoes
    1 vegetable bouillon cube
    2 cups half and half
    2 cups milk
    8-9 cloves minced garlic
    2 1/2 tablespoons butter
    2 1/2 tablespoons flour

Prepare mashed potatoes, remembering to save the cooking water. Dissolve bouillon cube in potato water. In a separate pan, heat half and half and milk gently on low heat. Sauté garlic in the butter in a medium fry pan, about 3 minutes. Add the flour and continue to sauté another 2-3 minutes. Whisk potato water into this roux till smooth and thickened. Whisk mashed potatoes into the warm milk and cream. Whisk roux into the cream and potato mixture. Serve immediately. If you reheat, do not boil.

Pepper Potato Chowder (4-6 servings)

This is a Dwayne Doner original. The juxtaposition of the hot chili and the mild potatoes and sour cream give your mouth a memorable ride. If you prefer a milder version, cut down on the ground red chili and increase the paprika. This gathered many followers who looked for it on the menu or asked us to put it on.

    2 cups water
    2 1/2 cups diced red potatoes/ 6-8 small potatoes
    1/2 red pepper, diced
    1/2 green pepper, diced
    1/2 cup diced onion
    4 cloves minced or pressed garlic
    1 tablespoon butter

1/2 4-ounce can chopped green chilies
1 1/2 teaspoons paprika
3/4 teaspoon ground cumin
1/4 teaspoon ground red chili
3/4 teaspoon dried basil
1 1/2 teaspoons minced fresh parsley/ 3/4 teaspoon dried
2 tablespoons flour
1/2 cup sour cream
Salt and pepper

Boil potatoes in water till potatoes are just fork tender. Drain and save the cooking water. In a large fry pan or heavy-bottomed soup pot, sauté red and green peppers, onion and garlic in butter till onions begin to wilt. Add green chilies, paprika, cumin, red chili, basil, parsley and flour. Continue to cook on low heat, about 10 minutes, stirring frequently. Whisk potato water into this mixture to make a stew-like consistency. Add potatoes and simmer 10 minutes, stirring frequently. Whisk in sour cream, salt and pepper just before serving.

Chilled Minted Pea (4 servings)

It sounds a little strange, but this is a refreshing and delightful dish to serve during that brief window when green shelling peas are in season. It came to us through Rosemary Dennis. It is full of fresh pea sweetness with just a hint of mint, cooling on a hot summer day.

3 cups shelled fresh green peas/ 3 pounds in the shell
1 1/2 cups shredded lettuce/ 1/2 medium head
1/2 cup sliced scallions/ 6 to 7 (1 bunch)
2 cups water
1/3 cup light cream or crème fraiche
3 tablespoons minced fresh mint leaves

Place peas, lettuce, scallions, mint and water in a saucepan. Cover and bring to a boil over medium heat. Reduce heat and simmer 20 minutes. Cool and puree in a blender or food processor. Whisk cream into blended mixture. Refrigerate to cool completely. Garnish with fresh mint leaves.

High School Education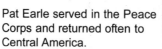

Thank you Betsy, Krista, Rosa and all the others who have
made the Daily Bread what it is. I often think I received my
most valuable education on Saturday mornings during high
school washing dishes at the Daily Bread.
Note from Patrick Earle for 20 year retrospective **(52)**

Pat Earle served in the Peace
Corps and returned often to
Central America.

From other sources:

Café Beaujolais:
Black Bean Chili
Curried Cream of Zucchini
Spring Pea
Chilled Bulgarian Cucumber

Vegetarian Epicure:
Corn Chowder

Natural Gourmet:
Borscht with Beans and Greens
Fresh Corn Puree

Natural Foods:
Golden Nugget Stew

Amber Waves of Grain:
Leek and Barley Stew

Enchanted Broccoli Forest:
Chilled Peach and Cantaloupe
Green Gazpacho

Moosewood Cookbook:
Cream of Asparagus
Cream of Broccoli
Cauliflower Cheese
Cream of Celery
Gypsy Stew
Hungarian Mushroom
Minestrone
Mushroom Barley
Russian Cabbage Borscht
Spicy Tomato
Split Pea
Cream of Summer Vegetable
Gazpacho
Chilled Berry

Salads

Potato (about 6 cups)

Gemma Rinn is responsible for this version of the classic. We originally envisioned having the same salads every day, but soon found that cooks and customers preferred variety. This became one in a rotation.

    6 cups peeled and cubed potatoes
    2 eggs
    2 scallions, chopped
    2/3 green pepper, chopped
    2/3 red pepper, chopped
    2 stalks celery, chopped
    1 tablespoon minced fresh parsley
    1 tablespoon dried dill weed
    1 teaspoon black pepper
    2 teaspoons prepared Dijon-style mustard
    1 cup mayonnaise
    2 tablespoons red wine or balsamic vinegar

Cook potatoes and whole eggs together in water till potatoes are just fork tender. Drain and rinse under cold water. Take out eggs. When cool, peel and chop eggs. In a mixing bowl, combine scallions, green and red pepper, celery, parsley, dill weed and pepper. Add cooled potatoes and chopped eggs. Toss lightly to combine. In a separate bowl stir together mustard, mayonnaise and vinegar. Pour over vegetables. Toss to distribute dressing. Cover and refrigerate.

Gonzo Potato (about 6 cups)

The Corvallis, Oregon restaurant, Nearly Normal's, loaned this "gonzo cuisine" recipe via Mare Kuhlman. This non-dairy alternative to the standard, mayonnaise-type potato salad was well received. The black olives and sesame oil give this a distinctive taste. I often brought this to summer potluck meals.

    5 1/2 cups unpeeled, cubed red potatoes, cooked till tender
    8 minced scallions
    1/2 cup flavorful black olives
    1/4 cup minced fresh parsley
    1/4 cup wine vinegar
    1/4 cup sunflower or other light oil
    2 teaspoons toasted sesame oil
    1-2 teaspoons tamari

Prepare potatoes (trim only occasional bad spots). Drain and rinse under cold water. Combine them with the scallions, olives and parsley in a mixing bowl. In a separate bowl, stir together vinegar, sunflower oil, sesame oil and tamari. Pour over vegetables and toss to coat everything well. Cover and chill.

Solid Ground ....

Dougie McLean's song "Solid Ground" was a bakery favorite, requested by young and old alike. The refrain reminds us that, "you do not own the land, the land owns you."

Without soil, water and sun we would not have vegetables, fruits, flowers or life! I began gardening organically in Vermont in the early 1970s, when dairy farms were disappearing and manure not always easy to find. My laying flock of chickens provided some manure. Even with all the bakery waste, it wasn't enough to keep my quarter acre vital and fertile. So I turned to compost and green manure crops to fertilize and condition my soil. I came accross a reference to a book called *Topsoil and Civilization* by Vernon Gill Carter and Tom Dale in my gardening research and got a copy out of the library. Their exhaustive study of our legacy as caretakers of the soil does not paint a very promising picture of our future. The authors write:

> With the progress of civilization, man has developed many skills; but rarely has he learned to preserve his main source of food, the soil. Paradoxically, man's most brilliant achievements have usually led to destruction of the natural resources on which his civilizations were based.... **(53)**

We need to use and encourage wise farming practices which conserve and build soil, not allow it to run off into lakes and streams or blow off on the wind. It truly is our greatest national treasure.

Dancing to the four directions in the garden at the Sunray Peace Village.

Chicken Pasta Salad (about 6 cups)

This basic pasta salad recipe evolved over time. It made its first appearance during the reign of cooks Gemma Rinn and Alison Forrest, but neither of them claims it as her own. It lends itself to a number of variations. Use any leftover meat, fish or drained, cooked beans. Add olives or artichoke hearts.

    1/2 chicken breast, cooked (or 6 ounces cooked shrimp)
    3 cups dry rotini or fusili pasta, cooked al dente and drained
    1/2 green pepper, diced
    1/2 red pepper, diced
    1/4 cup minced red onion
    1/3 cup minced fresh parsley
    1/2 cup red wine or balsamic vinegar
    1/4 cup olive oil
    3/4 teaspoon salt
    2 teaspoons dried basil/ 1 1/2 tablespoons fresh

Prepare chicken or shrimp. Cook pasta, drain and rinse with cold water. Combine peppers, onion and parsley in a mixing bowl. Add vinegar, olive oil, salt and basil. Whisk to combine. Add pasta and chicken or shrimp. Toss lightly. Cover and refrigerate.

Chicken Cashew Pasta (about 6 cups)

Mare Kuhlman's husband Dan Hambrock put in time as a cook too. He encountered this salad while working at Ogelvey's, a restaurant in Taos, New Mexico. He thought Bread customers would enjoy it, and they did. The chicken has lots of flavor, and the dish is tangy with ginger and garlic.

Chicken:
1 full chicken breast, with bones
1 cup orange juice
1/2 cup tamari
1/2 cup water

Pasta and dressing:
12 ounces linguine, cooked al dente then rinsed in cold water
3 tablespoons cider vinegar
1/2 cup toasted sesame oil
1/3 cup tamari
2 tablespoons grated fresh ginger
6 cloves garlic, minced or pressed
1/4 teaspoon crushed red pepper
Pinch dried thyme
1 drop Tabasco
3 tablespoons minced fresh parsley
Pinch black pepper
2/3 cups cashews, oven roasted and coarsely chopped, for garnish
1/3 cup chopped scallions/ 8 to 10 scallions, for garnish

Cook chicken breast in a small saucepan with the orange juice, tamari and water till chicken is fork tender. Drain and discard cooking juice. Dice chicken when cool enough to touch. Prepare pasta. Whisk vinegar, oil, tamari, ginger, garlic, red pepper, thyme, Tabasco, parsley and black pepper together. Combine chicken, pasta and dressing in a mixing bowl and toss to coat everything. Cover and chill. Chop cashews and roast about 15 minutes in a 375 to 400 degree oven. Just before serving, sprinkle scallions and cashews on top of salad, or serve separately for people to garnish as they choose.

Tofu Cashew Pasta (about 6 cups)

Carnivore customers enjoyed the chicken version so much that envious vegetarians asked if we couldn't offer a veggie alternative. Rose Warnock developed the following variation, substituting the tofu for chicken. Otherwise, the pasta and dressing are the same as above.

Tofu:
8 ounces firm tofu, cut in 1/2 inch cubes
1 cup orange juice
1 cup tamari
2 tablespoons toasted sesame oil
1 tablespoon nutritional yeast
1 teaspoon granulated garlic or 3 fresh cloves, minced or pressed
Pasta and dressing: from above

Prepare the tofu. Simmer the tofu in a small saucepan with orange juice and tamari for 10 to 15 minutes. Drain and discard the cooking liquid. Heat the sesame oil in a sauté pan over high heat. Sprinkle or toss the tofu with the nutritional yeast and garlic. Sauté tofu, turning cubes to brown them on all sides. Remove from pan and drain on a brown paper bag or paper towels. Use amounts from above to prepare the pasta, dressing and garnishes. Add prepared tofu. Toss and chill.

Vegetable Pasta (about 6 cups)

Another authorless recipe, though it derives from versions served on tables around the world. It is full of texture and taste and quite filling. A green salad on the side, a loaf of bread and it feels like a meal to me.

2 cups raw rotini pasta, cooked, drained and rinsed under cold water
1/4 cup minced red onion
1/2 cup chopped black olives, the more flavorful, the better
1/3 cup cooked and drained pinto or kidney beans
1/2 green pepper, chopped
1/2 red pepper, chopped
1/2 cup quartered artichoke hearts
1 stalk celery, chopped
1/3 cup diced fresh tomatoes
1 tablespoon minced fresh parsley
1/3 cup red wine or balsamic vinegar
1/3 cup olive oil
1/2 tablespoon dried basil or 2 tablespoons fresh
1/2 teaspoon salt

Prepare pasta. Cool to room temperature. Combine onion, olives, beans, green and red pepper, artichokes hearts, celery, tomatoes and parsley in a mixing bowl. In a separate bowl, stir together vinegar, oil, basil and salt. Pour over vegetables. Add pasta. Toss everything to distribute well. Cover and chill.

Summer Green Beans with Peanuts and Pasta (6 cups)

The original for this recipe came out of the *Christian Science Monitor,* in the late 1980s. Gardeners who plant green beans usually plant more than they can eat. Farmer and bakery friend George Safford planted enough to feed the county and challenged us to come up with new and interesting ways to use them. Rose Warnock played with the original to come up with this tasty, spicy pasta salad with nice color and crunch. Reduce or remove the ground red chili if you and your household prefer a milder salad.

2 cups dry pasta, cooked al dente, drained and rinsed
1 1/3 cups thinly sliced raw green beans/ 1 1/2 pounds
1 1/2 sweet red peppers sliced in thin strips
1 cucumber, peeled, seeded and sliced
8 scallions, diagonally sliced
1/3 cup peanut butter
1 1/3 tablespoons tamari
1 tablespoon lemon juice
3 tablespoons olive oil
1/4 teaspoon ground red chili
1/8 teaspoon ground cumin
Pinch turmeric
1/2 cup coarsely chopped peanuts, oven roasted

Prepare pasta and cool to room temperature. Cut the vegetables decoratively. Peel the cucumber, slice it in half lengthwise, scrape out the seeds with a tablespoon and then slice into half moon shapes. Combine the green beans, red pepper, cucumber and scallions in a mixing bowl. In a separate bowl, stir together the peanut butter, tamari, lemon juice, olive oil, ground red chili, cumin and turmeric. Pour over the vegetables. Add the pasta and toss to coat everything. Cover and chill. Sprinkle the roasted peanuts on top just before serving.

Marcia's Sesame Noodles (about 6 cups)

Grandmother Marcia Rhodes lived next door in Richmond village and had a studio upstairs for many years. She was an excellent cook besides being a gifted artist. Her long dance with breast cancer turned her to a light, nearly macrobiotic diet, and she requested we offer some dishes she could eat without guilt. Marcia's recipe left much to the creativity of the cook. So, play around with the dressing and find a version you like.

4 ounces cooked and cooled shrimp, if desired
8 ounces linguine, cooked al dente, rinsed and cooled
3 cups julienne (matchstick) sliced raw vegetables: carrots, red cabbage, cucumbers...

Dressing:
Tamari
Toasted sesame oil
Brown rice vinegar
Minced garlic
Grated fresh ginger
Toasted sesame seeds, for garnish

Prepare the shrimp, if you choose to add them, and the pasta, allowing time for them to cool completely. Prepare vegetables, slicing them into very thin, matchstick diameter strips (you can do this in a food processor). Make 1/2 cup dressing altogether, combining tamari, sesame oil, vinegar, garlic and ginger. To serve, arrange noodles on a platter or individual plates. Arrange vegetables and shrimp, if using, on top of noodles. Pour dressing over these, and sprinkle the sesame seeds on top of the whole thing.

Richmond's Downtown Booming.....................................

Many environmentally engaged businesses found office space in Richmond convenient and affordable. The town was happy to play host because the organizations brought activity and provided clean jobs.

Richard Donovan, of SmartWood, a group that promotes environmentally friendly forest practices worldwide, liked being in the village because it contributed less to sprawl.

Tom Butler, editor of *WildEarth* and Kirsten Bower, Northeast Organic Farmer's Association of Vermont office manager, cited proximity to Daily Bread as another plus. Many meetings moved to the dining room for lunch or a goodie break.

A flurry of activity in 1999 brought many changes to the village. A 16-unit, low-income apartment complex opened. The Richmond Corner Market went up for sale. Daily Bread and Bridge St. Cafe moved into larger quarters. A gift shop called Joyful Estrogen opened. Richmond Beverage was developing a reputation as a "boutique" convenience store with an excellent selection of wines and micro brew beer.

Richmond Beverage owner Craig Colburn told reporter Matt Sutkoski in a *Burlington Free Press* interview: "Although Richmond is economically a little more affluent, it's not becoming elitist. It's just the total spectrum of people, from diverse and alternative life-styles to blue-collar work. It's just making it a neat place to live and work. ...Everybody doesn't always get along, but everybody is willing to sit down and work out their problems, maybe after a little chest-pumping."(54)

Garden Salad (4-6 servings)

We offered small, soup bowl-sized, or the large, dinner plate-sized, garden salads as regulars on our lunch menu. We used red and green leaf lettuce for the base, with a medley of vegetables including carrots, red cabbage, cucumber, red and green peppers, mushrooms, celery, tomato and clover sprouts, topped with tamari-roasted sunflower seeds and bakery-toasted croutons. We prepared our own dressings in house, from scratch. It is a toss-up whether soup and bread, the TLT (tofu, lettuce and tomato) sandwich, or the garden salad was the most frequently ordered lunch item.

1 medium to large head of red or green leaf lettuce
1 medium carrot, grated
1/2 cup grated red or green cabbage
8 to 10 slices cucumber, peeled as necessary/ 1/2 medium cucumber
1/4 red pepper, sliced or diced
1/2 green pepper, sliced or diced
2 mushrooms, pared and sliced
1/2 cup chopped celery/ 1/2 rib
1 tomato cut in eighths
1 handful clover or alfalfa sprouts
1/4 to 1/3 cup tamari roasted sunflower seeds (see page 261)
Croutons (see page 261)

Rinse and prepare vegetables, being mindful to drain off any excess water. Tear lettuce into bite-sized pieces and line a medium-sized bowl. Arrange prepared vegetables artfully with sprouts, seeds and croutons on top. Serve dressing/s on the side. See recipes below or use your own favorite.

Note: If you prepare this ahead of time, leave the tomatoes till just before serving or they may become mushy.

House Dressings and Extras

Yogurt Dill Dressing (2 1/2 cups)

Gemma Rinn brought this recipe to the Bread. It is tasty, rich and thick enough to use on a sandwich or as a dip.

1 cup yogurt
1 cup mayonnaise
2 teaspoons red wine or balsamic vinegar
4 tablespoons olive oil
3 tablespoons dried dill weed
2 cloves garlic, minced or pressed
1/2 teaspoon black pepper

Whisk all together in a small bowl. Transfer to a bottle, jar or other covered container and refrigerate until you need it. Shake or stir before using.

Vinaigrette (2 cups)

This is your basic oil and vinegar with a little Dijon mustard thrown in for zip and interest.

1/3 to 1/2 cup red wine or balsamic vinegar
1 1/2 cups olive oil
1/2 tablespoon Dijon-style mustard
3 to 4 cloves garlic, minced or pressed
Salt and pepper

Combine all ingredients in a pint or larger jar. Whisk or shake before using. Store, covered, in the refrigerator.

Lo Fat Honey Dijon Dressing (2 cups)

In the mid-1990s, we began hearing requests for low- or no-fat options. Rose Warnock found a version of this in a *Cooking Light* magazine and worked on it till it met her standards. It is a sweet and tangy dressing with plenty of body and none of the guilt.

1 cup low fat yogurt/ 8 ounces
1/3 cup no-fat mayonnaise
1/3 cup honey
2 1/2 tablespoons prepared Dijon mustard
2 1/2 tablespoons coarse grained mustard
1 1/2 tablespoons rice vinegar

Whisk all together in a small bowl. Transfer to a bottle, jar or other covered container and refrigerate until you need it. Shake or stir before using.

Tamari-roasted Sunflower Seeds (2 cups)

This simple garnish made the garden salad eating-out special. Tuck them in when you have your oven pre-heating for another project.

2 cups hulled sunflower seeds
1 tablespoon tamari or other soy sauce

Preheat oven to 350 degrees. Mix tamari with seeds in a small mixing bowl to coat. Spread seeds on a cookie sheet. Put in heating or hot oven. Stir every 5 or 10 minutes until they are aromatic and beginning to brown. Cool. Store in a tightly-lidded container.

Croutons

We had plenty of ageing bread around. We served bakery fresh bread for lunch, offering the day-before's for breakfast toast. Any that we didn't take home became croutons or compost. The ovens were going all the time, so as soon as we accumulated enough for a large roasting pan, we made up a batch. The following is a basic method. Experiment!

Preheat oven to 350 degrees. Spread cubed bread in a roasting pan or casserole. Drizzle melted butter or olive oil over it. Sprinkle granulated garlic or garlic powder, dried parsley, basil, oregano and thyme and black pepper over the bread. Toss with a spatula or large spoon. Put in oven and stir every 10 minutes until croutons are crunchy and beginning to brown.

More Salads

Tomato and Mozzarella (about 6 cups)

This salad is as flavorful as your ingredients. It is especially good in high summer when garden tomatoes and fresh basil are available. Gemma Rinn prepares this with fresh mozzarella, but regular will do. Gemma suggested we try this, and I developed this particular version. With some grilled veggies and a fresh crusty bread, this makes a filling summer meal.

2 to 3 cups diced fresh tomatoes
1 cup minced red onion
1 cup mozzarella , in 1/2 inch cubes/ about 8 ounces
1 cup flavorful pitted black olives, sliced or quartered

Dressing:
1/2 cup olive oil
1/4 cup red wine or balsamic vinegar
Salt or tamari
2 teaspoons dried basil/2 tablespoons fresh
Black pepper

Prepare tomatoes, onion, cheese and olives and combine in a mixing bowl. In a separate bowl, stir together olive oil, vinegar, salt or tamari, basil and black pepper. Pour over the vegetable and cheese mixture. Toss to coat all. Cover and chill.

Tomato and Artichoke (6 1/2 cups)

This recipe is quite simple and tasty. It is another which is best with fresh garden tomatoes, full of flavor. If preparing this out of season, try for tomatoes with some good color, not the frequently cardboard-like spheres which pass for tomatoes during the winter months. If you are in a hurry, you can use already marinated artichoke hearts and skip making your own dressing.

2 14-ounce cans artichoke hearts, quartered
1 pint cherry tomatoes, halved or 2 cups diced fresh tomatoes/ 2-4 tomatoes

Dressing:
2/3 cup olive oil
2 1/2 tablespoons red wine or balsamic vinegar
2 teaspoons dried basil or 2 tablespoons fresh
1 teaspoon granulated garlic or 3 cloves, minced or pressed
1 teaspoon dried oregano or 2 tablespoons fresh

In a mixing bowl, combine artichoke hearts and dressing ingredients. Cover and refrigerate 8 hours or overnight. Just before serving, add tomatoes and toss to coat everything.

Greek Rice (about 6 cups)

Mare Kuhlman brought in this recipe and we called it "Mare's" for years until bakery friend Barbara Dubois took credit for introducing it to Mare. It is a refreshing and filling dish, perfect for a hot summer's day. It is especially tasty with briny, Kalamata-style olives and a fruity full-bodied olive oil.

1 2/3 cups brown rice, cooked and cooled
1 sweet red pepper, diced
8 scallions, chopped
1 stalk celery, diced
1 1/3 cups feta cheese/ 8 ounces
2/3 cups Greek olives
1/2 cup olive oil
1/4 cup feta brine or red wine vinegar
1 1/2 tablespoons lemon juice

Prepare rice. Cook in three cups water till rice is soft but not mushy. Cool and set aside. Combine red pepper, scallions, celery, feta and olives in a mixing bowl. In a separate bowl, stir together olive oil, brine or vinegar and lemon juice. Pour over vegetables. Add cooled rice and toss to distribute vegetables and dressing. Cover and chill.

Wild Rice and Hazelnut (about 6 cups)

Andrew Paschetto made this recipe up when our Jubilee Farm partner, Sarah Jane Williamson, brought us some of her fennel bounty. It is one of those crops she just loves to grow! The sweet tangs of orange and fennel give this a delightfully fresh flavor.

Andrew writes:

Try to avoid bargain wild rice: it's cheap usually because it's all broken up bits. This will make the salad look more like taboule. Adding some thin slices of fresh fennel bulb takes this salad to truly remarkable levels. This is OK as a leftover, but alas really doesn't age well.

3/4 cup uncooked wild rice
1 cup uncooked brown rice
1 cup hazelnuts, oven roasted and coarsely chopped
2 1/2 stalks celery, diced
1/2 red onion, minced
1/4 cup chopped fresh parsley
1 cup orange juice, fresh squeezed is especially good
Zest of 1 orange peel, grated fine
1/3 cup red wine vinegar
1 teaspoon sea salt
1/2 teaspoon ground anise or fennel seed
1/3 to 1/2 cup olive oil
1/4 bulb fresh fennel, optional

Prepare grains. Cook wild rice in 1 1/2 cups water until tender. Cook brown rice separately in 2 cups water until done. Cool both to room temperature then combine. Spread the rice out in a baking or other flat pan to speed up the cooling process.

Prepare nuts and vegetables. Add nuts, celery, onion and parsley to the rice mixture. In a separate bowl, stir together orange juice, grated rind, vinegar, salt, seeds and olive oil. Pour over rice and vegetable mixture and toss to coat all. If you have fresh fennel, slice enough to make 1/2 cup and add now. Cover and chill before serving.

Rice and Sunny (about 6 cups)

This recipe is light and simple but filling. I first met this salad when Rika Henderson served it at Sunray Meditation Society retreats. Cooking the rice with flavoring of its own gives the kitchen and the salad a nice aroma. Serve it with a choice of salad dressings. It keeps well, undressed and refrigerated, for up to 5 days.

1 tablespoon toasted sesame oil
1/4 teaspoon dried thyme
1 1/3 cups raw brown rice
2 1/2 cups water for cooking rice

1 1/3 cups diced celery/ 3 to 4 stalks
2/3 cup toasted sunflower seeds (see page 261)
1/3 cup minced fresh parsley
1 cup fresh or frozen green peas, thawed
1 1/2 teaspoons lemon juice
Salad dressing/s of choice (see pages 260)

In a medium fry pan which has a lid, sauté thyme in sesame oil till fragrant. Add the rice and stir until coated. Add the water and bring to a boil. Reduce heat, cover and cook till all liquid is absorbed, about 30 minutes. Put rice into a mixing bowl. Add celery, sunflower seeds, parsley, peas and lemon juice. Toss to combine. Cover and chill. Serve with choice of dressings.

Black Bean, Corn and Shrimp (about 6 cups)

This colorful and unusual salad originated with a recipe in the *Christian Science Monitor*. We prepared it with our house vinaigrette, but you may find another dressing which pleases you more. Fresh summer corn makes it extra special, but frozen or canned will do.

3 cups fresh, frozen and thawed or drained canned kernel corn
8 ounces cooked shrimp
1 14-ounce can black beans, drained/ 1 1/3 cups
1/3 cup minced red onion
1/2 sweet red pepper, sliced thin
1/2 cup vinaigrette dressing (see page 260) or your choice

Make sure corn and beans are well drained. Mix everything in a bowl. Toss lightly to combine. Cover and chill.

From other sources:

Moosewood Cookbook:
Taboule
March Hare
Fresh Fruit
Hummus
Raw Vegetable

Enchanted Broccoli Forest:
Swiss Green Beans

Natural Gourmet:
Pico De Gallo
Nori Rolls

Vermont Fresh Network

The Vermont Department of Agriculture and the New England Culinary Institute invited farmers, restaurateurs and agricultural bureaucrats to a cold 1996 winter meeting and lunch. How could we work together more profitably for everyone? How could farmers provide what restaurants wanted to buy? How could chefs use more local meat, cheese and produce?

We found that local organic lettuce compared favorably with commercial California when usable product was taken into account rather than a straight price per head comparison. We found that farmers were happy to plant more of what we were sure we wanted and were committed to buy.

The Vermont Fresh Network was born as a means of pairing growers directly with chefs.

"In this win-win situation, the crisp sugar-snap peas that grower Sarah Jane Williamson picks at 8 a.m. in Huntington appear on a plate at the Blue Seal restaurant in Richmond by suppertime," wrote *Burlington Free Press* reporter Debbie Salomon. (55)

Many of us had informal "partners" in local farms who had been providing us for years. I grew a lot of produce, as did Judy Bush, George Safford and Heidi Racht. My old friend Neal Mauck, who had sold me garlic and maple syrup for years, hooked us up with Arcana Farm in Jericho when he started working there.

With the weather always a variable, farmers and chefs had to communicate regularly to make accommodations. Chefs learned to be more flexible with their menus. At the first meeting, lamb producers challenged chefs to use more than just the chops. Putney Inn's executive chef put the "Lamb Sampler" on the menu and found it to be a customer favorite. Her chefs prepared a variety of dishes from sausage, chop and roast to ragout, and found they could use the whole animal.

We found that Daily Bread's two main farm partners complemented each other well. Arcana's sandy Jericho soil warmed early, while Sarah Jane's Huntington bottom land supported lettuce well into the summer.

Sarah Jane's Jubilee Farm hosts the annual Huntington Valley Arts Fair. One year, you could go for a wagon ride besides seeing an amazing display of local artists' work.

DAILY LUNCH 11 – 4

...prepared daily from the freshest & best ingredients the season will allow...

SOUPS

Bowl	$1.95 $2.50	with today's bread
Half Bowl	$1.25 $1.79	with today's bread

SALADS

Simple Side	$1.50
Small Garden	$2.85
Large Garden	$3.85

DRESSINGS

Yogurt Dill • Vinaigrette
Low Fat Honey Dijon • Oil & Vinegar

COMBOS

Soup & Side Salad	$3.25
Sandwich & Side Salad	$4.25
Soup & Sandwich	$4.95
Salad Plate	$3.95

BAKERY SPECIALS

Monday	Pizza	$1.56–$1.73
Tuesday	Potato Smokers	$2.25/plain
		$2.40/with veg.
Wednesday	Quesadilla	$3.32
	with salsa or spicy, hot red chili?	
Thursday	Pizza	$1.56–$1.73
Friday	Savory Spirals	$1.73

VERMONT SOURCES

Cheddar is Cabot Mild Cheddar
Tempeh is from Vermont Soy
Salsa is Green Mountain Salsa
Eggs from Shadow Cross Farm
Seitan from Sheffield Seitan
Mozzarella is from Richmond Cheese Company

SANDWICHES

on today's fresh bread with your choice of lettuce, tomato or sprouts, mayo or mustard, or check out the optional extras

Grilled Cheddar & Tomato	$2.99
Egg Salad	$2.99
Tuna Salad	$3.09
Tuna Melt	$3.79
Tofu, Lettuce & Tomato	$3.49
Tempeh, Lettuce & Tomato	$3.69
Hummus	$3.49
Dwayne's Grilled Veggie	$3.79
Seitan Melt Deluxe	$3.69

"steak" or barbecue sauce

Basics

without vegetable option

Grilled Cheddar	$2.65
Peanut Butter & Jam	$1.95
Grilled PB&J	$2.35
Bread & Butter	.79

Optional Extras

...on toast .25 ...extra cheese .25
...extra veggies .30–.50

☆ CAFE SPECIALS ☆

Check the boards for delectable daily specials: casseroles, burritos, salads, sandwiches, stir fry, curries, stews, gumbos, rice & beans

FARM FRESH PARTNERS

Jubilee Farm Huntington
Arcana Gardens Jericho

Add 9% for Vermont Rooms & Meals Tax • Eat In or Take Out

Sandwiches

We offered the standard tuna salad, egg salad and grilled cheese options, leaving grinders and lunch meat sandwiches to Dolan's, later the Richmond Corner Market, which served reasonably priced and generous ones right next door. Zachary's, a pizza joint around the corner, and later Bridge Street Cafe right across the street, an American-home-cooking-diner-style restaurant, offered lots of familiar Italian and meat and potatoes specials. We developed a large repertoire of mostly vegetarian sandwich options. Something for everyone!

Early café cook Heidi Champney introduced us to the TLT, a marinated tofu, lettuce and tomato sandwich which was extremely popular. When local organic tempeh became available in the late 1990s, we added a number of tempeh sandwiches to our regular options. Dwayne Doner and Donovan Ward lobbied for seitan, and won many new converts. The secret to successful tofu, tempeh and seitan dishes is based on flavorful marinades.

TLT Tofu (to marinate 1 pound tofu, 5 to 6 2 slice servings)

Heidi Champney was introduced to the TLT at Oberlin College. Her roommate Susan Rosadina simply drenched the sliced tofu in tamari and then rolled it in nutritional yeast before sautéing. At the Bread, the marinade gained oil, ginger, dill and garlic. We sprinkled a little nutritional yeast and granulated garlic on the tofu while grilling, and served it on fresh bakery bread.

Plain or fancy, this tofu can be used in stir fries, for Eggless Benedict (see page 258) and numerous other dishes. It keeps for a week to 10 days in the refrigerator. This sandwich became one of our most popular. Many were challenged to try it, with the promise of anything else on the menu if they did not like it. They were often pleasantly surprised and gave the much maligned tofu another chance.

1 pound extra firm tofu, sliced into 1/4 inch thick slices

Marinade:
1 1/2 cups tamari
1/2 cup sunflower or other light oil
1/2 tablespoon dried dill weed
1/2 tablespoon powdered ginger
4 to 5 cloves garlic, minced or pressed
Water to cover

Slice and drain tofu. In a small bowl, stir together tamari, oil, dill, ginger and garlic. Add tofu. Add enough water to just cover. Cover and refrigerate at least overnight before using. Rotate the slices occasionally, as the ones on the bottom will absorb more of the tamari and become quite salty.

To assemble (per sandwich):
2 slices marinated tofu
1 teaspoon light oil for sauté
Nutritional yeast
Granulated garlic or garlic powder
2 slices fresh bread
Mayonnaise or mustard, optional
Tomato slices
Leaf lettuce

Heat a small sauté pan or griddle to medium high. Add 1 teaspoon oil. Heat to sizzling. Place two slices tofu per sandwich in the hot pan. Sprinkle with nutritional yeast and garlic. When one side has browned, turn over and sprinkle a little bit more yeast and garlic on the tofu. Serve on bread with mayonnaise and/or mustard, slices of fresh tomato and lettuce.

Orange Ginger Tempeh (for 4 sandwiches)

George Abele wanted a tempeh sandwich for the menu: the TempehLT. His favorite marinade was this orange ginger variety. We grilled it like the tofu, served with tomato and lettuce on fresh bakery bread.

4-ounce block of tempeh cut into 8 triangles (see drawing)

Marinade:
1/2 cup sunflower or other light oil
Juice of 1 orange
1 1/2 tablespoons finely grated orange zest
1 1/2 tablespoons grated fresh ginger root
1/2 cup tamari
Water to cover

Slice tempeh in half horizontally. Divide into 2 squares. Cut each square into 2 triangles.

Slice tempeh horizontally across the middle. Cut each half into 4 triangles. In a mixing bowl, stir together oil, orange juice, zest, ginger and tamari. Add tempeh pieces. Add enough water to cover. If you won't use the tempeh within a few days, rotate the slices, carefully as they can be fragile, from the bottom to the top. Those on the bottom will absorb more tamari and tend to be saltier. Cover and refrigerate until ready to grill.

To assemble (per sandwich):
2 triangles marinated tempeh
Nutritional yeast
Granulated garlic or garlic powder
2 slices fresh bread
Mayonnaise, mustard, salsa, optional

Heat a small fry pan or griddle. Add 1 teaspoon oil and heat until it sizzles. Grill 2 slices tempeh per sandwich. Sprinkle nutritional yeast and garlic on top. Flip over to brown second side. Serve with mayonnaise and/or mustard, sliced tomato and lettuce. Some customers liked cheese along with this tempeh.

Tempeh Reuben (for 4 Reuben sandwiches or Tempeh Taters)

Dwayne Doner was a master of seasonings. He came up with just the right mix to approximate popular "meat" tastes translated for tofu, tempeh and seitan. This marinade is a combination of sweet and savory. It complimented our home-fried potatoes quite nicely. Our tempeh version of the corned beef Reuben sandwich was made with fresh, crunchy Hill Farm of Vermont sauerkraut, Swiss cheese and a house-prepared Thousand Island dressing on bakery rye, pumpernickel or sometimes oatmeal bread. Only diehard meat eaters, or those who didn't really care for the Reuben to begin with, could resist this one.

4-ounce block of tempeh, thinly sliced on the diagonal (see diagram)

Marinade:
1/2 cup sunflower or other light oil
1/3 cup tamari
2 1/2 tablespoons maple syrup
1/3 cup water
3 to 4 cloves garlic, minced or pressed
1 tablespoon prepared Dijon-style mustard
1/3 cup very finely minced onion
1/3 teaspoon dried rosemary
2/3 teaspoon black pepper
2/3 teaspoon dried dill weed
2 teaspoons dried parsley
2/3 teaspoon Liquid Smoke
Pinch powdered ginger

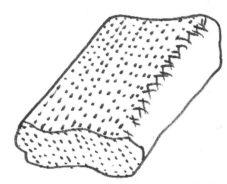

Take full 4-ounce block of tempeh. Begin along the long side. Make as many thin slices as you can on a slight diagonal.

Lay out your thinly sliced tempeh in a shallow dish or pan. These slices are fairly fragile, so handle them as little as possible. Whisk together oil, tamari, syrup, water, garlic, mustard, onion, rosemary, pepper, dill, parsley, liquid smoke and ginger in a small bowl. Pour over tempeh. Cover and marinate overnight.

To assemble (per sandwich):
2 slices rye, pumpernickel or your choice of bread
1 tablespoon butter
1 ounce sliced or grated Swiss cheese
3 to 4 slices Reuben-marinated tempeh
1/4 cup fresh sauerkraut
1 tablespoon Thousand Island Dressing: (mayonnaise, ketchup and sweet pickle relish)

Heat a heavy fry pan or griddle. Butter one side of each piece of bread. Place on pan, butter side down. Top with Swiss cheese. Place tempeh on griddle and cook till lightly browned. Flip over. Add sauerkraut to the grill. When tempeh is browned, place on top of bread and cheese. Put sauerkraut over tempeh. Spoon dressing over sauerkraut. Cover with second slice of bread and cheese. Serve hot.

Devil's Own Tempeh (to marinate 4 ounces, enough for 4 sandwiches)

Dwayne Doner played a mean blues harp, and had an extensive collection of blues tapes and CD's, which he shared with the rest of us. Being somewhat of a blues fanatic myself, I did not complain. One day, Dwayne came up with this new tempeh sandwich, featuring a spicy marinade and hot peppers. Legend has it that father of the Blues, Robert Johnson, made a pact with the devil to play the way he did. In his honor, we called this "The Devil's Own Tempeh Sandwich," and the name stuck.

4-ounce block tempeh, cut into 8 triangles

Marinade:
1/2 cup sunflower or other light oil
1/2 cup Louisiana-style hot sauce
1/4 cup tamari
1/2 teaspoon hot oil
1/2 tablespoon ground cayenne pepper
6 to 9 cloves garlic, minced or pressed
1/2 teaspoon dried thyme
1 1/2 tablespoons fresh lemon juice
1/4 cup finely minced onion
3 minced fresh basil leaves/ 3/4 teaspoon dry basil

Slice tempeh in half horizontally. Cut each half into 4 triangles. In a bowl big enough to hold the marinade and the tempeh, whisk together oil, hot sauce, tamari, hot oil, cayenne, garlic, thyme, lemon juice, onion and basil. Add the tempeh to the marinade. Cover and refrigerate overnight.

To assemble (per sandwich):
Sliced green and/or red pepper
Sliced onion
1 teaspoon oil for grilling
2 slices bread
1 tablespoon butter
1 ounce sliced or grated cheddar cheese
2 slices Devil's Own marinated tempeh
1 tablespoon salsa or red chili sauce

Heat heavy fry pan or griddle over medium heat. Sauté enough pepper and onion for one sandwich (1/4 to 1/3 cup). While they're grilling, butter bread and place on pan, butter side down. Top with cheddar. Add tempeh to the pan and grill it until it is brown on both sides. Place tempeh on top of one slice of grilled bread and cheese. Top with grilled peppers and onions. Top with choice of salsa or red chili sauce and second piece of grilled bread and cheese. Serve immediately.

California Tempeh (to marinate 4 ounces tempeh, enough for 4 sandwiches)

This is another Dwayne Doner original. This is more subtly flavored than the other marinades. It is especially nice on a hot summer day. It compliments the artichoke hearts, avocado, olives and sprouts for the California sandwich or can be used in stir fries or a pasta salad.

4 ounces tempeh cut into 8 triangles

Marinade:
1/2 cup olive oil
1/2 cup pizza sauce or flavored tomato sauce
1/2 cup water
1/2 cup tamari
3 cloves garlic, minced or pressed
1 tablespoon dried basil/ 2 tablespoons fresh
1 tablespoon red wine or balsamic vinegar
1 tablespoon dried parsley/ 2 tablespoons fresh
1 1/2 tablespoons fresh lemon juice
1 teaspoon finely grated lemon zest
1/4 cup pureed black olives, the more flavor the better

Slice block of tempeh horizontally in half. Cut each half into 4 triangles. In a bowl big enough for marinade and tempeh, whisk together oil, sauce, water, tamari, garlic, basil, vinegar, parsley, lemon juice, lemon zest and pureed olives. Add tempeh, cover and refrigerate overnight.

To assemble (per sandwich):
2 slices grilled California marinated tempeh
2 slices fresh bread
Mayonnaise or mustard
Sliced avocado
Quartered artichoke hearts
Alfalfa or clover sprouts
Sliced Greek olives
Tomato slices
Lettuce

Heat heavy fry pan or griddle. Brown tempeh on both sides. Place tempeh on bread slices spread with your choice of mayonnaise, mustard or both. Pile avocado slices, artichoke hearts, sprouts, olives, tomato and lettuce on top. Cover with second slice of bread.

Tempeh for Tempeh Terkey and Tempeh Salad (for 4 ounces tempeh/ 4 servings)

Another in the long list of Dwayne Doner originals. His secret, he said, was in duplicating the seasonings of meat dishes. The combination of parsley, sage, rosemary and thyme give that poultry taste without the meat. After the tempeh is baked, it can be cubed and dressed for tempeh salad or sliced and gravied and accompanied with bread stuffing and cranberry sauce for the Hot Tempeh Terkey Sandwich.

4 ounces tempeh left in one block

Marinade:
1/2 cup olive oil
1/4 cup tamari
1/2 tablespoon dried thyme
1 tablespoon dried parsley
1/2 teaspoon black pepper
1/2 teaspoon dried sage
1/2 teaspoon dried rosemary
4 to 5 cloves garlic, minced or pressed
1/4 cup finely minced onion

In a shallow baking dish, whisk together olive oil, tamari, thyme, parsley, pepper, sage, rosemary, garlic and onion. Place whole block of tempeh in it. Cover and refrigerate overnight. Preheat oven to 350 degrees and bake the marinated block 35-45 minutes until browned. Cool. For Hot Terkey, slice. For salad, dice small.

Sandwich:
Sliced Terkey
Stuffing
Cranberry sauce
Mushroom gravy

Salad:
4 ounces Terkey-baked and diced tempeh
1/2 cup diced celery/ 1 stalk
1/2 cup grated carrot/ 1/2 carrot

Dressing:
1 7-ounce block tofu
1/4 cup olive oil
1/2 tablespoon cider vinegar
1/2 teaspoon celery seed
1/2 teaspoon Spike or other seasoned salt
1/4 teaspoon black pepper
1 clove garlic, minced or pressed
3 tablespoons water

Toss together diced, baked tempeh, celery and carrot in a small bowl. In a food processor or blender, buzz tofu, oil, vinegar, celery seed, Spike, pepper, garlic and onion to make a smooth dressing. Pour dressing over tempeh and vegetable mixture and toss lightly to combine. Use on sandwich with favorite accompaniments or on a salad plate.

The Food was Good Too . . . .

Daily Bread's following made for long lines for weekend brunch and frustrated cooks and bakers who couldn't put the food out any faster. Just before we decided to increase the dining room and kitchens, freelance reporter Marialisa Calta visited and wrote a review for *Seven Days*:

...I walked into Daily Bread ... and was immediately transported nearly 25 years and 3,000 miles away. It was the mid-'70's, and the staff at the Seattle alternative newspaper I worked on met at our neighborhood hangout....So in the same way Daily Bread suits me just fine. It manages, unself-consciously, to preserve some of that relaxed, free spirit feeling of the '70's without the overweening sense of self-righteousness that was also an unfortunate hallmark of the era....It even has a chalkboard for public graffiti. On the day I visited last week someone had scribbled the semi-subversive admonition: "Phone in sick."
... While I was taken with the ambiance...the food was pretty good too....My friend Sue ordered the chicken pot pie, which is one of the best I've ever tasted-and that includes my own, which I think is pretty great...The homefries were nicely spiced and just crispy enough. Other specialties include yam burritos, tempeh Reuben, and a wide variety of homemade soups. **(56)**

Grilled Cheese

Just about everyone has his or her own version of the grilled cheese sandwich. Our secrets to success were fresh bakery bread, liberal amounts of butter and a weight to press the sandwich while grilling. Here are the basics.

2 slices fresh bread
1 tablespoon butter
2 to 4 slices cheddar cheese

Heat a heavy fry pan or griddle over medium heat while assembling your sandwich. Arrange bread, cheese, bread. Butter the top of the sandwich. Turn over into your hot pan. Grill until bottom is lightly browned and cheese begins to soften. Butter the top of the sandwich. Turn over sandwich. Place a heavy pan on top of sandwich while second side browns and cheese melts.

Grilled Cheese and Tomato: add sliced tomato between cheese slices before grilling

Tuna Melt: layer 1/3 cup tuna salad between cheese slices before grilling

Grilled Eggplant Parmesan Sandwich

This is a shortcut eggplant parmesan sandwich. The eggplant may be prepared ahead of time or just before assembling. Using mozzarella, pizza sauce and sliced pepper inside the sandwich with the eggplant gives the mouth the eggplant parmesan experience without all the mess.

For the eggplant:
1 large eggplant, sliced and lightly salted to remove excess moisture
1 cup milk
1 egg
1 1/2 to 2 cups breadcrumbs
1/4 cup parmesan cheese

Slice eggplant, salt it and let it sit at least half hour. Beat egg and milk together in a shallow dish. Stir together breadcrumbs and parmesan cheese in another shallow dish. Grease a baking pan. Heat oven to 350 degrees. Dip slices of eggplant in batter, then breadcrumb mixture and arrange on baking sheets. Bake 15-20 minutes until lightly brown.

The sandwich:
2 slices fresh bread
1 to 2 slices Parmesan baked eggplant slices
Sliced tomato
Sliced green pepper
2 tablespoons pizza sauce
Sliced or grated mozzarella cheese

Prepare grilled cheese sandwich using bread, cheese, eggplant, tomato, peppers, sauce, cheese and bread. Grill until cheese is melted and outside of sandwich is browned on both sides.

Seitan Deluxe Sandwich

This is another from Dwayne Doner's incredible culinary repertoire. We often described it to customers as a "vegetarian Philly cheese steak." Caramelized grilled onions and thinly sliced grilled seitan were stuffed inside a grilled cheese sandwich with either steak or barbecue sauce, both made in house.

Steak sauce:

2 tablespoons sunflower or other light oil
1/4 cup finely minced onion
3 cloves garlic, minced or pressed
1/4 teaspoon dried thyme
1/4 teaspoon black pepper
1/2 tablespoon minced fresh parsley
1 cup raisins pureed with 1/2 cup water
1/2 teaspoon finely grated lemon zest
1/2 teaspoon lemon juice
2 tablespoons tamari
2 tablespoons catsup
2 1/4 tablespoons cider vinegar

Sauté onion, garlic, thyme, pepper and parsley in sunflower oil till onions are translucent. Puree raisins in a blender or food processor. Add to the sauté, stirring constantly. Reduce heat and add zest, lemon juice, tamari, catsup and vinegar. Simmer 20 minutes, stirring frequently to prevent scorching. This sauce also forms the base for the seitan marinade for breakfast steaks.

Barbecue sauce:

1/2 cup finely chopped onion
5 to 6 cloves garlic, minced or pressed
1 1/2 teaspoons dried basil
1 1/2 teaspoons minced fresh parsley
2 tablespoons sunflower or other light oil
1 1/4 cups catsup
1/4 teaspoon dried thyme
1/8 teaspoon dried rosemary
1/4 teaspoon Liquid Smoke
2 tablespoons maple syrup
Pinch ground red chili

Sauté onion, garlic, basil and parsley in sunflower oil until onions are translucent. Add the catsup, thyme, rosemary, Liquid Smoke, syrup and chili. Reduce heat and simmer 10 minutes, stirring frequently to prevent sticking.

To assemble:
Few slices seitan
Few slices onion
Few drops sunflower or other light oil
2 slices fresh bread
1 tablespoon butter
2 to 4 slices cheddar cheese
1 tablespoon Steak or Barbecue sauce

Heat a heavy fry pan or griddle over medium heat. Sauté onions till they just begin to caramelize. Sauté the seitan next to the onions. Add 1 tablespoon sauce of your choice to the seitan. Butter bread slices. Place cheese on unbuttered sides of bread. Place onions on one, seitan on the other. Place, butter side down, in the fry pan. Grill until cheese has melted and bottoms are browned. Put together and serve immediately.

Seitan Breakfast Steaks

The Worthington Company, which produces many vegetarian meat substitutes, ran short of their vegetarian sausage, Prosage, which we served at Daily Bread. We needed something to serve in its place, and Dwayne Doner came up with this option. The "steaks" may be served with breakfast or in a sandwich, or come up with your own concoction.

1 pound bulk seitan, sliced thin on the diagonal
1/3 cup steak sauce (see above)
1/3 cup water
1/3 cup sunflower or other light oil
3 tablespoons tamari
1 teaspoon dried rosemary
1 teaspoon dried thyme
3 cloves garlic, minced or pressed

Slice seitan on the diagonal into thin strip steaks. In a bowl large enough to hold marinade and seitan, whisk together steak sauce, water, oil, tamari, rosemary, thyme and garlic. Cover and marinate at least overnight. Brown on a hot fry pan or griddle to serve.

Market Share II . . . .

Vermont's Chittenden County continued to grow. It was home to IBM, IDX and General Electric-by-another-name. It's five colleges flourished. Burlington topped the Ten-best-places-to-live list. Neighbors in Williston fought a plan for one quadrant of Tafts Corner; the other three were developed into at first a few strip malls and then, by the mid-1990s, the full complement of big box stores.

When Hannaford's, a New England grocery chain, opened its Williston store, it featured organic produce, soy milk and locally produced fresh breads. There was a bank branch in the store and others nearby. Its pharmacy prices were the lowest around. It had wine. There was lots of parking.

Daily Bread's gross sales dropped by 10%, about $20,000. The same story reverberated around the village. Everyone, from the post office to the bank, from the corner market to the beverage store, the shoe store, the florist, felt the pinch. It was sobering. More than one of us began to consider for the first time whether and when to get out.

Business rebounded some, but it became more of a struggle to compete against the low, low, low prices ten miles down the road.

Veggie Burgers

There is now a selection of frozen veggie burgers in almost every supermarket across the country. They have overcome their former bad reputation based on failed early experiments with tofu, textured protein, and the like. Here are two burgers which Daily Bread customers enjoyed. Both of these burgers may be frozen once cooked, then thawed and warmed or microwaved at a later date.

Sun burgers (6)

Mare Kuhlman brought this recipe to the Bread when we first opened the café. These tasty, hearty burgers are made from sunflower seeds and vegetables with egg to bind. We served them with lettuce and tomato on bakery fresh bread or buns. We had many requests for these, though those who do not care for sunflower seeds are not likely to care for them.

Burger:
2 cups sunflower seeds, ground fine in a blender or food processor
1/4 cup finely minced onion
1/2 cup finely minced carrot/ 1/2 large carrot
1/2 cup finely minced celery/ 1 large stalk
1 clove garlic, minced or pressed
1/3 teaspoon salt
3/4 teaspoon tamari
Pinch Spike or other seasoned salt
3/4 teaspoon dried basil
1 1/2 tablespoons light oil
1 1/2 tablespoons minced fresh parsley
1 lightly beaten egg

Lettuce and tomato for accompaniment
12 slices bread or 6 burger buns for accompaniment

Grind sunflower seeds to a fine meal in a blender or food processor. If using a blender, buzz small amounts at a time so as not to over-stress the blender. Combine all ingredients in a medium mixing bowl and blend. Form into patties to fit the bread or buns you will be using. Heat a heavy fry pan or griddle. Grill burgers till toasty brown on both sides. Serve on bread with lettuce, tomato and your favorite mayo, ketchup, salsa, mustard or other condiments. Or freeze some for later.

Kris' Veggie Burgers (6)

Kris Hulphers served these to her housemates and her then two-year-old daughter Anathea. Her housemates asked me to try them. "Garden Burger Mix" is available at most health food stores. We offered these on fresh bakery bread or buns with burger fixings. They hang together better if the mixtuure chills overnight or all day before grilling.

Burger:
1 cup cooked oatmeal/ 1/2 cup uncooked
1 large raw beet, peeled and coarsely grated
1 large carrot, peeled and coarsely grated
1/3 cup minced onion
1/2 cup Garden Burger Mix
1 egg, lightly beaten
1 tablespoon tamari
Pinch Spike or other seasoned salt
Pinch nutritional yeast, optional
Lettuce and tomato
12 slices bread or 6 buns

Kris & butter can at the grill.

Prepare oatmeal, or save some from breakfast. Grate beets and carrot. Mix oatmeal, beet, carrot, onion, Garden Burger mix, egg, tamari, salt and yeast (if you are using) in a medium mixing bowl. Cover and refrigerate overnight or at least 6 hours. When ready to cook, heat heavy fry pan or griddle. Form mix into patties to fit the bread or buns you have. Grill over medium heat to brown well on both sides. Serve with your favorite condiments.

From other sources:

Moosewood Cookbook
Falafel--made into patties rather than balls, grilled not fried

Growing Pains: Out to the Street......................................

Richmond's success brought pressure to expand. The old dining room was small, and customers waited an hour for a table on weekend mornings. The café kitchen was tight and at the limit of efficient production. The front of the building became available. Jeb came forward to design and carry out the neccessary renovations. Plumber Rick Pemberton and electrician Pete O'Brien took care of the licensed work.

The new dining room extended all the way to the front of the building, opening onto a porch facing Bridge Street, the main thoroughfare through Richmond's business section. Many customers missed the old windows, which we had removed to install a real pastry case, so we used them to create a windscreen and some privacy for the new dining room. A few Bread employees and friends assisted in the refit. The fire inspector insisted we install automatic extinguishing, a mere $5,000 item. Julius Dychton and Jeb made three larger versions of our original wrought iron and wood tables.

We increased the number of seats from 20 to 40, added a second bathroom, doubled the café prep area and added a second stack of deck ovens. I borrowed $15,000 from a friend and paid that back after the sale of the business. Even so, the many extra costs of expansion ate up the bank account.

It was the late 1990s: the economy appeared to be booming. McDonald's was offering an $8/hour starting salary; my longtime cooks were only making $10. Unemployment rates were reported to be the lowest in thirty years. It was a worker's market. There was a tremendous turnover of workers. Training required time and attention, above and beyond the regular schedule of prep, production and clean-up.

Headaches went from occasional to chronic. The bakery and the café kitchen were not contiguous anymore. We traded a certain sense of whole for more productive work spaces. The numbers grew to require management, which we had side-stepped for years. I had to become much more of a manager and boss than I ever cared to be. I rarely got to bake. I missed customer-time at the counter. Bills piled up while I paid off expansion-related expenses.

The thrill was gone for me. It seemed time for someone else to take Daily Bread into its next incarnation, take it into the 21st century. I put the business up for sale.

Mexican Suite
Kris' Veggie Enchiladas (6)

Kris Hulphers learned to make these from a California friend. Her housemates urged her to try them at the Bread. She advises that spinach smooths out the filling, otherwise any choice of vegetables will do. These are smooth and cheesy, and the chocolate in the mole (that's pronounced mo-lay) sauce gives it an unusual background flavor. We used fresh flour tortillas, but you can use store bought without seriously diminishing the dish.

1 recipe flour tortillas (see page 113)

Sauce:
3 tablespoons olive oil
3 tablespoons ground red chili, or use part paprika for a milder sauce
1/2 cup flour
2 teaspoons ground cumin
3 cloves garlic, minced or pressed
3/4 teaspoon dried basil
4 1/2 cups boiling water
3/4 cup tomato sauce, 1/2 14-ounce can
3 tablespoons chocolate chips

Filling:
6 cups mixed vegetables with some spinach
Steamed broccoli
Lightly steamed winter or summer squash
Celery, onion, your choice
3 cups grated Monterey Jack or cheddar cheese/ 12 ounces

Prepare tortillas. Grill them lightly till golden brown and still flexible.

Prepare sauce. Heat olive oil in a large fry pan and toast chili till aromatic and bubbling. Add flour and cook another 2-3 minutes, stirring constantly. Add cumin, garlic and basil and continue to cook 2 minutes. Whisk boiling water into flour and spice mixture and continue to cook till smooth and thickened. Whisk in tomato sauce and chocolate chips. Remove from heat.

Prepare vegetables. Preheat oven to 350 degrees. Spread a thin layer of sauce in the bottom of a 10"x14" baking pan. Fill each tortilla with 1/4 cup cheese, 1 cup vegetables and a few tablespoons sauce. Roll and place seam side down in baking dish. Sprinkle the remaining cheese over the rolled enchiladas and top with the rest of the sauce. Bake 45 minutes till all bubbling.

3 Sisters Burrito (6 servings of 2 each)

Bakery friend and extraordinary macrobiotic cook Robin Hopps advised college food services and individuals on healthier vegetarian food options. Robin took an idea she found in Mary Estella's *Natural Foods* cookbook and offered this variation to the Bread. Rose Warnock and Dwayne Doner both tweaked it to present a dish which pleased our palates.

12 corn tortillas, your favorite brand

Sauce:
3/4 cup olive oil
1/3 cup minced fresh parsley
6 to 9 cloves garlic, minced or pressed
1/2 teaspoon salt

Filling:
1 tablespoon olive oil
2 cups diced winter squash/ 2 pounds butternut, buttercup or Hubbard
1 teaspoon ground cumin
1/4 teaspoon black pepper
1/4 teaspoon crushed red pepper
2 tablespoons minced fresh cilantro
2 cups cooked and drained kidney beans/ 1 14-ounce can
2 cups fresh, frozen or canned kernel corn, drained
2 tablespoons tamari

Garnish:
4 ounces alfalfa or clover sprouts
3/4 cup diced tomatoes

If corn tortillas are frozen, thaw so they will be pliable. Prepare sauce by pureeing the 3/4 cup oil, parsley, garlic and salt in a blender or food processor. Set aside. Preheat oven to 350 degrees. In a skillet or heavy saucepan with a lid, sauté squash, cumin, black pepper, crushed red pepper and cilantro in 1 tablespoon olive oil till spices are fragrant. Reduce heat and cover to simmer till squash is fork tender. Add the drained kidney beans, corn and tamari and cook another 5 minutes to mingle flavors. Remove from heat. Grease 6 soup bowls or a 9"x13" baking pan. Distribute filling among the 12 corn tortillas, arranging open side up in your bowls (2 per bowl) or pan. Pour the sauce over them. Bake 20-25 minutes. Garnish and serve.

Mexican Pie (10"x14" casserole/ 6-8 servings)

I first encountered this dish at a Sunray Meditation Society weekend retreat. Rika Henderson found it a well received addition. I sometimes described it as southwestern lasagna. A cornmeal polenta crust gets layers of beans, vegetables, sauce and cheese. Add a simple salad and you have dinner.

Crust:
1 cup cornmeal
2 1/2 cups boiling water
4 tablespoons butter/ 1/2 stick
1/2 teaspoon salt

Casserole:
1 16-ounce can refried beans/ or 2 cups homemade (see p. 215)
2 cups sliced mushrooms/ 8 ounces
2 cups diced green pepper
2 cups kernel corn/ 1 14-ounce can
2 cups pizza sauce/ 1 14-ounce can (or see p. 108)
1 cup salsa
1 cup grated cheddar or Monterey Jack cheese/ 4 ounces

Preheat oven to 350 degrees. Prepare crust. Whisk cornmeal into boiling water. Reduce heat and continue whisking until mixture thickens. Whisk in butter and salt. Spread into the bottom of your casserole. Bake 30 minutes.

Sauté mushrooms, pepper and corn till just wilting. Spread refried beans over the corn crust. Spread vegetables over the beans. Stir pizza sauce and salsa together. Pour over the vegetables. Sprinkle cheese evenly on top of the sauce. Bake another 45 minutes until the whole is bubbly and the cheese is lightly browned.

Chilies Rellenos (6 servings)

Mare Kuhlman brought this out from her personal stash of recipes in early Café days. These rellenos are baked, not fried, and can be prepared ahead of time. They reheat well. The stuffed chilies are baked in a soufflé-like batter and served with a topping of sour cream and salsa or red chili sauce.

12 whole roasted green chilies/ 1 16-ounce can
8 ounces cheddar or Monterey Jack cut into 12 "fingers"

Batter:
2/3 cup flour
1/2 teaspoon baking powder
1/2 teaspoon baking soda
1 teaspoon ground cumin
2 teaspoons ground coriander
3 eggs, separated
1/3 cup buttermilk or yogurt
1/3 cup milk

Toppings:
1 cup sour cream
1/2 cup salsa or Red Chili Sauce (see page 216)

Drain chilies, if using canned. Cut cheese to fit inside peppers. Stuff one cheese "finger" into each chili. Place 2 stuffed chilies in each soup bowl or arrange in a 10"x14" casserole. Preheat oven to 350 degrees. Prepare the batter. Whisk together flour, baking powder, baking soda, cumin and coriander in a medium-sized mixing bowl. Separate eggs, placing whites in a beater bowl. Stir yolks with buttermilk and regular milk in a small bowl. Stir yolk mixture into flour mix. Whip egg whites to firm peaks and fold gently into yolk and flour batter. Pour or spoon batter over peppers and bake 15-20 minutes until tops lightly browned. Serve with sour cream and salsa or red chili sauce.

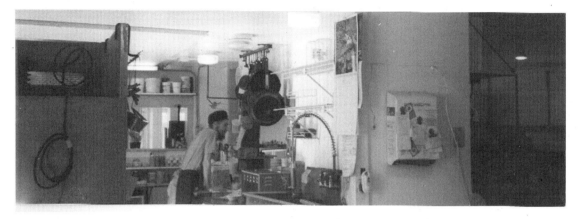

Cook David Babson ready for an order.

New, improved, and the silverwear still doesn't match. . . . .

Customers were relieved that we kept the funky feel of the old dining room while adding natural light from three sides. There was more space between the tables. The window divider lent privacy to the front space. The new bathrooms created a wall enclosing a cozy corner with a view to the street where adults could easily corral busy toddlers while enjoying tea or lunch with friends. People donated toys and books their own kids had outgrown.

Our version of "online" ordering was a clothes line and pulley system to send written orders from the front counter to the kitchen.

We kept our menu of bakery breads and sweets, daily bakery and cafe specials, breakfast, lunch and weekend brunch. We continued to use as many local products as possible.

Burlington Free Press food columnist Debbie Salomon reviewed the expanded space, and put it well: "Last month, Bott pushed her space forward to the street....Thank goodness Bott hasn't succumbed to cuteness. Nothing matches, not even cutlery." (57)

Noodles and ...

Ginger Fried Noodles (4-6 servings)

Cook Andrew Paschetto writes of this dish:

This is what happens when the cook really wants lo-mein but only has an enormous flat griddle to work on! This is always done *mis en place*, ingredients all cut, placed and ready to go. Don't be shy with the seasoning; this is intended to be very fresh and very flavorful. When your pan and oil are hot, grab a fistful of veggies and let 'em rip. Be unafraid of a hot pan and jumping oil. Brief flare ups are more showy than dangerous. This dish cooks faster in the pan than in a microwave, and is 10 times tastier for it.

1/2 pound linguine, cooked al dente, drained and cooled
6 to 8 ounces extra firm tofu, diced and lightly toasted in pan or oven
3 cups shredded bok choy, Chinese or regular cabbage/ about 10 ounces
3/4 cup diagonally sliced celery/ 1 1/2 stalks
1 1/4 cup julienne or matchstick cut carrots/ 2 carrots
3/4 cup thinly sliced onion
4 diagonally sliced scallions
3 tablespoons grated or finely minced fresh ginger root/ 3-4 inches
1 teaspoon toasted sesame oil
1/8 teaspoon ground red chili, optional
Tamari
Toasted sesame oil

Have all ingredients ready to go. Cook pasta. Toast the tofu. Heat a heavy fry pan, a wok or griddle on high heat till a drop of water sizzles immediately. Add a squirt of toasted sesame oil. Throw in a fistful each of cabbage and celery, keeping it moving, letting it fry about 30 seconds before adding carrots and onion. Keep it stirring and frying another 30 seconds. Add scallions, ginger and tofu. Sprinkle a little red chili on if desired. Stir and fry another 30 seconds. Add a handful of noodles and a squirt each of tamari and toasted sesame oil. Toss and heat till noodles just start to brown. Serve piping hot.

Alison's Lasagna (10"x14" casserole/ 8-10 servings)

Alison Forrest learned to make this as a youngster from her mother. It is a tasty, hearty vegetarian version of the Italian classic. Alison serves this to Huntington's Brewster Pierce Elementary School students, who love it. She often substitutes Swiss chard for the spinach!

15 long or 18 short lasagna noodles plus a few extra for the pot
6 cups pizza sauce (see page 108) or prepared seasoned tomato sauce
1 pound frozen spinach/ 1 1/2 pounds fresh
2 pounds ricotta cheese/ 4 cups
2 cups grated parmesan cheese/ 8 ounces
3 eggs
Black pepper
4 cups grated mozzarella cheese/ 1 pound

Cook noodles in plenty of water with a squirt of olive oil. Drain and rinse in cold water. Chop spinach, if using fresh, or thaw frozen. Combine spinach with ricotta, parmesan, eggs and black pepper. Stir to blend.

Preheat oven to 350 degrees. Oil your baking pan. Spread a thin layer of sauce in the bottom of your pan. Arrange a layer of noodles on top of sauce. Spoon about 1/3 of the ricotta mixture over the noodles. Sprinkle about 1/4 of the mozzarella over the ricotta. Spoon about 1/3 of the sauce over all this. Repeat noodles, ricotta, mozzarella, sauce two more times. Top with last of the mozzarella. Cover with aluminum foil. Bake, covered, at least 45 minutes. Remove foil and bake another 15 minutes or until cheese on top is browned and all is bubbly.

If you want to prepare this ahead of time, you may use uncooked noodles, assemble the whole casserole and freeze or refrigerate until ready to bake. The noodles must sit at least overnight to work this way. Thaw at least an hour. Preheat oven to 350 degrees. Bake as above.

Lentil Stroganoff (4-6 servings)

Rose Warnock found the inspiration for this low fat vegetarian variety of the classic noodle dish in a *Cooking Light* magazine. She played with the quantities and arrived at this recipe. It is a surprisingly tasty and satisfying casserole, creamy and flavorful with plenty of mushroom taste.

3 cups egg noodles, cooked al dente and rinsed/ about 10 ounces
1 1/4 cups green lentils cooked in 3 1/2 cups water/1 16-ounce can, drained
1/2 teaspoon oil for sauté
2 1/2 cups sliced mushrooms/ 10-12 ounces
1 cup chopped onion
2 cloves garlic, minced or pressed
2 tablespoons flour
2 teaspoons dried mustard
1 can fat-free mushroom soup
1/2 cup lowfat yogurt
1/2 teaspoon black pepper
2 tablespoons minced fresh parsley

Prepare lentils, if starting with dry, and noodles. Set aside. Preheat oven to 350 degrees. Grease your baking pan. In a medium fry pan, sauté mushrooms, onion and garlic in oil till onions wilt. Sprinkle flour and mustard onto sauté and continue to cook another 2 to 3 minutes. Stir together in a small bowl the soup, yogurt and black pepper. Add this mixture to the sauté and stir to make a thick sauce. Toss with the lentils and noodles in a mixing bowl and then spread into your prepared pan. Sprinkle parsley on top. Bake 30 minutes.

Mushroom Pea Noodle Delight (4-6 servings)

Heidi Champney brought this recipe from the Oberlin College coop dining hall kitchen, where she cooked when she was a student there. A fellow student ate a similar dish while visiting The Farm community in Tennessee. *The Farm Cookbook* does offer a recipe for Tofu Pot Pie, which closely resembles this. The nutritional yeast gravy ties together the noodles, tofu and vegetables, and gives it a rich smoky flavor. The turmeric gives it a beautiful golden color. People not fond of nutritional yeast will likely not enjoy this. But try it for a delicious and nutritious casserole.

1 1/2 cups egg noodles, cooked al dente and drained/ 5-6 ounces
1 1/2 to 2 cups fresh or frozen green peas
1 teaspoon olive oil for sauté
3 cups sliced mushrooms/ 12 ounces
8 ounces cubed tofu/ about 2 cups
1/3 cup diced scallions/ 6 to 7 scallions
1/8 teaspoon black pepper

Sauce:
1/4 cup olive oil
2 tablespoons toasted sesame oil
6 tablespoons soy or other margarine/ 3/4 stick
3/4 cup flour
2 cups hot tap water
3 tablespoons tamari
3 to 4 cloves garlic, minced or pressed
1 cup nutritional yeast
1/2 teaspoon turmeric
Paprika to dust top

Prepare noodles. Shell or thaw peas. Set aside. Heat oil in a fry pan over medium heat. Sauté mushrooms, tofu, scallions and black pepper in butter till scallions and mushrooms begin to wilt. Remove from heat and mix with cooked noodles. Preheat oven to 350 degrees. Grease casserole pan.

Make sauce. Heat olive and sesame oils with margarine in a medium saucepan. Add flour and toast 2-3 minutes. Whisk hot water into this roux to make thick gravy. Add tamari, garlic, nutritional yeast and turmeric and heat another 2-3 minutes, stirring frequently.

Stir peas and half the gravy into the noodles. Spread into greased casserole. Pour rest of the gravy over this and sprinkle paprika on top. Bake 30 minutes until casserole is bubbling and top lightly browned.

Linguini al Forno (10"x14" casserole; 4-6 servings)

Forno means oven in Italian, translating this dish's name to baked linguine. Andrew Paschetto wanted a pasta and vegetable dish without cheese. He writes of this:

Fancy Italian for baked noodles and veggies. This can take about whatever you have, but make sure your ingredients compliment tomatoes. Fresh tomatoes are most flavorful, but canned whole ones will do in a pinch. Use plenty of your favorite olives, capers, even anchovies. Herbs and a good fruity olive oil. Imagine a hot, salty pasta salad.

1/2 pound dry linguine, cooked al dente, drained and rinsed
1 tablespoon olive oil for sauté
1 cup sliced onions
2 cups sliced mushrooms/ 8 ounces
1 green pepper, minced
1 sweet red pepper, minced
1 1/2 diced ripe tomatoes/ 1 16-ounce can
1/2 cup ripe olives, as flavorful as possible
1 1/2 tablespoons dried basil/ 3 tablespoons fresh
2 tablespoons dried oregano/ 4 tablespoons fresh
Pinch crushed red pepper
2 dashes red wine vinegar
Salt and pepper
1/2 to 3/4 cups bread crumbs for top

Prepare noodles. Set aside. Grease baking pan. Preheat oven to 350 degrees. Heat olive oil in a large fry pan. Sauté onions till translucent. Add mushrooms, green and red peppers to sauté and continue to cook until mushrooms soften and turn brown. Remove from heat.

In a roomy mixing bowl, toss together noodles, sautéed vegetables, fresh tomatoes, olives, basil, oregano, pepper, vinegar and salt and pepper. Spread into prepared baking pan. Sprinkle breadcrumbs on top. Bake 35-40 minutes.

Seitan Goulash (10"x14" casserole/ 8 cups)

This is a Dwayne Doner's veggie variation on an American comfort food, American Chop Suey. Roasting the seitan with herbs and tamari gives it good flavor. This is an easy crowd-pleaser at potlucks.

6 ounces seitan diced small
1/2 teaspoon dried thyme
1/4 teaspoon dried rosemary
2 1/2 tablespoons olive oil
2 1/2 tablespoons tamari

3 cups dry elbow macaroni, cooked and rinsed/ 12 ounces
1 medium onion, diced
1 large pepper, red or green, diced
3 to 4 cloves garlic, minced or pressed
2 1/2 teaspoons dried basil
1 14-ounce can canned diced tomatoes/ 1 1/2 cups
1 14-ounce can pizza sauce (or see page 108)/ 1 1/4 cups

Preheat oven to 350 degrees. Toss seitan with thyme, rosemary, oil and tamari in your casserole pan. Bake 12-15 minutes until seitan begins to brown. Boil macaroni. Sauté onion, pepper, garlic and basil in a little olive oil until vegetables just begin to wilt. Combine seitan, macaroni, tomatoes, cooked vegetables and sauce in a large bowl. Spread into casserole and bake, covered, for 25-30 minutes.

Prosage Goulash (10"x14" casserole/about 8 cups)

This is another Dwayne recipe using a vegetarian sausage instead of meat. We used Prosage at Daily Bread. Any veggie or meat sausage will do.

2 1/2 cups dry macaroni, cooked and rinsed
1 green pepper, diced
1 red pepper, diced
1 small carrot, peeled and diced
4 ounces Prosage or other vegetarian or meat sausage, diced small
2 tablespoons olive oil
1 14-ounce can tomatoes/ 1 1/2 cups
1 8-ounce can tomato sauce/ 3/4 cup
1 1/2 tablespoons dried basil
3 cloves garlic, minced or pressed
3/4 teaspoon dried oregano
1/4 teaspoon black pepper

Preheat oven to 350 degrees. Boil macaroni till tender. Sauté peppers, onion, carrot and Prosage in olive oil until veggies tender. Add tomatoes, sauce, basil, garlic, oregano and pepper to vegetables. Mix with the cooked noodles in a large bowl or cooking pot. Spread in your casserole and bake, covered, 30 minutes.

Vegan Mushroom Macaroni (10"x14" casserole/about 8 cups)

The Bread served an egg and cheese based Mushroom Macaroni for years. Vegan master Dwayne Doner developed this tasty non-dairy version.

2 1/2 cups dry elbow or rotini noodles, cooked and rinsed/ 8 ounces
2 cups sliced mushrooms/ 8 ounces
1 cup chopped mushrooms/ 4 ounces

1/2 cup chopped onion
1/4 cup minced fresh parsley
1/4 cup minced celery/ 1/2 stalk
1 red pepper, diced
2 cloves garlic, minced or pressed
3/4 teaspoon Spike or other seasoned salt
3/4 teaspoon thyme
1/2 cup olive oil
1/2 cup flour
1 tablespoon tamari
1/2 cup soy milk
1 cup water

Cook pasta; drain and set aside. Preheat oven to 350 degrees. Slice and chop mushrooms. Sauté onion, parsley, celery, red pepper, garlic, Spike, thyme and olive oil together in a large fry pan. When vegetables have wilted, add flour and continue to stir and cook 5-10 minutes on low low heat. Slowly whisk in the tamari, soy milk and water. When mixture begins to bubble, add mushrooms. Cook and stir till mushrooms are tender, about 5 minutes. Toss with pasta. Spread in casserole and bake 25 minutes to heat through.

Scene for a Day-or Was It Two? . . . .

A month after we opened the new dining room, a business card from Steve Price, representing 20th Century Fox, landed on my desk. News was circulating that our neck of the woods was to be the set for an upcoming Jim Carrey movie. Price returned to discuss the possibility of using the new Daily Bread for one of their filming locations. Staff and customers got all excited. I hadn't watched television for twenty-five years and rarely went to a movie. I had no idea what I was getting into.

I explained that to close off Bridge St. closed off the only route through the village and that other businesses and services would be affected; Fox would have to get permission from the town. Price had to strike deals with individual business people. Not everyone felt adequately compensated.

As it turned out, the crew did not finish in the allotted two days and had to finish some shots at a nearby sound stage.

The Go Go Gas station on Susie Wilson Road in Essex Junction was also contracted as a set location. The station swarmed with so many police and security guards that some passersby thought it was a crime scene. Around the county and state, the long list of pesky details the film makers asked for surprised us who suddenly found ourselves negotiating contracts and fulfilling obligations.

The props people, the electricians, the designers, the painters were great visitors: pleasant and professional. They frequently stopped in for something to eat on their way to other locations. *Burlington Free Press* reporter Casey Seiler quoted one of the producer brothers Farelly saying:

"You get some of these small towns and it's like a carnival, when you're bringing in 125 or 150 people," he said. "Some people can get a little rankled because they had to re-route their way home-but that's just part of making movies. But I'd say here we've had a lot less disturbance than we've had in other places." **(58)**

The state of Vermont had set up an office to court Hollywood location business. It seemed to me that many other programs were suffering from lack of government funds, and the money could have been used more wisely. The movie directors, the Farrelly brothers, wanted an out of the way location for their movie. For them it was business as usual.

Rice and...

Karen Wagner's Tempeh and Rice (4 servings)

Gemma Rinn contributed this recipe, which Andrew Paschetto fine tuned. The tempeh marinade is in the orange ginger tradition. The vegetable mixture of cabbage, onion, yam or carrot and mixed peppers is both colorful and delicious. The whole combination is served over rice, and makes a light but filling meal. It is best to marinate the tempeh overnight or all day to develop the full flavor.

4 ounces tempeh cut into 16 triangles

Marinade:
3/4 cup tamari
1/4 cup honey
6 to 8 cloves garlic, minced or pressed
1 1/2 tablespoons finely chopped or grated fresh ginger root/ 1-2 inches
1/4 cup orange juice
1/4 cup cider vinegar

The dish:
1 1/2 cups raw brown rice, cooked in 3 to 4 cups water
1 cup sliced yam or carrot, lightly steamed
1 cup thinly sliced cabbage, red or green
1 cup sliced onion
1/2 green pepper, in thin strips
1/2 red pepper, in thin strips
Light oil for sauté

Prepare the tempeh. Slice the tempeh in half horizontally. Cut each half into 8 triangles. Stir together tamari, honey, garlic, ginger, orange juice and vinegar in a bowl large enough to hold marinade and tempeh. Add tempeh to marinade. Cover and refrigerate overnight or all day.

When ready to prepare dish, cook brown rice. Lightly steam sliced yam or carrot over boiling water about 8 minutes. Toss cabbage, onion, yam or carrot and peppers together in a mixing bowl. Heat oil in a heavy fry pan, wok or griddle. Lift tempeh pieces with a slotted spoon. Add to hot oil. Saute till tempeh begins to brown. Add vegetables and continue to toss till onions and peppers wilt. Serve rice with tempeh and vegetables on top or mix.

Red Beans and Rice (4 servings)

Counter person and local masseuse extraordinaire Marcia Levison gained an appreciation of Cajun inspired food from her husband Jake. She thought Bread customers would appreciate a good Red Beans and Rice. Cook Andrew Paschetto added to her basic recipe and came up with this version.

Andrew's African American wife Deirdre and her relatives have educated him on the fine points of rice and beans. Here are his words of wisdom:

Since coming to Colorado, I have learned that when it comes to rice and beans, there is no substitute for fat. Seaweed gives beans body (and allegedly makes them less windy, but really after cooking and eating these things for twelve years I find the difference negligible--whether blowing at four knots or six, it still stinks). There are more naturally flavored vegetable oils available if you can't bring yourself to use pork fat. Be liberal with the "aromatics" onions, garlic and herbs. Make this as spicy as you can stand, let it cook a long time, let it be almost a soup, and add just a whisper of liquid smoke. Oh, and if you add the salt to the beans at the beginning, you can count on having to have your barber make a house call before they get tender.

2 cups raw kidney beans/ 3 1/2 cooked (2 16-ounce cans)
1/3 stick Kombu sea vegetable
1/2 cup diced onion
1 cup diced carrot/ 2-3 carrots
2/3 cup diced celery/ 2 stalks
2 2/3 tablespoons wine vinegar
1/3 teaspoon Liquid Smoke
1 teaspoon dried thyme
2/3 teaspoon dried sage
1 tablespoon paprika
2 teaspoons ground red chili
1 tablespoon miso
Salt and pepper

1 cup raw brown rice, cooked

Combine beans, Kombu, onion, carrot, celery, vinegar and Liquid Smoke in a heavy saucepan with enough water to cover plus about 2 inches. Cook over medium heat, stirring frequently until beans are tender, about 2 hours. Take out Kombu, dice and return to the pot. Cook brown rice. Pan toast thyme, sage, paprika and chili in a heavy fry pan till quite aromatic but not browning. Add toasted spices to beans and simmer at least 10-20 minutes or until rice is done. Add salt and pepper to taste. Dissolve miso in a little of the bean liquid. Return to pot. Do not boil once miso has been added. Serve beans over or alongside rice.

Marcia Levison extended her massage work to attend births as a Doulah. Marcia, son Aaron & daughter Sarah.

Black Beans and Rice (6 servings)

Heidi Champney brought this recipe with her from her Oberlin College coop dining days. The beans are flavorful without being overly spiced. Add your own spice with your choice of salsa or chili sauce. Many customers enjoyed yogurt or sour cream alongside.

2 1/2 cups dry black beans, soaked overnight/ 2 14-ounce cans
8 cups water
3 cloves garlic, minced or pressed
1/2 teaspoon thyme
1/2 teaspoon oregano
1/2 teaspoon ground cumin
1/2 teaspoon mustard powder
Pinch cayenne pepper
Pinch black pepper
1 teaspoon salt
2 tablespoons olive oil
2 medium onions, diced
2 green peppers, diced
3 tomatoes, chopped

1 1/2 cups raw brown or basmati rice, cooked

For accompaniment:
1-2 cups yogurt or sour cream
Salsa (see page 217)
Red chili sauce (see page 216)

Drain soaked beans and combine with water, garlic, thyme, oregano, cumin, mustard, cayenne and black pepper in a large saucepan. Bring to a boil over high heat. Reduce to a simmer and cook till beans are tender. Or add spices to canned beans and heat through. The time will vary with the beans. Add salt after beans are fully cooked. Cook rice. Heat oil in a small fry pan. Add onions and pepper and sauté until onions become transparent. Add tomatoes to heat. Add cooked vegetables to beans and continue to simmer while rice cooks. Prepare any accompaniments.

Curried Lentils and Rice (4 servings)

Andrew Paschetto brought this recipe with him.
The cook who taught me to make Indian dhal taught me that basically you've only used too much spice in this dish when you detect a chalky powderyness from the sheer volume of spices. South Asia has come up with some of the finest weddings of sweet and savory tastes....Basmati rice will make this a perfect Asian "rice and beans".

2 cups dry green lentils, soaked overnight
7 cups water or veggie stock
2 cups diced onion/ 2 medium onions
3 to 4 cloves garlic, minced or pressed
2 tablespoons olive or sesame oil
1 1/2 tablespoons curry powder
1/2 tablespoon Garam Masala Indian spice
1 teaspoon ginger juice
1 tablespoon lemon juice

1 cup raw basmati rice, cooked

For accompaniment:
Plain yogurt or *raita* (see other cookbooks for recipes)

Drain water from soaked lentils. Combine lentils and water or stock in a medium saucepan. Cook over medium heat until lentils are tender. Cook onions and garlic in oil in a medium sauté pan until golden brown. Add curry powder and garam masala to onions and continue to sauté 2-3 minutes to toast spices thoroughly. Add ginger and lemon juices to sautéed vegetables, and then add all to cooked lentils. Simmer lentils at least a half hour to develop flavors. Cook rice. Serve with yogurt or *raita* (cooling mixtures of yogurt and mild fruits or vegetables).

Zucchini Rice Casserole (9"x13" casserole/6 servings)

Heidi Champney brought this one from Oberlin too. It is a simple and satisfying casserole, if a little bland for some. Any summer squash may be used, and a combination is nice for color and texture. For a lighter result, reduce the ricotta and cheddar and increase the rice.

2 pounds zucchini, or other summer squash, sliced thin
3/4 cup raw brown rice, cooked in 2 cups water
2 cups ricotta cheese/ 1 pound
2 eggs
1 cup diced onions
1 tablespoon minced scallions
1 teaspoon marjoram
1 1/2 cups grated cheddar cheese/ 6 ounces

Lightly steam squash in a steamer basket or colander over boiling water, retaining some of its firmness. Prepare rice. Preheat oven to 350 degrees. Mix ricotta, eggs, onion, scallions and marjoram in a small bowl. Add to rice and stir to combine. Oil the casserole. Layer half the rice mixture, half the squash, the rest of the rice, the second half of the squash, and top the whole with the grated cheddar. Bake 45 minutes until top is lightly browned.

Civil Unions..

I recognized a number of Vermont Supreme Court Justices among the customers at the Bread the Saturday morning following their as yet unannounced landmark decision striking down the state marraige law as unconstitutional. We knew they had been considering the case and wondered if their breakfast choice was any indication of the outcome. This ruling made way for Vermont's legislature to pass a law allowing same sex partnerships to be sanctioned by the state extending many rights previously available only to married couples. Vermont's Gay, Lesbian, Bi-, and Trans-gendered newspaper *Out in the Mountains* had their office upstairs from the Bread. Or maybe they were just hungry.

Many outsiders thought we were a "queer" business because there were so many women employees. Some were, and we were supportive of all life choices. We also had married and un-married mothers, grandmothers and men workers.

As I told *Out In The Mountains* reporter Chris Tebbets:

I think that the queer community, the old hippie community--there's a lot of a so-called alternative net-work in this area. I think that we're more of a force than a lot of the straight world recognized. I really think that we need to support one another in our various ventures; we can be who we are and be in this world and live a good life. **(59)**

Pies and Potatoes

Chicken or Tofu Pot Pies (3 6-inch pies)

Judy Bush credits common sense for this recipe. Food writer Marialisa Calta described this version as, "… one of the best I've ever tasted--and that includes my own, which I think is pretty great. The crust was light, flaky and a bit salty, a perfect compliment to the creamy comfort-food filling." **(60)**

For the tofu option, we substituted tofu for the chicken, margarine or oil for the butter and veggie stock for the chicken.

1 recipe pie dough for 2 crust pies or 1/2 recipe for a top crust only (see page 105-6)

Filling:
1 1/2 pounds chicken, cooked and boned or 1 1/2 pounds diced tofu
2 1/2 tablespoons butter, margarine or oil
2 1/2 tablespoons flour
2 1/2 cups chicken broth or veggie stock
1/8 teaspoon dried thyme
Pinch nutmeg
Pinch salt
Pinch parsley
1/3 cup minced onion
1 cup diced potatoes/ 1 small potato
1 cup diced carrots/ 2 carrots
1/2 cup diced celery/ 1 stalk

Prepare pie dough and chill. Prepare chicken or tofu. Preheat oven to 375 degrees. Toast together butter, margarine or oil and flour in a large sauté pan 2-3 minutes. Add stock, thyme, nutmeg, salt and parsley to pan and whisk to make a smooth gravy. In a separate pan, sauté onion, potatoes, carrots and celery until vegetables begin to soften. Add to gravy and chicken or tofu. We used oven-safe soup bowls. If using bottom and top crusts, roll out your bottoms to line bowls with a little hanging over the lip. Roll out tops just big enough to cover the top. Fill the bowls just before you put them in the oven to prevent crust sogginess. Place top crust over the filling. Press top crust firmly onto the lip or bottom crust. Poke a few vent holes in the top. Bake 30-40 minutes till the filling is bubbly and the tops are golden brown.

Cornish Veggie Pie (10"x14" casserole/ 12 inch pie/ 6-8 servings)

I defer to Andrew Paschetto's personal notes on this casserole version of the famous Cornish Meat Pies or "Pasties," (the "a" pronounced as in "past"), which Andrew developed to save preparation time.

> The trick with this is to slice the vegetables thin enough to cook before the pastry burns. Each layer retains its own flavor and only influences the others: potatoes on the bottom, then carrots, rutabaga, onions, Prosage or beef, and then the butter and seasoning. This dish relies on trickle-down, so you want the most flavorful and juicy stuff on top.

This is a wonderful dish to prepare in the cold fall and winter months when root vegetables are at their sweetest.

1 1/2 recipes pie dough (see page 105-6)

5 cups thinly sliced potatoes
2 cups thinly sliced rutabaga
2 cups thinly sliced carrots
2 cups thinly sliced onion
8 ounces Prosage or other flavorful veggie or meat sausage, sliced thin
8 tablespoons butter or margarine/ 1 stick
1 tablespoon thyme
1 1/2 teaspoons salt
1 1/2 teaspoons black pepper

Prepare pie dough. Roll out 2/3 of the dough into a rectangle to line your casserole pan. Preheat oven to 375 degrees. Prepare vegetables, sliced as thinly as possible. Layer potatoes, rutabaga, carrots, onion and Prosage onto bottom crust. Dot butter or margarine over the top. Sprinkle thyme, salt and pepper over all. Roll out remaining 1/3 pastry into a rectangle to cover casserole. Pinch edges and cut vent holes in the top to let steam out. Cover with foil and bake 1 1/2 to 2 hours. Take foil off and bake another 15 minutes to brown.

Potatoes Romanoff (10"x14" casserole/ 6-8 servings)

The original version of this recipe came from the first *Vegetarian Epicure* cookbook, which appeared on the scene in the early 1970s. We affectionately referred to it as "potatoes with all your dairy groups." Mare Kuhlman altered the original.

    8 cups peeled and diced potatoes
    1 1/2 cups ricotta cheese/ 12 ounces
    1 cup sour cream
    4 medium cloves garlic, minced or pressed
    1/4 cup minced onion
    1/4 cup minced fresh parsley
    1 1/2 teaspoons salt
    1 1/2 teaspoons black pepper
    1 cup grated cheddar cheese
    Paprika

Parboil potatoes in water till just fork tender, not soft and mushy. Drain. Preheat oven to 350 degrees. Combine ricotta, sour cream, garlic, onion, parsley, salt and pepper in a small bowl. Add to potatoes and stir to cover. Spread in casserole and top with grated cheddar. Sprinkle paprika on top for a little color. Bake 35 minutes until bubbly and the cheese is lightly browned.

Colcannon (9"x13" casserole/6 servings)

This is my own version of the old Irish favorite, traditionally boiled together in one pot and without the cream cheese. We served it often. George Safford kept us well supplied with cabbage all winter and into the next spring. And we always had a large supply of potatoes on hand for home fries, roll dough and for feeding sourdoughs.

    3 to 4 cups cooked, mashed potatoes/ 4-6 potatoes
    2 tablespoons butter
    5 cups thinly sliced green cabbage/ 1 good sized head
    6 ounces cream cheese
    1 egg
    2/3 cup diced onion
    1 clove garlic, minced or pressed
    1/8 teaspoon black pepper
    1/3 teaspoon salt
    1/2 cup breadcrumbs

Prepare the potatoes. Sauté cabbage in butter in a large fry pan or heavy-bottomed sauce pan until cabbage is wilted. Preheat oven to 375 degrees. Combine mashed potatoes, cream cheese, egg, onion, garlic, pepper and salt. Grease your casserole pan. Layer half the cabbage, half the potato mixture, second half of the cabbage and the rest of the potato mix into the casserole. Top with breadcrumbs. Bake 25 minutes.

From other sources:

Vegetarian Epicure:
Kasha Knish-used this filling inside our basic pastry wrapper
Russian Veggie Pie
Eggplant and Potato Curry
Stuffed Pumpkin
Potato Latkes

Moosewood Cookbook:
Arabian Squash Casserole
Russian Macaroni and Cheese
Mushroom Moussaka
Spinach Mushroom Kugel
Stuffed Winter Squash

New Recipes from Moosewood
Casserole Milanese
Mexican Brunch Pie

The Sale

It was time for a few personal adventures; I was ready for a change of pace.
I wrote up a sign and posted it in the front window:

"I'm hoping to find a like-minded individual or partners who will carry on with the same energy and tradition that Daily Bread has established over the years."

I met with a local accountant to arrive at an asking price. Three or four people showed enough interest to look at the financials, but expressed dismay at the low net profit.

Customers and employees said they understood, but hoped the place wouldn't change too much. Upstairs neighbor Kirsten Bower said, "Every town needs their local town gossip-eatery."

Craig Colburn, owner of Richmond Beverage across the street, said in a *Burlington Free Press* interview, "The café has helped foster a unique community that draws people of all types. We'll miss her." (61)

As potential buyers came and went, employees looked into buying the restaurant and turning it into a worker cooperative. They wanted to keep their jobs and keep the funky, unofficial town meeting place.

The New Leaf Cooperative Enterprise, a program administered by the Burlington Community Land Trust to help people start cooperatives or convert existing businesses into cooperatives, met with the group to look into the details.

Many customers offered to help with start up money and I fully supported the effort. At least the employees knew and supported the non-traditional approach. Most business owners want or need a bigger return on their investments. Many of the employees were young and eventually decided that they could not make enough of a time commitment to make the coop work.

The new young Richmond Corner Market owner, Aaron Millon, had said on a number of occasions that he needed two years and then wanted to buy the Bread. Aaron came to Vermont as a student at the New England Culinary Institute. He wanted to expand the market and add a small high-end dining room upstairs. We talked on and off and eventually Aaron brought in a fellow NECI graduate, and we came to an agreement that seemed it would work for all of us.

Friends, customers and coworkers threw me a going away party, with Selectboard member Linda Andrews reading a proclamation of thanks from the Town.

A rainbow even showed up at the party!

Selectboard member Linda Andrews read an official proclamation. People demanded a speech, which brought smiles from young and old alike.

Under New Management

The new Daily Bread started to use mixes for their baked goods. The "professional" baker threw away the old recipes; she had to call up for the Orange Tea Cake recipe to avoid a local revolt. Café fare became more omnivorous than vegetarian and took on a decidedly nouvelle character.

A *Seven Days* review a year later wrote:

Richmond's Daily Bread keeps both "veggie and omnivorous options on our menu," says chef-owner Aaron Millon. "We only carry responsible, local meat products labeled 'all natural' and 'free roaming.' Our vegetarian dishes include a Morel Mushroom Risotto with fresh English peas, fava beans, shaved parmesan and a persillade of parsley, garlic and lemon. One special is a Roasted Portabella and Eggplant Stack, with summer squash, baby spinach, roasted peppers, fennel potatoes and Vermont Butterworks goat cheese. For vegans, we can leave out the goat cheese. **(62)**

The People's Kitchen

I was somewhat disappointed that so much of the old Bread had disappeared. I also realized that it was no longer in my hands.

One spring 2001 evening, Liz Shukwit, a young woman at African dance class needed a ride. I asked what she was up to. She was part of the "V-Mob" who were organizing support for the influx of people planning to voice their opposition to the FTAA (Free Trade Area of the Americas) at a meeting to be held in Quebec City. It inspired me. I helped out with a few bulk orders and menus. One day I walked in to find April Howard, ex-Bread baker there making sandwiches. She and a number of friends had traveled from Bard College, outside of New York City, up to Burlington to help.

Many meals were dished out from the storefront kitchen. Carloads were sent up to the Canadian border. "Full bellies equal happy people," Liz told *Seven Days* reporter Susan Green while hosting a "sandwich-making party" at the makeshift but magical People's Kitchen on North Street. (63)

The V-Mob, which organized medical and legal teams in addition to food, was the contact organization for Burlington and was one of many Northeast convergence points.

The food was turned back at the border because it was homemade rather than prepackaged. The border officials claimed it would take two days to thoroughly inspect the handmade food before it could safely cross into Canada.

The End of an Era

The undertaking was more than the new owners had bargained for. By the end of 2002, Aaron had put it up for sale. Daily Bread officially closed its doors for good at the end of February 2003. The space is now under new ownership, operating as a Mediterranean restaurant and wine bar called Toscano's.

On the Rise •••

Sometime during 2003, Ben Bush, his wife Raechel and members of Ben's band began to fantasize about a new eatery.

Raechel, Ben and Judy behind the counter at On the Rise

They found a storefront in the main block, next door to Richmond Beverage and across the street from the old Bread, a tiny space in comparison, requiring creative use of every cubic inch. They worked out some new recipes and consulted about some of the oldies but goodies. They enlisted Judy's and Chelsie's help. Chelsie's partner Betsy Orvis planted extra spinach and greens for them. They purchased a few essential pieces of equipment and fabricated others themselves. Government paperwork and bureaucratic footdragging caused a few frustrating delays, par for the course.

They opened their doors in June 2004, to cheers, tears, and smiling, salivating customes. Visitors will find many old Daily Bread favorites there plus bagels and many new and exciting breads, sweets and savories. They are also equipped to whip up lattes, mochas, cappucino, fruit smoothies and frozen coffee drinks. They offer a daily soup option for take out.

On the Rise and its new building next to Volunteers Green, with cafe seating, stone oven and show gardens is a huge success. Music, movies, muffins, melons!

Dedication •••••••••••••••••••••••••••••••••••••

I dedicate this story to the children, that they may have safe food in a safe world. May we face truth with courage and humility. May we love with open hearts and laugh deeply. May we sweat honestly and work for the benefit of all.

Ben and Raechel's son Ezra
2 years old, kneading bread at his
Grandma Judy's house.

Appendix 1. Seasonal Eating

One way to live more harmoniously with the planet, to lower our impact , is to eat more seasonally. Cornell University's Northeast Regional Food Guide is very helpful in looking at the options, which are more diverse than you might at first believe. Over time, the Bread planned its menus around the availability of fresh and root-cellared produce to a large extent. Here are some recommendations of available items in the New England area and recommended recipes. Those with an asterix are found in this cookbook. There are many recently published cookbooks featuring seasonal recipes. Check your local public library or favorite bookstore.

July, August, September, October

Vegetables:

Beets	Broccoli	Cabbage
Carrots	Cauliflower	Celery
Cucumbers	Eggplant	Fennel
Garlic	Green beans	Lettuce
Mushrooms	Okra	Onions
Peppers	Potatoes	Scallions
Sprouts	Summer squash	Sweet Corn
Spinach	Green Peas	Tomatoes
Leeks	Fresh herbs	

Soups:

Chilled:

*Chilled Minted Pea	Gazpacho
Green Gazpacho	Chilled Peach and Cantaloupe

Hot:

*Pesto Vegetable	*Chicken Vegetable
*South of the Border Chicken	*Egyptian Red Stew
*Greens Gumbo	*Japanese Vegetable
Cauliflower Cheese	Corn Puree with Roasted Red Pepper
Corn Chowder	Cream of Celery
Curried Cream of Zucchini	Cream of Summer Vegetable
Black Bean Chili	Minestrone

Salads:

*Vegetable Pasta
*Chicken Pasta
*Greek Rice
*Marcia's Sesame Noodles
*Tomato and Artichoke Heart
*Garden Salad
Swiss Green Beans
Nori Rolls

*Potato
*Tomato and Mozzarella
*Rice and Sunny
*Summer Green Bean and Pasta
*Black Bean, Corn and Shrimp
Pico de Gallo
Taboule

Casseroles and Main Dishes:

*Tofu Lettuce and Tomato Sandwich
*Tempeh Lettuce and Tomato Sandwich
*Curried Tempeh Flatbread
*Zucchini Pie
*French Shrimp Rolls
*Pasta al Forno
*Zucchini Rice Casserole
Casserole Milanese
Mushroom Moussaka
*Calzone

*Devil's Own Tempeh Sandwich
*California Tempeh Sandwich
*Grilled Eggplant Sandwich
*Quesadillas
*Mexican Veggie Pie
*Spinach Lasagna
Spinach Turnovers
Eggplant and Potato Curry
*Pizza
*Fresh Tomato Cheese Dreams

Fruits:

Strawberries
Peaches
Plums
Cherries

Blueberries
Melons
Pears
Cranberries

Raspberries
Nectarines
Apples

November, December, January, February
Vegetables:

Beets
Celery
Greens
Mushrooms
Rutabaga
Turnip

Cabbage
Daikon
Kale
Onion
Sprouts
Winter squash

Carrots
Garlic
Leeks
Potatoes
Sweet potatoes

Frozen:

Corn   Peas   Pesto
Broccoli   Cauliflower

Fermented:

Pickles   Sauerkraut

Soups:

Cream of Celery   Russian Cabbage Borscht
*Betsy's Beet Borscht   *Pesto Vegetable
*Wedding Stew   *Greens Gumbo
*Fish Chowder   *Zen Stew
*Garbanzo Stew   *Curried Yam and Lentil
Split Pea   Gypsy Stew
*Zuni Stew   *Sherry's Veggie Stew
*Veggie Bean Stew   *Potato Kale
Mushroom Barley   *Alison's Lentil
*Chicken Barley Corn   Leek and Barley Stew
*Potato Tomato   *Caldo con Queso
*Judy's Creamy Tomato   Corn Chowder

Salads:

*Wild Rice and Hazelnut   Russian Beet
*Chicken Cashew Pasta   *Tofu Cashew Pasta
*Gonzo Potato   Mixed Vegetable
Nori Rolls   Coleslaw

Casseroles and Main Dishes:

*Tempeh Reuben Sandwich   *Seitan Deluxe Sandwich
*Ginger Fried Noodles   *Spinach Lasagna
*Cornish Veggie Pie   Un-stuffed Squash
Russian Veggie Pie   Arabian Squash Casserole
*Onion Prosage Turnovers   *Kris' Veggie Enchiladas
*3 Sisters Burrito   *Black Beans and Rice
*Dwayne's Yam Burritos   Tuna Noodle
Scalloped Potatoes   *Potatoes Romanoff
*Curried Lentils and Rice   *Potato Smokers
*Pizza   *Calzone
*Garlic Gateau   *Yankee Soul Pie

Fruits:

Apples	Pears	Pumpkin

Dried:

Apricots	Cherries	Cranberries
Raisins	Crystallized ginger	

Frozen:

Berries	Rhubarb	Plums
Peaches		

March, April, May, June
Vegetables:

Asparagus	Baby Beets	Bok Choy
Baby carrots	Cabbage	Celery
Fiddleheads	Garlic	Greens
Wild leeks	Lettuce	Mesclun
Mushrooms	Onions	Parsnips
Potatoes	Radishes	Scallions
Snap Peas	Spinach	Sprouts
Turnips	Winter Squash	

Greenhouse:

Cucumbers	Mesclun	Hot Peppers
Tomatoes		

Frozen:

Corn	Herbs	Peas

Soups:

Cream of Asparagus	Borscht with Beans and Greens
*Creamy Onion	*Creamy Garlic
*Garbanzo Stew	*South of the Border Chicken
*Chicken Barley Corn	Mushroom Barley
*Mushroom Lentil	*Greens Gumbo
*Fish Chowder	Golden Nugget Stew
Split Pea	*Japanese Vegetable
Russian Cabbage Borscht	*Caldo con Queso
Black Bean Chili	Spring Pea
Hungarian Mushroom	Spicy Tomato
*Alison's Lentil	*Curried Carrot
*Potato Kale	

Salads:

    *Chicken Cashew Pasta
    *Gonzo Potato
    Spinach

    *Tofu Cashew Pasta
    *Marcia's Asian Noodles
    *Garden

Casseroles and Main Dishes:

    Scalloped Potatoes
    *Cornish Veggie Pie
    Macaroni and Cheese
    Russian Macaroni and Cheese
    *Colcannon
    Un-stuffed Squash
    Spinach and Mushroom Kugel
    Falafel or as burgers
    Kasha Knishes
    *Potato Smokers
    *Becca's Samosas
    *Seitan Deluxe Sandwich

    *Potatoes Romanoff
    Russian Veggie Pie
    *Mushroom Macaroni
    *Lentil Mushroom Stroganoff
    *Red Beans and Rice
    Tuna Noodle
    *Kris' Veggie Burgers
    *Onion and Prosage Turnovers
    *Pizza
    *Kris' Veggie Enchiladas
    *Garlic Gateau

Fruits:

Apples	Rhubarb	Early Strawberries

Frozen:

Berries	Peaches	Plums

Appendix 2. School to Work: A Case for the Manual Arts

At least half of the more than 160 employees who worked at Daily Bread were high school students. These young people were, for the most part, excellent employees.

School administrators teased me that I had only the cream of the crop. Many were honor students. There were also many who, for one reason or another, were not thriving in the academic classroom.

Some worked on life skills like spoken communication, making purchases, counting change and carrying a task to completion. Some wanted experience in a commercial kitchen to see if they wanted to pursue a culinary career. Some just wanted a paycheck.

All were computer literate. Most either drove cars or were enrolled in a driver's education class. Some had learned practical skills at home, but most were dumbfounded by a loose screw, a leaky faucet or plugged toilet--never mind a minor car repair!

Taxpayers have funded one generation after another of computers, while the mechanical/industrial arts are sacrificed to the promise of white collar "Information Age" jobs for everyone where no one gets his hands dirty. What about the service trades which provide a community a semblance of self-sufficiency?

Vermont's Chittenden County provides a first hand example of how this nod to high tech plays out on the local level. The trades are quickly vanishing. High incomes and a booming economy make replacement more expedient than repair. High housing costs for rents, ownership and tax bills push tradespeople further and further away from the metropolitan Burlington area.

We and our children need to acknowledge and respect those who repair our automobiles, build our houses, fix our plumbing, grow and prepare our food. The plumber, cook, farmer, heavy equipment operator, logger, welder, cheesemaker, home health aid, trash hauler--all these folks--allow the rest of us to pursue our "clean" jobs, provide a car for every adult, dinners to go, health insurance coverage, health club memberships and otherwise to live a "high" quality of life. Students, school faculties and family members can all benefit from greater familiarity with the basic skills of tool usage and safety.

Medieval scholars referred to the seven mechanical or "useful" arts of: clothmaking, armaments and building, commerce, agriculture, hunting and food preparation, medicine and theatrics." These were to balance the seven "liberal" arts of: "grammar, dialectic, rhetoric, geometry, arithmetic, astronomy and harmony." Maybe it is time to reconsider this balanced approach.

I am troubled by what I observe to be a disconnect in our current culture between what is "real" and what is "on screen." Real is hitting the thumb more often than the nail until you get into the swing of it and hit the nail most of the time. Real is feeling the dough with your hands, smelling the aroma while it bakes and then tasting a slice of your fresh hot bread. Real is often lying on the ground breathing petrochemical fumes while attempting a car repair beside the road. Real is getting up every morning to milk the cows. No amount of mouse clicking will thaw the frozen pipes down in the crawl space.

Useful skills and knowledge give a person the ability to be a contributing member of any group. They increase the potential for responsibility to self and others. In light of recent recognition of multiple intelligences, manual projects offer some students their first opportunity to succeed, even excel, in a school setting.

Trial and error are both required for success. The first, or sometimes second or third, attempt may lead to a solution; or it may produce a pile of kindling. Success tempered with perseverance and the limitations of the materials themselves, helps build life skills and common sense.

Technical education has long been the step-child of primary and secondary American schooling. In Europe, traditional aprenticeships and a variety of specialized secondary schools provide students with options. Future writers, scientists and mathematicians follow the academic track. Hands-on learners, those not interested or attuned to academics-as-we-know-it, are cycled through the "general" program.

Some U.S. students attend regional technical centers if they are fortunate enough to have assertive parents and/or pro-active guidance counselors. The pre-tech program offered at the Burlington and Essex Junction centers allow students to sample the variety of courses available. They can then choose a concentration. Technical studies can also be more fully integrated through internships and paid employment within the community.

High school studio arts classes give some students relief from the steady diet of book learning. Aspiring farmers, chefs, contractors and videographers travel, spending more bus time than their counterparts. This also takes students out of their circle of friends, out of sight, out of mind. Few of these students give keynote graduation addresses. Where would we be without these skilled hand workers? Hungry, wet and cold!

Familiarity begins at home and continues throughout life. Schools can participate in exposing students to a wide variety of work carried out in their communities. School can also "go to work" as early as Head Start. Before the Richmond Elementary School moved from the village to its current campus up on the hill, rows of school children lined up two by two were constantly spotted walking to or from a local business, the post office or other town resource. On the school campus itself, custodial, mechanical and culinary jobs are done every day, which students could assist.

Basic hand tools and hand work are not as new, improved, exclusive or fashionable as the latest model car, software or computer chip. They have not changed in the last year, ten or even a hundred years! Many tools can be fabricated in any reasonably well-equipped wood and metal shops. Imagine the wonder, pride and satisfaction in forging your own hammer or hoe and then using it to construct or cultivate a coldframe where greens are grown for the school lunch program?

Every Vermont school campus is required to have open space. Why not devote a portion of that land to grow food? The food could also be donated to the local food pantry to help others. Experiences in generosity invite positive feedback and form solid connections with the wider spheres of community and environment. Everyone likes to feel needed, and there are too few ways in which today's young people feel useful or necessary.

Hands-on experiences also give students real life situations to observe academic theory in practice: measurement, computation, communication, geometry, problem solving, physics, history, aesthetics, politics--the applications are endless. Students see for themselves that what they are studying have practical applications which might really help them or their neighbors in the future.

In Vermont, in 2000, one in seven young people between 18 and 21 years of age, were under the supervision of the Department of Corrections. It is unfortunate that through our cultural failure to pass along responsible use of alcohol, we criminalize vast numbers of young people with little change in behavior. Skateboards and graffitti offend mainstream adult sensibilities, creating more criminals. Youth violence actually dropped through the 1990s. Most of the charges against Vermont youth were "quality of life" offenses.

What is our message? That we do not trust our kids? That they are guilty and suspect until proven innocent? That zero tolerance justifies cancellation of the very constitutional rights championed in our classrooms? Is this any way to promote good citizenship?

Students tell me they have never found a place to work like the Bread. What made it different? I believe that a genuine interest and respect for co-workers, customers, vendors and service people permeated the workplace, despite apparent differences. I expected and freely gave responsibility: employees calculated their own pay and taxes. There was a diverse adult staff: moms, musicians, artists, social workers, community organizers, writers, nurses, ecologists. Conversations were wide-ranging, and we listened to each other's music.

We did not cry over spilt milk or dropped sweet rolls. Some weeks the chickens ate well. I shared my failures: I baked my share of door stops before producing an edible loaf. We were all dedicated to turning out good food, from scratch, mostly vegetarian, with as many local ingredients as possible. Perseverance and elbow grease were required, and we still had a good time.

I believe that returning the mechanical arts and handwork to their rightful places of honor, practice and appreciation will go a long way to inspire young people. The intoxication of success is often the jump start necessary to lead a student on his or her way to self-directed pursuits of knowledge.

When all ways of knowing and learning are appreciated, we are more tolerant of differences. Our future depends on it.

Bibliography

Early inspiration:

Selected Poems Yevtushenko, Yevgeny Yevtushenko, Penguin Books, 1963
Air Conditioned Nightmare, Henry Miller, New Directions Corp., 1970

Breads and Bread Baking

Baba a Louis Bakery Bread Book, John McLure, distributed by Chelsea Green Publishing Company, 1993
Beard on Bread, James Beard, Ballantine Books, 1973
Bread, Bread and Puppet, Glover, VT, 1984
Bread Baking, Catherine Clark, Bulfin Printers, Inc., 1976
The Bread Builders, Daniel Wing & Alan Scott, Chelsea Green Publishing Company, 1999
The Tassajara Bread Book, Edward Espe Brown, Shambhala, 1970
Uncle John's Original Bread Book, John Rahn Braue, Pyramid Books, 1977
A World of Breads, Delores Cassela, Independent Pub. Group, 1974

Cakes, Cookies & Sweets

Brownies, Sharon Moore, Simon & Schuster, (not absolutely sure this is the same book; bakery copy lost and no listing closer in any indexes)

The German Cookbook, Mimi Sheraton, Random House, 1965

The Joy of Cheesecake, Jeremy Iggers et al., Barrons Educational Series, 1980

The Maple Syrup Baking and Dessert Cookbook, Ken Haedrich, American Impressions Book Company, 1985

Maida Heatter's Book of Great Chocolate Desserts, Maida Heatter, Knopf, 1980

The New York Times Cookbook, Craig Claiborne, Harper & Row, 1961

The New York Times Natural Foods Cookbook, Jean Hewitt, Morrow/ Avon 1983

Rosie's Bakery All Butter Fresh Cream Sugar Packed No Holds Barred Baking Book, Judy Rosenberg, Workman Publishing, 1991

Super Natural Dessert Cookbook, Lois Fishkin & Susan DiMarco, Creative Arts Book Company, 1985

Uprisings: The Whole Grain Baker's Book, Cooperative Whole Grain Education Association Staff, Book Publishing Co., 1990

Savory Dishes and Vegetarian Cooking

Amber Waves of Grain: American Macrobiotic Cooking, Alex Jack, Japan Publications (USA),1992

Cafe Beaujolais, Margaret S. Fox and John Bear, Ten Speed Press, 1984

Diet for a Small Planet, Frances Moore Lappe, Random House, Inc., 1971

Enchanted Broccoli Forest, Mollie Katzen, Ten Speed Press, 1982

The New Farm Vegetarian Cookbook, Louise Hagler/ Dorothy Bates, Book Publishing Co., 1988

Jane Brody's Good Food Book, Jane E. Brody, W.W. Norton & Company, 1985

The Joy of Cooking, Irma S. Rombauer & Marion Rombauer Becker, Bobbs-Merrill Company, Inc., 1964

Low Fat Thermometer Cookbook, unable to find publication information

Moosewood Cookbook, Mollie Katzen, Ten Speed Press, 1977

Natural Foods, Mary Estella, Kodansha Amer Inc., 1985

Natural Gourmet, Anne Marie Colbin, Ballantine, 1991

Northeast Regional Food Guide, Jennifer l. Wilkins & Jennifer Bokaer-Smith, Cornell University, 1996 (available through Cornell University Resource Center 607-255-2080)

Recipes for a Small Planet, Ellen Buchman Ewald, Ballantine Books, 1973

Tassajara Recipes, Edward Espe Brown, Shambhala, 2000

Vegetarian Epicure, Anna Thomas, Alfred A. Knopf, 1972

Related Topics

Building Soils for Better Crops, Fred Magdoff, University of Nebraska Press, 1992

The Chain Gang, One Newspaper versus the Gannett Empire, Richard McCord, University of Missouri Press, 1996

The Drum and the Hoe, Harold Courlander, University of California Press, 1986

Flash of the Spirit, Robert Farris Thompson, Vintage, 1983

How to Grow More Vegetables than you thought possible on less land than you can imagine, John Jeavons, Ten Speed Press, 1991

The Interstate Gourmet New Haven to Burlington, Neal O. Weiner and David M. Schwartz, Oak Cottage Press, 1981

The Interstate Gourmet, a guide to good eating along Interstate 89, 1986

Land, Bread, and History: A Research Report on the Potential for Self-Sufficiency in Vermont, George Burril, James R. Nolfi, Vermont Institute of Community Involvement, 1976

Much Depends on Dinner, The Extraordinary History and Mythology, Allure and Obsessions, Perils and Taboos, of an Ordinary Meal, Margaret Visser, McClelland and Stewart, 1986

The Original Vermonters, William Haviland, University Press of New England, 1994

Recipes Into Type, Joan Whitman and Delores Simon, Biscuit Books Inc., 1993

Shadow work, Ivan Illich, Marion Boyars Publishing, Inc., 1981

Snow Bakery, Bread and Puppet, Troll Press, 1984

Solviva, Anna Edey, Trailblazer Press, 1998 (508-693-3341)

Tools for Conviviality, Ivan Illich, Harper & Row, Publishers, 1973

Topsoil and Civilization, Vernon Gill Carter and Tom Dale, University of Oklahoma Press, 1974

Voices of Our Ancestors, Dhyani Ywahoo, Shambhala Press, 1987

Illustrations

Dedication, Mary Bott's family photos
p 1. bakery archives, unknown
p 2. Bott family archives, unknown
p 3. Bott family archives, unknown
p 4. original line-drawing Mary Bott
p 4. Bott family archives, unkown
p 6. Eisenkramer family collection
p 7. Bott family photos, NY Post photographer
p 7. Bott/ Mayer photos, unknown
p 11. Bott photo, Andrea Escher
p 11. Daily Bread scrap book, Betsy Bott
p 12. County Weekly photo, Randall Gillett
p 12. Bush family photos, unknown
p 12. "Winter Morning", Judy Bush
p 13. Daily Bread label, Judy Bush design
p 14. Daily Bread scrapbook, unknown
p 14. Daily Bread archives
p 14. Daily bread archives, Joan Knight
p 15. Daily Bread archives, Joan Knight
p 15. Daily Bread archives, Joan Knight
p 16. Bott personal collection
p 17. Bush family photos, Jeb Bush
p 17. Daily Bread archives, unknown
p 17. Daily Bread scrapbook,
p 18. Daily Bread scrapbook, unknown
p 18. Daily Bread scrapbook, unknown
p 18. Daily Bread scrapbook, Jeffords campaign
p 19. Daily Bread scrapbook, unknown
p 19. Daily Bread scrapbook, unknown
p 19. Daily Bread scrapbook, unknown
p 21. drawings, Betsy Bott
p 26. Daily Bread scrapabook, unknown
p 31. Daily Bread scrapbook, John Bott
p 32. Bott personal photos, Henry Bush
p 34. drawing, Betsy Bott
p 34. Daily Bread phtos, unknown
p 35. Daily Bread photos, unknown
p 35. drawing, Betsy Bott
p 37. Daily Bread photo, unknown
p 37. tag, Betsy Bott
p 38. Jim Painter memorial service program
p 39. Daily Bread photo, unknown
p 40. tag, Betsy Bott
p 43. Daily Bread photos, unknown

p 43. Bott personal photos, Irene Horbar
p 44. Daily Bread ad, Heidi Racht design
p 49. tag, Betsy Bott
p 49. Daily Bread scrapbook, unknown
p 52. Daily Bread photos, unknown
p 57. tag, Betsy Bott
p 58. tag, Betsy Bott
p 59. tag, Betsy Bott
p 64. drawing, Betsy Bott
p 67. illustration for holiday card, Lynn E Alden
p 73. drawing, Betsy Bott
p 74. drawing, Betsy Bott
p 76. drawing and tag, Betsy Bott
p 77. tag, Betsy Bott
p 78. drawing, Betsy Bott
p 79. Daily Bread photos, unknown
p 81. Daily Bread photos, unknown
p 82. tag, Betsy Bott
p 84. drawing, Betsy Bott
p 87. Galligan-Sagars 2003 Christmas card
p 89. Daily Bread scrapbook, unknown
p 91. drawing, Betsy Bott
p 93. Labelle family photos, unknown
p 95. Daily Bread scrapbook, Betsy Bott
p 96. T-shirt art, Judy Bush
p 99. Daily Bread scrapbook, Heidi Racht
p 101. tag, Betsy Bott
p 102. tag, Betsy Bott
p 107. Daily Bread photos, unknown
p 109. Daily Bread photos, unknown
p 118. Daily Bread photos, unknown
p 123. Daily Bread photos,
p 125 Daily Breat photos,
p 126. Daily Bread photos, unknown
p 129. Daily Bread scrapbook, Becca Cunningham
p 134. Daily Bread scrapbook, unknown
p 136. Betsy Bott personal collection, unknown
p 137. Daily Bread scrapbook, unknown
p 139. Daily Bread photos,
p 140. tag, Betsy Bott
p 141. 5th Anniversary invitation, Betsy Bott
p 143. page 1, The Richmond Times, I, 1, November 1984, design Irene Horbar

p 367. On the Rise Coffee Card, Ben Bush design
p 367. Betsy Bott's personal photos, Jeb Bush
p 368. Betsy Bott's archives, Judy Bush

Footnotes

1. **A People's History of the United States**, Howard Zinn, Harper Collins, 1999
2. Interview with Studs Terkel, NPR
3. "The Staff of Life," **Air Conditioned Nightmare,** Henry Miller, New Directions Corp., 1970
4. "Zima Junction," **Selected Poems Yevtushenko**, Yevgeny Yevtushenko, Penguin Books, 1963
5. Letter to the Editor, *Seven Days*, April 1998
6. "The Hippie Convention," Susan Green, *Vanguard Press*, June 28--July 1, 1984
7. "In Richmond it's the People Making the Difference," Harriet Riggs, *Vermont Life*, Spring 1980
8. "Richmond: the Hills are Alive," Randall Gillett, *County Weekly*, June 4, 1979
9. Windsor, Ontario promotional material, 2000
10. **Bread**, Peter Schumann, Bread and Puppet Press, 1984
11. Richmond, A Community with Pride, 1994 Camels Hump Middle School project
12. postcard from Jim Painter
13. note from Rosie McLaughlin, 1999
14. quote jotted down during a 1980s WVPR radio interview with Allen Ginsberg
15. Marie Whiteford's job application, 1999
16. traditional German rhyme, translation Betsy Bott
17. "Baking, an Act of Love," Paul Benzaquin
18. **Interstate Gourmet--New Haven to Burlington**, Neal O. Weiner and David M. Schwartz, Oak Cottage Press, 1981
19. "Empty Bread Baskets", Diane Nazarowitz Mortier
20. traditional rhyme altered
21. "From the center," Kathleen Fitzgerald, *WildEarth*
22. Nominating letter to Vermont Dept. of Employment and Training, Gary Wills, 1996
23. "Craving Coffeecake," Debbie Salomon, *Burlington Free Press*, Nov. 11, 1997
24. Daily Bread archives, letter from Krista Willett, late '90's
25. Thank you letter from Jules Rabin, Upland Baker, Oct. 20,1989
26. "By the Bag, Barrel, or Ounce," Jack Cook, *Country Journal*, January 1976
27. Thank you letter from Bread and Puppet Theater, Linda Elbow, 1984
28. "A Day in the Life of... Pat Quinn: Meat Cutter," *Burlington Free Press* Sunday, Aug. 7, 1983
29. "Betsy Bott: Creating Space for Real Community," Matt Sutkoski, *Vermont Times*, June 27, 1991
30. " Pizza Genie slices up a magical taste", Debbie Salomon, *Burlington Free Press*, summer 1998
31. "Happy to Be Here," *The Richmond Times*, I, 1, November 1984
32. He Who Sings the Wolfsong, promotional flyer, Wolfsong, early '90's
33. "Richmond cafe bakes itself into the hearts of Vermonters," Debbie Salomon, *Burlington Free Press*, May 6, 1999
34. "Daily Bread, giving back to the community," Chris Tebbetts, *Out in the Mountains*, February, 1999
35. Note left on birch bark, early '90's, Daily Bread archives
36. "What Becomes a Legend?" Dick McCormack, *Vermont Vanguard Press*, 1987
37. personal note, Doug Perkins
38. personal note, Matthew Witten

39. personal note, Heather Ward

40. "How to keep enough development from becoming too much," Wilson Ring, *Vermont Times*, Sept. 22, 1992

41."Scoop shop magnates answer weird food questions," *San Francisco Examiner*

42. Janet Coles, note for 20th anniversary, 1999

43. note from the Murphy/ Havard family, 2004

44. **The Interstate Gourmet, a guide to good eating along Interstate 89**, 1986

45. "Toaster," Ezra Tishman, 1994

46. "Morning Glories," Amy Killinger, *Burlington Free Press*, March 28, 1991

47. "Sloppy Trough," *Fat Content*, July/ August 1995

48. "Lunch Comes with Lessons," Heidi Racht, *Burlington Free Press* Forum, October 18, 1998

49. Dwayne Doner job application

50. "Richmond cafe bakes itslef...", Debbie Salomon, *Burlington Free Press*, May 6, 1999

51. Tribute to George Safford, Mary Bowen Houle, *Times Ink!*, Dec. 2001

52. "For Twa," Betsy Bott, 1993

53. Patrick Earle note for 20th Anniversary, 1999

54. **Topsoil and Civilization**, Vernon Gill Carter &Tom Dale, University of Oklahoma Press, 1974

55. "Richmond Goes Green," Matt Sutkoski, *Burlington Free Press*, April 1,1999

56. "Vermont Network," Debbie Salomon, *Burlington Free Press*, 1996

57. "Eating Alternative," Marialisa Calta, *Seven Days*, Feb. 3,1999

58. " Richmond cafe bakes itself...," *Burlington Free Press*, May 6, 1999

59. "It's a wrap," Casey Siler, *Burlington Free Press*, 1999

60. "Giving Back...," Chris Tebbetts, *Out in the Mountains*, February 1999

61. "Eating Alternative," Marialisa Calta, *Seven Days*, Feb. 3, 1999

62. "Richmond mainstay for sale," Seth Blackman, *Burlington Free Press*, Sep. 18,1999

63. "Where's the tofu?" Susan Green,*Seven Days*, May 16, 2001

64. "Anarchy Never Sleeps," Susan Green, *Seven Days,* April 25, 2001

General Index

Recipe Index

From the people:

If you've ever lived in Vermont, if you were a human being in the USA any time between 1959 and 1985, or if you ever ate bread that said, "I am the staff of life," you will love this social history, memoir, eco-political philosophy, down-home recipe book. And you'll love the food you make with it, ... Barbara Dubois

George and I sat down to a lunch of Farmer's Market vegetables with your Maple-wheat bread and orange tea cake and I read aloud practically the whole opening autobiographical section.
It was wonderful!...to revisit so many of the events which had meant so much in the shaping of who George and I came to be.   Fin Drury

I never will be able to put together anything quite as delicious as your "Farmer's Market goodies," but it will be fun to try. Elvie Ramsdell

Betsy Bott has worked as a teacher, health counselor, baker, cook, reporter, editor and business owner. She is currently homesteading on 15 acres of overgrown woodlot with partner Jeb Bush, off the power grid in down east Maine. She grows a big garden, works as a public librarian and performs with the West African drumming group Baba Kevin and Ngoma. This is her first book.

photo by Lisa Looke

Is there a better compliment to a cookbook than pages marked and stained with bits and pieces of ingredients from a certain recipe? Yours already has several so marked…Melissa read it through the day it came. I savored it over many breakfasts and lunches. I had forgotten how integral the Bread was in a certain time of my life. Ken Carter

…your cookbook appeared in our home just when needed and is chock full of yummy things I remember but have never tried making myself….Now I can make hash browns the way I remember them! Brian is particularly fond of your polenta.

Somehow seeing and reading about the early days…begins to put in perspective that era of our lives.

And those packed evenings of song and good times with the coffeehouse seem like a faraway time…Oh but I am glad to have played a part in stirring the pot so to speak.

Lausanne Allen

I just finished reading/ drooling my way through "Made from scratch." Some of my fondest memories from my senior year of high school were permeated by the Daily Bread.

The bakery may no longer be in Richmond; now it is in the kitchens of the devoted that have found it hard to go without Amazons on Wednesday or Tea Cakes on Thursday. Lindsay Clark

From the Press:

Five years is a long time to wait for marinated homefries…Now, at last, Bott has come out with the company cookbook—a self-published, spiralbound tome that is as funky and full of love as the legendary eatery once was…a satisfying mix of food-flavored memoir, local hippie history, practical cookbook and employee tribute. In the same community spirit that distinguished the Daily Bread, Bott tells her story via the people who came through.

"Side Dishes," Paula Routly, *Seven Days* 11/16/05

Even homemade couldn't compare with Bott's baked goods. Her soups salads, and sandwiches were the universal antidote to manufactured food.

(Bott) has, thank heavens, written and self-published "Made from scratch," …that resurrects the recipes, people, politics and mission of this Richmond landmark.

"Yummy New Yorker bits whet appetite," Debbie Salomon, *Burlington Free Press*, 2/21/06

While *Made from scratch*…can't quite bring us the conversation or the coffee, it certainly brings us the food. And the accompanying history of the bakery and café goes a long way toward transporting us into that cozy, inviting world that was The Daily Bread.

Made from scratch is well organized. Recipes are clearly written and easy to follow. I especially appreciated how the bakery recipes provided options for making a large or small quantity—no need to do the math yourself. The story Betsy tells, accompanied by photographs, poems, and artwork, reads like a mini-memoir and will leave you longing for a place that has yet to be recreated here in Chittenden County.

Member Cookbook Review, Lauren Cleary, *The Onion Skin*, April 2006